Protocol Engineering

T0202913

Hartmut König

Protocol Engineering

 Springer

Hartmut König
Department of Computer Science
Brandenburg University of Technology Cottbus
Cottbus
Germany

Revised English Translation from the German edition:
Protocol Engineering. Prinzip, Beschreibung und Entwicklung von Kommunikationsprotokollen
by Hartmut König
Copyright © Vieweg+Teubner I GWV Fachverlage GmbH Wiesbaden, 2003
All Rights Reserved.

ACM Codes: C.2, B.4

ISBN 978-3-642-44093-9   ISBN 978-3-642-29145-6 (eBook)
DOI 10.1007/978-3-642-29145-6
Springer Heidelberg New York Dordrecht London

© Springer-Verlag Berlin Heidelberg 2012
Softcover reprint of the hardcover 1st edition 2012
This work is subject to copyright. All rights are reserved by the Publisher, whether the whole or part of
the material is concerned, specifically the rights of translation, reprinting, reuse of illustrations,
recitation, broadcasting, reproduction on microfilms or in any other physical way, and transmission or
information storage and retrieval, electronic adaptation, computer software, or by similar or dissimilar
methodology now known or hereafter developed. Exempted from this legal reservation are brief excerpts
in connection with reviews or scholarly analysis or material supplied specifically for the purpose of being
entered and executed on a computer system, for exclusive use by the purchaser of the work. Duplication
of this publication or parts thereof is permitted only under the provisions of the Copyright Law of the
Publisher's location, in its current version, and permission for use must always be obtained from
Springer. Permissions for use may be obtained through RightsLink at the Copyright Clearance Center.
Violations are liable to prosecution under the respective Copyright Law.
The use of general descriptive names, registered names, trademarks, service marks, etc. in this
publication does not imply, even in the absence of a specific statement, that such names are exempt
from the relevant protective laws and regulations and therefore free for general use.
While the advice and information in this book are believed to be true and accurate at the date of
publication, neither the authors nor the editors nor the publisher can accept any legal responsibility for
any errors or omissions that may be made. The publisher makes no warranty, express or implied, with
respect to the material contained herein.

Printed on acid-free paper

Springer is part of Springer Science+Business Media (www.springer.com)

To Charlotte, Christine, and Sven

Preface

Motivation for the book

Communication protocols – for short protocols – form the basis for the operation of computer networks and telecommunication systems. They are behavior conventions which describe how communication systems interact with each other in computer networks. Protocols define the temporal order of the interactions and the formats of the data units exchanged. Communication protocols comprise a wide range of different functions and mechanisms, such as the sending and receiving of data units, their coding/decoding, error control mechanisms, timer control, flow control, and many others. Protocols essentially determine the efficiency and reliability of computer networks. The processes in protocols, however, may be very complex and sophisticated. Concurrent processes and the nondeterministic appearance of events increase the complexity of protocol behaviors. The diversity of the involved mechanisms is often in conflict with the hoped for efficiency.

Communication systems use defined protocol hierarchies which are based on fixed architectural principles like in the Internet architecture. Protocols provide a specific functionality which is offered in the form of a service to other protocols or to an application. Different principles have been applied for the design of protocol hierarchies. Closed or proprietary architectures are dedicated to the requirements of a certain application or to the products of a company. Open architectures, in contrast, provide unified interaction principles which allow one to set up heterogeneous networks.

Communication protocols can be implemented in either hardware or software. Implementations in software prevail, especially in higher layers. The implementation of protocols is closely connected to the target execution environment, in particular to the given operating system. The manner in which a protocol is implemented influences its efficiency just as strongly as its design.

The experience of almost error-free use of services in the Internet hides the efforts needed for the development of communication protocols. Before protocols can be installed in a network they have to be designed, described, verified, adapted, implemented, and tested. The development of protocols – from design to installation – is a complex, tedious, and error-prone process which is only in part automated nowadays. Protocol development raises similar questions and problems as software engineering. Many of the typical phases and features of software development are also contained in the protocol development process. However, the distributed character of communication protocols raises a number of additional issues which go beyond traditional software development. For that reason, **Protocol**

Engineering[1] has become a sub-discipline in the telecommunication area which comprises the design, validation, and implementation of communication protocols.

The crucial aspect in protocol development is to find an appropriate description of the protocol. Informal descriptions have proved inappropriate due to their ambiguity. Therefore formal descriptions based on formal semantic models are preferred. The use of **formal description techniques (FDTs)** for the design, validation, and implementation of communication protocols is the characteristic feature of *Protocol Engineering*. Formal description techniques guarantee a unique interpretation of the protocol specification. They are the foundation for the systematic development of communication protocols as well as distributed systems as an engineering discipline. They establish the basis for providing tools to support the different development stages and to automate parts of the development phases.

What are the features of communication protocols which justify the establishment of *Protocol Engineering* as an independent sub-discipline? These features relate to a number of particularities which characterize protocol development and distinguish it from traditional software development:

- The protocol notion used commonly comprises, exactly speaking, two concepts: that of the service and that of the protocol. The *service* denotes the result of the interaction between network components, when running a protocol. It can be used by other protocols or an application. The *protocol* describes how the service is provided. It is quasi its "implementation". This has consequences for the description of services and protocols. In contrast to the traditional software specification not only a *What*-specification, which describes the "service", is required, but also a *How*-specification is needed to specify how this service is provided, i.e., its "implementation".

- Protocol entities, which form the communicating partners in a protocol, must be capable of reacting simultaneously to different events and communication requirements, respectively. This can result in concurrent execution threads and the nondeterministic appearance of events.

- Unlike many other areas in computer science, the protocol area is characterized by (international) standards. Many protocols are defined as a standard. This is necessary so that the protocol can be implemented multiple times in different execution environments. The various implementations must be able to work together, i.e., they must be interoperable. Standardization usually cuts off the design stage from subsequent phases, such as verification, implementation, and testing. It also requires specific methods, such as the conformance test, to prove compliance with the standard.

- Protocols are subject to high demands on efficiency and reliability. The complexity of protocols is often contradictory to these requirements. The distributed nature of protocols results in complex state spaces in which design and

---

[1] The name was first introduced by Piatkowski in 1983 [Piat83].

implementation errors are difficult to find. To prove the correctness of the design and implementations special methods have to be applied.

- The development of protocols is expensive. It binds much manpower over a long period. To make this process more efficient tools are required which implement the protocol-specific development methods.

With regard to the existence of a world-wide communication infrastructure like the Internet, one might assume that the development of new protocols is not required any more. This is not true. Novel technological possibilities and innovative developments put new demands on the communication infrastructure and their protocols. In recent years many new protocols have appeared, in particular for wireless communication or peer-to-peer applications. With the development of new Internet applications and technologies the development of new protocols will continue in the future.

Objective of the book

The book is dedicated to the fundamentals of *Protocol Engineering*. It introduces the reader to the world of protocols, their basic principles, their description, and their development. The book considers both the theoretical and the practical aspects of *Protocol Engineering* and tries to link both parts which are often considered independently. At the same time it aims to point out the possibilities and limitations of the various methods. Last but not least, the book aims to encourage the reader to apply these methods in their practical work.

The book is primarily a book about formal description techniques for communication protocols and related methods. In the introductory part it presents the fundamentals of communication protocols as they are needed for further reading. The book is not a general introduction to computer networks; this is given in the well-known teaching books of Tanenbaum and Whetherall, Stallings, Peterson and Davie, and Kurose and Ross. It deals with a specific, but important area of the development of computer networks and telecommunication systems and thus it supplements the above mentioned books.

For whom is the book written?

This book is written for students and engineers of computer science and communication technology who want to introduce themselves to the field of communication protocols and their development. It also addresses specialists who want to deepen their knowledge of *Protocol Engineering* or look up applied methods. The book may be also of interest to software engineers who work on the development of distributed systems. Many of the presented methods for describing and validating protocols can also be applied to distributed systems.

The book does not require special knowledge of this topic. It is merely assumed that the reader possesses basic knowledge in computer networks and software engineering.

Structure of the book

The book consists of three parts. The first part contains the fundamentals of communication protocols. It describes the working principles of protocols and implicitly also those of computer networks. In this part we introduce the basic concepts *service, protocol, layer*, and *layered architecture*. Applying analogies from everyday life we try to familiarize the reader with the in-part-complicated procedures in protocols. In parallel, we introduce the basic elements for the description of protocols using a model language. Thereafter we present the most important protocol functions. Finally we give as a case study an overview of the TCP/IP protocol suite.

The second part of the book deals with the description of communication protocols. We give a comprehensive overview of the various methods and techniques for describing protocols. Beginning with the requirements on formal description techniques we first introduce the fundamental description methods which are in part used as semantic models for the formal description techniques. Thereafter we give an example of the various approaches of formal description techniques together with an overview of a representative language. The languages considered in this way are SDL-2000, MSC, LOTOS, cTLA, and ASN.1. We also give an outlook on the use of UML for describing protocols.

The third part presents the protocol life cycle and the most important development stages. We consider the following phases: design, specification, verification, performance evaluation, implementation, and testing and present the most relevant methods applied in these stages. The reader gets acquainted with approaches for a systematic protocol design, with basic techniques for the specification of protocols, with various verification methods, with the main implementation techniques, and with strategies for their testing, in particular with the conformance and the interoperability tests. In the testing chapter we also give an overview of the test description languages TTCN-2 and TTCN-3.

The connection between the three parts of the book is formed by the XDT (*eXample Data Transfer*) protocol. XDT is a simple data transfer example protocol which applies the *go back N* principle. It is used as a reference protocol throughout the book to exemplify the different description techniques as well as to demonstrate important validation and implementation approaches. This is supposed to give the reader the possibility to compare the different techniques and methods. The complete formal descriptions of the XDT protocol in the various formal description techniques are available at the web site of the book (see below).

How should the book be read?
The first part of the book deals with the fundamentals of communication protocols. It introduces the principles and the elements for describing protocols as they are presumed in the following two parts. This part addresses readers who want to familiarize themselves with basic protocol principles. Readers who have a good knowledge about protocols can omit this part. It is recommended, however, to read the short introduction to the XDT protocol in order to understand the reference examples in the later chapters.

The second part deals with the description of protocols. It introduces the basic description methods and the most important formal description techniques. The way protocols are described plays a central role in the protocol development process, since the selection of the description technique, in particular of the associated semantic model, determines the applied design and validation methods. For that reason, we separate the introduction of the formal description techniques from the description of the protocol development phases. We recommend the reader first concentrates on the description methods and the basic concepts of the description techniques he/she is most interested in.

The third part describes the development phases typical for communication protocols. Since communication protocols are seldom developed continuously, i.e., from design to implementation/installation, many protocol engineers specialize in certain phases, e.g., verification. Therefore, it is up to the readers how deeply they immerse themselves in the respective subject.

We provide for almost all chapters exercises which should help the reader to better understand the presented contents and to practice various description techniques.

Website for the book
A website is available to provide online materials and additional information on the subject of the book. These materials are available via the following URL:

http://www.protocol-engineering.tu-cottbus.de

The website contains among others:

- lecture materials related to the book including exercises
- the informal description of the XDT protocol
- an animated simulation of the XDT protocol to visualize the protocol behavior
- formal descriptions of the XDT protocol in the various FDTs presented in the book
- additional information and references.

Cottbus/Dresden, Germany   Hartmut König
Autumn 2011

Contents

Acknowledgements

The writing of a book is seldom motivated by the author alone. It is the result of a long involvement with the topic as well as of discussions with colleagues which raised the idea to start this lengthy work. So it has been with this book. The work started with a translation of a previous version published in German several years ago which was step by step extended or rewritten reflecting various comments and new developments. In this regard I would like to thank several colleagues at this point who supported the preparation of the manuscript.

First I'm much obliged to Prof. Ulrich Herzog (University of Erlangen) who convinced me some years ago to make an English translation of the book.

Further I would like to thank a number of colleagues who supported me in the preparation of individual chapters. I thank Monika Heiner (BTU Cottbus), Peter Herrmann (NTNU Trondheim), Iksoon Hwang (Telecom Paris Sud), Heiko Krumm (University of Dortmund), and Bruno Müller-Clostermann (University of Duisburg-Essen).

I also thank Prof. Ana Cavalli (Telecom Paris Sud) and Prof. Peter Herrmann (NTNU Trondheim) for hospitality at their institutions, when writing the manuscript.

Special thanks go to my Ph.D. student Prabhu Shankar Kaliappan for reading and correcting the manuscript. I also thank my assistants Alek Opitz and Michael Vogel for supporting me in developing the exercises contained in this book.

I'm also much obliged to Ronan Nugent of Springer for assisting the book project from the beginning to the printing. Furthermore, I also thank the unknown Springer proofreader for his careful reading.

Last but not least I'm very grateful to Mrs. Katrin Willhöft who actively supported me in preparing the manuscript and the drawings as well as the final printed version.

Part I: Principles of communication protocols

The first part of the book deals with the fundamentals of communication protocols. It introduces basic concepts and mechanisms of protocols. Since many protocol mechanisms are borrowed from human communication paradigms, we exemplify in the beginning protocol principles using analogies from everyday life. Simultaneously we introduce important fundamentals for describing communication services and protocols.

The notions and concepts of this introduction follow the OSI reference model of the *International Organization for Standardization* (ISO) and the TCP/IP Internet architecture. We do not, however, give prominence to the architectures themselves, but focus on the introduction of the concepts relevant for protocol theory. The introduction is *top down*. We start with the service concept. Thereafter we introduce the notion of protocol and proceed to the layering principle, and finally to layered architectures. The experience of many classes has shown that this approach facilitates the understanding of the basic protocol concepts. Therefore, we consider the layered architectures only briefly at the end of this introduction.

The first four chapters on *Services*, *Protocols*, *Layers*, and *Layered architectures* are structured in the same way. In the section *Principles* we introduce the theoretical foundations of the respective concept. In *Description* we present the elements required for their (formal) description followed by a demonstration using the XDT (*eXample Data Transfer*) protocol in the section *Example*.

In order to explain the basics of formal protocol descriptions we use a model language which applies basic terms of the service and protocol concept. The language aims at an intuitive understanding of the concepts. It uses a multi-level approach that allows a differentiated consideration of the various aspects. In *Example* we describe the XDT protocol in the model language. XDT is a simple connection oriented data transmission protocol which applies the *go back N*-principle.

The protocol is used as a reference protocol throughout the book to demonstrate the various description, validation, and implementation approaches. It shall give the reader a means to compare the expressiveness of the various formal description techniques presented in the book.

Readers who are familiar with the foundations of communication protocols and their description may omit this part. We recommend, however, that they acquaint themselves with the introduction to the XDT protocol in Sections 1.3, 2.3, and 3.3, which we will refer to throughout the book.

1 Services

Computer networks provide **services**. These services allow us to exchange data, programs, music files, pictures, movies or other documents. They can be used to download programs, to start them remotely, to update remote data bases, or to access web sites; they can also help users to communicate with others partners, and much more. The term *service* is of fundamental importance for the understanding of the processes in computer networks. It is closely related to the term *protocol* and represents an essential element for their description, validation, and use. This chapter deals with services. We start with a short overview of the different kinds of services. Thereafter we introduce the model of a communication service and present the basic concepts for its formal description using a model language. Finally we describe the service provided by our example protocol XDT and give a formal description of it using the model language.

1.1 Principles

Kind of services

In computer networks two kinds of services are distinguished: asymmetric and symmetric services (see Figure 1.1/1). **Asymmetric services** are services which apply the client/server paradigm. The service, e.g., a web page, is provided by a server in the network. It is called by a user, the *client*, on demand. The majority of services provided in computer networks are asymmetric services. These are in particular those services which are directly perceived by network users. They are therefore also called network services. The interaction between the client and the server follows the elementary scheme of service request and service provision. It is mostly implemented by means of a *remote procedure call* (RPC). More complex applications today use so-called distribution platforms, such as CORBA, or web services, which support transparent service provision, i.e., the client does not need to know the location of the server. In addition, they provide supplementary services to handle security demands, timing, and other related problems [Tane 02].

Symmetric services in contrast are services that simultaneously provide the offered service at two or more service access points. They are **communication services** which serve the exchange of data. Network services use communication services to transport the service request and the results of the service provision. Hence, the execution of asymmetric services is connected to symmetric communication services (see Figure 1.1/1). Often a logical communication relation – a so-called *connection* – is established between the access points to guarantee reliable transmission. There are also symmetric network services. They have a prevailing communicative character, e.g., a peer-to-peer video conference service. In this book we mainly consider communication services, i.e., symmetric services. They are provided by network protocols. For asymmetric services, other realization approaches are applied. Introductions to asymmetric services are given among others in [Tane 02].

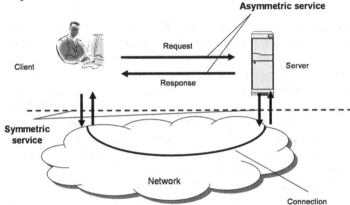

Figure 1.1/1: Asymmetric versus symmetric services

Application processes access symmetric services by calling functions of these services (see Figure 1.1/2). These functions are provided by special **communication software** embedded in the operating system of the hosts[1]. The structure of this communication software depends on the applied communication architecture. Different models and approaches may be applied. They are presented in subsequent chapters.

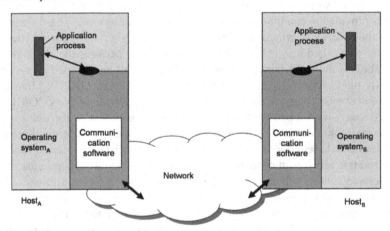

Figure 1.1/2: Communication software

---

[1] Computers in a network environment are usually called hosts.

Model of a communication service

The model of a communication service is shown in Figure 1.1/3. It distinguishes two basis concepts: that of the **service users**, which invoke the service, and that of the **service provider**, which offers the service. The interface between them is called the **service interface**. In order to use a service at least two service users are required. The service provider by contrast presents itself to all service users in the same way. This aspect can be exemplarily shown by means of the plain old telephone service (POTS). The telephone service is available everywhere where a telephone exists. It provides the same service at all telephones, but always two partners – the service users – are required when using the service.

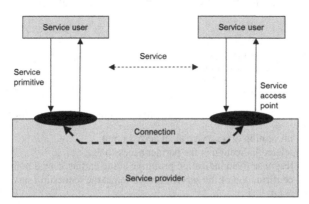

Figure 1.1/3: Model of a communication service

Service access points

A service user invokes a service via a **service access point (SAP)**, which possesses a unique address. A service access point can be compared, for example, with a post office, in which various postal services are offered. Other examples of service access points in everyday life are telephones or mobiles for the telephone service, and the mailbox for the mail service. The service users communicate with each other by handing over data at one service access point and reading them out at the other point. The transportation of the data is internally organized by the service provider. To facilitate the interaction a firm logical relation – a **connection** – can be established between the service access points (see below).

Service primitives

The invocation of a service is described through **service primitives** (SP). These are abstractions for describing the interactions between the service users and the service provider at the service interface. Service primitives do not prescribe how these interactions have to be implemented. The use of such primitives can be again exemplified with the telephone service. So the ringing of a telephone is nothing more than a service primitive of the telephone service that indicates a call request. The dial and the busy tone are other primitives of the service indicating that the line is free or that the partner's telephone is busy.

In the context of the OSI reference model (see Section 4.3.1) a notation for service primitives was developed, which is still used today, mostly a bit simplified. According to this notation service primitives are specified by a name, a type and parameters, e.g.,

CONNECT request(called address, calling address, QoS parameters, user data)
DATA indication(user data).

Further a label of the protocol layer may be added. We introduce them only in Chapter 3.

The *name* of a service primitive is not prescribed. It usually reflects the purpose of the service, e.g.,

CONNECT   - connection set up,
DISCONNECT - connection release,
DATA   - data transmission,
ABORT   - connection abort.

The *type* specifies the function of the primitive. Four types are distinguished:

request   - invocation of a service at an access point,
indication - related indication at the partner access point,
response   - response to an indication primitive at the partner access point,
confirm   - confirmation of the service invocation at the requesting service access point.

Service primitives of type *request* and *respond* are always triggered by the service user, while *indication* and *confirm* primitives are responses of the service provider (see Figure 1.1/4). The *parameters* are used to transport the data between the service user and provider. Typical parameters are addresses, options, and user data to be transferred. Nowadays the rather troublesome OSI notation is usually applied in a simpler form, e.g., *CONrequ*, *CONind*, or *DATrequ*. We also use such abbreviations in the following.

Service primitives are mostly not called accidentally. There are dependencies between the service primitives which require a defined invocation order. Such a defined order is, for instance, needed for setting up a telephone call. The following actions or "service primitives" prelude a telephone call: *pick up receiver →listen to dial tone → dial number → ringing* or *busy tone*. In order to specify dependencies between service primitives **time sequence diagrams** are used. They describe the sequence of interactions at the service access points. The time sequence diagrams "break up" the communication service model of Figure 1.1/3 by shifting the service provider into the middle of the presentation (see Figure 1.1/4a). The interaction sequence is specified along the time line directed downwards. Note that the comments given in Figure 1.1/4a serve for explanation and are usually omitted. Figure 1.1/4 contains examples of typical call sequences. Time sequence diagram a) depicts a **confirmed service** (see below), which contains primitives of all four types. Diagram b) represents an **unconfirmed service**, which only consists of a *request* and an *indication* primitive. Time sequence diagram c) gives an example for the abort of a connection by the service provider. The tilde indicates that there exist no time dependencies between the service primitives on the two sides.

Time sequence diagrams are not sufficient to represent all dependencies between service primitives at the access points. Each only describes a selected interaction sequence. In order to define, for example, the order between the connection set up and the subsequent data transmission additional representations are needed. For this, matrix representations or state diagrams are used. Matrix representations define the order between the various primitives. State diagrams describe the different states of the service provider at the two access points (see Section 1.3.1).

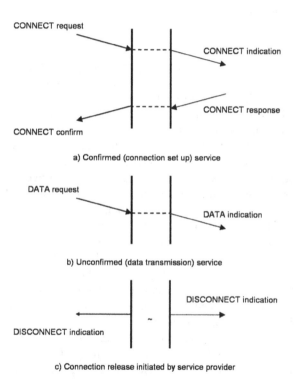

CONNECT request

CONNECT indication

CONNECT response

CONNECT confirm

a) Confirmed (connection set up) service

DATA request

DATA indication

b) Unconfirmed (data transmission) service

DISCONNECT indication

DISCONNECT indication

c) Connection release initiated by service provider

Figure 1.1/4: Time sequence diagrams

Connection-oriented services

The service users may establish a connection between the service access points. The associated services are called **connection-oriented services**. A **connection** is a logical relation between the communication partners for the duration of the communication. A connection can be compared with a connection established between two partners during a telephone call. A connection can support different kinds of data transmission: in one direction (*simplex*), alternating in both directions (*half duplex*), or simultaneously in both directions (*duplex*). Communication protocols mostly support duplex transmission.

Connection-oriented services are characterized by the following features: (1) they assure a complete data transmission, and (2) they preserve the transmission order of the sent data. This means that all data handed over at the sender SAP are delivered in the same order at the receiver SAP. This is the same principle as applied during a telephone call: all words spoken into the microphone are delivered in the same order at the remote receiver. The activities needed to ensure these features are not visible to service users.

Connection-oriented services consist of three phases:

- connection establishment,
- data transmission, and
- connection release.

These three phases represent **partial services,** which are characterized by defined interaction orders at the service interface. They can in principle be combined with other partial services to create another service.

The **connection establishment** or **set up** has the task to establish a connection between the service access points of the two service users. The interactions, which take place at the service interface, correspond to those of a *confirmed service* in Figure 1.1/4a. The connection set up is initiated by the service user, called the *initiator* in the sequel, by means of a *CONNECT request* primitive. The connection set up request is indicated to the partner – the *responder* – by a *CONNECT indication* primitive. The responder has the choice to accept or to reject the connection set up request. If the responder accepts the connection it responds with a *CONNECT response* primitive, which triggers a *CONNECT confirm* to the initiator to close the connection establishment successfully. In case of rejection, the responder sends a *DISCONNECT request* primitive. The initiator is informed about this by a *DISCONNECT indication*. Reasons for the rejection of the connection may be lack of resources to handle the connection. Usually the number of connections is limited by the implementation.

After setting up a connection the **data transmission** phase can start[2]. The data transmission corresponds to the *unconfirmed service* of Figure 1.1/4b. The data are handed over to the service provider using *DATA request* primitives. Their delivery at the receiver SAP is indicated by a *DATA indication* primitive. The connection ensures reliable transmission. An additional acknowledgment (at least at the service interface) is not required.

---

[2] The variant of the connection set up described here is called explicit connection set up. The complement is the implicit connection set up which allows the data transmission to start before the connection set up has been confirmed. It will be considered in Section 5.3.1.

The connection is released when the data transmission is finished. A **connection release** can be either explicitly started by a service user, when the data transmission is finished, or aborted by the service provider during data transmission due to internal reasons. The explicit release begins with a *DISCONNECT request* primitive followed by a *DISCONNECT indication* at the partner's access point. An abort is indicated by a *DISCONNECT indication* at all service access points (see Figure 1.1/4c).

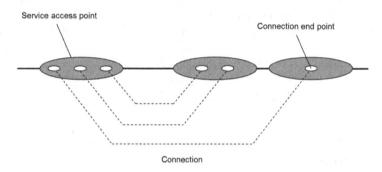

Figure 1.1/5: Connection end points

In the OSI context several connections can be established between service access points (see Figure 1.1/5). They are distinguished by means of **connection-end-point identifiers** (CEP *identifiers*). These identifiers can be used as connection references by the service users to manage the connections (see Section 2.1). This is not possible in the case of the Internet architecture. Here connections can only connect different access points (see Section 4.3.2 for this).

During connection establishment a **quality of service** (QoS) can be agreed between the service users and the service provider. The quality of service defines quantitative demands for service parameters that have to be fulfilled by the service provider. Examples of such parameters are data throughput, transmission delay, residual error rates, jitter, and others. Usually three main QoS classes are distinguished: best effort, statistical QoS, and guaranteed QoS. The classification *best effort* means that the demands are not mandatory for the service provider, but it tries to fulfill them without making any guarantees. It is also not obliged to inform the users about violations. *Best effort* is the typical quality of service of traditional communication services. It is still the most commonly provided quality of service in the Internet. In high performance communication, e.g., multimedia services with real-time requirements, statistical and guaranteed QoS are applied. These QoS classes provide the agreed quality depending on the available resources either with a certain probability or guaranteed.

Connectionless services

Connection-oriented data transmission causes an overhead to establish, maintain, and release the connection. This does not matter if larger amounts of data are transmitted and/or if a certain quality of service is demanded. In cases where only some short data units have to be exchanged this overhead is often not justified. In such cases **connectionless services** are preferred which do not require an explicit communication relation between the partners to send data. An example of a connectionless service in everyday life is the mail service. Letters are sent without informing the receivers beforehand. The destination is found by means of the address of the partner's access point which must be attached to the data unit sent. The reception of the data is not acknowledged. Connectionless services are therefore unconfirmed services according to Figure 1.1/4b. They do not guarantee reliable delivery of data units and they do not preserve their transmission order. Data losses must be detected by the service users which have to retransmit the data if required.

1.2   Description

1.2.1   Service specification

It is necessary for the service user to exactly know how to invoke a service. In normal life one also has to know how services have to be invoked. For example, the activities or "service primitives" sequence described above has to be performed to make a telephone call. The description of how to use a service is provided in the service specification. A **service specification** defines the requirements on a service and the steps of its invocation. Typical elements of the service specification are the provided (partial) services, the service primitives including the dependencies between them, their parameters and (mostly optionally) the dependencies between parameters. Time sequence diagrams are often used in practice to specify services, but they do not allow, as discussed above, a complete service description.

In international standards of ISO and ITU-T communication services and protocols are usually described in separate standards. The elaboration of service specifications is not self-evident. It is mainly applied in ISO and ITU-T documents, less so in the *Request for Comments* (RFCs) of the IETF (*Internet Engineering Task Force*). The notion of service appeared in the context of the OSI reference model in the 1980s. In the Internet world it is less explicitly used. For a systematic development of protocols, however, a service specification is essential, since only thus a systematic verification of the protocol design is possible (see Chapter 11).

The description of services (and protocols) in international standards is mostly informal using a verbal, textual description supplemented by time sequence diagrams, state diagrams, and tables. Informal descriptions, however, have proved insufficient for the specification and the development of communication services and protocols. The central issue is that they do not ensure a unique interpretation. Furthermore, they do not allow computer-aided analyses of the specification. For these reasons, the use of formal description techniques is recommended. Formal specifications are characterized by a formally defined syntax and semantics. In this section we introduce the elements required for describing services. We use a model language which applies terms of the service concept as well as well-known constructs of modern high-level programming languages. The model language distinguishes three nested description levels that are dedicated to the description of services, protocols, and the mapping of protocols onto the service of the lower layer. The language elements are introduced in the *Description* part of the three introductory chapters. They are then used to formally describe the example protocol XDT in the *Example* parts.

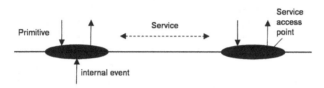

Figure 1.2/1: Description range of level S

In this section we introduce **level S** (*S=Service*) of our model language. It describes the provided services and the allowed interactions at the service interface (see Figure 1.2/1). The internal behavior of the service provider is only considered when it influences the interactions at the service interface. Such relations are described through internal events.

1.2.2   Services and service primitives

The service specification describes the service(s) provided. The description comprises the partial services (if any), the service primitives including their parameters, and the existing dependencies between them. Note that the service specification does not take into account the existence of several connections and the address scheme of the service access points. It is a generic description that applies to each connection. Connections and addresses are only introduced during implementation or configuration, respectively.

In our model language we describe services in the **service**-specification. It consists of an invocation specification and a behavior specification. The *invocation specification* specifies the partial services and their associated primitives:

service {
    invocation specification
    behavior specification
}

The following example depicts a fragment of the XDT service specification of Section 1.3 (comments are line bounded and start with //).

```
service {DATA_TRANSFER:                              // Service provided
    requested XDATrequ(conn: integer optional,
                       source_addr: address optional,
                       dest_addr: address optional,
                       eom: boolean,
                       data: array [] of byte
                       )
    responded XDATind(conn: integer,
                      eom: boolean,
                      data: array [] of byte
                      ),
               XDATconf(conn, sequ: integer),
                . . .
}
```

The service primitives are defined by their name, type, and parameters. We distinguish between two types of primitives: **requested** and **responded**. The **requested** primitives are primitives that are invoked by the service users; the **responded** primitives are triggered by the service provider. The parameters of the primitives must be specified with their data types. We do not explicitly introduce these data types; their context should make them self-explanatory. Some service primitives may contain parameters which are not included in every invocation of the primitive. These parameters are marked as **optional**. The **optional** feature can be used for describing variable data structures, which often appear in service and protocol specifications.

1.2.3 Dependencies between service primitives

To specify the causal dependencies between service primitives one has to distinguish between local and global behavior. The **local behavior** describes the allowed interactions between a service user and the provider at the service access point. The **global behavior** specifies the dependencies between the local interactions at the remote partners' access points (see Figure 1.2/2). The relation between local and global behavior can be illustrated by a telephone call. The dialing is a local behavior at the initiator site, the ringing the associated local behavior at the partner site. Only the global behavior defines that the dialing must precede the ringing. Time sequence diagrams are a means to partially describe global behavior.

The dependencies between service primitives are specified in the *behavior specification* of our model language (see above). The behavior specification consists of one or several **sap**-specifications.

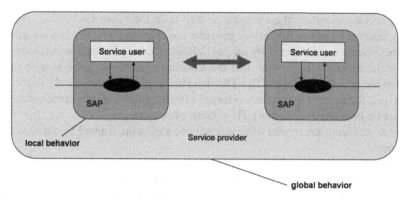

Figure 1.2/2: Local and global behavior

A **sap**-*specification* describes the interactions at a service access point and their relation with interactions at the partner interaction point. We apply a procedure-oriented representation for describing the interactions at a service access point. It reflects the sequence of the interactions (see Section 7.1 for this). Each **sap**-specification defines a certain type of access point. If the behavior at all service access points is the same, only one **sap**-specification is required. The **sap**-specification has the following syntactical structure. We explain the elements next.

> **sap** *name*   // **sap**-specification
> **signal** *name*$_1$, ... , *name*$_j$
> **phase**-specification
> **par event**-specification$_n$

Local behavior

In order to describe the interactions at a service access point we need a description model that specifies the semantics of the behavior. The description model applied is depicted in Figure 1.2/3. It describes a service access point as an asynchronous communication interface with two opposed event queues.

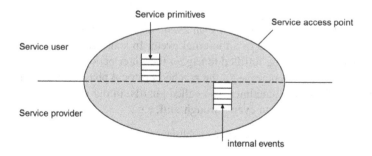

Figure 1.2/3: Description model of the local behavior

The service users put their service primitives in the downward queue. Analogously internal events of the service provider are enqueued into the upward queue. The local behavior is defined by all possible sequences of events which may appear at the service access point, and the associated reactions of the service users and service provider, respectively. The downward queue contains only requested primitives; the upward queue only **internal events,** which indicate certain states of the service provider (see below). How these events are triggered is not described (as we do not learn the reason when a telephone call is interrupted by a disconnection tone).

Although service specifications are primarily used for specifying the externally visible behavior at the service interface, internal events are applied to describe exceptional situations like the failure of the communication link, which lead to reactions at the service interface. The use of internal events is a trick to take the behavior of the service provider into account. The description of internal events is handled differently in the various formal description techniques. Automata-based description techniques use **spontaneous transitions** that are triggered without any input event. Algebraic description techniques define an explicit **internal action** (see Chapter 7).

In our model language we use different internal events to describe the various states of the service provider. They are interpreted as signals and must be declared at the beginning of the **sap**-specification in a **signal**-*declaration*, e.g.,

signal abort, break

A signal is set, when it enters the upward queue. It is not described how this is done.

The interactions appearing at the service interface are described in a so-called **behavior description**. For this, the same description principle is applied in almost all formal description techniques. This also relates to protocol descriptions, which we consider in the next chapter. The description of an interaction, or more generally of an action, has the following structure:

event [*condition*]$^{[0:n]}$: *action*

The (inter)action is triggered by an *event*. In a service specification an event may be a service primitive or an internal event. In some cases, one or more additional conditions must be fulfilled to trigger the (inter)action. These conditions describe context dependencies, e.g., the reached protocol phase or the value of some parameters. They are sometimes also called guards. In our example language conditions are connected to an event through **and**, e.g.,

XDATrequ **and** sequ=1: connection establishment

When the specified event occurs and all possible conditions are fulfilled, then the associated *action* is executed as a reaction to this event. Formal description techniques differ in the execution semantics of the action part. Some techniques apply an atomic execution, others not.

Since events do not occur continuously at the service interface, the service users and the provider are forced to wait. Furthermore, they usually do not wait only for one event but for several. In state-oriented descriptions like finite state machines, waiting is implicitly expressed through the state (see Section 7.4). The associated transitions describe the reactions to the awaited events. When an event occurs, the associated transition is triggered. In a procedure-oriented description, as here, an explicit wait-statement is needed. We introduce a **wait event**-*statement* for this purpose:

wait event{
    $event_1$ [*condition*]$^{[0:n]}$: $action_1$ |

        . . .

    $event_n$ [*condition*]$^{[0:n]}$: $action_n$
}.

The **wait event**-statement only reacts to the first occurring event. After executing the associated reaction it leaves the **wait event**-statement. For example, the statement

wait event{
        break_over: **respond** XDATconf |
        abort: **respond** XABORTind
                set CONNECT
}

would either trigger an *XDATconf*-primitive or abort the transmission by means of an *XABORTind*.

An associated *action* may consist of several statements which are executed sequentially. One possible statement is the **wait event**-statement itself. Another statement is the **respond**-*statement*:

respond *service primitive*(*parameters*),

e.g.,

respond XDATind(conn,eom,data).

The **respond**-statement describes the sending of a service primitive from the service provider to the service user including the associated parameter values. A **respond**-statement is triggered by an internal event.

Communication protocols often distinguish several phases, such as connection establishment, data transmission, and connection release. Protocol phases comprise a subset of the protocol procedures. They are a useful means to structure the protocol. This structuring is also reflected in the service specification. In most formal description techniques the specification of protocol phases is left to the specifier. In our model language we explicitly introduce phases to support better readability. A phase is considered as a condition which can be set and polled. Protocol phases are introduced in the **phase**-*specification*, e.g.,

> **phase** CONNECT: XDATrequ, XDATconf, XDISind;
> DATA TRANSFER: XDATrequ, XABORTind, XBREAKind;

For each phase, the service primitives that occur in this phase are specified. A phase is set in the *action* part by means of a **set**-statement, e.g.,

> **set** CONNECT.

This means that the protocol changes to the specified phase. The preceding phase is implicitly reset.

Global behavior

The global behavior describes dependencies between the local behaviors at the partners' service access points, exactly speaking between their service primitives. The representation of these dependencies is not that easy. There are no established means for this as can be seen in Chapter 8, where we introduce different formal description techniques. In our model language we define two special constructs to represent global dependencies: the *cause statement* and the *triggering event*. The **cause**-statement

> *local event*: ↳ *SAP.event*

describes a reaction to a *local event* that triggers the specified *event* at the partner *SAP* after a limited time. For example, a triggering *request*-primitive eventually causes an *indication*-primitive at the partner access point, e.g.,

> XDATrequ: ↳ receiver.XDATind

The statement does not describe how this happens. It only establishes a (global) relation between these two events. The names of the service access points used in the **cause**-statement must be introduced in a **sap**-specification. The triggering event is indicated without parameters.

The *triggering event* (without parameters) represents the counterpart to the **cause**-statement. It is used in the specification of the partner SAP to establish a relation to the causing reaction, e.g.,

wait event{
    ↳ sender.XDATrequ: **respond** XDATind
    . . .
}.

Another important feature of the service specification is the description of dependencies between the parameters of the service primitives. This is usually applied to indicate whether the values of the parameters change during transmission or not. In some ISO standards, e.g., for the transport service [ISO 8072], tables were used for this. In formal description techniques parameter relations are rarely specified, since the specifications may be pretty long winded. For that reason, we do not specify parameter relations here to simplify the examples.

1.2.4 Nondeterminism

An important element in describing services and protocols is the use of nondeterminisms. They are applied, when it is not possible or even not wanted to specify exactly the occurrence order of certain events. Two kinds of nondeterminisms are used in service and protocol specifications:

- the simultaneous occurrence of events and
- the assignment of different reactions to the same event.

Simultaneous occurrence of events

The simultaneous occurrence of events is caused either by simultaneous interactions at the service interface or by concurrent processes within the service provider that do not allow one to determine the exact order in which the events occur. There are two possibilities to handle concurrent events: (1) truly concurrently, what is often difficult to realize, or (2) in an interleaved manner. The latter is a common model for concurrent systems which is also applied in the protocol area. In the **interleaving model** all events of a concurrent execution of processes are arranged in a linear order, called the *interleaving sequence* [Clar 00]. The concurrently executed events appear arbitrarily ordered with respect to one another. All interleaving sequences represent possible externally observable behavior of the system. Figure 1.2/4 demonstrates the principle. All ordering combinations are possible interleaving sequences. It is only possible to define a partial order for the occurrence of events which determines that a certain event must occur before another one. In verification this has to be taken into account because it may lead to very large state spaces which are difficult to handle. For this purpose, methods have been introduced to reduce the state space by considering only selected interleaving sequences (see Section 11.3.2 for this).

Taking the simultaneous occurrence of events into account we can now completely describe the (local) behavior at an access point in our model language. For this, we introduce the **par event**-statement.

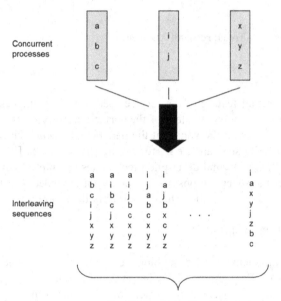

Figure 1.2/4: Principle of interleaving

par event {

   $event_1$ [condition]$^{[0:n]}$: $action_1$ ||

   ...

   $event_n$ [condition]$^{[0:n]}$: $action_n$

}

The **par event**-statement expresses the fact that some events may occur simultaneously and have to be handled concurrently. In contrast to time sequence diagrams, it allows one to subsume all interactions that may occur at a service access point under one statement. The **par event**-statement has a similar syntactical structure to the **wait event**-statement, but the actions are executed in parallel when the associated event occurs. The symbol "||" indicates concurrent execution.

par event {

   break: **respond** XBREAKind(conn)   // Break

      . . . ||

   abort: **respond** XABORTind(conn)   // Transmission abort

      set CONNECT ||

   eom: **respond** XDISind(conn)   // Regular connection release

      set CONNECT

}

The **par event**-statement runs endlessly. It is executed as follows. The service access point alternately reads the first event from one of the event queues (cp. Figure 1.2/3) and examines whether it is awaited in one of the alternatives. If the event is awaited then the associated execution is started, otherwise the event is discarded. If the same event occurs twice, while the first one is still being handled then the execution is postponed until the handling of this event is finished. In case of empty input queues the service access point waits for further incoming events. If a **wait event**-statement is included in a **par event**-statement then the service access point examines for both statements whether the event is awaited. The **par event**-statement has priority over the **wait event**-statement in this case, i.e., the event is assigned to the former statement.

Assignment of different reactions

In certain situations it is useful to assign several reactions to the same event. This allows one to describe alternative behaviors. At the specification level it remains open which of the specified reactions will be selected. The following example shows this situation:

```
wait event{
        XDATrequ: ↳ receiver.XDATind                    // connection set up
                wait event{
                        connected: respond XDATconf |    // confirmed
                        abort: respond XABORTind         // abort
                } |
        XDATrequ: ↳ receiver.XDATind                    // data transmission
}.
```

In this **wait event**-statement two different reactions are specified for an *XDATrequ* primitive. In the first case a connection set up procedure is finished (either successfully or not), while in the second case the received data are handed over to the receiver. This example might seem a little bit artificial, but at this stage of the introduction in our example protocol there are not that many options for presentation, yet. However, similar representations can be found in many specifications. The advantage of nondeterministic descriptions lies in the simplification of the description because alternative behaviors do not need to be assigned to different states. Furthermore, it increases flexibility because the decision, which alternative to be chosen, is postponed until implementation or another development phase. This allows it to adapt more flexibly to the target environment.

The application of nondeterminism in formal descriptions strongly depends on the abstraction level of the specification. More abstract description techniques use it more frequently than implementation-oriented techniques. In the implementation phase nondeterminisms are usually dissolved.

1.3   Example

At the end of this introductory chapter we apply the discussed elements of the service specification to our example protocol XDT (*eXample Data Transfer Protocol*). The protocol provides a reliable data transmission service over an unreliable medium. It is a connection-oriented protocol (see Figure 1.3/1). We introduce the XDT protocol stepwise in the next three chapters. The informal introduction is followed by a description in our model language. In this chapter we begin with the description of the XDT service.

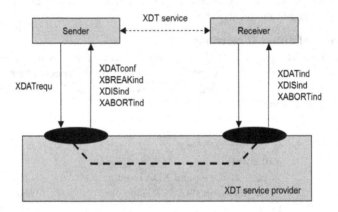

Figure 1.3/1: XDT service

1.3.1 XDT service

The XDT service provides a connection-oriented data transmission service for transferring a large amount of data. The connection is assumed to be unidirectional. The connection set up uses a 2-way-handshake (see Section 5.2). It starts with an *XDATrequ* primitive that can already contain user data. The initiator can only continue the transmission when a successful connection set up is indicated through an *XDATconf* primitive. The primitive contains a connection reference for identifying the connection. At the receiver side a new connection is indicated by an *XDATind* primitive. For simplification, we assume that the receiver is able to always accept new connections. An unsuccessful connection set up is indicated to the initiator by an *XABORTind* primitive.

We further suppose that the data are handed over to the XDT service provider in units of the same length. A sequence number is assigned to each data unit. The service provider confirms that a data unit is sent off by an *XDATconf* to the sender. Only then the next data unit may be handed over. For simplicity, it is assumed that a data transmission comprises at least two *XDATrequ*, i.e., the connection set up will be always finished. Furthermore, it is assumed that the sender continuously transmits data units (each time after getting an *XDATconf*), i.e., there are no larger breaks caused by the sender. However, it is possible that the service provider after receiving an *XDATrequ* primitive can interrupt the transmission by an *XBREAK-ind* for a certain time. The end of the break is indicated by the originally expected *XDATconf* primitive.

When the service provider is not able any more to ensure the transmission order of the data units, it aborts the transmission by an *XABORTind* primitive and releases the connection.

The transmission is finished when the last data unit is successfully transmitted. When transferring the final data unit, the *eom* field in *XDATrequ* and *XDATind* is set to true. The connection is released with an *XDISind* primitive at both sides.

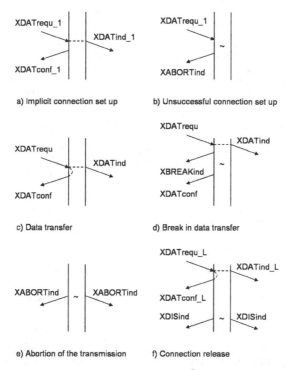

Figure 1.3/2: Time sequence diagrams of the XDT service[3]

Figure 1.3/2 contains the time sequence diagrams of the XDT service. The local dependencies between the various interaction sequences at the XDT service access points are represented by the state diagram in Figure 1.3/3.

---

[3] The subscripts 1 and L indicate the first and the last service primitive of the transmission, respectively.

1.3.2 Formal description

In this section we describe the XDT service in our model language (level S). The description begins with the invocation specification, which specifies the XDT services and its primitives. Thereafter we describe the interactions at the XDT service interface in the behavior description. Since XDT is an asymmetric protocol, we need two **sap**-specifications, which are denoted as *sender* and *receiver*. The XDT protocol phases are CONNECT for the connection establishment and DATA TRANSFER for the data transmission. There is no explicit connection release phase because the connection is implicitly released after receiving the last data unit.

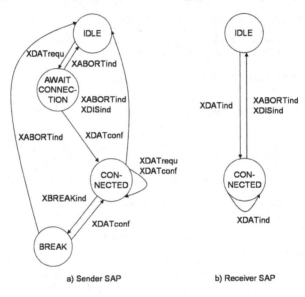

Figure 1.3/3: State diagrams of the XDT service provider at the two access points

The service provider indicates the following internal events: *connected* for a successful connection set up, *abort* for a transmission failure, *break* and *break_ over* for the beginning and the end of the break, and *eom* to indicate the successful transmission of the last data unit. There exists only one global relation. This is between the *XDATrequ* primitive at the sender side and the *XDATind* at the receiver side. All other service primitives are only of local importance.

The specification is enclosed by **specification** *name*{ ... }. We will add further parts to this specification in the following chapters.

specification XDT {
service XDT-DATA_TRANSFER: // PROVIDED SERVICE
    requested XDATrequ(conn: integer **optional**,   // Connection reference
                sequ: integer,   // Sequence number
                source_addr: address **optional**, // Source address
                dest_addr: address **optional**,   // Destination address
                eom: boolean,   // End of message
                data: **array** [] **of** byte   // User data
)
   responded XDATind(conn,sequ: integer, eom: boolean, data: **array** [] **of** byte),
        XDATconf(conn,sequ: integer),
        XBREAKind(conn: integer),
        XABORTind(conn: integer **optional**),
        XDISind(conn: integer)

sap sender{   // BEHAVIOR AT SENDER SAP
signal connected, abort, eom, break, break_over
phase CONNECT: XDATrequ, XDATconf, XDISind; // Connection set up phase
    DATA TRANSFER: XDATrequ, XABORTind, XBREAKind;
par event{   // Data transmission phase
XDATrequ(1,source_addr,dest_addr,eom,data)   // Connection set up
    and CONNECT:
        ↳receiver.XDATind
       wait event{connected: **respond** XDATconf(1,conn)
                                // Connection established
                          set DATA TRANSFER | // Phase change
                  abort: **respond** XABORTind   // Set up aborted
        } ||
XDATrequ(conn,sequ,eom,data)   // Data transfer phase
    and DATA TRANSFER: **respond** XDATconf(conn,sequ)
                    ↳ receiver.XDATind || // To receiver
break: **respond** XBREAKind(conn)   // Break
      wait event{
        break_over: **respond** XDATconf(conn,sequ) | // End of break
        abort: **respond** XABORTind(conn)   // Abort during break
                set CONNECT
        } ||
abort: **respond** XABORTind(conn)   // Transmission fails
      set CONNECT ||
eom: **respond** XDISind(conn)   // Connection release
      set CONNECT
} // Sender-SAP

```
    sap receiver{                                    // BEHAVIOR AT RECEIVER SAP
    signal abort, eom
    phase CONNECT, DATA TRANSFER: XDATind
    par event{
        ↳sender.XDATrequ and CONNECT:               // Connection set up
            respond XDATind(conn,1,eom,XDATrequ.data)
            set DATA TRANSFER  ||
        ↳sender.XDATrequ and DATA TRANSFER:         // Data transmission
            respond XDATind(conn,sequ,eom,XDATrequ.data)  ||
        abort: respond XABORTind(conn)              // Transmission abort
            set CONNECT  ||
        eom: respond XDISind(conn)                  // Connection release
            set CONNECT
    }// Receiver SAP
} //XDT
```

Further reading
Introductions to the service concept can be also found in all introductory books about computer networks, such as the books of Kurose and Ross [Kuro 08], Stallings [Stal 08], Peterson and Davie [Pete 07], and Tanenbaum and Wetherall [Tane 10].

Exercises
(1) What is a service? What kinds of services are distinguished? Explain the differences between them.
(2) Describe the model of a communication service. Explain the role and the function of its elements.
(3) Explain the service elements used for the following scenarios:
   - mail service
   - telephone service
   - directory assistance.
   Which of these scenarios represent symmetric services?
(4) What is a connection? Between what points is a connection set up: between the service users or between the service access points? What are the phases of a connection-oriented service?
(5) Explain the difference between a connection-oriented and a connectionless service. What are the advantages/disadvantages of each? When should they be applied?
(6) What is the purpose of the service specification?
(7) Explain the difference between local and global behavior in a service specification.
(8) What is meant by nondeterminism? How is it used in formal descriptions?
(9) What is interleaving? How is it expressed in formal descriptions? What is the alternative approach to interleaving?

(10) What is the purpose of internal events used in service specifications?

(11) Replace the implicit connection acceptance of the receiver in the XDT service by an explicit one, i.e., the receiver no longer accepts every connection; it can accept or reject a connection.

a) Describe this extension by means of time sequence diagrams. Introduce appropriate service primitives.

b) Change the state diagrams of Figure 1.3/3, which describe the local behavior at the XDT SAPs, appropriately.

c) Describe the changes in the model language.

(12) Extend the XDT service at the receiver side by a mechanism by which the service user may interrupt the reception of data for a certain time period. The time is given as a parameter to the service provider which controls the break duration and continues to deliver data after the time has elapsed. Describe the changes as in exercise (11) using time sequence diagrams, state diagrams, and the model language.

(13) Replace the implicit connection release in the XDT service by an explicit one that is triggered by the receiver by an *XDISrequ* when it has received the last PDU. The sender releases the connection with an *XDISind*, after which the receiver also releases the connection with *XDISind*.

a) Describe this extension by means of time sequence diagrams.

b) Change the state diagrams of Figure 1.3/3 appropriately to express global dependencies between the service primitives.

c) Describe the changes in the model language.

2 Protocols

In this chapter we consider how communication services are provided. For this, we look inside the service provider. We introduce the notion of protocol and explain the relations which exist between protocol procedures and the interactions at the service interface. Next we describe the basic elements of communication protocols and show how they can be described. Finally we continue introducing the XDT protocol.

2.1 Principles

Entities

Services are provided by the service provider using interacting entities (see Figure 2.1/1). **Entities** are active objects of the service provider that communicate with their environment by exchanging messages. The internal structure of the entities is not relevant from the modeling point of view. We only consider their capability to interact with other entities and with the environment.

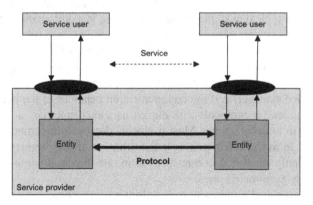

Figure 2.1/1: Service and protocol

The entities serve the service access points. A service access point is always assigned to one entity only, while an entity can simultaneously handle several access points (see Figure 2.1/2). The entities read the service primitives handed over at the service access points and analyze them. According to the address information transported in the service primitives they start to interact with the entity which serves the related service access point to provide the service. This entity is called a **peer entity**. The working principle of an entity can be compared with a letter distribution centre, which fetches the letters from the mailboxes, reads the addresses,

29

and forwards the letters to the peer distribution centre, which delivers the letters to the receivers' mailboxes.

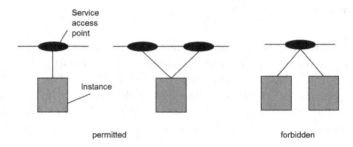

Figure 2.1/2: Relation between service access points and entities

Communication protocol

The interaction between peer entities follows firm rules. These rules are defined by a communication protocol or protocol, for short. A **communication protocol** is a behavior convention that defines the temporal order of the interactions between the peer entities as well as the format (syntax and semantics) of the messages exchanged.

In conversational language the term protocol possesses two meanings. It either denotes the minutes of a meeting, or it describes a firm procedure, i.e., a convention or a ritual. A typical example of the second case is a diplomatic protocol. The term protocol in computer networks corresponds to the latter meaning. It defines a communication procedure that iterates. Note that a protocol is not a dialogue, because a dialogue has mostly an unpredictable course that cannot be repeated.

Two kinds of protocols are distinguished: symmetric and asymmetric ones. A protocol is called **symmetric** if the communication behavior of the two entities is equal. This is given for protocols with duplex data exchange, i.e., a simultaneous data exchange in both directions. Most protocols deployed in computer networks are symmetric. In **asymmetric** protocols the behavior of both entities is different. Protocols that only support data transmission in one direction (simplex transmission) are usually asymmetric ones.

In order to graphically represent protocol interactions, time sequence diagrams are used. In contrast to the description of services, the interaction between the entities is now described by the messages exchanged. Figure 2.1/3 shows as examples the time sequence diagrams for a successful and a rejected connection set up. They include both the service primitives and the exchanged messages.

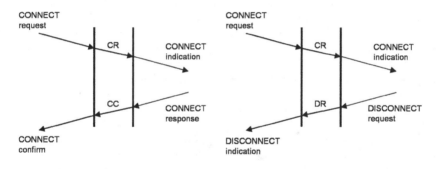

a) Successful connection establishment   b) Rejected connection set up

Figure 2.1/3: Protocol sequences as time sequence diagrams

Protocol data units

The messages that are exchanged between peer entities are called **protocol data units (PDUs)**. Their format, i.e., the structure and the semantics of the components, is defined by the protocol, which is known to both entities to ensure that the protocol data units are equally interpreted. A protocol typically uses several protocol data units, e.g., for connection set up, data transfer, and connection release. They are distinguished by their names and different internal code tags.

Principle of transparency

The protocol data units transport the user data which have been handed over to the service provider through service primitives. The user data are not accessible to the service provider, similarly to the context of a letter, which is not accessible to the postman, i.e., these data are transparent for the service provider. They must be delivered unchanged to the receiver. This is called the **principle of transparency**. Of course, the service provider could access these data, but what this principle exactly means is that the service provider should not use these data for controlling the protocol procedure. The principle of transparency forms the basis for the "tunneling" technique applied in the Internet, when protocol data pass through a network with another protocol architecture.

To implement the principle of transparency the user data, called **service data units (SDUs)**, are supplemented by protocol control fields, known as **protocol control information (PCI)**. The protocol control information and the service data unit form the protocol data unit (see Figure 2.1/4). Protocol control fields may precede and/or succeed the service data unit as *PDU header* and/or *trailer*. Most protocols only use a PDU header because it is easier to analyze. Typical protocol control data are, for example, the source and destination address, the length of the PDU, the PDU tag, quality of service (QoS) parameters, and the frame check sequence. The protocol control fields are removed at receiver side before the service data units are delivered to the service user.

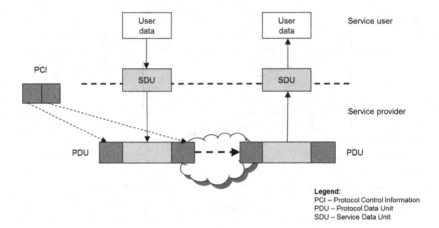

Figure 2.1/4: Principle of transparency

Protocol functions

Protocol entities contain various procedures and mechanisms which are repeatedly used in different protocols. These protocol procedures are called **protocol functions**. A typical protocol function is the error control which defines, for instance, the reactions of the protocol entities when a PDU has not been transmitted successfully. Other examples are the fragmentation of PDUs or the flow control, which controls the speed of the data exchange between the sender and receiver entities. We will comprehensively introduce the most important protocol functions in Chapter 5.

Connections

In connection-oriented protocols the peer entities have to manage the connections that are established between the service users at the service access points. The same protocol runs over each connection. The protocols are executed concurrently and do not influence each other. Connections are identified by **connection references,** which are only used as local context information. The connection references correspond to the connection end points of Section 1.1. The entities use **connection tables** (see Figure 2.1/5) to manage the connections and to store all information about them, e.g., the addresses of the access points, the state of the connection (*non-existent, establishing, existent, releasing*), and others. The connection reference can be used as table index.

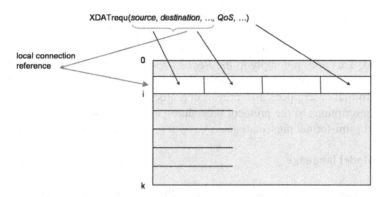

XDATrequ(*source, destination*, ..., *QoS*, ...)

local connection
reference

0

i

k

Figure 2.1/5: Connection table

Concurrency and nondeterminism

In the last chapter we discussed that concurrency and nondeterminism may appear at the service interface. Accordingly the protocol entities have to be capable of handling them. The entities must be able to simultaneously react to different communication demands and events. For example, during the coding of a PDU it can be indicated that the respective connection has been interrupted. In this case the entity has to take measures to re-establish the connection. These actions are performed **concurrently**. When several events appear simultaneously to the entity, it cannot be predicted in which order the entity handles them. It is even not prescribed, which event will be handled first and in which order the other events are handled. The selection is **nondeterministic**.

2.2 Description

2.2.1 Protocol specification

The manner in which entities interact with each other in a protocol is defined in the **protocol specification**. It describes the temporal order of interactions between the peer entities and defines the format of the messages exchanged. The protocol specification defines among others how the entities react to service primitives, incoming PDUs, or internal events. The protocol specification is basically the "implementation" of the service specification.

The protocol specification represents the reference document for the validation and the implementation of the protocol. From the service user's point of view, it is not necessarily required to know the protocol specification. It is relevant for the protocol engineer. A protocol specification is always independent of a concrete implementation, i.e., it only prescribes the interactions between the entities, but it does not prescribe how the protocol is integrated into a certain execution environment, i.e., the operating system. Thus it is guaranteed that implementations for different execution environments can be derived from the same protocol specification.

In former ISO specifications the service and protocol descriptions were strictly separated. This does not apply to the *Request for Comments* (RFCs) of the IETF, in which services are mostly not explicitly described. As with service specifications, informal descriptions also prevail in protocol specifications. They consist of textual descriptions of the protocol procedures supplemented by tables, diagrams, and other semi-formal presentations.

2.2.2 Model language

We again demonstrate the principles of the protocol specification using our model language. As next language level, we now introduce **level P** (*P=Protocol*). It describes the interactions between the entities under the assumption of a virtual communication between them (see Figure 2.2/1). Virtual communication means here that it is not said at this abstraction level how the interaction between the peer entities is implemented.

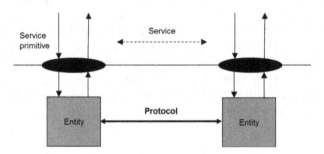

Figure 2.2/1: Description principle of level P

We start with the description of the PDU formats. Thereafter we consider the description of the protocol procedures.

2.2.3 Description of the PDU formats

The data units which are exchanged in a protocol form the "common language" of the communicating entities, which they have to interpret equally. Therefore their formats have to be specified unambiguously. The definition of the PDU formats is independent of the description of the protocol procedures. They are usually described separately.

The specification of the PDU formats is handled differently in the various formal description techniques. One of the earlier techniques, Estelle for instance, used PASCAL data types. This was very convenient for the user because PASCAL was pretty well-known at that time. But it introduced implementation dependencies into the description which might lead to different interpretations of the data formats. Therefore other languages introduced their own data description. The algebraic language LOTOS incorporated the algebraic data type language ACT ONE. This proved a failure because the data format specification appeared expensive. SDL first defined its own notation based on algebraic representations of abstract data types. Later it was integrated the abstract syntax notation ASN.1, which is preferred for describing the data formats of communication protocols nowadays. We will introduce it in Section 8.5.

In our model language we use for readability reasons elements of modern programming languages for describing the data structures, as we already did for the description of the service primitives at level S. The PDU formats are described in the **message**-specification which follows the **service**-specification of level S:

```
specification name{
    service specification                          // unchanged from level S
    message specification
    . . .
}
```

In the **message**-specification all protocol data units that appear in the protocol have to be listed, e.g.,

```
message{
    DT: struct(length: 0..255,                     // Data PDU
              code: bits,
              source-addr: address optional,
              dest-addr: address optional,
              conn: integer optional,
              sequ: integer,
              eom: boolean,
              data: [] byte
              )
    ACK: struct (code: bits,                        // Acknowledgment DT
               conn: integer,
               sequ: integer
               )
}
```

To describe the access to components of a protocol data unit, we use the dot-notation which is often applied in connection with **struct**- and **record**-constructs in high-level programming langages, e.g., DT.sequ or ACK.conn.

2.2.4 Description of protocol procedures

In general, there are two approaches to formally describe communication protocols: constructive and descriptive techniques (see Section 7.3). *Constructive techniques* describe the protocol by means of an abstract model. This is in essence a quasi-implementation of the protocol on a more abstract level. *Descriptive techniques*, in contrast, formulate properties usually in logical calculi which the protocol to be designed is to fulfill. In practice most formal description techniques apply the constructive approach. Typical semantic models of constructive description techniques are finite state machines or labeled transition systems (see Section 7.4 and 7.7). Our model language also belongs to this type of description techniques.

Semantic model

For simplicity reasons, we do not introduce a formal semantic model for our model language here. We present the description principle applied to interpret specifications. The semantic model of the level P of our model language is based on extended final state machines (see Section 7.5). It refines the behavior description based on the **par event**-statement used in level S. In contrast to many finite state machine representations, which use a state-oriented description, we apply *a communication-oriented description method* which focuses on the representation of interactions between the peer entities (see Section 7.1). The basic unit of this description principle is the so-called protocol part (see Figure 2.2/2).

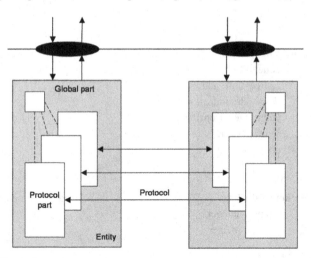

Figure 2.2/2: Protocol parts

A **protocol part** describes a dedicated communication behavior of an entity that is triggered by an external and/or an internal event. The reaction on this event is described sequentially using a procedure-like form. The protocol parts of the peer entities constitute the protocol. To illustrate the principle one can image a conversation. The phrases of each partner are recorded in a protocol part. When they are put together they present the conversation. At best a protocol consist of two protocol parts, those of the sender and receiver entities. In most cases, however, several protocol parts are needed. In symmetric protocols the entities consist of the same protocol parts; in asymmetric protocols they have different ones. The protocol parts of an entity are executed concurrently. In certain situations coordination between different protocol parts may be required. This is done by exchanging signals.

Interactions between the entities are *asynchronous*. Each entity possesses an event queue in which the incoming events for all protocol parts are stored. Events are service primitives, PDUs, timeouts, signals, and internal events. Figure 2.2/3 depicts the description model of a protocol entity.

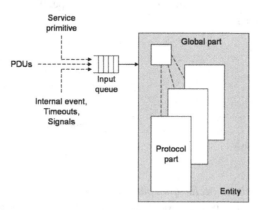

Figure 2.2/3: Description model of a protocol entity

Specifications and statements

In order to describe the protocol behavior we introduce two further specifications: the **protocol-** and the **entity**-specification. A level-P specification now has the following syntactical structure:

specification *name*{
    service *specification*   // unchanged from level S
    message *specification*
    protocol *specification*
    entity *specification$_1$*
    . . .
    entity *specification$_n$*
}

The **protocol-specification** declares which protocol parts constitute a protocol. A protocol may be divided into sub-protocols that run, for instance, in different phases. For each sub-protocol, the respective protocol parts have to be listed. The protocol parts are referred to by the name of the entity and the name of the part, e.g.,

protocol
    connection set up: XS.connect_s ⇔ XR.connect_r
    data transfer: XS.transfer_s ⇔ XS.ack_handler ⇔ XR.connect_r

The **entity-specification** constitutes the main part of the level-P specification. It describes the communication behavior of the protocol entities. In symmetric protocols only one **entity**-specification is needed; in asymmetric protocols separate **entity**-specifications must be introduced for describing the sender and the receiver entity. The **entity**-specification consists of a specification and declaration part and an action part.

entity *name*
sap-*specification*   // Specification and declaration part
signal-*declaration*
var-*declaration*
timer-*declaration*
par event{   // Action part
    . . .
}.

The *specification and declaration part* begins with the **sap**-specification, which is mandatory. The **sap**-specification specifies the service access points which are served by the entity. The given access points must relate to a service access point of the level-S specification, e.g.,

sap sender.

In the **signal-declaration**, which is optional like the other declarations, the signals must be declared which are exchanged internally between protocol parts, e.g.,

signal break, credit.

The signals indicate the occurrence of certain events in the respective protocol part, e.g., the change of the protocol phase or the arrival of a new credit for flow control. Internal events are also represented by signals. It is not described how these signals are set.

The **var-declaration** is used for introducing variables like in programming languages. Each variable has a data type. Here the same data types are allowed as introduced in the level-S specification. A variable may be initialized by indicating an initial value after **init**, e.g.,

var i, j: integer,
    sequ: integer **init**(1),
    last: boolean **init**(false)

The declared variables are valid for all protocol parts of the entity. They can be used to exchange data between protocol parts. Access to the variables is assumed to be exclusive, i.e., only one protocol part can read a variable or assign a new value at a given instant.

The **timer declaration** contains the timers used in the entity to detect message losses. The timers are also globally declared for the entity. For each timer, the time interval is specified including the used time unit (*ms, s, min, h*), e.g.,

> **timer** t1: 0..100 **ms**,
>   t2: 0..? **s**.

If no upper bound is to be specified at this specification level a question mark is indicated instead. The role of timers in protocols is discussed in detail below.

The *action part* of an entity is described through a **par event**-statement (cp. Section 1.2.4). It describes the parallel execution of the protocol parts. The invocation of a protocol part is described by the triggering event (service primitive, PDU, timeout, signal, and others) followed by the name of the protocol part, e.g.,

> **par event**{
>   XDATrequ: connect_s ||
>   data transfer: transfer_s ||
>   run_ah: ack_handler
> }

The protocol parts are represented by their name which acts like a call. A protocol part may have parameters (see below). For readability reasons, protocol parts are separately described. They follow the main specification **spec**{ ... }.

A protocol part is activated as follows. An entity reads the first event from its input queue and checks whether this event is an expected one. Expected events are those events that are awaited in a **par event**- or **wait event**-statement. If the event is awaited then the respective protocol part or the respective reaction in the **wait event**-statement is executed, otherwise the event is discarded. An event cannot be assigned if the respective protocol part is currently in execution. In that case it is delayed until the protocol part terminates. If the input queue is empty the entity waits for new incoming events.

The description of the **protocol parts** consists like the **entity**-specification of a declaration and an action part:

> **protocol part** *name* (**peer** *entity*)
> **signal**-*declaration*   // Declaration part
> **var**-*declaration*
> **timer**-*declaration*
> *event*: **begin**   // Action part
>   *statements*
> **end**

In the header of the protocol part after the key word **peer** the peer entity (or entities) is specified. This is a formal parameter that represents the communication partner. It must be replaced by the name of the entity when the protocol part is invoked. In symmetric protocols the peer entity can be omitted.

The declaration part corresponds to that of the **entity**-specification. All three declarations are optional. In the **signal**-declaration all signals must be listed that are expected in this protocol part. Variables and timers declared in a protocol part are only valid within that protocol part.

The action part of a protocol part consists of the triggering event and the corresponding reaction. A triggering event may be a service primitive, a PDU, a timeout, or a signal. The event must be the same as specified in the action part of the respective **entity**-specification. The reaction, embedded in **begin** ... **end**, consists of one or several statements which are executed sequentially. We introduce these statements next. Some of them are already known from the S-specification.

Interactions with the peer entity are described by the **send-statement**, e.g.,

DT → receiver.

It describes the sending of a message to the peer entity. The message must be specified in the **message**-specification, the name of the receiver entity correspondingly in the header of the protocol part. The receiving of a message is correspondingly represented by an arrow in the reverse direction, e.g.,

ACK ← receiver.

The receiving of a PDU represents an event, the so-called *receive event*. It may appear as triggering event of a protocol part or in a **wait event**-statement.

The sending of a service primitive to the service user is described by the **respond-statement**, e.g.,

respond XDATrequ.

The waiting of the entity in a protocol part is described by the **wait event**-statement, which was introduced in Section 1.2.3. Triggering events may be: service primitives, PDUs, time-outs, and signals. As in the service specification, awaited events may be connected to an additional condition to express context dependencies, e.g.,

wait event{
    DT ← sender **and** DT.sequ = 1: ...
}.

In this case, the respective alternative is only selected if also the additional condition is fulfilled.

The sending of a signal to another protocol part is described by means of a **set-statement**, e.g.,

set break.

The **set**-statement causes the signal to be written into the event queue like any other event. It has now the value *true*. After the signal has been read out and triggered some reaction, its value is set to *false* again. The change of protocol phases can be handled by signals, if this is taken into account in the specification.

Timers

Timers are used in protocols to monitor communication procedures to avoid waiting indefinitely for certain events. If an event does not occur in a defined time interval, a so-called time-out is triggered. A **time-out** is handled as an event that triggers an alternative reaction to the awaited one, e.g., an error procedure. This prevents the entity from running into a deadlock state.

The representation of time and the declaration of timers are differently handled in formal description techniques. Some languages do not or only partially support time, others do support it. In our model language we assume a continuous progress of time. Timers are declared in the **timer**-declaration introduced in the preceding section, e.g.,

timer t1: 0..100 **ms**,
    t2: 0..? **s**.

The upper value of the time interval defines the time-out. Different time units can be used: *h*, *min*, *s*, and *ms*. Timers that are declared in an **entity**-specification are valid in all protocol parts, whereas timers declared in a protocol part are only valid locally in this part.

Timers are started by means of a **start-statement**, e.g.,

start t.

A running timer may be stopped using the **reset-statement**, e.g.,

reset t.

If a **start**-statement is applied on a running timer, the timer is implicitly reset first. A time-out is indicated by a *timeout* event in a **par** or **wait event**-statement, e.g.,

start t
wait event{
    DT ← sender: **reset** t   // awaited event
              . . . |
    timeout t: *reaction*   // alternative reaction after time-out

}

A time-out causes the *timeout* event to enter the event queue (cp. Figure 2.2/3). When it is an awaited event, it is read-out, otherwise it remains in the input queue and might be selected if the **par** and **wait event**-statements are executed again. To avoid any trouble from this it is recommend to reset timers when an awaited event is processed, as is done in the example above. The **reset**-statement does not just stop the timer. It also removes the *timeout* event from the input queue.

Local actions

Protocol specifications describe the external behavior of communicating entities, i.e., their interactions. To run a protocol actions are also needed which are only of local importance, e.g., the coding/decoding of PDUs, the analysis of the received values, cyclic redundancy checks, start and reset of timers, and others. We call these actions **local actions** in the following. To what extent local actions are considered in a protocol specification depends on the abstraction level of the applied description technique. To represent and to verify the protocol flow they are unlikely to be required because mainly the interactions between the entities are of interest here. Local actions, however, are required for the implementation of the protocol. Therefore, more abstract formal description techniques, such as LOTOS [ISO 8807], scarcely consider them, while less abstract techniques like SDL [ITU-T 100] do.

In our model language we describe local actions. We use statements for the description of the control flow which are known from high-level programming languages, such as the **if**-statement, the **case**-statement, the **loop**-statement, and the empty statement **skip**. Thereby loops are unlimited. They can be unconditionally left by means of **exit** or conditionally by specifying a condition after **exit when**. Increment and decrement statements (**incr**, **decr**) can be used for counting the number of loops. Moreover, we introduce the statement

exit *name*

to prematurely leave a protocol part. In exceptional cases it might be useful to cancel the protocol execution. This is expressed by

cancel protocol

It terminates all protocol parts, resets the variables and timers, and removes all events from the input queues.

Coding and Decoding of PDUs

The coding of PDUs at sender side and their decoding and analysis at receiver side are another example of local actions. They represent a large part of the protocol code and can take a considerable part of the protocol execution time. Coding/decoding is also differently handled in the various formal description techniques. Abstract techniques, such as LOTOS or Petri nets, do not consider them, whereas the coding/decoding can be described in more implementation-oriented techniques like SDL.

In our model language we also forego for readability reasons an explicit description of PDU coding/decoding. Instead we represent them by means of a predefined procedure *coding_PDU* using the concrete PDU names for *PDU*, e.g.,

coding_DT(data,sequ).

Parameters are the data that have to be coded. For simple PDUs, which do not transport user data, the coding is sometimes omitted. The decoding at receiver side is indirectly described by using selections, e.g.,

DT.data,

when PDU data are used in a **respond-** or another statement.

Informal descriptions
Informal descriptions do not belong in a formal description. Nevertheless they are allowed, for example, in SDL. Informal descriptions may be useful during the design phase to describe protocol steps the formal representation of which would not be useful or needed at this level of abstraction. In this sense informal descriptions are also used in our model language. We mainly describe local actions this way to avoid a too implementation-oriented representation. The same applies to the description of conditions in **if-**, **case-**, and **exit when-**statements.

Instantiations
Up to now we have only considered language features for describing the protocol behavior. Several formal description techniques, e.g., SDL, also provide the possibility to create instances of their description elements (modules, objects, and others). This allows, for example, in addition to the description of the protocol flow to describe the establishment of a connection. This might be useful for the prototyping of the specification. However, it often requires the explicit setting up of communication paths, e.g., channels, between these instances. This requires a lot of additional language features and rules which are actually not related to protocols, but may constitute a large part of the protocol description (see the SDL XDT specification in Section 8.1.4). In our model language we confine ourselves to the pure protocol description.

2.3 Example

We now continue the description of the XDT protocol started in Section 1.3.

2.3.1 XDT protocol

The XDT protocol provides a reliable transmission of a larger, but limited sequence of data units over an unreliable medium preserving the order in which the
data units are sent. It uses the *go back N*-principle to retransmit lost PDUs (see
Section 5.1). This method retransmits all PDUs starting from the last not confirmed PDU, even if some of them have already been successfully transmitted.

The data units handed over from the *sender* by means of an *XDATrequ* primitive are mapped on *DT*-PDUs (see Figure 2.3/1). Each *DT*-PDU possesses a sequence number. The successful transmission of a *DT*-PDU is confirmed by the receiver entity *XR* with an *ACK*-PDU which contains the sequence number of the
PDU increased by 1. A correctly transmitted data unit is delivered to the *receiver*
via an *XDATind* primitive. *DT*-PDUs that do not arrive in the correct order are
discarded. No confirmation is sent. If the transmission order cannot be re-
established within a time interval *t* the receiver entity *XR* aborts the transmission,
sending an *ABO*-PDU to the sender entity *XS*. The service users at both sites are
informed about this by an *XABORTind* primitive.

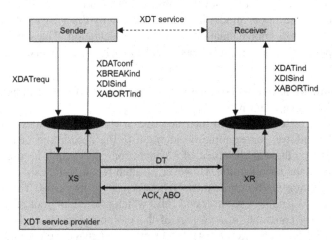

Figure 2.3/1: XDT service and protocol

The first *DT*-PDU also establishes the connection between the communication
partners. The *sender* can only continue the data transmission when the connection
set up is confirmed by an *XDATconf* primitive (2-way-handshake (see Section
5.2)). For simplicity reasons, we assume that the receiver always accepts a new
connection. The connection set up is confirmed by the receiver entity *XR* through
an *ACK*-PDU which contains the connection reference *conn* assigned by the receiver entity. This reference is indicated to the *sender* with the first *XDATconf*
primitive. If the connection set up is not confirmed within a time period *t1* it is
aborted by an *XABORTind*. The possible protocol procedures for a connection set
up are depicted as time sequence diagrams in Figure 2.3/2. The question mark in

Figure b) is to indicate that the reason for the abort remains unknown (loss of the *DT*- or the *ACK*-PDU).

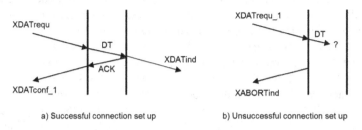

a) Successful connection set up   b) Unsuccessful connection set up

Figure 2.3/2: Possible protocol sequences for XDT connection set up phase

After establishing the connection, the other data units can be sent. They are handed over to the XDT service provider by *XDATrequ* primitives, where they are mapped on *DT*-PDUs. The sending of a *DT*-PDU is indicated to the sender by an *XDATconf*. Only then can the sender hand over a new data unit to the service provider. (Note that for simplicity reasons it is not proved in the protocol that this presumption is fulfilled by the sender.)

After sending the second *DT*-PDU, a timer t_2 is started that monitors the arrival of *ACK*-PDUs. It is restarted each time an *ACK*-PDU is received. When $t2$ times out the *go back N*-procedure is called, i.e., all not acknowledged *DT*-PDUs are retransmitted. During *go back N* no further *XDATrequ* primitives are accepted from the service provider. For the *go back N*-procedure, a copy of each *DT*-PDU is stored in a buffer. It is erased when the respective acknowledgement is received. The size of the buffer, however, is limited. When the buffer is full, *XS* indicates a break to the sender by means of an *XBREAKind* primitive. During this break no further *XDATrequ* primitives are accepted. The break terminates when an *ACK*-PDU of a stored *DT*-PDU arrives and its copy is removed from the buffer. The end of the break is indicated to the sender through the outstanding *XDATconf*.

The sender entity *XS* monitors the activity of the receiver entity *XR* using the activity timer *t1*. If no *ACK*-PDU arrives within a defined time interval the sender entity aborts the transmission and delivers an *XABORTind* primitive to the *sender*. This prevents a deadlock at sender side.

The connection is released after the successful transmission of the last *DT*-PDU. This is indicated to *sender* and *receiver* by an *XDISind* primitive. The last data unit is signaled by setting the parameter *eom true* in the last *XDATrequ* primitive and the last *DT*-PDU. Some of these protocol procedures are depicted in Figure 2.3/3.

Note that the assumptions we made for the use of the XDT service in Section 1.3 also apply to the XDT protocol.

2.3.2 Formal description

The formal description of the XDT protocol at level P of our model language is given below. Since XDT is an asymmetric protocol, the sender entity and the receiver entity both have to be specified. The sender entity *XS* contains three protocol parts: *connect_s*, *transfer_s*, and *ack_handler* that describe the connection set up, the data transmission, and the reception of the acknowledgements, including the *go back N* procedure. The receiver entity *XR* possesses two protocol parts: *connect_r* and *transfer_r* which describe the connection set up and the data reception. The protocol parts *connect_s* and *connect_r* constitute the sub-protocol for the connection establishment, the protocol parts *transfer_s*, *ack_handler* and *connect_r* are the respective sub-protocol for the data transmission.

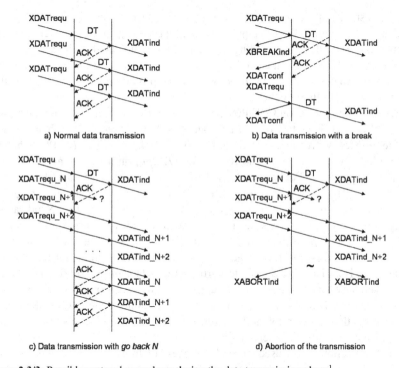

Figure 2.3/3: Possible protocol procedures during the data transmission phase[1]

The different number of protocol parts is caused by the fact that the sending of *DT*-PDUs and the reception and analysis of the acknowledgements are activities that are independent of each other and can be executed concurrently. For that reason, they are represented in separate protocol parts.

---

[1] For clarity reasons, we abstain from representing the *XDATconf* primitive for confirming each *XDATrequ* primitive in figures a), c), and d).

specification XDT{
service   // XDT-S specification remains preserved
message
    DT: **record**(length: 0..255,   // Data PDU
        code: bits,
        source-addr: address **optional**,
        dest-addr: address **optional**,
        conn: integer **optional**,
        sequ: integer,
        eom: Boolean,
        data: array [] of byte)
    ACK: **record**(code: bits,   // Acknowledgement PDU
            conn: integer,
            sequ: integer)
    ABO: **record**(code: bits,   // Abort PDU
            conn: integer)
protocol   // Sub-protocols
    connection set up: XS.connect_s $\Leftrightarrow$ XR.connect_r
    data transfer: XS.transfer_s $\Leftrightarrow$ XS.ack_handler $\Leftrightarrow$ XR.connect_r
entity XS   // SENDER ENTITY
  sap sender   // associated SAP
  signal DATA TRANSFER   // indicating data transmission
  var conn: integer,   // Connection reference
    sequ: integer **init**(1),   // current sequence number
    last: integer **init**(0),   // Sequence number of last PDU
    buffer: **array** [1..m] **of** DT,   // *DT*-Buffer with upper limit *m*
    go_back_N: boolean **init**(false),   // *true*, if *go back N* is running
    break: boolean **init**(false)   // *true*, if break
  par event{
    XDATrequ
      and XDATrequ.sequ = 1: connect_s || // Connection set up
    XDATrequ
      and not go_back_N
      and not break: transfer_s || // Data transfer phase
    DATA TRANSFER: ack_handler   // ACK monitoring
  } // XS

entity XR   // RECEIVER ENTITY
  sap receiver   // associated SAP
  signal DATA TRANSFER   // indicating data transmission
  var conn: integer   // Connection reference
  par event{
    DT $\leftarrow$ sender **and** DT.sequ = 1: connect_r || // Connection set up
    DATA TRANSFER: transfer_r   // Data transfer phase

```
} // XR
} // XDT
```

The protocol parts *connect_s* and *connect_r* describe the connection set up at the sender and receiver side. They are the only protocol parts that are active during the connection set up phase.

```
protocol part connect_s (peer receiver)      // CONNECTION SET UP SENDER
timer t: 0..? ms                             // Timer: ACK monitoring
XDATrequ and XDATrequ.sequ = 1:              // triggering event
   begin
      coding_DT (XDATrequ.source-addr,XDATrequ.dest-addr,1,XDATrequ.data)
      DT → receiver                          // sending DT_1
      start t                                // start ACK monitoring
      wait event{                            // awaiting ACK
         ACK ← receiver and ACK.sequ=1:      // ACK received
                  reset t                    // stop ACK timer
                  conn:= ACK.conn
                  respond XDATconf(conn,1)    // connection is set up
                  set DATA TRANSFER |         // change of the phase
            timeout t: respond XABORTind      // abort connection set up
      }
   end //connect_s

protocol part connect_r (peer sender)        // CONNECTION SET UP RECEIVER
DT ← sender and DT.sequ = 1:                 // Timer: ACK monitoring
   begin
      determine connection reference(conn)
      respond XDATind(conn,1,DT.data,DT.eom)  // deliver XDATind_1
      coding_ACK (conn,1)                     // coding ACK_1
      ACK → sender                            // sending ACK_1
      set DATA TRANSFER                       // change of the phase
   end //connect_r
```

During data transmission the protocol parts *transfer_s* and *ack_handler* are activated at sender side, at receiver side only the protocol part *transfer_r* is activated. The protocol part *transfer_s* maps the data units received from the sender into *DT*-PDUs and sends them to the receiver. A copy of each PDU is stored in a buffer. When the buffer is full, a break is indicated to the sender through an *XBREAKind* and the condition *break* is set. No break is triggered when the DT-PDU is transmitted, i.e., *eom = true*.

```
protocol part transfer_s (peer receiver)     // DATA TRANSMISSION SENDER
XDATrequ
   and not go_back_N and not break:
```

```
begin
    incr sequ                                    // next sequence number
    coding_DT (conn,sequ,XDATrequ.data)
    if (DT.eom)                                  // last data unit?
        {last:=sequ}                             // number of the last data unit
    copy DT in buffer
    DT → receiver                                // sending DT
    if (buffer is full and not last=sequ)
        {break:=true                             // break
          respond XBREAKind(conn)
        }
        else respond XDATconf(conn,sequ)         // deliver sending confirmation
end //transfer_s
```

The protocol part *ack_handler* monitors the arrival of the acknowledgements from the receiver. It runs in parallel to *transfer_s*. All arriving correct acknowledgements erase the respective *DT*-copy in the buffer. If the entity is in a break state the break is finished. After receiving the acknowledgement of the successful transmission of the last *DT*-PDU the connection is released with an *XDISind* to the sender. If no correct *ACK*-PDUs arrive within time interval *t2* the *ack_handler* calls the *go back N*-procedure. Since the *ack_handler* is always active, it also accepts the *ABO*-PDU in case of a connection abandonment and terminates the protocol. Moreover, it monitors the activity of the receiver entity. If no *ACK*-PDU arrives from *XR* within the time period *t1* the *ack_handler* assumes that the *XR* is not active any more and releases the connection at sender side.

```
protocol part ack_handler(peer receiver)    // MONITORING ACKNOWLEDGEMENTS
var N: integer init(1),                          // last confirmed PDU
    i: integer                                   // auxiliary variable
timer t1: 0..? ms                                // timer: activity receiver
     t2: 0..? ms                                 // timer: ACK monitoring
DATA TRANSFER:                                   // starting event
  begin
    start t1                                     // start activity timer
    loop{
      start t2                                   // start ACK monitoring
      wait event{                                // awaiting ACK
        ACK ← receiver:                          // ACK arrival
            reset t1                             // stop activity timer
            reset t2                             // stop ACK timer
            if (ACK.sequ>N)                      // ACK correct?
              {N:=ACK.sequ                       // store sequence number
                erase DT copy
                if (break)
                  {respond XDATconf(conn,sequ)   // terminate break
                   break:=false
                  }
```

```
                    if (N=last+1)                    // all ACKs received?
                       {respond XDISind(conn)        // connection release
                        sequ:=1                       // reset sequ, last
                        last:= 0
                        exit ack_handler              // leaving ack_handler
                       }
                    }
                 start t1 |                           // restart activity timer
      timeout t2: go_back_N:=true                     // missing ACK
                  i:=N+1
                  loop{                               // starting go back N
                       coding_DT (buffer[i])
                       DT → receiver                  // resending DT[i]
                       exit when i=sequ               // end of retransmission
                       incr i
                  }
                  go_back_N:=false |                  // end go back N
   ABO ← receiver: respond XABORTind(conn)  // protocol abortion by receiver
                       sequ:=1                        // reset sequ, last
                       last:= 0
                       exit ack_handler |             // leaving ack_handler
      timeout t1: respond XABORTind(conn)             // inactive receiver
                  sequ:=1                             // reset sequ, last
                  last:= 0
                  exit ack_handler                    // leaving ack_handler
   }
   }
end //ack_handler
```

The protocol part *transfer_r* describes the reception of the *DT*-PDUs in the receiver entity *XR*. *DT*-PDUs that arrive in correct order are confirmed by an *ACK*. The user data are delivered to the receiver. PDUs out of order are discarded. If the sending order cannot be re-established within the time interval *t transfer_r* aborts the transmission by means of an *ABO*-PDU. The timer *t* also acts as an activity timer to track whether the sender entity *XS* is still active. After receiving the last *DT*-PDU the connection is released at receiver side.

```
protocol part transfer_r (peer sender)       // DATA TRANSFER RECEIVER
var N: integer init(2)                        // awaited sequence number
timer t: 0..? ms                              // timer: order monitoring
DATA TRANSFER:                                // triggering event
    begin
        start t                               // start order monitoring
        loop{
            wait event{                       // awaiting DT
          DT ← sender: if (DT.sequ = N)       // correct sequence number?
                          {reset t            // correct order / stop timer t
                           respond XDATind(conn,N,DT.data,DT.eom)
                                              // delivering data to receiver
                           ACK(conn,incr N) → sender
```

```
                                            // sending ACK
                    if (DT.eom)             // last data unit ?
                       {respond XDISind(conn)
                                            // connection release
                       set CONNECT          // change of phase
                       exit transfer_r      // leaving transfer_r
                       }

                       start t              // restart order monitoring
                       }
                    else discard DT    |    // DT out of order
        timeout t: respond XABORTind(conn)  // order not re-established
                    ABO(conn) → sender      // abort transmission
                    set CONNECT             // change of phase
                    exit transfer_r         // leaving transfer_r
        }
    }
end //transfer_r
```

Further reading

As for services, introductions to the protocol concept can be also found in all introductory books on computer networks, such as [Kuro 08], [Stal 08], [Pete 07], and [Tane 10].

Exercises

(1) What are entities? What is their role within the service provider?
(2) What is a protocol? What is its relation with services? What is the difference between symmetric and asymmetric protocols?
(3) Why has the structure of protocol data units to be known to both entities?
(4) Explain the principle of transparency. Why is it needed? Which well-known network method is based on this principle?
(5) What are typical parameters of the protocol control information?
(6) How are connections handled in a protocol?
(7) What is the purpose of the protocol specification?
(8) What is the task of timers in protocols? What are the basic timer functions?
(9) Explain the need for the reset function. What could happen if no reset function is available?
(10) Concurrency is a characteristic feature of protocol entities. Consequently, interleaving is a possible model to describe concurrent behavior. The XDT sender entity executes the sending of data PDUs and the reception of acknowledgements concurrently. Give some possible interleaving sequences.
(11) Replace the implicit connection acceptance in the XDT protocol according to exercise (11) in Chapter 1 by an explicit one, i.e., the receiver no longer accepts every connection; it can accept or reject a connection.
     a) Describe this protocol extension by means of time sequence diagrams. Introduce appropriate PDU names.
     b) Describe the protocol changes for both entities in the model language.

(12) When the transmission order in XDT cannot be re-established the receiver entity *XR* aborts the transmission with an *ABO*-PDU. The reception of *ABO* at the sender entity *XS* is not monitored by *XR*. How does the protocol behave when *ABO* gets lost?

(13) In exercise (12) of Chapter 1 we extended the XDT service at the receiver side by a mechanism by which the service user may interrupt the reception of data for a certain time period. The time was given as a parameter to the service provider which controls the break duration and continues to deliver data after this time has elapsed. Extend the XDT receiver entity specification appropriately to handle this extension. Describe the protocol changes in time sequence diagrams and in the model language.

(14) Replace the implicit connection release in the XDT protocol by an explicit one that is triggered by the receiver through an *XDISrequ* when it has received the last PDU. The sender releases the connection with an *XDISind*, after which also the receiver releases the connection with an *XDISind*.

a) Describe this extension by means of time sequence diagrams. Introduce appropriate PDU names.

b) Describe the changes for both entities in the model language.

3 Layers

After introducing the notion of protocol as the basis for the provision of services in the last chapter, we now consider how the communication between the peer entities is implemented. This leads us to the notion of layer. The wide range of tasks to be fulfilled in a computer network forces one to structure the communication software. For this, a horizontal layering of functions has prevailed. This chapter introduces the concept of layering. The structure of the chapter corresponds to that of the previous ones. We begin with the principles of layering. Next we discuss their description. We finish the chapter with the introduction of the last part of the XDT protocol in which it is integrated into a layered architecture.

3.1 Principles

A **layer** comprises all entities that provide the same functionality. Each layer may provide one or several services. The principles of service provision are the same as described in the previous chapter. Thereby it is not described and even not of interest how these services are provided. In a layered architecture the entities use the services of the adjacent lower layer for exchanging messages (see Figure 3.1/1). Thus, an entity becomes both service user and service provider.

The layering principle is a design approach which has been borrowed from everyday communication. For example, a mailing service is based on the use of transport services, e.g., railway, airway, or shipping services, which perform the transport of the letters to the destinations. The transport services receive the letter at an agreed service access point, e.g., at a railway station. The further transport is their responsibility. The transport services may hire other companies to perform the transport for certain routes. At the destination the transport service delivers the letters to the mailing service at an agreed service access point.

Notation

In order to denote the layers and their elements in a layered architecture the following notation is often applied. A certain layer is denoted as the (N)-layer, the adjacent higher layer as the (N+1)-layer, and the lower layer as the (N-1)-layer. An (N)-layer provides an (N)-service to the (N+1)-layer. Accordingly, other elements of the (N)-layer, such as service access points, protocol, protocol data units, etc., are denoted as (N)-SAPs, (N)-protocol, and (N)-PDUs, respectively (see Figure 3.1/1). In some communication architectures like the OSI reference model the layers are named. Then the abbreviations, e.g., *T* for transport layer, are used to denote elements of the layer, e.g., T-CONNECT request, T-SAP and so on (cp. Section 1.1)[1].

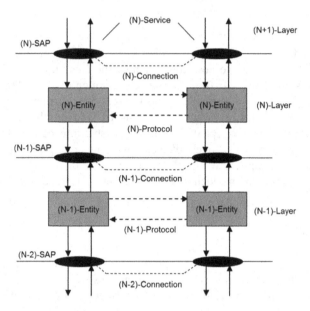

Figure 3.1/1: The layering principle

Peer entities

Communication between entities in a layered architecture is based on fixed rules. A protocol always defines the communication rules between entities of the same layer, i.e., between (N)-entities. These entities are called therefore **peer entities**, i.e., there is a peer-to-peer communication relation[2] between them. The peer entities communicate with each other using (N-1)-services. Other communication relations, e.g., between an (N)-entity at sender side and an (N-1) entity at receiver side, are not allowed.

Example

Tanenbaum uses a debate between two philosophers in Africa and Asia to demonstrate the layering principle in his book [Tane 03]. We use this example here due to its good clarity. The example considers a 3-layer communication (see Figure 3.1/2).

---

[1] We did not use the abbreviation for layers in Section 1.1 because the notion of layer was not introduced yet.

[2] Note that the notion of peer-to-peer is today mainly used as a design approach for applications. In layered architectures it has been used already for 30 years.

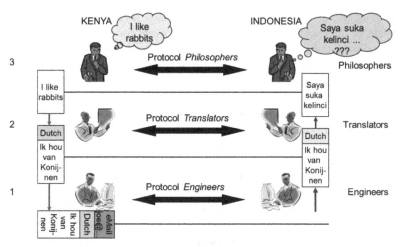

Figure 3.1/2: Layered structure of the philosophers' example (from [Tane 03])

We assume two philosophers (*peer entities of level* 3), who live in Kenya and Indonesia. They intend to have a debate. Since they do not speak the same language, they each engage a translator (*peer entities of level* 2). These again each engage an engineer to assist them in establishing and maintaining the communication (*peer entities of level* 1). The African philosopher begins the debate with a thesis which is formulated in his mother language Swahili. He transfers the thesis to his translator (*service interface* 3/2) who translates it either directly into Indonesian or into a transfer language, e.g., English, French, or Chinese. His colleague in Asia then translates the thesis, if required, into Indonesian and delivers it at the service interface 3/2 to his philosopher. This procedure requires a separate interaction between the translators (*protocol of level* 2) in which they agree about the transfer language and later during the debate about possible different interpretations of words or phrases. The translators transfer the (translated) theses as well as their own messages to the engineers for transmission (*service interface* 2/1). They receive their answers in the same way. The engineers have a separate interaction (*protocol of level* 1) to agree about the applied communication method, e.g., e-mail, SMS, or Twitter, and to discuss technical aspects for maintaining the transmission.

The example does not only exemplify the layering principle, it also applies some important features of the layering principle which we want to emphasize separately:

- The interaction between the acting persons is horizontal, i.e., between peer entities. They use the service of the underlying layer to communicate, but they are not interested in how this service is provided or which protocol options have been chosen as long as the service interface remains unchanged. So the philosophers, for example, do not need to know which transfer language has been agreed upon or whether it changes during communication.

- The principle of transparency is applied at each layer (cp. Section 2.1). The content of the exchanged messages is not relevant for acting persons at lower layers. So the translators do not discuss the philosophical content of the theses, and the engineers in turn do not comment on the content of the messages of the philosophers and translators.
- Apparently simple interactions at the upper level, e.g., the exchange of only one thesis, do not automatically induce less communication at lower levels. It may, in contrast, cause an extensive message exchange in these layers. This is because each message exchanged at the upper level triggers the same protocol mechanisms for assuring a correct transmission (e.g., agreement on the transfer language, connection re-establishment after a breakdown, re-transmission of lost messages, and others).
- Problems or errors appearing during communication at lower levels may not necessarily be noticed at the upper layers because protocols usually try to repair these problems. For example, the philosophers may not learn about a breakdown of the connection between Africa and Indonesia, if the engineers can re-establish it in a reasonable time. Only if the fault is serious will they be informed.

Principle of transparency

In a layered architecture the principle of transparency causes the length of the protocol data units to enlarge at sender side, when they pass downwards, while it correspondingly shrinks at receiver side (see Figure 3.1/3). Each layer adds its protocol control information (PCI), which is considered as part of the (transparent) user data at the (N-1) layer, where the (N-1)-PCI is added to the (N-1)-SDU. This may lead to very large PDUs that cannot be transmitted efficiently. Such PDUs can be fragmented while preserving the principle of transparency and transmitted separately (see Section 5.6).

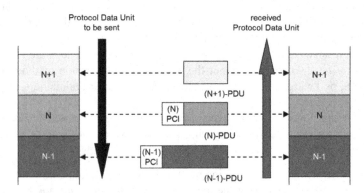

Figure 3.1/3: Principle of transparency in a layered architecture

Mapping on the (N-1)-layer

A considerable part of a protocol concerns the mapping of the (virtual) communication between the peer entities on the services of the underlying layer. Here similar rules apply as introduced in Section 2.1 for the relation between (N)-entities and (N)-SAPs (see Figure 3.1/4). Accordingly an (N)-entity may use several (N-1)-SAPs. An (N-1)-SAP, however, is only assigned to one (N)-entity, otherwise no unique assignment of data to (N)-entities is possible.

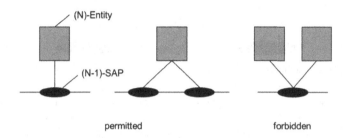

Figure 3.1/4: Allocation rules between (N)-entities and (N-1)-SAPs

The (N)-protocol has further to adapt to the (N-1)-service and the quality provided. This requires functions in the (N)-protocol that perform this mapping. For example, to use an (N-1)-connection the (N)-protocol has to provide functions to set up, manage, and release the connection. Moreover, in order to increase transmission efficiency it might be useful to multiplex several (N)-connections over an (N-1)-connection or vice versa to split up an (N)-connection onto several (N-1)-connections. Besides, large PDUs may be fragmented into smaller units or smaller PDUs may be chained to a larger unit, respectively (see Chapter 5 for more details).

3.2   Description

Most formal description techniques do not offer specific means to express layering aspects. This is because the description focuses on the protocol, i.e., the interaction sequences, while the layer forms the logical framework around the protocol. However, a separate description of the mapping of the protocol onto the (N-1)-service has proved useful. In our model language we follow this approach. We introduce the third and last language **level M** (M – *Mapping*) which then represents the complete protocol specification. The description principle of the M-specification is shown in Figure 3.2/1.

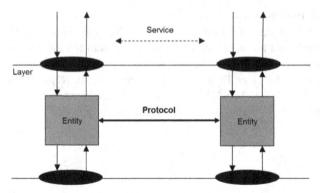

Figure 3.2/1: Description principle of level M

The M-specification differs from the P-specification by one language element: the **SAP handler** (see Figure 3.2/2) which describes the use of the (N-1)-service by the protocol entity. For better readability, the SAP handler is separately described like the protocol parts. In the **entity**-specification the SAP handler is referenced by

   sap handler *name*,

where *name* refers to the associated protocol entity. The SAP handler is always executed in parallel with the protocol parts, but this does not need not to be expressed in the **protocol**-statement.

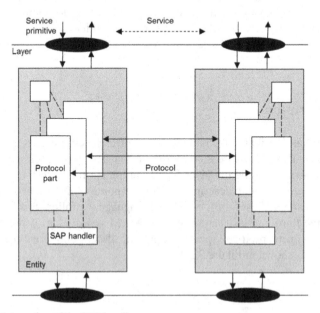

Figure 3.2/2: Integration of the SAP handler

The SAP handler possesses its own input queue which admits the following events: (N-1)-service primitives, (N)-PDUs (*sending events*), signals, and time-outs triggered in the SAP handler. Figure 3.2/3 shows the complete description model of an entity in our model language.

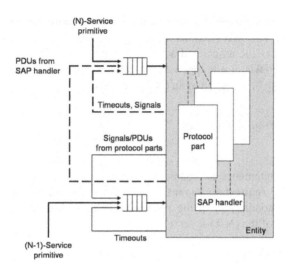

Figure 3.2/3: Complete description model of a protocol entity

The SAP handler has a syntactical structure like that of a protocol part. It consists of a specification and declaration part, and an action part.

```
sap handler name
service-specification                    // Specification and declaration part
signal-specification
var-declaration
timer-declaration
loop{                                    // Action part
    wait event{
        event₁: action₁      |
        event₂: action₂      |
            . . .
        eventₙ: actionₙ
    }
}
```

In the specification and declaration part the (N-1)-services and their primitives are described, e.g.,

service Y-DATA_TRANSFER: **requested** YDATrequ
                            responded YDATind

The parameters of the service primitives as well as the relation among them is not specified because this information is contained in the (N-1)-service specification. The **signal**-specification serves for indicating signals which are expected from other protocol parts. Furthermore, variables and timers may be declared locally.

The action part is simple. It consists of an endless **loop** that comprises a **wait event**-statement. The SAP handler always reads the first event from its input queue and executes the associated action. It might be possible that some events, e.g., sending of PDUs, are mapped on the same service primitive. In such cases several events may be assigned to an (N-1)-action, e.g.,

```
wait event{
    ABO, ACK: request YDATrequ
}
```

Two further statements are required to describe the protocol behavior in the SAP handler: the **request-statement** and the **set event-statement**. The **request**-statement is the counterpart of the **respond**-statement. It describes the call of a service primitive of the (N-1)-layer, e.g.,

request YDATrequ.

The **set event**-statement serves for indicating events, e.g., the arrival of a PDU, to the protocol parts, e.g.,

set event DT.

The **set event**-statement writes the event into the upper waiting queue to (re-) activate a protocol part which is waiting for this event.

3.3   Example

3.3.1 XDT protocol

In order to demonstrate the layering principle in our example we assume that XDT runs over a layer *Y* (see Figure 3.3/1). The Y-layer provides a connectionless data transmission service that can be used in both directions. The service primitives of the Y-service are *YDATrequ* and *YDATind.* All XDT connections are mapped on this service.

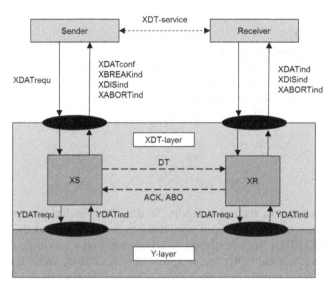

Figure 3.3/1: XDT protocol with Y-layer

3.3.2 Formal description

The M-specification completes the formal description of the XDT protocol. It only differs from the P-specification by the SAP handler. Therefore we confine ourselves here to the **entity** specification and the associated SAP handlers.

```
entity XS                                    // Sender entity
   sap sender
   signal go_back_N
   var  sequ: integer init(1),
        last,conn: integer,
        break: Boolean init(false),
        buffer: array [1..m] of DT
   par event{
      XDATrequ
         and XDATrequ.sequ = 1: connect_s ||     // Connection set up
      XDATrequ
        and not go_back_N
          and not break: transfer_s       ||     // Data transfer phase
      DATA TRANSFER: ack_handler                 // ACK monitoring
   } //XS

sap handler XS
   service Y-DATA TRANSFER:  requested YDATrequ
                            responded YDATind
```

```
loop{
   wait event{
      DT: request YDATrequ |
      YDATind: Assign arriving PDUs to their connection conn
                case code of {
                   ACK: set event ACK |
                   ABO: set event ABO
                 }
   }
 }
} //XS
```

The SAP handler of the sender entity *XS* describes the handover of the *DT-*PDUs by means of the *YDATrequ* primitives to the Y-layer and the arrival of *ACK-* and *ABO*-PDUs from this layer. For the latter, first it has to be determined to which connection the PDUs are assigned. This is done by using the *conn* parameter. This is informally described here. After that the type of the PDU is determined by means of the *code* field in the PDU. Finally the PDU is moved to the upper input queue by the **set event**-statement.

The integration of the SAP handler into the receiver entity *XR* is similar. Note that the PDUs *ACK* and *ABO* are assigned to the same action.

```
entity XR                                    // Receiver entity
   sap receiver
   var conn: integer
   begin
      DT ← sender and DT.sequ = 1: connect_r  ||   // Connection set up
      DATA TRANSFER: transfer_r                    // Data transfer phase
   end //XR

sap handler XR
   service Y-DATA TRANSFER: requested YDATrequ
                            responded YDATind
   loop{
      wait event{
         ACK, ABO: request YDATrequ |
         YDATind: Assignment of the received DT-PDUs to their connection
                  set event DT
      }
    }
} //XR
```

Further reading

The layering principle is usually explained together with the service and protocol concept in introductory books on computer networks, such as [Kuro 08], [Stal 08], [Pete 07], and [Tane 10].

Exercises

(1) What is the advantage of the deployment of the layering principle in networking? Give an example of its use in everyday life.

(2) Explain the layering principle. Between which entities is a communication allowed? What does an (N)-layer know about the (N-1)-layer? What happens if protocol errors occur at lower layers?

(3) What is the consequence of the principle of transparency for layering?

(4) Assume that the Y-layer in our XDT example provides a connection-oriented service. Introduce the necessary changes in the specification in our model language given above. What has to be done when the connection is broken?

4 Layered architectures

In computer networks and communication systems defined layered architectures are used, in which the communication protocols are embedded. These architectures define the functionality of the different layers and specify the interaction principles between them. They are mostly specified by standardization bodies or industrial consortia. Layered architectures are usually the product of a lengthy development process that is often influenced beside technical requirements by companies' strategies and political trade-offs. Protocol developers have little influence on this process and must accept the architecture as given. In this chapter we present several examples of layered architectures and discuss the differences among the approaches. We first introduce related terms. Next we present as examples the OSI reference model, the TCP/IP architecture, and the B-ISDN reference model.

4.1 Principles

Layered architectures can be principally differentiated into closed and open architectures.

Closed architectures

A layered architecture that aims at a specific application area and that takes particular requirements of this area into account is called a **closed architecture**. These are dedicated architectures that have a limited application area, usually that of homogenous networks which consist of computers of the same type or family. A special variant of closed architectures are *producer-oriented closed architectures* that are optimized in connecting the hardware and software products of a certain producer. These architectures are called **proprietary architectures**. Famous examples are SNA (*Systems Network Architecture*), DNA (*Digital Network Architecture*) and Novell Netware, which were used in the past as the basis for network products of the firms IBM, DEC, and Novell over a long time. The advantage of closed architectures is that they are optimized for the application area. They also can be quickly adapted to changing conditions. Their main disadvantage is that the integration of non-proprietary systems is expensive because special adaptors/gateways have to be implemented. The same applies to the adaptation to other network concepts. For this reason, closed architectures are not suitable for setting up heterogeneous networks as we find them in the Internet. Closed architectures have lost their importance in the Internet age. Their use is confined to specific applications. Existing proprietary architectures have opened to the Internet architecture.

Open architectures

Open architectures define a unified communication interface for communicating with other computers. Hence, open architectures aim at establishing heterogeneous networks. The term *open* means that each system that follows these rules can be integrated into the respective network. The best known examples of open systems are the OSI communication architecture [ISO 7498], [Tane 03] and, of course, the Internet architecture [Kuro 08], [Stal 08], [Tane 03].

Standardized protocols

The objective of an open communication can be achieved only if the protocols contained in the different layers of the layered architecture are also standardized. This happened for both aforementioned architectures, but in different ways. The services and protocols of the OSI architecture were standardized by the *International Organization for Standardization* (ISO) in the 1980s after standardizing the OSI reference model. This was a very lengthy process, which hampered the broad practical deployment of the protocols and the development of commercial products. The Internet protocols were standardized by the *Internet Engineering Task Force* (IETF). In contrast to the ISO approach, the core protocols TCP, UDP, and IP existed and could be used from the very beginning. The development of new protocols proved to be more flexible as well because they were not developed in standardization bodies but in working groups of experts. The proposals were/are published in the *Request for Comments* (RFC) and are open for discussion worldwide. To become a standard, two independently developed implementations must be reported.

Protocol profiles

Specifications of communication protocols often contain options. These options concern protocol parameters and procedures. The decision which option is taken is made as a rule by the protocol implementer. Depending on the application context, different options may be selected. In addition, there often exist several versions of a protocol. This may lead to the situation that different implementations of the same protocol cannot work together, i.e., they are not interoperable because they support different options and/or versions (see also Section 14.4 for this). To avoid this situation so-called protocol profiles were introduced, which were used especially in the OSI context. A **protocol profile** is a tailored protocol hierarchy dedicated to a certain application that specifies the protocol options and versions used in the different layers. Protocol profiles require pretty large efforts for their specification, implementation, and testing. Therefore, a large number of protocol profiles appeared disadvantageous.

Communication versus protocol architectures

There are two ways of defining layered architectures. The OSI architecture defined a **communication architecture** by introducing architectural elements for describing the basic model elements, e.g., entities, service access points, and others. These elements had to be implemented, but it was not prescribed how this was to be done in the respective implementation context, i.e., they did not define implementation rules. In the Internet protocol architectures are applied. **Protocol architectures** are in some ways similar to protocol profiles. They define a dedicated layering of protocols which are often used for a certain class of applications, e.g., conference applications. Protocol architectures differ from communication architectures by the fact that the interfaces between the protocols are defined by the protocols themselves and not by some generalized architectural element like a service access point or a specific layer concept. Protocols may thus appear in various protocol architectures. Nowadays protocol architectures are mainly used because they have proved more flexible, although they require a detailed knowledge of the interfaces of the protocols (see Section 4.3.2 for this).

Protocol stack

Another term which is often used is that of the protocol stack. It is more a colloquial term. A **protocol stack** refers to a dedicated protocol hierarchy in a communication or protocol architecture that specifies the protocols used.

Communication software

The software that implements a communication or protocol architecture is called **communication software**. This software does not actually belong to the operating system under which it runs, although protocol implementations are always integrated in the context of a certain operating system. This is because communication protocols are designed independently of a concrete execution environment. They do not relate to a certain computer type or operating system. Their task is to connect computers independently of the system software applied. Therefore, communication protocols are principally independent of operating systems. When implemented, however, communication protocols use operating system functions to fulfil their task (see Chapter 13). In this sense communication software can be considered as operating system software with an enhanced meaning.

4.2 Description

Layered architectures are variously described. No special descriptions beside graphical representations are used for describing protocol architectures because the definition of the protocols is given by their service and protocol architectures. Communication architectures, in contrast, were described by using reference models.

A **reference model** is quasi the specification of the communication architecture. It is a framework from which different concrete communication architectures may be derived. The reference models describe the components of the communication architecture and the interaction principles applied. They further define the number of layers and their functionality. The terminology applied in the various models is often different. Usually reference models also specify the protocols that are used in the different layers. Well-known examples of such reference models are the already mentioned OSI reference model and the B-ISDN reference model. The Internet TCP/IP architecture is a protocol architecture rather than a reference model, although it is often called so in the literature. We discuss this below.

Reference models are mostly described informally owing to their complexity. There were some approaches to formally describe architectural concepts, e.g., in the LOTOS context with the development of the concept of **architectural semantics** [Viss 88]. They argued that architectural elements like service access points, entities, or connections have some influence on the implementation and must therefore be semantically correctly defined. This approach was demonstrated in [Turn 93] by describing the architectural elements of the OSI reference model using the standardized formal description techniques Estelle, LOTOS, and SDL. The architectural semantics concept did not achieve practical relevance later because of its complexity and the fact that the Internet context mainly uses protocol architectures.

4.3   Examples

In this section we give as examples an overview of three layered architectures and discuss some of their features. They are the OSI reference model, the Internet architecture, and the B-ISDN reference model. We introduce further principles of layered architectures in the context of this discussion.

4.3.1   OSI reference model

The **OSI reference model** (*Open Systems Interconnection Reference Model*, OSI/RM) [ISO 7498] was the reference model of the *International Organization for Standardization* (ISO) which was developed for setting up open heterogeneous networks. Development began in the late 1970s. The model fell short of the high expectations which arose especially in the 1980s. It lost its practical importance with the breakthrough of the Internet. Its importance now lies in the theoretical contributions of its development.

The OSI reference model consists of seven layers (see Figure 4.3/1), which were selected according to specific design criteria (cp. [Tane 03]). The lower four layers are called *transport-oriented layers*; the upper three *application-oriented layers*. The interface between them is called the *transport interface*. It represents an important interface in a layered architecture because it separates transmission-oriented aspects from application-oriented ones in communication.

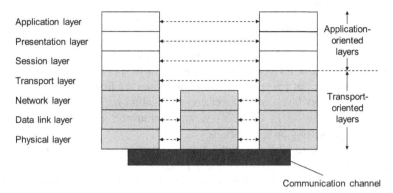

Figure 4.3/1: OSI reference model

The OSI reference model defines the structure of the layer and the interaction principles between them. It specifies how services are provided and determines the principles of protocol execution. The basic architectural concepts of the model were already introduced in the previous chapters. We therefore consider only the functionality of the layers here. Since it has been described in many books, we confine ourselves to a short survey.

The OSI reference model was originally designed for wide area networks (WANs) with a meshed topology based on point-to-point links between network nodes. This determines the functionality of the single layers. We first consider the transport-oriented layers, starting from the bottom this time:

The **physical layer (PH)**[1] transmits the data in the form of signals over the communication channel. This layer does not contain any protocol as we got to know in previous chapters. It is characterized by the hardware requirements of signal transmission. The physical layer specifies the mechanical, electrical, functional, and procedural requirements on data transmission. Besides the access procedure to the communication medium, it also comprises the mechanical requirements, such as the norm of the plugs and the cables as well as electrical specifications for the voltage level.

The **data link layer (DL)** ensures the correct transmission of bit sequences – called *frames* – between two network nodes connected by a point-to-point link. Typical tasks of this layer are framing, the synchronization of frames, and error control.

The **network layer (N)** is responsible for forwarding and relaying data in the network. One of its main tasks is routing which is used to find the optimal route for the protocol data units from the source to the destination node. The network layer is mainly used for connecting networks, so-called *internetworking*.

---

[1] In the OSI reference model each layer possesses an initial. This is used as part of the notation for naming service primitives, PDUs, and other layer elements (cp. Sections 1.1 and 3.1).

The **transport layer (T)** establishes an **end-to-end relation** between the source and destination nodes – the *end systems* – which is also called **end-to-end communication**. While the communication relation in the lower layers is point-to-point, the transport layer obscures this by considering only the communication between end systems. The reference model expresses this by the fact that the intermediate protocol stack of passed nodes only comprises the first three layers. Starting from the transport level, only direct communication between end systems is considered (cp. Figure 4.3/1). For this reason, the transport interface is an appropriate interface for setting up applications.

The concepts pursued with the application-oriented protocols of the OSI reference model did not prevail. Many of these functions are nowadays realized in a different and more flexible manner through middleware which is superimposed on the transport interface. For this reason, we briefly mention the functionality of these layers for the sake of completeness.

The **session layer (S)** serves for the synchronization of the communication concerning the contents. This comprises among others the resynchronization of the communication after interrupts, the resuming of the communication, and the assignment of sending rights. The session concept, however, is reused in various protocols, e.g., in the security area.

The **presentation layer (P)** ensures a uniform interpretation of data in heterogeneous network environments independently of their possibly different representation on the particular computer systems. The function of the presentation layer corresponds to that of the translators in our philosophers example in Section 3.1. The presentation layer negotiates in cooperation with the application layer a so-called *presentation context*. It defines an abstract syntax to describe the data formats of the application. A transfer syntax is derived from the abstract syntax for exchanging the application data. The abstract syntax notation ASN.1 was developed for describing these abstract syntaxes. It is often applied for describing data formats in protocol specifications (see Section 8.5).

The **application layer (A)** provides means to implement the transition between the protocol stack and the application. Like the physical layer, it is not a layer as introduced in Section 3.1. There are, for instance, no service access points. OSI defined a special model for the application layer which was very complex and did not find acceptance.

In the 1980s the OSI reference model was adopted by the committee 802 of the American *Institute of Electrical and Electronics Engineers* (IEEE) for the definition of a reference model for local area networks (LAN), which emerged in the 1970s. Unlike WANs with their meshed topology, LANs originally used a shared medium that connected all end systems (*stations*). Typical topologies were/are the bus, the ring, and the star. The stations compete for access to the shared medium by means of special access procedures. The most important ones are CSMA/CD (*Carrier Sense Multiple Access/Collision Detection*), which is the base of Ethernet, and the token methods. To integrate the different topologies and access methods a trade-off was found, which is still used in this form today in the Internet architecture. The trade-off consisted in dividing the data link layer of the OSI/RM into two sub-layers: the MAC and the LLC sub-layers which contain protocols of the same name (see Figure 4.3/2). The **MAC** (*medium access control*) **protocol** implements in cooperation with the physical layer the access method to send and receive frames to/from other stations. The **LLC** (*logical link protocol*) provides a unified interface to the upper layers that covers the applied access method. Communication in the LLC sub-layer is end-to-end. It has a similar task as the transport layer. LLC provides a connectionless and a connection-oriented data transmission service. The physical layer in LANs is also divided into two sub-layers: one sub-layer for handling communication aspects and one for the medium access. Their functions vary for the different access methods.

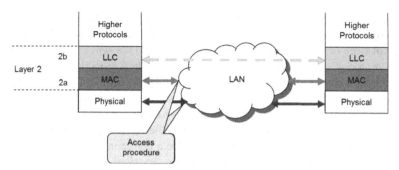

Figure 4.3/2: IEEE 802 LAN architecture

The high expectations associated with the OSI development were not fulfilled. There are several reasons for this. They range from strategic decisions over weaknesses of the model to the slow standardization process. A detailed discussion can be found in [Tane 03]. Last but not least, the breakthrough of the Internet ended the OSI development because the rival network architecture became dominant. The OSI reference model has proved altogether as too complex. Some model decisions appeared less practicable, others were made obsolete by new requirements, e.g., from high performance communication. Another fatal error was the standardization procedure. It took more than 10 years from the beginning of the OSI development until all protocols were standardized. The standardization proceeded in a bottom-up manner according to the research progress on the respective protocol layers. In this process inconsistencies appeared between the specified functionality of the layers and the requirements of the protocols. This led to inefficiencies, divergences, and extensions, such as the repeated use of certain protocol functions in several layers (e.g., error control, flow control etc.) (see Chapter 5), the introduction of sub-layers in layer 3 to handle internetworking, the late introduction of connectionless transmission, and the already mentioned development of a specific model for the application layer.

What remains are most of all the architectural concepts and the systematic approach. Therefore, the OSI model is still used as a reference model to characterize communication architectures in practice because it is more comprehensive than other models which describe the functionality of computer networks. Further merits of the model are some important conceptual contributions, in particular the distinction between service and protocol. This is an important presumption for the description and validation of protocols, which is the subject of this book. Finally, it must be mentioned that much research work was done during the OSI development which had a fundamental influence on the development of computer networks. One example is the development of a testing methodology for communication protocols that we introduce in Chapter 14.

4.3.2   TCP/IP protocol suite

The TCP/IP protocol suite is the layered architecture of the Internet. It originates from the first wide area network of the world, the ARPANET. The **TCP/IP protocol suite** does not represent a reference model in the sense introduced above. It is a protocol architecture which has been established around the core Internet protocols: the connectionless network protocol IP (*Internet Protocol*), the connection-oriented transport protocol TCP (*Transmission Control Protocol*), and the connectionless transport protocol UDP (*User Datagram Protocol*). In contrast to the OSI reference model, these protocols were the starting point of the development. The TCP/IP architecture does not provide a common framework for the design of communication architectures. It mainly describes the cooperation of the core protocols with other protocols of the Internet. This is the reason why we avoid the notion "TCP/IP reference model" here, although it can be found in the literature.

TCP, IP, and UDP owe their success primarily two things: their simplicity and their early integration in Berkeley UNIX which was freely available at that time and very popular in the academic community. With the Internet established as the global computer network infrastructure, TCP/IP will remain the dominant layered architecture for computer networks for a long time. Changes will be introduced in an evolutionary manner, e.g., by introducing new protocol versions like for IP.

The TCP/IP architecture consists of four "layers" (see Figure 4.3/3), of which exactly speaking only the IP layer (corresponds to OSI layer 3) and the TCP/UDP layer (OSI layer 4) are layers in the sense introduced above. Their objective is to provide stable transmission of data between end systems in the Internet independently of changing network conditions. Unlike OSI, the TCP/IP architecture included the concept of internetworking from the very beginning. The solution has been to apply the connectionless data transmission protocol IP in the network layer. The connection-oriented TCP above ensures reliable communication between end systems in the transport layer, when needed. Applications that do not require reliable transmission, e.g., in multimedia communication, can use the connectionless UDP instead.

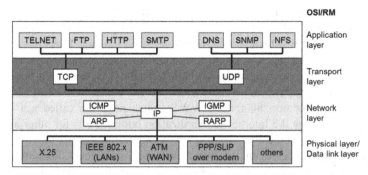

Figure 4.3/3: TCP/IP architecture (compared with the OSI/RM)

The other two "layers" describe the integration of underlying networks and applications in the architecture. The lowest "layer" specifies the underlying networks. In contrast to OSI, there is no distinction between layers 1 and 2, although their functionality is presumed. The TPC/IP architecture deliberately leaves it open which network is used underneath (e.g., LAN, ATM, Frame Relay, MPLS, mobile networks etc.). This is in part useful because some networks use different layering concepts (see also Section 4.3.3 for this). When considering a concrete network, the respective network architecture has to be added to the TCP/IP stack.

The "application layer" is likewise unstructured. There is no specific model. Moreover, the TCP/IP architecture does not contain a session and a presentation layer like in the OSI/RM. Both protocols have proved unnecessary for many applications. If these functions are required then they have to be included in the application.

There are several possibilities to superimpose an application on the transport interface. An application can be placed directly on the interface, e.g., as a service. The Internet provides several standard network services, such as *telnet*, *ftp*, *smtp*, and others, which can be directly used by the network user. However, there is also the possibility that further application-oriented protocols have to be included above the interface to enable the application. We discuss the various possibilities in Section 6.3.

There are still other essential differences between the Internet architecture and the OSI reference model beside the aforementioned differences in the layered structure. The TCP/IP protocol stack allows several protocols to run within a layer. This is useful and makes the protocol architecture more flexible. As a consequence, other interaction principles between protocols are required. TCP/IP has no explicit service concept as introduced in Chapter 1. This one of the most important differences between the two approaches. The TCP/IP architecture only knows the concept of protocol and layer. There is no architectural concept of the service access point. Hence, it applies an essentially more complex scheme of interaction points which is discussed next.

The TCP/IP architecture applies several concepts of interactions in the protocol stack (see Figure 4.3/4). We start from the application point of view. An application is bound to a port, which is identified by a 16 bit number. **Ports** are communication end points. They correspond to the OSI/RM service access points. One can say likewise that an application is characterized by its associated port. Standard Internet applications possess fixed port numbers, e.g., ports 21 and 22 for ftp, port 23 for telnet, or port 80 for the WWW. Such ports are called *well-known ports* and assigned by the Internet standardization bodies. Ports for other applications are assigned dynamically.

The application accesses the transport interface via a socket. **Sockets** are the *application programming interface* (API) of the transport interface to support the porting of applications and services. The interactions are programmed by means of special routines. Each socket is identified by an address that consists of the IP address and the (local) port number. Sockets are the end points of connections. Unlike OSI, connections are not characterized by references but by the tuple ($socket_i$,$socket_j$). TCP/IP does not know the concept of connection end points as introduced in Section 1.1.

The interaction between the transport protocols and IP is controlled by the protocol number. This is an entry in the IP protocol header. The **protocol number** determines the receiver protocol of the user data in the IP payload part. In other words: it addresses the "service user" the user data are assigned to. The concept of protocol numbers applies not only to the transport protocols but to all protocols which run in the IP layer, such as ICMP (*Internet Control Message Protocol*), IGMP (*Internet Group Management Protocol*), ARP (*Address Resolution Protocol*), and others. IP defines this kind of handover for about 100 protocols. Some of them, like ICMP, also interact with it. The protocol number is the tag for IP to deliver the user data to the correct receiver protocol or respective "service user".

Access to the IP layer is defined by the **IP address** that at the same time also defines the interface to the network. Each host in the Internet possesses an IP address, which may be statically or dynamically assigned. A host may simultaneously have several IP addresses to access different networks. Such systems are called *multi-homed*. Furthermore, a host can support different protocol stacks, e.g., for IPv4 and IPv6. The distinction and selection of the protocol stack takes place at the network interface by means of the **version** indication in the IP header.

If a host is located in a local area network the network interface is determined by the MAC address. A **MAC address** is a flat address that does not contain any information about the location of the host. In contrast to the point-to-point communication paradigm of IP, the data delivery in shared medium LANs applies a broadcast transmission principle which ensures that the frames pass along all connected stations. Therefore the IP address has to be mapped onto the MAC address. For this, the *Address Resolution Protocol* (ARP) is used, and the *Reverse ARP* (RARP) for the opposite mapping.

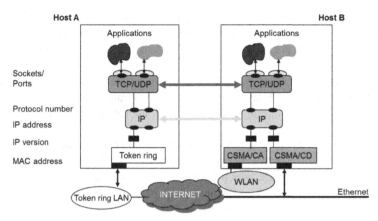

Figure 4.3/4: Interaction points in a TCP/IP (after [Stai 97])

4.3.3 B-ISDN reference model

The B-ISDN reference model has been the reference model for the **Broadband-ISDN** (*Integrated Service Digital Network*), the successor of the (narrow band) ISDN in telephony. It was developed in the 1980s and 1990s to enable multimedia communication. The basic transmission method of B-ISDN is ATM (*Asynchronous Transfer Mode*) [Stal 08], [Tane 03]. Although B-ISDN did not achieve the expected success, it is worth mentioning the reference model here because of some differences with the previously discussed models.

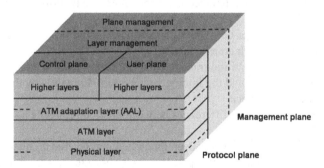

Figure 4.3/5: B-ISDN reference model

The B-ISDN reference model differentiates three layers (see Figure 4.3/5), which do not directly correspond to those of the OSI/RM. They can be related approximately to OSI layers 1 and 2. The first difference to the former models is the distinction between a **control** and a **user plane**. The B-ISDN reference model separates all activities for establishing, maintaining, and releasing connections. These activities – usually called signalling – are assigned to the control plane; the data transmission correspondingly to the user plane. In both planes run separate protocols. This principle is called *out-of-band signalling* contrary to *in-band signalling*, in which, as introduced in Section 2.1, connection management and data transmission run over the same connection. The separation of signalling and data transmission is convenient for the transmission of large data volumes as in multimedia communication. It allows fast transmission of the signalling data between the partners which is not delayed by the user data stream. Out-of-band signalling is typical for protocols in high performance communication. Many Internet protocols also apply this principle.

The second difference is the integration of the **network management** into the reference model. This is based on experience gained with the OSI reference model and the TCP/IP architecture which originally did not include network management. It was supplemented by separate models in both architectures only in the late 1980s.

Further reading

As in the chapters before layered architectures are also described in many introductory books about computer networks, such as [Kuro 08], [Stal 08], [Pete 07], and [Tane 10].

Exercises

(1) Explain the difference between closed and open layered architectures. What are their benefits and shortcomings? Which of these layered architectures is often called a proprietary architecture? How do you characterize the Internet architecture?

(2) What is the role of standardized protocols in the context of layered architectures?

(3) What is the difference between a communication and protocol architecture? Give examples of such architectures.

(4) The transport layer and the transport interface play an important role in the OSI reference model and the Internet architecture. Explain why this is so and what is their importance.

(5) Give some of the major differences between the OSI reference model and the TCP/IP protocol suite.

(6) How have local area networks been integrated into layered architectures?

(7) What possibilities exist to set up applications above the transport interface?

(8) What are the end points of connections in TCP? Are several connections allowed between the same end points?

(9) Describe how the interaction between layers and protocols is realized in the Internet architecture. Explain in particular the role of the protocol number in the IP protocol.

(10) What is the difference between in-band and out-of-band signalization? Give examples of their application.

5 Protocol functions

After introducing the basic concepts of services, protocols, and layered architectures in previous chapters we return once more to the protocol as the main concept to have a closer look at it. Communication protocols typically contain a number of procedures and mechanisms which appear in many protocols. These procedures are usually called **protocol functions**. Many of these protocol functions in turn use other protocol functions. Which protocol functions are applied in a protocol depends on the purpose of the protocol. Protocols in higher layers usually apply other functions than those in lower layers. There are, however, many functions that are applied in many protocols, such as connection management, flow control, error control, or synchronization. These and other protocol functions are introduced in this chapter. With this introduction, we want to give the reader a deeper insight into the most important protocol mechanisms, the diversity of their procedures, and the complexity resulting from this.

5.1 Error control

One of the most important tasks of (connection-oriented) communication protocols is to ensure that the protocol data units are correctly and reliably transmitted, even if the underlying communication channel is unreliable. Protocols must, therefore, possess means to detect transmission errors and to react appropriately to them. This is the task of the **error control** which is one of the most important protocol functions. There are different error control methods which are deployed in varying contexts. Some of these methods are fundamental for protocols. For that reason we begin this chapter with this protocol function.

Confirmations

When an entity sends off a PDU, it wants to know whether it reached the receiver entity. For this, **explicit acknowledgements** are used which are sent back by the receiving entity if the PDU arrived completely and correctly. Acknowledgements are the simplest and most frequently used means to confirm a successful transmission. There are two principle approaches: positive and negative acknowledgments. Mostly positive acknowledgments are used to confirm the reception of a PDU. The sequence number is usually added to the confirmation, as a rule increased by one to indicate the next expected sequence number (see Figure 5.1/1). To reduce the number of acknowledgments and thus the network load **cumulative acknowledgments** may be used that confirm several PDUs with one acknowledgement (see Figure 5.1/1).

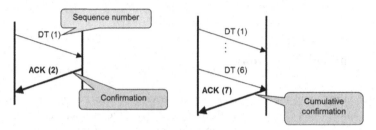

Figure 5.1/1: Confirmations

Negative acknowledgements are used to explicitly indicate faulty transmissions or outstanding PDUs. Often particular error PDUs are used for this which contain fault information. This kind of error control in which the receiver actively participates is also called **active error control**. The counterpart is **passive error control,** where the error control is incumbent upon the sender. The reaction of the peer entity on errors is diverse. This may range from retransmissions over particular error reactions to the release of the connection.

A special variant of sending confirmations is **piggybacking**. Here no explicit acknowledgment PDUs are sent, but the confirmation is added ("piggybacked") to a PDU in the opposite direction. This principle can only be used in duplex communication. It is applied in TCP (see Section 6.2.1).

Timers

Acknowledgements can also get lost. Therefore confirmations are only useful if their possible loss is supervised, otherwise the waiting entity runs into a deadlock situation. In order to avoid this, the arrival of acknowledgements is monitored by a clock or **timer** (see Figure 5.1/2).

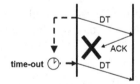

Figure 5.1/2: Timer

When a timer is started, a time interval is specified within which the acknowledgement is expected to arrive. If no confirmation arrives in this time period a **time-out** is triggered that invokes a predefined reaction. The timer is usually started after sending the PDU, just before the protocol entity enters a wait state, e.g.,

timer t: 0 .. 100 ms

DT → receiver

```
start t                                    // Start timer
wait event{
    ACK ← receiver:  reset t
                     decode ACK |
        timeout t: respond XABORTind       // Reaction to time-out
}
```

The time-out represents an alternative event to the events being expected in a waiting state. It allows the entity to leave the waiting state and thus to avoid a deadlock. The time-out is handled like other events (e.g., a PDU or a service primitive). Note that the timer must be stopped when one of the other expected events occurs. This is usually done by a **reset** operation.

Another important application of timers is activity monitoring of the communication partner, i.e., the peer entity. When the peer entity for whatever reason stops communicating, the active partner may also deadlock. Such situations can be avoided using an **activity timer** to signal the inactivity of the peer partner. The activity timer is restarted each time a PDU arrives. The timer must have a reasonably large time-out value to distinguish PDU delays from inactivity of the peer entity. The following specification fragment from Section 2.3 depicts the use of the activity timer $t1$ in the XDT protocol. In this case the sender entity closes the connection when the receiver is signalled inactive.

```
start t1                                   // Start activity timer
loop{
    start t2                               // Start ACK monitoring
    wait event{                            // Await ACK
        ACK ← receiver: reset t1           // Reset activity timer
                        reset t2           // Reset ACK supervision
                        . . .              // ACK decoding
                        start t1 |         // Restart activity timer
                . . .
        timeout t1: respond XABORTind(conn)  // Receiver entity inactive
                    set CONNECT              // Sender closes connection
                    sequ:=1; last:=0         // Reset variables
                    clear_queue(conn)
                    exit ack_handler         // Leaving protocol part
    }
}
```

It must be mentioned that timer management is one of the most important tasks when configuring a protocol. The crucial task is to appropriately determine the time-out interval for end systems in different, sometimes far away networks. If the time interval is too small then this causes frequent time-outs and unnecessary retransmissions or connection releases, while too large time-out intervals lead to delayed reactions of the entities. The determination of reasonable time-out intervals in TCP is a comprehensive example of the complexity of this problem (see [Stal 08], [Tane 03]).

PDU loss and duplication

During data transmission the receiving entity has to detect missing and duplicated protocol data units. This is done by using sequence numbers (see Section 5.7). **PDU losses** are revealed if an expected PDU does not arrive within the specified time-out interval and/or PDUs with higher sequence numbers have already arrived. The sender can be informed about a PDU loss in two ways: indirectly by a missing acknowledgement or directly by repeating the acknowledgment which was received last.

PDU duplications can occur if acknowledgements being awaited are assumed to be lost due to time-out. In this case the sender retransmits the PDU after time-out (see Figure 5.1/3). But if the acknowledgements are only delayed then the peer entity receives these PDUs twice. It perceives the duplication by means of the sequence number and discards them.

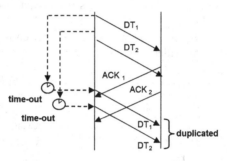

Figure 5.1/3: PDU duplications

Automatic repeat request

The acknowledgment principle introduced above corresponds to a stop and wait scheme. The sender waits until either the receiver confirms the transmission positively (or negatively) or a time-out triggers retransmission. When larger sequences of data PDUs have to be transmitted this is too long-winded. It is much more efficient if the PDUs are sent continuously. The problem is how to react when aPDU in the sequence has not been confirmed, while its predecessors and successors are? In this case **automatic repeat request (ARQ)** methods are applied. There are two basic approaches:

- go back N, and
- selective repeat.

Go back N

The *go back N* method repeats the transmission of all PDUs starting from the Nth unconfirmed PDU independently of whether some of these PDUs are already confirmed (see Figure 5.1/4a). This requires that the sender stores a copy of all PDUs until they are acknowledged. In the error case the receiver entity discards all PDUs following the Nth PDU in sequence. They are also not confirmed. The lack of the N-acknowledgement leads to a time-out at sender side and triggers the retransmission of the Nth and all following PDUs.

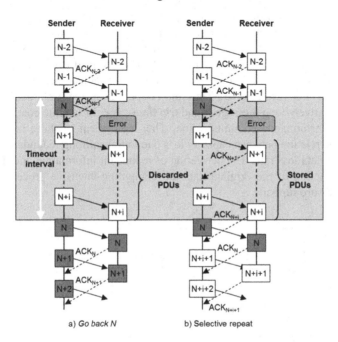

a) *Go back N*   b) *Selective repeat*

Figure 5.1/4: ARQ methods

Selective repeat

Selective repeat is the alternative approach to *go back N*. The difference is that in selective repeat only the missing PDU is retransmitted (see Figure 5.1/4b). Later successfully transmitted PDUs are stored in the receiver entity until the transmission order is re-established. Thereafter the PDUs can be delivered to the service user. The successful transmission of all PDUs can be confirmed by a cumulative acknowledgement.

A comparison of the two methods shows similar performance for traditional protocols [Stal 08]. Selective repeat requires that a sufficient large number of buffers should be provided at receiver side to intermediately store the PDUs. For *go back N*, only the copies of the unconfirmed PDUs have to be stored at sender side. Therefore the *go back N* method is preferred in traditional protocols. In high performance protocols it is different. Due to the high transmission rate, a data volume can be transmitted between PDU loss and error correction in *go back N* which corresponds to the double bandwidth-delay product. This data volume has to be retransmitted. In addition, approximately the same amount of data has to be delayed at sender side until the re-transmission is finished. This is not acceptable so *go back N* is not applied here, whilst selective repeat shows a similar performance to traditional protocols.

Forward error control

An alternative approach to the retransmission of PDUs is forward error control, which applies methods of coding theory. **Forward error control (FEC)** tries to re-construct lost PDUs at receiver side using redundant information, which is additionally transmitted. The principle of the approach (see Figure 5.1/5) is to add *h* redundant data units to *k* original data units that are derived from them. If up to *h* of the original data units are lost it is possible to re-establish them using the *h* redundant units. Forward error transmission is applied for real-time data transmission with relatively long message round trip times, e.g., in satellite communication or in high performance communication. The deployment of these methods depends on the relation between capacity loss due to transmitting redundant information and the data loss rate. The derivation of redundant information and the possible reconstruction of the original data are computing-intensive processes which require hardware support.

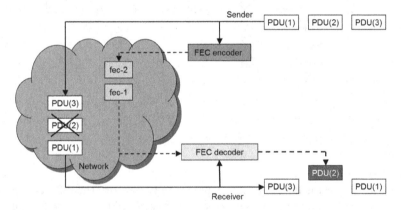

Figure 5.1/5: Forward error control

Cyclic redundancy checks

Finally we still have to consider how the receiver entity detects that a PDU arrived faulty, incomplete, or distorted. This can be detected with help of **cyclic redundancy checks (CRCs)**. They are usually deployed in lower layer protocols but can also be used in higher protocols. Cyclic redundancy checks also add redundant information to the PDU. This information is called the *frame check sequence* (FCS). It is generated by the sender entity. The frame check sequence is determined in a manner such that the PDU extended with the frame check sequence is divisible without remainder by a previously determined value. Upon receiving the extended PDU the receiver entity divides it by the same value. If there is no remainder it is assumed that the transmission was error-free. For determining the frame check sequence, polynomial codes are used. A detailed description of the method is given in, among others, [Stal 08] and [Tane 03]. Protocols that apply this protocol function vary regarding the PDU fields which are taken into account in the cyclic redundancy check. Many protocols, e.g., TCP, take the whole PDU into account, while others, especially in lower layers like ATM, calculate the checksum only for the header. Regarding the protocol description, the calculation of the frame check sequence represents a local action of the protocol entities (cp. Section 2.2.4).

5.2   Synchronization

An important protocol function is **synchronization** which is usually applied in the context of other functions, e.g., during connection set up. In certain situations of the protocol execution it is required that the communicating entities are in defined states in order to ensure the consistency of certain protocol operations. Typical examples are connection set up and release. In duplex communication, for instance, both sides have to confirm the connection set up before they can start sending data, otherwise data losses may occur. The need for synchronization in protocols results from the autonomous operation of the peer entities. They can only synchronize with each other by exchanging messages. These, however, may get lost or be delayed.

For synchronization, handshake procedures are applied. Two types are mainly used in protocols: the 2-way and the 3-way handshake. Their principle is depicted in Figure 5.2/1.

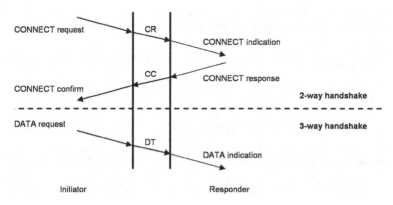

Figure 5.2/1: 2- and 3-way handshake

2-way handshake

The 2-way handshake consists of a simple message exchange between the peer entities. The *initiator* side starts with a connect request PDU, the *responder* side confirms the connection set up. The following example shows the principle for the XDT protocol in a slightly simplified way:

Initiator	Responder
XDATrequ_1:	
DT → responder	**wait event{**
wait event{	DT ← initiator:
ACK ← responder:	**respond** XDATind
respond XCONconf	ACK → initiator
set DATA TRANSFER	**set** DATA TRANSFER
}	}

After confirming the connection set up, the responder assumes that the connection is successfully established. This is sufficient for a unidirectional transmission. The responder receives with the connection set up message all parameters from the initiator and can wait for the messages. Even if its confirmation gets lost the connection is established and the receiver is ready to accept protocol data units. In a bidirectional or duplex communication, which is usually assumed for connections, this might become a problem. Assume that the responder starts sending PDUs immediately after sending its set up confirmation. If the confirmation message gets lost the communication between initiator and responder becomes inconsistent because the connection set up has not been confirmed to the initiator. This may lead to data loss or message reordering which contradicts the connection-oriented transmission paradigm (cp. Section 1.1). The use of timers does not remedy the problem because it only leads to a reaction at one side, whilst the other side continues to assume that the connection is set up. Only a further handshake provides a safe solution.

3-way handshake

The 3-way handshake requires that the initiator confirms the reception of the confirmation with a further message. Only when receiving this message the responder may begin sending its data units. Thus, it is ensured that both sides have the same knowledge about the state of the connection. It is not necessary that a special connection set up PDU is used for the second confirmation. This can be done by means of the first data PDU. Even if this PDU gets lost the initiator can rely on the successful connection set up and send further messages which are then interpreted as the second confirmation by the responder. When applying a 3-way handshake the XDT example changes as follows[1]:

Initiator	**Responder**

```
XDATrequ_1:
    DT → responder                    wait event{
    wait event{                           DT ← sender:
        ACK ← responder:                  respond XDATind
        respond XCONconf                  ACK → initiator
        set DATA TRANSFER                 wait event{
    }                                         DT ← sender:
    . . .                                     set DATA TRANSFER
    DT → responder                    }              .   .   .
                                  }
```

5.3 Connection management

Connection management comprises all activities that are required to set up, to maintain, and to release a connection in connection-oriented protocols. These comprise many more activities than the three phases – *connection establishment*, *data transfer*, and *connection release* – foreshadow at first glance.

5.3.1 Connection establishment

To set up a connection two activities are required: to establish the connection and to negotiate the quality of service parameters (QoS). The connection establishment requires that both partners synchronize for the acceptance or refusal of the connection. For this, the aforementioned handshake procedures are applied. A responder may also refuse a connection establishment offer. The reasons for this are mostly a lack of resources, i.e., the responder is not able to handle the connection, or the incapability to fulfill the desired QoS requirements. The latter play a less important role in traditional protocols. Here only a few parameters are used, such as throughput, transmission delay, residual error rate, or error probabilities. The negotiation procedure is simple. The initiator submits an offer to the responder that it accepts, reduces, or rejects. In case of a reduction the initiator now has the choice to accept or reject it. By this the negotiation is finished. In traditional protocols quality of service rules were applied rarely. In modern protocols, in particular for high performance and multimedia communication, more complex mechanisms are applied. Special models have been developed to make contracts

---

[1] Note that the XDT protocol actually does not require a 3-way handshake because it only supports unidirectional transmission.

between the service users and the provider, and to enforce these contracts. These models are complex and do not directly relate to protocols. We do not consider them further here.

There are two principal ways to set up a connection: explicitly or implicitly.

Explicit connection set up

Explicit connection establishment is applied in the majority of protocols. It is characterized by a separate set up phase before the data transmission phase starts (see Figure 5.3/1). Depending on the protocol context a 2-way or 3-way hand-shake is applied.

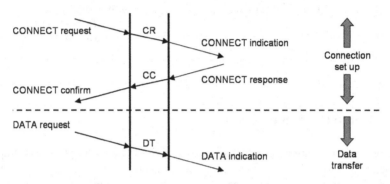

Figure 5.3/1: Explicit connection set up

Implicit connection set up

Explicit connection set up is not expedient for high performance protocols with transmission rate of several megabits per second. The reason is that with an in-creasing transmission capacity the volume of data in transmission becomes sig-nificantly larger so that delays like that of the connection set up phase are not ac-ceptable anymore. Figure 5.3/2 shows this difference related to the bandwidth-delay product for a low and a high performing link. The bandwidth-delay product denotes the product of the transmission rate (bandwidth) and the transmission de-lay. The latter comprises the delays for sending and receiving data and their transmission as well. In this example we assume a link length of 1000 km with a signal delay of 100 µs per bit for the low performing network and of 1 ns per bit for the powerful one. As a consequence, multiple messages are in transmission in the high performance network compared to the traditional one. The round trip time (sending and confirming) in the traditional network, needed for a 2-way hand-shake, is about 20 msec. During this time 20 Mbyte of data could be transmitted in the high performance network. This delay as well as delays by retransmitting data is usually not tolerable in high performance networks.

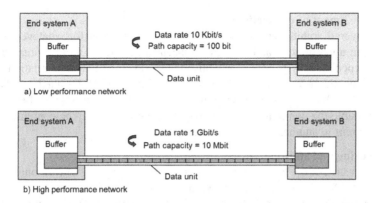

Figure 5.3/2: Bandwidth-delay product in networks with different transmission rates (source [Brau 95])

The implicit connection set up differs from the explicit one by the fact that data transmission starts immediately after sending the first connection set up message without waiting for the confirmation of the set up. Thus, the gap between triggering and confirming the set up is fully used for sending data. Figure 5.3/3 shows the principle. If the responder refuses the connection the data PDUs get lost. They must be retransmitted, if this is still needed, during the next set up attempt. This drawback is accepted for the benefit of a better transmission rate. For the implicit connection set up, also specific PDUs may be used as for the explicit set up.

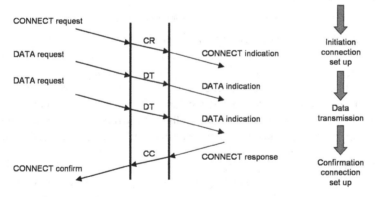

Figure 5.3/3: Implicit connection set up

5.3.2 Connection maintenance

During data transmission various measures are required for maintaining the connection which remain unnoticed by the service user. These measures mainly concern reactions to a breakdown of an (N-1)-connection and the mapping between (N)- and (N-1)-connections.

Re-establishment of connections

In a layered architecture the breakdown of a connection for whatever reason requires an appropriate reaction of the adjacent higher layer. In this situation the upper protocol usually tries to re-establish the (N-1) communication relation. This can be done either by resynchronization or by reassignment. **Resynchronization** means that the broken (N-1)-connection is re-established by the (N)-entities. If this is not possible the communication via the (N)-connection may be continued by a **reassignment** to another (N-1)-connection.

Multiplexing and splitting

Another task of the connection management is the mapping of (N)- onto (N-1)-connections. Mostly a one-to-one mapping is applied. In some situations it might be favorable to map several (N)-connections onto one (N-1)-connection (*multiplexing*) or vice versa one (N)-connection onto several (N-1)-connections (*splitting*) (see Figure 5.3/4).

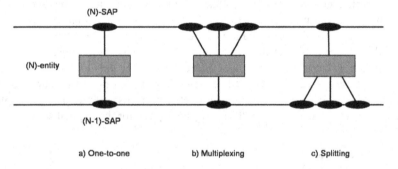

a) One-to-one   b) Multiplexing   c) Splitting

Figure 5.3/4: Mappings of (N)- onto (N-1)- connections

Multiplexing of (N)-connections is useful when it is not favorable to maintain several (N-1)-connections for efficiency reasons. Sometimes it may be useful that for certain reasons several (N)-connections are set up over an (N-1)-connection to support different functions, e.g., error handling. **Splitting** of connections is vice versa useful, when the reliability of the transmission is to be increased by transmitting the (N)-communication over several (N-1)-connections.

Multiplexing and splitting, however, require additional measures which are not needed in a one-to-one mapping. These measures imply further protocol functions that bring along an additional overhead. Therefore, it must carefully be assessed whether this overhead is acceptable when layering protocols.

For multiplexing, these are:

- *Scheduling of (N)-connections regarding an (N-1)-connection* to control the simultaneous arrival of PDUs on (N)-connections,

- *Flow control[2] on (N)-connections* to regulate the capacity of the (N-1)-connection,
- *Assigning arriving (N-1)-PDUs* to their associated (N)-connections. For this, connection references are used.

For splitting, the following additional functions are required:

- *Scheduling of the PDU assignment to (N-1)-connections* when splitting the (N)-connection,
- *Re-establishing the (N)-PDU sequence* when reuniting the (N-1)-connections at receiver side due to varying arrival times.

5.3.3 Connection release

Connection release is usually initiated by the service users when the data transmission is finished or other circumstances (e.g., errors) force the transmission to be terminated. It can also be triggered by the service provider due to internal conditions.

There are two kinds of connection release:

- explicit connection release and
- abrupt connection release.

Explicit connection release

The explicit connection release is triggered by one of the service users (or sometimes also simultaneously by both). When closing a connection the service provider has to solve two problems:

- to synchronize the connection release between partners and
- to ensure complete data delivery.

The objective of the synchronization during connection release is to ensure that both entities close the connection. Otherwise, this might result in a half-open connection in which one entity is in the state *closed*, the other one in state *connected*. Unfortunately, this problem is not as easy as it looks. The problem is known as the "two army problem" and is described in detail in [Tane 03]. The two army problem describes a situation in which a blue army intends to attack a white army in a valley. The blue army, however, is split on two hills and has to coordinate the attack. To do so they send a messenger to the other side to deliver the time of the attack and to return with the confirmation. The problem is that the messenger can be captured. This can happen at very different moments. Figure 5.3/5 shows some of these situations related to the connection release.

---

[2] For flow control, see Section 5.8.

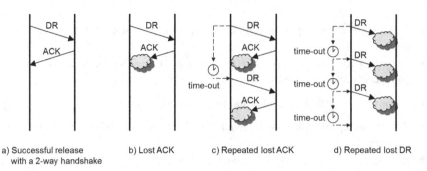

a) Successful release   b) Lost ACK   c) Repeated lost ACK   d) Repeated lost DR
   with a 2-way handshake

Figure 5.3/5: Variants of an unsuccessful connection release

It can happen that the first message reaches the peer entity but the confirmation gets lost, or that even the DISCONNECT request (*DR*) PDU to initiate the connection release does not reach the partner entity. Of course, the PDUs may be repeated. However, what happens if they are lost again? We can never reach a situation in which both sides can be sure that the other side is fully informed about the connection release. The problem is not solvable. A feasible solution is presented below. But prior to that, we consider the data delivery issue.

To completely deliver the data still in transmission several constraints have to be taken into account. We first consider a unidirectional transmission between the entities E_1 and E_2. The first question to consider is who should release the connection (see Figure 5.3/6a)? If E_2 closes the connection it cannot be sure that there are no further data in transmission. The solution is that only the sender may release the connection.

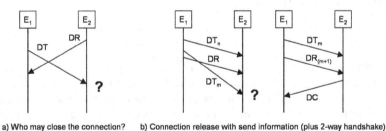

a) Who may close the connection?   b) Connection release with send information (plus 2-way handshake)

Figure 5.3/6: Variants of an incomplete data delivery

In the next situation we consider the case that E_1 sends two messages DT_n and DT_m and then releases the connection with a *DR*-PDU (DISCONNECT request). It might happen that the release indication arrives before DT_m (or even DT_n) (see Figure 5.2/6b). A solution to this problem might be that the release indication informs E_2 about the PDU sent last. This can be done by including the sequence number of that PDU in the *DR*-PDU, usually increased by one (see Section 5.7). What happens, however, if the release request does not arrive at E_2? If E_2 confirms the reception of DT_n and DT_m, E_1 does not notice that E_2 is not informed about the release. A 2-way handshake, i.e., an acknowledgement of the release request by a *DC*-PDU (DISCONNECT confirm), could be applied. In this case, E_1 can repeat the release indication if the confirmation is missing. This may ensure with a certain probability that E_2 will be informed about the release, but this does not solve the synchronization problem discussed above.

In a duplex connection the described procedure has to be applied in both directions to deliver the data completely. Each direction has to be closed separately. This is called *half close* and is applied in TCP, for instance. A half close terminates the data transmission in one direction, while data transmission can be continued in the other direction. Figure 5.3/7 shows the principle.

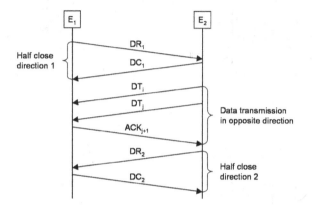

Figure 5.3/7: Connection release with 2 half closes

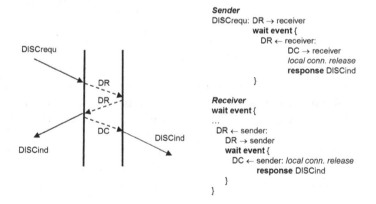

Figure 5.3/8: Connection release with a 3-way handshake

If both directions are closed simultaneously then the half closes can be subsumed into a 3-way handshake (see Figure 5.3/8), but this also does not solve the problem of a permanent PDU loss.

To solve the synchronization problem the following feasible approach is usually applied. The initiator of the connection release closes the connection also in the case when it cannot verify whether the partner entity does the same. For this, timers are deployed. Each side starts a timer when it starts the connection release or is informed about it for the first time. A missing acknowledgement triggers a time-out and the respective entity closes the connection locally. Figure 5.3/9 depicts two different situations for the loss of release PDUs.

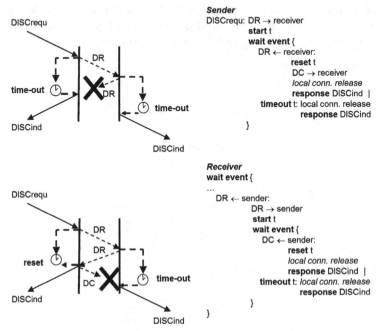

Figure 5.3/9: Timer-controlled connection release

However, even this solution can fail if the first *DR*-PDU never arrives at partner side. The deployment of only one timer is not sufficient because it can induce the initiator to give up after *n* unsuccessful attempts and close the connection onesidedly. This again would result in a half-open connection. To avoid this problem a second timer – the **activity timer** – is required at both sides which reacts after a defined period of time if the peer entity is not active any more (see Figure 5.3/10). It is restarted each time a PDU arrives from the other entity (cp. Section 5.1).

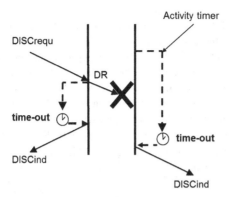

Figure 5.3/10: Detecting DR loss with an activity timer

Timer-controlled connection release is also expedient in other applications, e.g., in client/server applications. Here connections are often short-term and convey sometimes only small amounts of data. A handshake-based connection release needs comparatively much time. In situations with a high demand for client/server connections the available connections may quickly be exhausted. A timer-controlled connection release can improve the situation, since it releases the connection without exchanging PDUs. This presumes, however, that the time-out value is chosen appropriately so that all messages can be delivered. It also requires storing the connection context for a certain time to detect PDU duplications. The time interval depends on the transmission time of the PDUs in the network, which fluctuates. Sometimes synchronized clocks are deployed which are synchronized by protocols or radio-controlled clocks. The lifetime of the PDUs in the network is limited in absolute time. This allows it to exactly determine the time to release the connection.

Abrupt connection release

Abrupt connection release leads to an immediate connection break-up. All data in transfer are lost. Therefore, this kind of release is usually applied in exceptional situations, such as irreversible transmission errors. This abort causes another problem though: the reuse of connection references (cp. Section 2.1). If the references are reused immediately it may happen that PDUs arrive on a new connection, although they still belong to the old one. Therefore references have to be "frozen". **Freezing of connection references** is another protocol function that ensures that references are not reused for a certain time period. This time is determined by the round trip time of the messages.

5.4   Soft states

Soft states are a mechanism for the management of communication relations which is applied when control information has to be stored in network nodes along the communication path. This information has to be periodically refreshed (see Figure 5.4/1). A soft state expires when a refreshment-PDU does not arrive within a defined clean-up interval. Thereby the clean-up time-out is set so that it can tolerate occasional losses of refreshment PDUs. The soft states are explicitly deleted when the communication relation terminates. Maintenance of soft states is considered more flexible compared to that of the "hard states" in cases when the data delivery path may change. The soft state approach became popular in connection with the *resource reservation setup protocol* RSVP [RFC 2205] which is a QoS reservation signaling protocol for application data streams. Here soft states are used to store reservation information to provide a defined bandwidth in the routers. The RSVP PDUs are sent as IP packets (see Section 6.1.2 for this). Recent communication and signaling protocols for mobile ad hoc networks and overlay networks use similar principles.

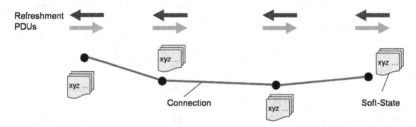

Figure 5.4/1: Soft states

5.5   PDU coding/decoding

The coding of PDUs before sending and their decoding and analysis after reception in the receiver entity represents an important part of each protocol. These actions essentially determine the efficiency of a protocol implementation. In protocol descriptions coding/decoding does not take up much space. The PDU formats are defined in the data part of the specification. The coding/decoding itself is often described by a function as we did in Section 2.2. These are local actions of the entities which are not visible in the protocol interactions. Protocol descriptions rarely describe the coding/decoding of PDUs because it is not relevant for modeling and validating the protocol flow. In implementations, however, PDU coding/decoding is one of the most expensive protocol functions because a lot of statements have to be executed to write data into PDUs and to read them out. In addition, the handover of PDUs between layers within the protocol stack has to be organized. A crucial issue in this context is to avoid the copying of PDUs which has a significant negative influence on the implementation efficiency. We go into detail on this in Section 13.5.

There are several possibilities to improve the efficiency of the coding/decoding process. A common approach is to align the PDU components to certain positions

to simplify access to them. Another is the simplification of protocol headers by using only a few bytes to faster evaluate them in routers and at the receiver. This is,
for example, supported by protocols that use out-of-band signaling (cp. Section
4.3.3) because it allows reducing protocol headers. Additional parameters and protocol options can be included in the more efficient signaling protocols. At application level this problem is usually bypassed using **text-based protocols**, such as
HTTP and SIP. In text-based coding PDUs are not coded using significant bit positions but as consecutive ASCII text. This much simplifies the coding/decoding
process. This can be done, since the protocol interaction at the application layer is
less intensive than at lower layers. It often consists only of simple request/res-
ponse mechanisms.

5.6   Adjustments of PDU size

Some network links and thus related protocols limit the size of the PDUs transferred. In the Internet a *maximum transfer unit* (MTU) is used which defines the
maximum packet size that can be transmitted over a link. It is actually determined
by the applied transmission procedure on the communication media. Therefore the
mapping of a protocol on an (N-1)-layer may also require an adaptation of the
PDU size. There are various possibilities.

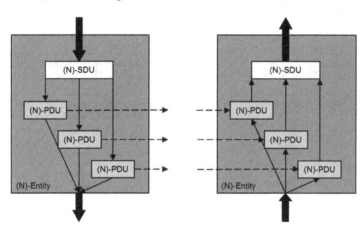

Figure 5.6/1: Segmenting and reassembling

Segmentation and reassembling
   Segmentation means that an (N)-service data unit is decomposed into several
segments in the (N-1)-layer. Each segment is converted into an (N-1)-PDU which
besides address information contains the segment length and sequence information
to re-establish the PDU order at receiver side. The segments are separately transmitted and reassembled in the receiver entity (see Figure 5.6/1). Note that segmentation does not hurt the principle of transparency discussed in Section 2.1 because

segmentation does not take the contents of the PDUs, i.e., the user data, into account. The adding of new headers does not touch the content. The SDU can be reestablished unharmed.

In the Internet this procedure is called **fragmentation**. It is applied, for instance, in the IP protocol (see Section 6.1). In IPv4 the header already contains fields to take the fragmentation header, if required. In IPv6 this is solved by means of a header extension. Fragmentation is not necessarily end-to-end. It can be applied in each router if the link MTU demands this.

The limitation of the transfer size may not be the only reason to apply segmentation. Smaller PDUs are in general better to handle. Error control, resynchronization, and internal handovers are more efficient. On the other hand, a greater organizational overhead and more traffic are required to ensure complete delivery. Therefore, segmentation has to be applied with care and reduced to a meaningful minimum.

Chaining and Separating

In some cases the opposite approach might be useful by uniting smaller data units to a larger one to reduce the overhead for their transmission. The pros and cons of this function are more or less vice versa to those of segmentation (see above). There are two ways to do this. One method is to write several PDUs into an (N-1)-SDU and send them together (*chaining and separating*) (see Figure 5.6/2). Another way is to connect several (N)-SDUs to one (N)-PDU. This called *blocking and disassembling*.

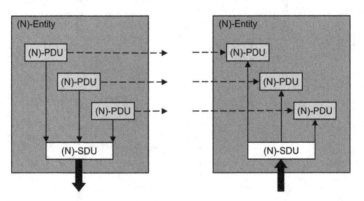

Figure 5.6/2: Chaining and separating

5.7   Use of sequence numbers

Connection-oriented transmission provides an ordered transmission. This means that the PDUs are delivered to the receiver in the same order as they were sent off, independently of the arrival order at the receiver entity. In order to re-establish the transmission order sequence information has to be tagged to the

PDUs. For this, **sequence numbers** in the PDU headers are used. They allow the receiver entity not only to re-establish the transmission order but also to detect missing PDUs or duplications. Sequence numbers are further used for the acknowledgment of PDUs (cp. Section 5.1). The starting sequence number has to be communicated between the two entities during connection set up to synchronize regarding this number. The use of sequence numbers implies two issues: (1) the assignment of PDUs to a later-established connection with the same reference and (2) sequence number overflow.

Avoiding wrong PDU assignments

The first issue is caused either by delayed PDUs or by a connection abandonment due to system failure in which all information about the established connection is lost. After system restart and re-establishing a connection with the same reference it might happen that PDUs, in particular acknowledgements, of the old connection, which are still in transmission, are assigned to the new connection. In protocols which use connection references this can be avoided by "freezing" the connection reference, i.e., by not assigning this reference to a new connection for a certain time. Internet protocols, e.g., TCP, do not use this mechanism because only one connection can be established between two sockets. In order to avoid this situation in these protocols several measures can be taken. First, the life-time of PDUs in a network should be limited. This is usually done by a *Time-to-Live* counter (TTL) that is decreased every time it passes a router. When the counter is equal to zero the PDU is discarded. Second, it should be ensured that two identically numbered PDUs are never outstanding at the same time. This can be achieved by bookkeeping of the assigned sequence numbers at both sides for each connection. Bookkeeping is to prevent sequence numbers from being reused for a certain time. These numbers form the forbidden zone (see Figure 5.7/1).

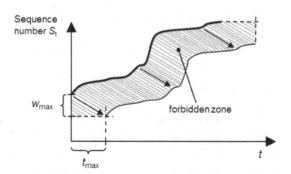

Figure 5.7/1: Forbidden zone

The *forbidden zone* is characterized by two parameters: the maximum lifetime t_{max} of the PDUs in the network and a safety margin w_{max}, e.g., number of PDUs the receiver agreed to accept (receiver window) (see Section 5.8 for this). The safety margin takes into account that PDUs may be resent.

Bookkeeping does not work in the case a connection breaks down. Therefore bookkeeping is not applied in practice. Instead entities wait until all PDUs still in transmission must have arrived or are discarded. Only then they are again ready to set up a new connection. This waiting time depends on the protocol applied (see Section 6.2.1 for this).

Sequence number overflow

Sequence numbers are assigned modulo a maximum number, since only a finite number of bits can be reserved for the sequence number in the PDU header. Sequence number overflow is not checked in the protocol. It is performed automatically. An important issue is, therefore, to determine an appropriate maximum value for the sequence number. If the maximum value is too small then new sequence numbers can correlate with outstanding PDUs. TCP uses a maximum value of 2^{32} (see Section 6.2.1). In high performance communication this causes problems. If we assume a maximum PDU lifetime t_{max} of 2 minutes the overflow is reached when transmitting 286 Mbps. To ensure a conflict free reuse of sequence numbers high performance protocols have either to provide a sufficiently large range for them or to limit the lifetime of the PDUs correspondingly. Another solution is the additional use of time stamps to correlate PDUs with equal sequence numbers.

5.8   Flow control

Flow control regulates the number of PDUs exchanged between sender and receiver entities. Its objective is to protect the receiver entity from overload situations, which may occur when the receiver is not able to accept all incoming PDUs due to differences in processing power of the hosts or available buffer capacities. There are two types of flow control:

- window-based flow control, and
- rate-based flow control.

5.8.1 Window-based flow control

In the **window-based approach** the receiver provides the sender a range of PDUs – the "window" – within which the sender can send PDUs. Window-based flow control is a pure end-to-end regulation between sender and receiver entities which only takes the receiver's situation into account and not that of the network connecting them. This regulation only relates to the first transmission of PDUs but not to retransmissions due to PDU loss or transmission errors. Retransmissions are performed independently. There are several methods for implementing window-based flow control:

- start/stop procedures,

- credit procedures, and
- the sliding window protocol.

Start/stop procedures

The simplest way to install a flow control is a **start/stop mechanism** in which the receiver sends a stop signal to the sender entity when it is not capable to accept further PDUs. The drawback of this approach is that frequent start/stop signals engender a discontinuous, bursty data flow which is usually not desired. In addition, the receiver entity has to provide sufficient buffer to store all PDUs which are still in transmission when the stop signal is sent out.

Credit procedures

An essentially more elegant method represents the **allocation of credits**. The receiver entity allocates the sender entity a credit, usually specified as a range of sequence numbers. The sender can use up the credit by sending out PDUs whose sequence numbers are in the specified range. When the credit is used up, the sender has to stop transmission until a new credit is allocated. Normally, credits are allocated continuously so that interruptions and bursty data flow are avoided. We demonstrate the principle of credit allocation taking XDT as an example. For this purpose, we extend the data transmission phase by a credit mechanism. Credit allocation and acceptance are activities which run in parallel to the sending and receiving of data PDUs. They are, therefore, represented by concurrent activities in the **par event**-statement. We first consider the behavior of the sender.

```
message DT = ...
         UPDATE = record (code: bits; credit, credit_nr: integer)
         ACKupdate = record (code: bits; credit_nr: integer)

   . . .

entity sender
signal new_credit
var credit: integer
par event{
    XDATrequ: code_DT                              // SENDING DT
              if (credit > 0)
                  {DT → receiver}
              else wait event{                     // Wait for credit
                  new_credit: DT → receiver
                  }
              decr credit ||                       // a credit unit is used up

    UPDATE ← receiver:                             // RECEPTION CREDIT
             if (UPDATE correct)                   // New credit-PDU?
                 {credit := UPDATE.credit
                 code_ACKupdate (incr UPDATE.credit_nr)
                 ACKupdate → receiver      // Confirmation credit
```

```
                    set new_credit                        // Signal to SENDING DT
                    }
    } //sender
```

The sending of *DT*-PDUs now depends on whether the sending entity still has credit. When the credit is used up, the entity has to wait. The *UPDATE*-PDUs, which arrive independently of sending *DT*-PDUs, increase the credit and decontrol a waiting *DT*-PDU. For each *UPDATE*-PDU, it is checked whether it contains a new credit or represents a duplication of an already received *UPDATE*-PDU. Only in the first case, the credit is increased. Furthermore, it is necessary to detect losses of credit PDUs. Otherwise, a deadlock may eventuate because the sender is unable to send data, whereas the receiver believes that no data are ready to be sent. For that reason, the sender has to acknowledge the reception of credits with an *ACKupdate*-PDU which contains the sequence number of the *UPDATE*-PDU increased by one.

The receiver supervises the credit acknowledgments with a timer which is started when sending the *UPDATE*-PDU. If no acknowledgement arrives the credit allocation is repeated.

```
entity receiver
timer t: 0..? ms
var new_credit, credit_nr: integer init(1)
par event{
    DT ← sender: ...  ||                      // RECEPTION DT
    loop{                                      // PT: CREDIT ALLOCATION
        determine credit(new_credit)
        code_UPDATE (new_credit)
        loop{
            UPDATE → sender                    // New credit to sender
            start t
            wait event{                        // Await credit confirmation
                ACKupdate ← sender:
                        credit_nr := ACKupdate.credit_nr
                        exit |
                timeout t: skip                // Repeat credit allocation
            }
        }
    }
} //receiver
```

Usually the credit values are chosen so that they correspond to the sequence numbers of the PDUs. They show the sender entity which PDUs it can send next. In this case one can waive the explicit credit acknowledgement, since the receiver knows from the PDU sequence number that the sender received the credit.

Sliding window protocol

This principle is used in the **sliding window protocol,** which is the most commonly applied variant of the credit principle [Tane 03]. A "sliding window" is here applied for credit allocation to define the credit range. This range is negotiated between the peer entities during connection set up. Figure 5.8/1 shows this principle for a credit range of three units. The window indicates the sequence numbers of the PDUs which may be sent. The sender may use up the credit range and send the PDUs with the specified numbers. The receiver displaces the window by its acknowledgements and thus allocates new credit. The expected next sequence number is used as confirmation. An acknowledgement can cumulatively confirm several data units. Note that the window during sending temporarily attenuates as long as the sent protocol data units are not confirmed. In Figure 5.8/1 we do not take PDU losses and changes in the transmission order into account. A description of the sliding window protocol which also considers these aspects is given in [Holz 91].

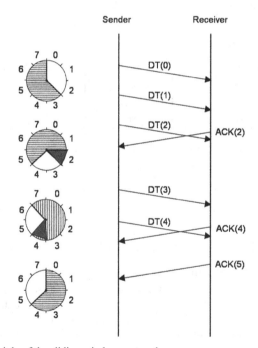

Figure 5.8/1: Principle of the sliding window protocol

5.8.2   Rate-based flow control

In contrast to window-based flow control which only carries out an end-to-end regulation between sender and receiver entities, rate-based flow control takes the actual load situation of the network into account. It controls the data flow which the sender injects into the network in such a manner that overload situations in the network are avoided or at least mitigated. Such regulation is required in high performance communication, e.g., for transmitting multimedia data streams. Rate-based flow control allows one to guarantee a possibly uniformly continuous data stream which enables a good presentation quality at the receiver side. Window-based mechanisms cannot guarantee this for two reasons: the high data volume in transmission and the purely receiver-related regulation which protects the receiver but does not take the network situation into account. Figure 5.8/2 illustrates the problem.

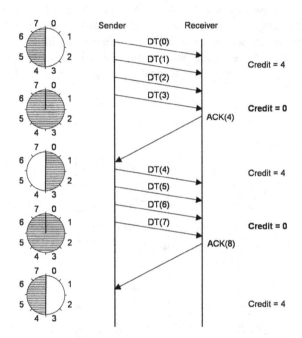

Figure 5.8/2: Sliding window with high transmission rates

The crucial point is that the receiver window is too small compared to the transmission rate. Consequently the window is often closed because the credit range is used up, although the sender entity could send further data. It has to wait for acknowledgements from the receiver to reopen the window. Until this point the data units have to be stored. This can cause discontinuous, bursty data traffic. Larger credit ranges, however, cannot simply be allocated without providing larger buffer capacities at the receiver. Additionally, appropriate resources in the routers to handle large data streams and to avoid jams have to be allocated.

Rate-based flow control provides a solution to this problem. It regulates the speed at which the sender introduces the PDUs into the network. Thus, the sender can control the transmission rate, which it agrees upon during connection set up. This is done by defining the data volume which can be sent in a certain time period, the so-called **burst**, and by controlling the minimum gap between bursts. During a burst phase the sender can send as many data packets as the burst size allows. When the limit is reached or the burst period is over, the sending procedure is interrupted. The efficiency of this regulation depends on the precision of the deployed timers. Here differences exist between software and hardware timers. Software timers are not precise enough to determine the interval between the data units to accurately approximate the burst rate. This may cause a bursty data flow. Hardware timers are more exact in this respect and guarantee a continuous data flow. Rate-based flow control further differs from window-based control by also taking retransmissions into account.

In practice rate-based flow control is often applied together with window-based control to avoid both network congestion and overloading of the receiver. Rate-based flow control, however, allows one to define larger windows. An example of the combined use of both mechanisms is the slow start concept of TCP, which we consider in Section 6.2.2.

Further reading

The basic protocol functions are described in varying levels of detail in most of the well-known introductions into the fundamentals of computer networks, such as the books of Kurose and Ross [Kuro 08], Stallings [Stal 08], Peterson and Davie [Pete 07], and Tanenbaum and Wetherall [Tane 10]. These books also describe the handling of corrupted protocol data units which is not considered here because it is not in the main focus of the book.

A broader introduction into protocol design principles is given in the book of Sharp [Shar 08] which besides protocol principles and functions deals with addressing schemes, routing, PDU encoding principles, security protocols, application protocols, and other related topics.

Exercises

(1)   Explain the role of protocol functions.

(2)   Which are the most important mechanisms for error control used in communication protocols? Give a short summary of each function.

(3)   For various reasons, the transmission of PDUs over a network may be disturbed. The probability of such problems is much higher than for a communication within a computer. Assume now that entity A sends six PDUs to entity B. The transmission of the third PDU is disturbed; that of the others not.

   a) What are the possible practical implications of such a disturbance of this PDU?

   b) How can some of the effects of a) be avoided without feedback to the sender entity?

   c) Instead of (or in addition to) b) feedback measures are used to correct the effects mentioned under a). What might this feedback look like?

  d) The feedback mentioned under c) has the goal to retransmit the PDU.
     Describe the two different versions of the retransmission of the PDU.
     What are the consequences for the transmission of the PDUs and the re-
     quired buffer resources?
  e) In d) we discussed two retransmission methods. Discuss now to what ex-
     tent in both approaches single and cumulative acknowledgments should
     be used.
  f) The feedback mentioned under c) can also be lost. What are the possible
     consequences of this? How can the problem be solved?

(4) What are the reasons that the receiver entity may receive the same PDU
     twice? Give a time sequence diagram to illustrate the reasons.
(5) We assume a connection-oriented protocol in which entity A sends the PDUs
     1 to 5 to entity B at intervals of 2 msec. The propagation delay is 3 msec; the
     serialization delay is neglected. Entity B confirms promptly each correctly
     received PDU. Entity A repeats the transmission of a PDU when it does not
     receive a confirmation within 10 msec. Repeated confirmations are also sent
     immediately by entity B.

  a) We assume that the first transmission of PDU 3 gets lost. Present the
     transmission of PDUs 1-5 in a time sequence diagram, once for the *go
     back N*-method and once for the *selective repeat*-procedure. Indicate the
     times for sending and receiving packets as well as, if needed, which
     PDUs are dropped by the receiver entity.
  b) Now we assume that it is not PDU 3 that gets lost but the acknowledge-
     ment for this PDU. Present also this case in two time diagrams. Indicate
     again the times for sending and receiving of the PDUs and the packets
     that are dropped by the receiver entity.
  c) Finally we assume that the transmission of PDU 3 is not delayed only 3
     msec but 9 msec. Present the time sequence diagrams for this situation
     for both methods. Indicate the times and the dropped packets as above.

(6) Replace the *go back N* procedure in the XDT protocol by a selective repeat.

  a) Describe this extension by means of time sequence diagrams. Introduce
     appropriate PDU names.
  b) Describe the changes to both entities in the model language.

(7) What are handshake procedures used for? What is the difference between a
     2-way and a 3-way handshake? When are they recommended to be applied?
(8) The XDT protocol uses a 2-way handshake. Explain why this can be done.
     What changes to the XDT protocol would require the use of a 3-way hand-
     shake?
(9) What is the difference between an explicit and implicit connection set up? In
     what situations are they used?

(10) XDT uses an explicit connection set up although no special PDUs were introduced for this. Replace the XDT connection set up by a confirmed implicit one. For this, we remove the constraint that the service user only hands over a new data unit after receiving an *XDATconf* primitive. Represent the solution in a time sequence diagram for an accepted and a rejected connection.

(11) Explain why a 2-way or 3-way handshake does not ensure a reliable connection release.

(12) A feasible solution for a reliable connection release is a timer-controlled release. Describe the procedure of this approach. What is the role of the activity timer in this context?

(13) When the order of the PDUs cannot be restored in the XDT protocol, the receiver entity *XR* aborts the connection sending an *ABO*-PDU. However, the reception of *ABO* by the sender entity *XS* is not checked by *XR*. How does the protocol behave if *ABO* gets lost?

(14) XDT in its current specification contains a "blemish". It may happen that all *DT*-PDUs are transmitted successfully, but some acknowledgments are lost. This can cause the receiver entity to indicate the service user a successful transmission, while on the sender side an abandonment of the transmission is signaled. Discuss whether this problem can be resolved and how the protocol must be changed to guarantee the same protocol outcome for both sides.

(15) Replace the implicit connection release in the XDT protocol by an explicit one that is triggered by the receiver with an *XDISrequ* when it has got the last PDU. The sender releases the connection with an *XDISind*, after which also the receiver releases the connection with an *XDISind*.

 a) Describe this extension by means of time sequence diagrams. Introduce appropriate PDU names.

 b) Describe the changes for both entities in the model language.

(16) Explain the difference in coding PDUs in normal protocols and in text-based protocols. Why do application level protocols often prefer the text-based coding?

(17) Sequence numbers play an important role in protocols. Why are they so important and what problems occur with their use?

(18) What is the purpose of flow control? Why is it needed?

(19) What are the methods applied for window-based flow control?

(20) The XDT protocol uses a break function (*XBREAKind*) at the sender side which represents a special variant of a flow control procedure. What flow control method does it correspond to? Who are the sender and the receiver here, i.e., which data flow controls this function? Why is it needed?

(21) The credit mechanism represented in Section 5.8.1 as an extension of the XDT protocol contains concurrent protocol procedures. As argued in Section 1.1, this can be described by an interleaving semantics. Give some possible interleaving sequences for this example.

(22) Extend the XDT protocol with the sliding window protocol. Describe the extension in the model language.

(23) Assume a connection between entity A and B. On this connection only PDUs of constant size are exchanged. The serialization delay is always 1 msec, the propagation delay 2 msec. For flow control, a sliding window protocol is applied, the window size is 3 PDUs, the sequence numbers are assigned modulo 8. A sends PDUs to B at the following times: 0 msec, 1 msec, 3 msec, 7 msec, 8 msec. B confirms each received PDU at the following times: 3 msec, 7 msec, 9 msec, and 10 msec. (The times relate to the first bit of the PDU.)

   a) Draw a time sequence diagram of the exchanged PDUs DT and ACK with the contained sequence numbers (acknowledgements increased by one). The first PDU has the sequence number 0. Specify for the following times the sequence number range and the remaining free size of the sliding windows: 2.5 msec, 6.5 msec, 14.5 msec.

   b) Does A adhere to the sliding window protocol at any time? Justify your answer! If A does not always conform to the sliding window protocol: what was the reaction of B and why has B acted so?

(24) What is the difference between a window- and a rate-based flow control?

(25) We assume again a connection between entities A and B. The propagation delay is 2 seconds in both directions; the serialization delay can be neglected. Now a rate-based flow control is applied. Initially one PDU may be sent per second. After 5 seconds, B informs A that it can send only one PDU every three seconds from now on. Draw the corresponding time sequence diagram in which A is to send 10 PDUs as soon as possible. Indicate for each packet the sending and receiving time.

6 Case study: The Internet protocol stack

At the end of the first part of the book we want to show how the protocol mechanisms introduced in the previous chapters are applied in protocols used in practice. What modifications are applied? What additional features and mechanisms are used to meet various requirements? We use the currently most important protocol architecture for this: the Internet protocol stack. Note that it is not the objective of this chapter to give a detailed introduction to the relevant Internet protocols. This can be found in many introductory books about the Internet. We restrict ourselves to selected aspects of these protocols to complete our overview of the basic protocol principles.

As discussed in Section 4.3.2, the TCP/IP protocol suite represents a specialized protocol architecture in which the protocols IP, TCP, and UDP form the kernel (see Figure 6/1). The network access and the application layer do not represent layers in the sense that we introduced in Chapter 3. The Internet architecture supports a wide range of network types. Each of them has to be specified separately. The same applies to the application layer. Here different possibilities exist of how to build applications on top of the transport interface. Therefore we focus in this chapter on the protocols of the IP and the transport layer. Finally we give an outlook on how to set up applications.

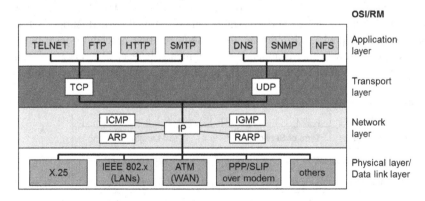

Figure 6/1: TCP/IP protocol suite

6.1 IP layer

The IP layer is determined by the **Internet Protocol (IP)**. It is the core protocol of the Internet which connects the various networks and "sticks them together". IP was designed by Cerf and Kahn at the beginning of the 1970s [Cerf 74]. In contrast to the OSI architecture and related layer-3 protocols, IP was designed to support the interconnection of networks, the so-called **internetworking**. IP is a connectionless protocol which provides an unreliable data transmission service. Connectionless data transmission in the Internet is also called datagram transmission. A datagram corresponds to a PDU which is denoted as **packet** in IP. There exist two IP versions: IPv4 and IPv6. IPv4 denotes the older version of IP which is still prevailingly used in the Internet. IPv6 is the successor version which introduces a new address scheme and new features needed in modern networks. The replacement of IPv4 has proved to be more complicated and long-winded than expected. About fifteen years after starting the development, a general transition to IPv6 is still not predictable.

At first glance IP as connectionless protocol seems to be a simple protocol. It possesses, however, quite a number of unique features compared to other protocols which we consider below. We first introduce the structure of the IP packet for both protocol versions. After that we consider interaction with other protocols.

6.1.1 Structure of IP packets

When describing connectionless protocols the structure of the protocol data units forms the core of the description. All important information is contained in the header and the trailer (if used) of the PDUs. An IP-packet consists of a header and user data part. The header structures are different in the two versions.

IPv4

The structure of the IPv4 header is depicted in Figure 6.1/1. The header consists of a 20 byte fixed part and a variable length optional part. IP supports fragmentation of the packets. In contrast to the segmentation procedure described in Section 5.6, no new header is added to the fragments. Instead IP reserves information fields in the header for that case. These fields are contained in the second row.

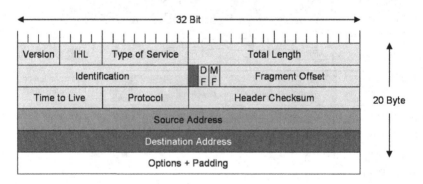

Figure 6.1/1: IPv4 header

The IPv4 header fields have the following meaning:

- *Version:* Indicates the protocol version, i.e., IPv4 or IPv6. According to this information the respective protocol stack is selected if the host supports both protocol stacks (cp. Section 4.3.2).
- *IHL:* Length of the IP header in 32-bit words. The minimum value is 5, if no options are applied, and the maximum value is 15, i.e., 40 bytes can used to describe options (see below).
- *Type of Service:* This field is provided for specifying the handling of packets in routers. It is often not used in practice. Type of service specifies how packets are handled related to delay, throughput, and reliability, and which service parameters are applied (e.g., minimum delay, maximum throughput, maximum reliability and others). In order to support modern applications with dedicated quality of service demands this field is used differently, when the differentiated service model is applied. It indicates the supported QoS class.
- *Total length:* Indicates the total length of the IP packet, i.e., header and user data. The maximum length is 65,535 bytes.
- *Identification:* Identifier to denote all fragments of an IP packet. It allows the receiver host to distinguish fragments of different packets.
- *DF (Don't Fragment):* Flag that indicates to the router that the packet may not be fragmented.
- *MF (More Fragments):* Flag that indicates that further fragments of this packet will follow. In the last fragment MF is not set.
- *Fragment Offset:* Indicates the position of the fragment based on which the receiver re-establishes the packet.
- *Time to Live:* Counter to limit the lifetime of the packet. It is supposed to count in seconds. The maximum value is 255 sec. The counter is decremented each time the packet passes a router. When the value is zero, the packet is discarded and a message is sent back to the source host. The *time to live* counter prevents packets from ceaselessly wandering around in the network and thus overloading it.
- *Protocol:* Indicates the receiver protocol of the user data carried with the IP packet. We discussed this principle in detail in Section 4.3.2. The protocol numbers are specified in RFC 1700.
- *Header Checksum:* Check sequence to prove the correctness of the transmission (cp. Section 5.1). Note that in IP this checksum only relates to the header. The checksum must be proved and recalculated at each node because at least the time to live value changes.
- *Source Address, Destination Address:* IP addresses of the source and destination hosts. They have their origin in the well-known class-oriented address scheme of IPv4 and are usually written in the dotted decimal notation, e.g., 141.43.10.3. As argued in Section 4, we do not consider address schemes in this book.

The *options* allow defining additional constraints for the transmission of the IP packets. The original intention for introducing options was to provide room for (experimental) features and extensions not foreseen in the original design. Options are of variable length beginning with a 1-byte identifier and some options with a length field. The defined options can be used to specify the security of the packet, to prescribe the route to be followed, to record the passed note, and to use time-stamps. This information may be used for debugging routing algorithms.

IPv6

The IPv6 header differs from the IPv4 header by two essential features. It possesses a simplified structure and considerably enlarged address fields. These changes pursue the objective to increase the analysis speed of IP packets in the routers and to enlarge the address space of the Internet. Figure 6.1/2 shows the structure of the IPv6 header.

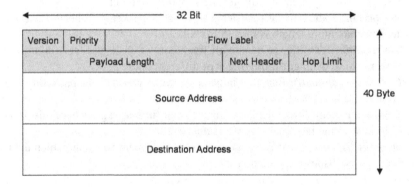

Figure 6.1/2: IPv6 header

The address field is extended by 24 bytes to a total of 32 bytes. It contains the sender and the receiver addresses. The total length of the IPv6 header, however, does not exceed 40 bytes. This is due to the reduction of the control information transported in each header. The elements of the IPv6 header are:

- *Version*: Indicates the protocol version, i.e., IPv6.
- *Priority*: Specifies the priority of the data packets of a source. There are 16 different priorities. The range from 0 to 7 is assigned for normal data traffic; the range 8-15 is provided for the service classes when using *Differentiated Services*.
- *Flow Label*: End-to-end indicator for data flows as they appear in multimedia communication. By means of the flow label, a router can decide how to handle the data packets belonging to this flow. All packets are handled equally.
- *Payload Length*: Length of the user data (max. $2^{16} = 65536$ bytes).
- *Next Header*: Indicates the header which follows the IPv6 header. This may be either the header of a packet contained in the user data field, e.g., ICMP, TCP, UDP and others, or an extension header (see below).

- *Hop Limit*: Indicates the number of routers (*hops*) a packet may pass until it is discarded. The *Hop Limit* corresponds to the *Time to Live* field in the IPv4 header.
- *Source Address, Destination Address*: 128 Bit IP addresses of the source and destination host.

The **extension headers** are the most interesting change compared to IPv4 from the protocol design point of view. They are a means to flexibly handle options in IPv6. Extension headers describe a protocol option. They are only included when the option is selected. This reduces the information transported in the protocol header. Note that, in contrast to IPv4, fragmentation is considered optional in IPv6. Therefore the required parameters are no longer contained in the IP header. They are only included in the fragmentation header, when fragmentation occurs. If extension headers are used, the *Next Header* field of the IPv6 header points to the first extension header (see Figure 6.1/3).

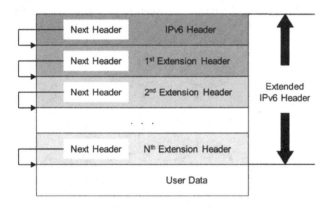

Figure 6.1/3: Principle of the IPv6 extension header

An IPv6 header may contain several extension headers. Each of them contains a *Next Header* and a *Header Extension Length* field which specify the following extension header and the length of the current header. IPv6 defines different extension headers: the *Hop-by-Hop Options* header for router options, the *Destination Options* header for router and destination system options, the *Routing* header to fix routes, the *Fragment* header containing the fragment control parameters, the *Authentication* header and the *Encapsulation Security Payload* header for authentication and encryption of data. The latter correspond to IPsec which is fully integrated into IPv6. The extension headers except the *Destination Options* header can only appear once in an IPv6 header. The sequence of the headers is fixed and corresponds to the order in which we introduced them here. The *Destination Options* header can be contained twice, whereby parameters for the destination system must be put to the end.

6.1.2   Interaction with other protocols

IP is not the only protocol which runs in the IP layer. The TPC/IP architecture allows several protocols to run in a layer. This is one of the most important differences compared to the OSI reference model. IP as the fundamental protocol of the Internet could not fulfill its task if it was not supported by other protocols which fulfill additional tasks and provide additional functions. Only the interaction with these protocols ensures the path of the IP packets through the network including feedback from the network nodes to the source node which is necessary for reliable operation of IP. This is a characteristic feature of IP which makes it different from other connectionless protocols, which only provide a simple data transmission service. Figure 6.1/4 shows the most important protocols which are associated with IP. Note that the routing protocols do not belong to the IP layer in the TCP/IP architecture. OSPF and the reservation protocol RSVP are protocols of the fourth layer, whilst RIP and BGP even run above the transport layer. The protocols ARP and RARP run at the border between layer 2 and 3; often they are considered as layer-2 protocols.

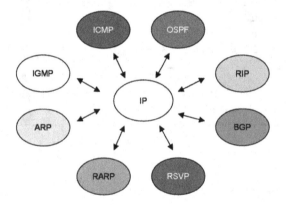

Figure 6.1/4: Protocols associated with IP

The protocols have the following tasks:

- **ICMP (*Internet Control Message Protocol*)**
  ICMP and IP are closely connected. It possesses various functions to provide feedback between the sender and the receiver as well as the passed routers. This feedback can be used, for example, to optimize the transmission paths, when better routes are found, or for error indications, if a destination is not reachable or the *Time to Live* value of an IP packet has elapsed. Furthermore, ICMP provides functions which support the network user like the well-known *ping*, to prove the reachability of a destination, or *traceroute*, to pursue the used

routes in the network. The close dependency between IP and ICMP explains why a new version ICMPv6 has been required for IPv6.

* **IGMP** (*Internet Group Management Protocol*)

  IGMP applies to the management of multicast groups in IP multicast. It is used to indicate the join or leave of group members.

* **ARP** (*Address Resolution Protocol*)

  ARP is used to determine the respective MAC address for a given IP address, if the destination host is located in a local area network. It is needed because the communication paradigms in WANs and LANs are different. In WANs we have point-to-point communication at layer 3, in LANs broadcast-like communication at layer 2. MAC addresses are flat addresses which do not contain any information about the location of the host in the LAN. Before forwarding the packet to the LAN the MAC address of the destination hosts has, therefore, to be determined at the interface between the networks using ARP.

* **RARP** (*Reverse Address Resolution Protocol*)

  Contrary to ARP, RARP determines the IP address of a given MAC address. It is applied if hosts do not possess a hard disc on which they can store their IP address.

* **RIP** (*Routing Information Protocol*)

  RIP is a routing protocol that applies the distance vector routing approach. It is a so-called intra-domain protocol which is used for path finding in autonomous systems, i.e., in network structures with their own administration authority. It is preferentially applied in smaller or medium-sized wide area networks.

* **OSPF** (*Open Shortest Path First*)

  OSPF is also an intra-domain protocol which takes the states of the links into account (*link state routing*). It is used in large wide area networks and is the more powerful and flexible protocol compared to RIP.

* **BGP** (*Border Gateway Protocol*)

  BGP is an inter-domain routing protocol for path finding between autonomous systems. It is not directly related to IP, but it is essential for the path finding of IP packets and currently one of the most important protocols in the Internet.

* **RSVP** (*Resource ReserVation Protocol*)

  RSVP is used for the reservation of resources along the transmission path [RFC 2205]. It is mainly used in the context of high performance and multimedia communication to ensure a defined transmission quality.

Another characteristic feature of ICMP and IGMP is that they use IP, i.e., a protocol of the same layer, to transport their PDUs. The "internal service user" is indicated by means of the protocol number, as explained in Section 4.3.2. Such a design of a "service interface" is possible because IP represents a connectionless protocol which provides only a data transmission service.

6.2   Transport layer

In the transport layer of the Internet protocol suite two basic transport protocols are used: the connection-oriented TCP and the connectionless UDP. Another protocol which has also been defined for the transport layer is the *Stream Control Transmission Protocol* (SCTP). SCTP is a session-oriented transport protocol which provides a reliable transport service together with a number of functions that are critical for telephony signalling transport [RFC 3286]. It does not have the importance of TCP and UDP. We confine ourselves to the latter here.

6.2.1   TCP

The **Transmission Control Protocol (TCP)** is the connection-oriented transport protocol of the Internet. It was designed, as previously mentioned, together with the IP protocol. TCP ensures a reliable end-to-end transmission between two communication partners over the unreliable IP. TCP as one of the oldest protocols uses a set of mechanisms which were not applied again in such a manner in other protocols. But TCP is the most used transport protocol and above all a living protocol, which has been supplemented again and again by new mechanisms which have taken many years of experience with TCP into account.

The original version of TCP is specified in [RFC 793]. Later this specification was corrected and extended [RFC 1122], [RFC 1323]. In this section we introduce the most important mechanisms of TCP. As with the introduction to IP, we focus on those aspects which are of interest for protocol theory. Comprehensive introductions to TCP can be found today in many books about the Internet. We subdivide the introduction for the sake of clarity into the description of the TCP service interface and the TCP protocol, even if the term TCP service is not explicitly used in the standard.

TCP service interface

TCP provides a connection-oriented reliable transport service. Data losses and changes to the sending order are recognized and repaired during the transmission, i.e., the data are delivered to the receiver in the same order as they were handed over to the protocol. The data exchange over a connection is duplex, i.e., in both directions. There is also the possibility of an accelerated data transmission.

Byte stream principle

One of the most important singularities of TCP is **byte stream transmission**. TCP does not use the concept of a service data unit as we introduced it in Section 2.1. It regards the data to be transmitted as a sequential byte stream. As a consequence, the data units handed over by the sender to the protocol do not have to be identical with the data units delivered to the receiver (see Figure 6.2/1). So, for example, the protocol can deliver instead of four units of 1024 bytes handed over to it a unit of 4096 bytes to the receiver, but the sequence of the bytes remains preserved! Unlike many protocols, there is no obligation for the accepting and delivering protocol entities to forward the received bytes immediately after reception. They can be buffered until more favorable transmission sizes are reached.

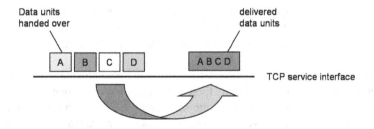

Figure 6.2/1: Byte stream principle of TCP

Ports

Ports are the access points of the applications in TCP (cp. Figure 4.3/4). They correspond to the service access points introduced in Section 1.1. A port is addressed by a 16 bit number; altogether 65,535 ports can be addressed. Port numbers are not only addresses. They also characterize the applications assigned to them. For that reason, port numbers are divided into two groups: the *well-known port numbers* (0-1023) and the *ephemeral port numbers* (>1023). The latter can be freely assigned to applications. They are released after the application has been terminated. In contrast, the *well-known numbers* are firmly assigned to certain applications. The assignment was/is carried out by the *Internet Assigned Numbers Authority* (IANA) and the *Internet Corporation for Assigned Names and Numbers* (ICANN). Examples of such allocations are: 20, 21 - FTP, 23 - TELNET, 25 - SMTP, 80 - WWW. These applications and/or services are accessed on all systems via the assigned ports to TCP. The assignment of firm port numbers supports in particular client/server applications (cp. Section 1.1) because it ensures that a service can always be called by different clients via the same port number.

Sockets

Sockets are the *application programming interface* for the applications to describe the interaction with TCP (cp. Section 4.3.2). A socket is addressed by the IP address of the host and the port number of the application. Sockets are also the end points of connections. In contrast to the OSI approach, only one connection is allowed between two sockets. A TCP connection is thus characterized by the tuple (*socket*$_i$,*socket*$_j$). In order to describe the interaction at the socket interface defined procedures are used. The most important ones are:

socket	-	generate a new socket,
bind	-	bind a local address to a socket,
listen	-	indicate readiness to accept a connection,
connect	-	send a connection request,
accept	-	accept a connection request,

send	-	send data,
receive	-	receive data,
close	-	close a connection and erase the socket,
shutdown	-	close a connection but preserve the socket,
status	-	inform about the status of the connection, i.e., socket address, state of the connection, window size.

Figure 6.2/2 gives an example of setting up, using, and closing a TCP connection for a client/server application. First both sides have to create a socket by means of the *socket*-procedure. With the succeeding *bind*-call, the port number is assigned to the IP address. Next, the server executes the procedure *listen* to wait actively for incoming connection set up calls. At client side these procedures are not executed because the client initiates the connection. This is done by calling the *connect*-procedure. The server accepts the connection through the *accept*-procedure. After that both sides can exchange data using the procedures *read* and *write*. When the connection is released, the sockets can be either entirely or partly closed using the procedures *close* or *shutdown*, respectively. With each procedure call, several parameters are exchanged containing various context parameters which are not considered further here. More details about so-called socket programming can be found in [Tane 03]. One can ask, what is the relation between socket programming and the interaction scenarios as we described them by means of time sequence diagrams in Section 1.1? Socket programming is a concrete implementation of interactions at the service interface. Time sequence diagrams describe such interactions in a more abstract way.

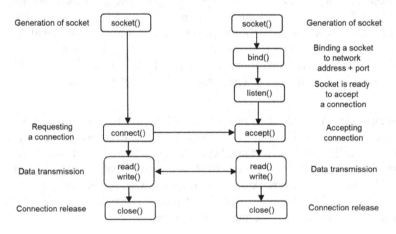

Figure 6.2/2: Socket programming

TCP protocol

TCP maps the byte stream received from the application onto protocol data units which are called **segments** here. The use of segments does not dismiss the byte stream principle because the latter only relates to the data exchange at the service interface. It does not affect the kind of data exchange applied within the protocol. A TCP segment consists of a TCP header and a user data part. The structure of the TCP header is important for understanding the protocol. It is introduced first. Beforehand, however, it is necessary to explain some further singularities of the protocol.

Some singularities of TCP

In contrast to many other protocols, TCP possesses only one protocol data unit type, i.e., all segments have almost the same structure. The unified segment structure facilitates the handling of the segments in the sender and receiver entities. Necessary functional differences of the segments are expressed by means of **flags** (see Figure 6.2/3). Depending on the flag set, the segments possess a different semantics which is exploited in the protocol procedures. In many TCP descriptions the flags are used to name the segments. One speaks of SYN- or RST-segments. Thus, different segment types are introduced indirectly, although there is only one segment structure.

A further characteristic feature of TCP as well as of UDP is its close relation with IP. So TCP segments do not address the hosts. They only contain the port numbers which identify the application. The host addresses are contained in the IP packet which also transports the TCP segment as user data. Therefore the TCP/UDP header extended by the IP header is sometimes called a "pseudo header".

Another special feature of TCP concerns the sending of data. The data handed over to the protocol have not to be sent immediately. They can be stored until enough data are collected to form a segment of reasonable size. If, however, the PSH-flag (see below) is set the data are sent off immediately. As a consequence, the segments may have different lengths. In order to restore the transmission order the TCP sequence numbers do not refer to the number of the segment but to the position of the first byte of the transported data in the byte stream.

Furthermore, segments are not confirmed by an explicit confirmation segment. The confirmation is rather "stuck" to an arbitrary segment sent in the opposite direction by **piggybacking** (cp. Section 5.1). The sequence number used for confirmation is contained as the *Acknowledgement Number* in the segment header. Simultaneously the ACK flag is set. The *Acknowledgement Number* also refers to the position in the byte stream. It indicates the number of the byte expected next.

TCP segment

The TCP segment consists of a header of at least 20 bytes and the user data part. The header is divided into a firm part (20 bytes) and an optional one. The maximum size of a segment can be negotiated during connection set up. The default value is 536 bytes. The structure of a TCP segment is presented in Figure 6.2/3.

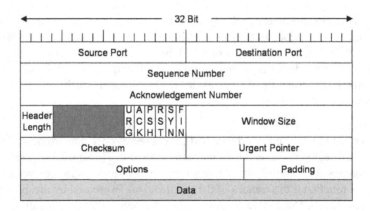

Figure 6.2/3: Structure of a TCP segment

The elements of the TCP segment header have the following meaning:

- *Source port*: Number of the source port
- *Destination port*: Number of the destination port
- *Sequence number*: Sequence number of the segment. Indicates the position of the first byte in the byte stream.
- *Acknowledgement number*: Confirmation of a received segment through pig-gybacking. Indicates the next expected byte.
- *Data offset*: Length of the segment header. Indicates the position in the segment where the user data part begins.
- *Control Flags*: Flags for activating certain protocol functions. They simultaneously indicate the validity of related data fields of the segment header, i.e., only if these flags are set are the related header fields interpreted.
  - URG: *Urgent*-flag. Indicates that the urgent pointer is active (see below)
  - ACK: *Acknowledgement*-flag. Indicates that an acknowledgement is piggybacked to the segment, i.e., the value in the *Acknowledgement Number* field is the next expected byte.
  - PSH: *Push*-flag; if this flag is set the data are not buffered in the TCP entity when they are handed over from the application. They are immediately forwarded to the network and to the application at receiver side. Nowadays most implementations automatically set the flag, so that it cannot be influenced by the receiver.
  - RST: *Reset*-flag. Used to reset a connection if required. It is also set when a connection establishment indication is rejected.
  - SYN: *Synchronization*-flag; Used to indicate the desire to set up a connection.
  - FIN: *Final*-flag; Used to release a connection. It indicates the termination of the transmission in one sending direction.

- *Window*: Current window size for flow control based on the sliding window protocol.
- *Checksum*: Check sequence to prove the correct transmission (cp. Section 5.1); it comprises the header and the user data.
- *Urgent pointer*: Pointer to the end of urgent data which are transferred immediately after the segment header. The urgent pointer is activated when the URG flag is set.

The option field provides functions which are not relevant for all applications. Examples are the definition of the maximum segment size, the use of time stamps, selective confirmation, and others. The option field may be followed by a padding field which contains zeros to guarantee that the header has a 32-bit-limit before the user data part begins.

Connection set up

TCP applies a 3-way-handshake for establishing a connection (see Figure 6.2/4). The connection establishment is triggered by the initiating entity by a segment in which the SYN-flag is set. Beside the port numbers of the two communication partners, the segment also contains the current position in the byte stream as sequence number. The peer entity accepts the connection by sending a segment in which the SYN- and the ACK-flags are set. The sequence number indicated refers to the current position in the byte stream for the transmission in the opposite direction. The acknowledgement number contains the sequence number of the initiator increased by one. If the connection is rejected an RST-segment is sent back. The 3-way-handshake is completed by another segment from the initiator which contains the acknowledgement for the opposite direction. Simultaneously the first user data can be transmitted in this segment. The sequence number is now increased by one in relation to the first segment, i.e., the connection establishment consumes a sequence number in each direction.

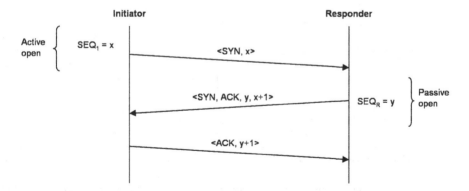

Figure 6.2/4: Connection establishment in TCP

A connection establishment attempt by the initiator (usually a client application) is called an *active open*, the reaction of the responders (usually a server application) accordingly a *passive open*.

The attempt of two service users to simultaneously set up a connection results in only one connection, since connections in TCP end at the sockets. There is no distinction of connection end points (cp. Section 4.3.2).

Connection release

Connections must be explicitly released in TCP. Apart from this, there is also the possibility to abort a connection. The connection release consists of a separate closing of the transmissions in each direction. The closing of a connection in one transmission direction is called a *half close*. Inducing a connection release by one of the communication partners is called an *active close* similarly to the connection establishment, the reaction of the opposite side accordingly a *passive close*. A *half close* begins with a FIN-segment (see Figure 6.2/5). The FIN-segment must be confirmed by an ACK-segment with the sequence number increased by one. Thus, the connection is closed in one direction. The application is informed accordingly about it. In the other direction data transmission can be continued until this transmission direction is closed, too. Similarly to the connection establishment, the transmission directions can also be closed at the same time (*simultaneous close*).

After executing both half closes the connection is de facto closed. The two associated sockets, however, are not released immediately. A certain time interval is waited to prevent late arriving segments from being assigned to a possible new connection (cp. Section 5.7). With today's TCP implementations the double maximum segment running time (maximum segment lifetime), about 240 seconds, is usually taken for this interval. All TCP segments which arrive after half of this time are discarded.

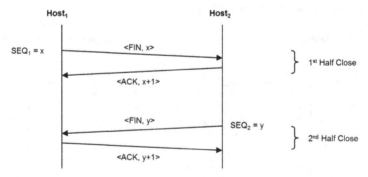

Figure 6.2/5: Connection release in TCP

TCP does not use complex mechanisms to recognize losses of the FIN- or the ACK-segments during connection release. The release procedure is timer-controlled (cp. Section 5.3.3). If the FIN-segment is not confirmed in a defined time period the connection is closed. The partner will eventually notice the inactivity of the opposite site, when the activity timer elapses.

Data transmission

After setting up the connection both sides can send data. If the PSH-flag is set the data are not buffered. They are transferred immediately. This is, for instance, useful in the case of remote access to another computer by means of *telnet* to transmit the entered characters. Otherwise the data are transmitted when the segment is full. The correctness of the transmission is proved by means of the checksum in the segment header. The receipt of each segment which contains data must be confirmed by a (piggybacked) ACK. When a confirmation is missed, a retransmission is triggered. This monitoring is performed by the **retransmission timer**. For retransmission, the *go back N*-principle is applied (cp. Section 5.1).

The flow control in TCP is based on the **sliding window protocol** (cp. Section 5.8.1). TCP does not use explicit credit PDUs. Instead it indicates the current window size in the *Window*-field together with an ACK to the sender. If this window update contains the value zero the window is closed and the transmitter must wait. The window reopens when the application on the receiver side reads data from the receiving buffer. This is communicated to the sender with another ACK-segment containing the window update. TCP permits, however, the sending of data in two exceptional cases, when the window is closed. First urgent data (URG-flag is set) can always be sent. This can, for example, be used to cancel a process at receiver side. Secondly 1-byte-segments may be sent to resend a segment with a window update. This can be used to prevent deadlocks, when the announcement of the re-opening of the receiver window has been lost.

The piggybacking principle for the confirmation of received segments causes another specific protocol mechanism, the **delayed acknowledgement**. Piggybacking becomes a problem when no segments are available for transmission in the opposite direction to carry the acknowledgement, because a missing confirmation triggers the retransmission of the segment. The delayed acknowledgement mechanism prevents this by forcing an explicit acknowledgement, if in a defined time period no segment will be transferred in the opposite direction. Figure 6.2/6 shows the principle. The acknowledgement process is monitored by the **delayed acknowledgement timer**, which triggers an additional ACK-segment when the delayed acknowledgement timer times out. The time-out value is generally adjusted to 200 msec, at the most however to 500 msec.

Extensions

TCP has been extended several times. These extensions are based on experience with the practical use of TCP in the Internet over many years. They concern the performance of the protocol as well as defects in certain protocol procedures. Examples of such extensions are the Nagle algorithm, the silly window syndrome, the slow start algorithm, the Internet congestion algorithm, and the dynamic timer management. We limit ourselves here to explanation of the slow start and congestion control algorithms, which are interesting additions to the flow control and the timer management. For introductions to the other mechanisms mentioned, the interested reader is referred to [Tane 03].

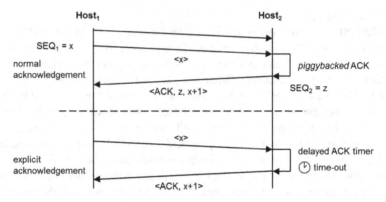

Figure 6.2/6: Delayed acknowledgement

The **slow start algorithm** represents an extension of the flow control mechanism in order to take the current network situation into account. It was proposed by Van Jacobson in 1988 [Jaco 88]. Flow control, as introduced in Section 5.8, is a pure end-to-end adjustment for data exchange between the sender and receiver entities to prevent the receiver from being overloaded with packets. It does not take the load situation in the network into account. In networks as well overload situations may occur, which can lead to packet congestion in certain network nodes which can in turn cause packet losses. This may especially occur if the end-to-end communication relationship spans several networks as is often the case in the Internet. The slow start algorithm adjusts the data stream sent into the network so that it does not overload either the receiver or the network, i.e., it passes the network possibly without congestion. For this purpose, a second window is introduced, the *congestion window*, which adjusts the data flow transferred to the network (see Figure 6.2/7). The size of the congestion window is one maximum segment at the beginning. The sender can send a segment. If it is acknowledged the window size is doubled. Now the sender can use this window size. If the segments are acknowledged the window size is double again and so forth, i.e., the window grows exponentially until it reaches the size of the receiver window which defines the amount of bytes the receiver is able to accept. The window growth is carried out on the condition that all segments sent are successfully acknowledged in time. If a segment is not acknowledged congestion is assumed in the network. The window is reset to its initial size and the procedure restarts. The slow start thus gradually increases the data flow of the sender to the window size of the receiver. If the network does not permit this the sending entity sends with smaller capacity.

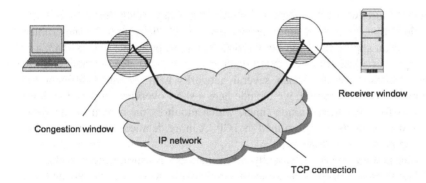

Figure 6.2/7: Principle of the slow start

The slow start algorithm has been extended to the Internet congestion control algorithm which is supported by all TCP implementations (see Figure 6.2/8). This algorithm introduces as a third parameter a threshold for the window's growth. When the window size reaches this threshold, initially 64 Kbytes, the window further increases linearly by only one maximum segment size, i.e., the sender adapts more slowly to the maximum window size. When a time-out occurs the threshold is set to half of the reached window size, the congestion window itself to one maximum segment, and the procedure continues. This allows a more fine-grained adaptation to the network situation.

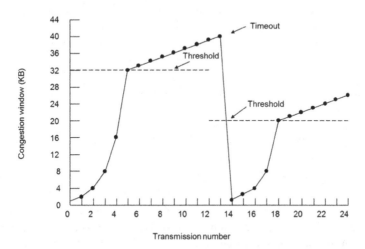

Figure 6.2/8: Principle of the Internet congestion control algorithm

Timer management

Timer management is another interesting feature of TCP. As argued in Section 2.2, time control is an abstract element in protocol design because it only specifies the procedure, whilst the concrete time-out values are usually left open to protocol configuration. In practice timer management is a challenging task. The problem is to define an appropriate time-out interval. Transport protocols like TCP are a good example for illustrating the determination of time-outs due to their end-to-end characteristics that may span several networks with probably different traffic situations. For that reason, we include here a short overview of how the time-out interval for the retransmission timer, which monitors the arrival of the segment acknowledgements, is determined in TCP. A more detailed description of this issue can be found in [Tane 03].

The time-out interval is usually determined by measuring the *round trip time* RTT of the segments, i.e., the time interval between sending a segment and receiving the acknowledgement. Figure 6.2/9 depicts two possible outcomes. Figure 6.2/9a shows a dense arrival of acknowledgements. In this case it is easy to determine the time-out interval by setting the value a bit higher than the measured round trip time. This is usually typical of lower layer protocols over a direct link. In TCP as an end-to-end protocol, which often covers many links, the outcome often corresponds rather to that of Figure 6.2/9b. The time-out value is much more difficult to determine in this situation. A too small value, e.g., T_1 in our example, triggers unnecessary retransmissions which put additional traffic load on the network. In the opposite case, i.e., T_2 is too large; receivers will wait too long for retransmissions. This reduces the network performance.

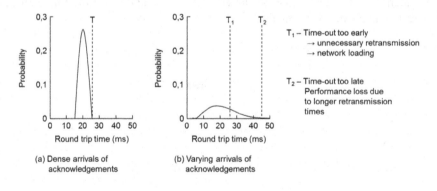

(a) Dense arrivals of acknowledgements

(b) Varying arrivals of acknowledgements

Figure 6.2/9: Different ACK arrival times (source [Tane 03])

In TCP a dynamic method is applied which constantly adjusts the time-out interval. The algorithm originates again with Van Jacobson. It is based on a constant measurement of the *round trip time* RTT_{Samp} for each segment sent. This value is used to update the estimated round trip time RTT_{Est} for this destination according to the formula

$$RTT_{Est} = \alpha RTT_{Est} + (1-\alpha)RTT_{Samp}$$

The smoothing factor α is usually set to 7/8. It indicates the weight given to the old value of RTT_{Est}. The time-out value is then set to

$$time\text{-}out = \beta\ RTT_{Est}$$

where β represents the standard deviation. It was initially set to 2. This approach proved too inflexible for strongly varying RTT_{Samp}. Karel and Van Jacobson later refined the calculation by using the mean deviation as a correcting factor

$$D = \alpha D + (1\text{-}\alpha)|RTT_{Est}\text{-}RTT_{Samp}| \ .$$

The time-out value is now set to

$$time\text{-}out = RTT_{Est} + 4 \times D \ .$$

This calculation is applied in most TCP implementations. Another issue of the original approach concerns the retransmission of segments after time-out. It cannot always be uniquely decided whether an acknowledgement relates to the first or repeated segment. To solve this problem today's implementations do not, following a proposal of Karn, update RTT_{Est} when a segment has been retransmitted. Instead they double the time-out interval for each loss until the segment is confirmed.

6.2.2 UDP

For a lot of applications and higher protocols, a reliable connection-oriented transmission like in TCP is not needed and/or it is too inefficient. Multimedia applications, for instance, do not meet the real-time constraints, when segments are retransmitted in case of loss or incorrectness. Such applications and protocols use the connectionless transport protocol UDP (*User Datagram Protocol*) [RFC 768].

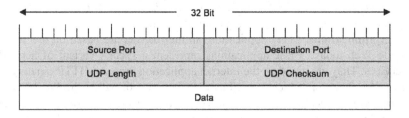

Figure 6.2/10: Structure of a UDP packet

UDP as connectionless protocol does not provide reliable transmission. Packets may be lost and the sending order is not preserved. Since connectionless protocols do not have a real protocol procedure, their specification mainly consists of the description of the packet header. In UDP this is quite simple; the header has only eight bytes (see Figure 6.2/10). As already argued for TCP, UDP is closely related to IP. The UDP header only indicates the port numbers of the application. The IP addresses are contained in the IP header. The computation of the checksum is not necessarily demanded, but it is supported by many implementations. Protocols that run over UDP are, for example, RIP (*Routing Information Protocol*), SNMP (*Simple Network Management Protocol*), RPC (*Remote Procedure Call*), LDAP (*Lightweight Directory Access Protocol*), RTP (*Real-time Transport Protocol*), SIP (*Session Initiation Protocol*), and others.

6.3   Applications and high-level protocols

The application layer comprises the applications and services that the network user perceives as proper network services (cp. Section 1.1). These applications and services are provided in cooperation with the underlying protocol layers as described in the previous chapters. Within the protocol stack, the transport interface represents the border between the communication and the application-oriented protocols. The latter are dedicated to support the applications. How applications are put on the transport interface is not prescribed in the Internet architecture. There are several possibilities:

- **Network services.** Many well-known Internet services like *telnet, ftp, email, dns, the web,* and others are directly provided above the transport layer (cp. Figure 4.3/3). These services use a connection-oriented or connectionless transport service according to their requirements. They are assigned to fixed port numbers known as the well-known port numbers (cp. Section 6.2.1). Each of these services uses its own protocol, e.g., SMTP or HTTP (see below). These application-oriented protocols are usually much simpler than the protocols described beforehand. They mostly comprise only a few interactions. In addition, application-supporting features are included like the *Multipurpose Internet Mail Extensions* (MIME) for the *Simple Mail Transfer Protocol* (SMTP) to represent different languages and alphabets.
- **Web applications.** Many applications in the Internet are based on the World Wide Web today. These applications represent a special variant of network services. They are based on the Internet application protocol HTTP (*HyperText Transfer Protocol*) which is used as transfer protocol within the World Wide Web. Web applications are client/server applications (see below) in which the client by means of a browser accesses content on a web server. The design of web applications applies a wide range of rules and methods which are beyond the topic of this book.
- **Self-developed applications.** Every user can develop its own application on top of the transport interface. There are different ways to build applications. Simple applications can be directly implemented on the transport interface. In this case the application developer has to directly program the interactions with

the transport layer at the respective socket, as explained in Section 6.2.1. Most applications, however, need additional protocol support. This can be either a specific middleware (see below) or additional application-oriented protocols, e.g., RTP (*Real-Time Transport Protocol*) for the transmission of multimedia data [RFC 1889]. The number of these protocols is not limited and depends on the application.

- *Middleware platforms.* Many distributed applications require a lot of generic functions or services, e.g., a name service, a mediation service, a timer service, security management, and others. These functions are nowadays subsumed in middleware platforms that are provided on the top of the transport interface. CORBA has been a typical example. Middleware platforms ensure distribution transparency, e.g., concerning the location of objects, access to servers, and errors. They also comprise functions which were formerly assigned to layers 5-7 of the OSI reference model (cp. Section 4.3.1). Middleware platforms are also described by reference models though these are different to those considered here. Nowadays web services [Alon 04] are often applied to provide these functions. Web services are software applications identified by a URI (*Unique Resource Identifier*) which can be bound over the Internet. For their advertisement, search, and binding, XML-based protocols are used, such as SOAP.

- *Client/server applications.* The majority of applications in the Internet apply the client/server paradigm. Client/server applications are asymmetric services in which a client accesses a service which is remotely provided by a server (cp. Section 1.1). To provide and call these services a middleware is usually deployed. For the design of client/server applications, separate layered models, e.g., 2-tier or 3-tier models, are applied [Alon 04].

- *Peer-to-peer applications.* In the last decade peer-to-peer applications have emerged which represent an alternative to the client/server paradigm. Peer-to-peer applications are distributed applications among equally privileged and acting participants. So a peer can be simultaneously a client and/or a server. Peer-to-peer systems often implement an abstract overlay network on top of the transport interface. These networks use their own protocols. Well-known examples are Chord, Kademlia, Gnutella, Skype, and others.

Further reading

Introductions to Internet protocols can be found nowadays in many books and articles, among them the books we referred to in previous chapters. These books as well as [Shar 08] also contain descriptions of application-oriented protocols and functions.

Exercises

(1)   What distinguishes the Internet Protocol from other connectionless protocols?

(2)   IP is often used by other protocols to transport their data. How does IP learn what is the receiving protocol?

(3)   Currently two versions of IP are deployed, IPv4 and IPv6. What are the most important differences between the two versions?

(4)   For fragmenting packets, the second row of the IPv4 header is reserved. What solution is applied in IPv6? What is the benefit of this approach?

(5)   Explain the byte stream principle of TCP. What is the difference to the protocol principles introduced in Section 2.1? How does the byte stream principle influence the TCP segment header information?

(6)   Explain why a 3-way handshake must be applied in TCP. How many sequence numbers are consumed during connection set up? Why are the sequence numbers different in the two directions?

(7)   How many connections can be set up between two sockets?

(8)   Why are sockets not immediately released after a connection has closed?

(9)   What is the difference between the sliding window protocol used in TCP and that described in Section 5.8.1?

(10) TCP exceptionally allows data to be sent when the window is closed. Explain why this is useful.

(11) Piggybacking has been supplemented by the delayed acknowledgement mechanism. Why this is needed?

(12) How must the XDT protocol be changed in principle in order to apply piggybacking?

(13) Explain the principle of the slow start and the congestion avoidance algorithms. Why have these algorithms supplemented TCP? Discuss in particular how we determine the size of the window that indicates how many bytes can be sent.

(14) There is no fixed time-out value for the retransmission timer. The value is dynamically adapted based on the response time. Explain how this is done.

(15) Determine the time-out value of the retransmission timer for the following situation. We assume that the estimated round trip time is currently 80 msec and the estimated standard deviation 20 msec. The smoothing factor α should be 7/8. Calculate the time-out value when the next acknowledgements arrive after 64, 150, and 200 msec.

(16) UDP is a connectionless unreliable protocol like IP. Why do applications use UDP and not directly IP?

(17) Describe the various possibilities to put applications on the transport interface.

Part II: Description of communication protocols

The accurate description of the procedures in communication protocols is an important precondition for their correct implementation and successful operation. Informal descriptions have proved to be insufficient for this because they permit ambiguous interpretations of the specification text. The goal of an accurate description can only be achieved by the deployment of formal description methods and techniques. The use of formal methods for the design, description, and validation of communication protocols and distributed systems forms the essence of *Protocol Engineering*. They are an important precondition for the development of tools to support computer-aided validations of protocol designs, specifications, and implementations. Furthermore, practical experience has shown that the elaboration and examination of formal descriptions are helpful for a better understanding of the protocol procedures.

The second part of the book is dedicated to the formal methods and description techniques applied to describe services and protocols. We begin with a short discussion of the need for formal descriptions for communication protocols and their requirements. Next we present the most important constructive and descriptive description methods which form the basis for the semantic models of the derived formal description techniques (FDTs). In particular, we consider finite state machines, extended finite state machines, Petri nets, process calculi, and temporal logics.

The main part of the representation is dedicated to introductions to various formal description techniques used in the protocol field. We introduce one representative technique for each of the main description approaches. So we consider the standardized FDTs SDL and LOTOS as examples of descriptions based on extended finite state machines and process calculi. Further we present MSC as an example of a communication-oriented description. In addition, we present with cTLA an example of a language which is related to descriptive methods. For the description of the data formats in protocols, ASN.1 has proved useful and is deployed as a supplement to other FDTs. It is introduced as well. Finally, we discuss the use of UML 2 for protocol development.

The introduction to the various description techniques (besides UML) follows a fixed structure. We first give an overview of the basic concepts of each language. Next we introduce the most important language elements. The principles of the applied formal semantics are described as well. For each language, we present a description of the XDT service and protocol or a fragment thereof to demonstrate the expressiveness of the considered formal description technique in a more complex application. This is to allow the reader to compare the various description principles. The complete specifications in this chapter are available at the book web site. The introduction concludes with a discussion of the pros and cons of each technique.

7 Formal description methods

Various methods are used to describe communication protocols. The search for suitable description methods for communication protocols in the 1980s yielded a broad range of approaches out of which some fundamental methods have crystallized. These methods constitute the basis of the semantic models of the various formal description techniques. Therefore we first consider the most important description methods in this chapter before we turn to the formal description techniques. From these, finite state machines, Petri nets, process calculi, and temporal logics have crystallized as the most important and most common ones. Apart from these methods, other approaches were also investigated, such as the use of grammars, data flow languages, and functional languages. They did not receive wider attention because they were not applied to real-life protocols. The use of high-level programming languages was considered likewise. Programming languages support the algorithmic description of protocol procedures as well as the generation of prototypes, but they usually do not possess a formally defined semantics. In addition, programming languages are primarily implementation languages and not specification languages. They often yield descriptions which are close to an implementation. For that reason, high-level programming languages are not used for protocol description. Many formal description techniques, however, use programming language features.

We begin this chapter with a discussion of the requirements on service and protocol specifications. Thereafter we give a classification of the various approaches followed by the introduction of the methods themselves.

7.1 Service and protocol specifications

Communication protocols are prevailingly implemented in software. This software is called **communication software**. Their production principally follows the same procedures as the development of software (see Chapter 9). Communication protocols, however, are characterized by a set of singularities which shape this process as well as their description.

The description and/or specification (the terms are used synonymously here) of communication protocols forms the basis of the protocol development process. It documents the requirements on the services and protocols. The service and the protocol specification serve further as a reference for their implementation and validation (verification, testing, etc.). They form quasi "the blueprint" for the protocol developer based on which all contentious questions are decided later.

The requirements on the description of communication protocols are similar to those of the software specification. The description should be *accurate, unique, complete*, and *sufficiently* abstract. Behind the term *abstract* hides the demand of implementation independence of the specification. The description must separate substantial requirements from insignificant, implementation-oriented ones. Thereby those requirements are considered substantial which determine the externally visible behavior of the protocol entities. Internal, implementation-dependent procedures are insignificant. Service and protocol specifications describe only the functional aspects of the design. Implementation-related aspects like the existence of several connections or the applied addressing scheme are mostly not considered. For the same reason, no statements are made likewise about the integration of the protocol into a concrete execution environment (operating system, protocol stack). These aspects are part of a later implementation-oriented specification (see Chapters 9 and 13 for this). Furthermore, a protocol description allows different implementations which comply with the specified functional behavior. These implementations are compliant or *conformant* to the specification. The protocol description abstracts from the implementation-specific details in which the implementations may vary. It is an abstraction of all possible implementations.

Description levels

The specification of communication protocols differs from conventional software specification above all by the fact that two description levels are needed: one level to describe *what* service is provided and another level to prescribe *how* this service is provided. The **service specification** embodies the *what*-specification (see Figure 7.1/1). It corresponds to the conventional software specification. The **protocol specification** represents the *how*-specification. Figure 7.1/2 depicts the domains of both specifications from a communication-oriented point of view.

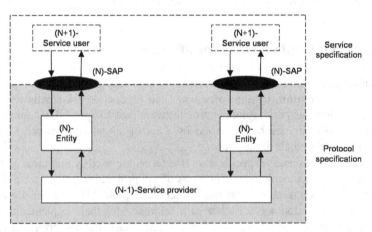

Figure 7.1/1: Service specification versus protocol specification

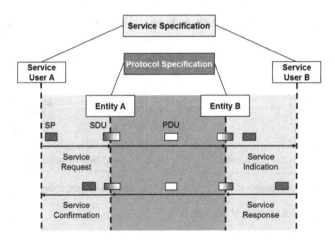

Figure 7.1/2: Domains of service and protocol specification

The service specification describes how the service users can call and use a service at the service interface. It solely considers the interactions between service users and service provider at the service interface. The specification contains the description of all (partial) services provided together with the associated service primitives and parameters as well as existing dependencies between them. The behavior of the service users themselves is not represented. This is why they are represented by dotted lines in Figures 7.1/1 and /2.

The protocol specification prescribes how the specified service has to be provided by the peer entities. It specifies the timed order of the interactions between them as well as the formats of the data units exchanged. The protocol specification represents the abstract implementation of the service specification. It defines the public interface for communication with other computers. Usually the protocol specification also describes how an (N)-protocol is mapped onto the (N-1)-service.

The different goals of the two specifications also determine their users. The service specification is relevant for the potential service user to know how to activate the service. Service users are either application or protocol developers who must know how to include the service in their application or protocol, respecttively. The protocol specification, in contrast, forms the working basis for the protocol engineer who deals with the validation, the evaluation, and the implementation of the protocol. This is hardly relevant for the service users.

Description principles

When describing a communication protocol two different representation principles can be applied: the behavior-oriented and the communication-oriented representation. The **behavior-oriented representation** describes the protocol by the behavior of the communicating entities (see Figure 7.1/3a). The communication between the entities is not represented directly. It results indirectly from the behavior of the entities. The **communication-oriented representation**, in contrast, describes the communication sequences between the entities, i.e., both communication partners are considered in the description (see Figure 7.1/3b).

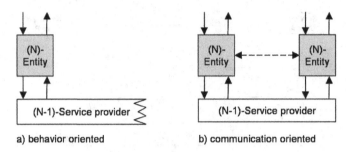

a) behavior oriented   b) communication oriented

Figure 7.1/3: Principles of protocol description

Most formal description techniques use the behavior-oriented representation because it corresponds to the often applied semantic model of a finite state machine. The drawback of the behavior-oriented description consists of the fact that the protocol flow, i.e., the interaction sequence between the entities, can only be derived with great effort. In many cases, however, the representation of the protocol interactions is desired. The communication-oriented representation, as used, for instance, in time sequence diagrams (cp. Section 1.1), corresponds more strongly to the nature of protocols. It is though much more difficult to write down this representation because dependencies between different partial sequences have to be taken into account [Boch 87]. In addition, the mapping onto the underlying semantic model is usually more complicated. Communication-oriented representations, however, have proved very useful and helpful for the design and understanding of protocol procedures. Therefore nowadays communication-oriented representations are frequently applied as a supplement to behavior-oriented descriptions. Message Sequence Charts (MSC) [ITU-T 120], which we will introduce in Section 8.2, is a typical example of a communication-oriented representation. Our model language used in the first part of the book supports it likewise.

7.2   Need for formal descriptions

In international standards the majority of services and protocols are described informally. The procedures are formulated verbally as text supplemented by state diagrams, state tables[1], time sequence diagrams, and parameter tables. The specification usually does not contain a closed description of the overall protocol procedure. It rather consists of a description of the reactions of the protocol entities to

---

[1] State tables describe the states of the protocol entity interpreted as a finite state machine (see Section 7.4)

the various events. The protocol implementer has to assemble these partial descriptions to set up the protocol in a puzzle-like manner.

Informal descriptions appear at first glance easily accessible and understandable. They have proved, however, insufficient for a systematic protocol development. There are above all two reasons for this:

- Informal descriptions are ambiguous. This may lead to different interpretations of the descriptions by the protocol developers resulting in incorrect and incompatible implementations.
- Informal descriptions represent an insufficient basis for the development of tools. A computer-aided validation of the single development steps is not possible on this basis.

The necessity of formal descriptions for the protocol development is generally recognized and uncontested therefore. The development of appropriate formal descriptions, however, is a lengthy and complicated process as we will see later in the third part of the book. For this reason, the use of formal descriptions in practice is still limited.

A **formal description** of a service or protocol is a specification written using a formal description technique (FDT). **Formal description techniques** are characterized by a formal syntax and semantics. The latter represents the decisive distinction from informal descriptions because it allows avoiding ambiguous interpretations of the specification. The formal semantics or the respective semantic model ensures the unique interpretation of the specification (see Figure 7.2/1).

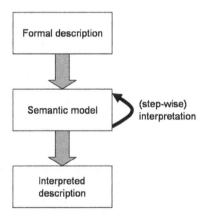

Figure 7.2/1: Interpretation of a formal description

The requirements on formal descriptions correspond to those of protocol descriptions discussed above, such as *exactness*, *clarity*, *completeness*, *abstraction* and *implementation independence*. Further desirable requirements are a *modular structure* to facilitate their handling as well as changes, and *comprehensibility*, to support intuitive understanding and to prevent misinterpretations.

7.3   Classification of formal description methods

The description of services and protocols consists in general of two components: the description of the communication procedures and the definition of the formats of the exchanged protocol data units. For this, complementary techniques are used. The communication procedures are described through formal methods or description techniques, while specific data description languages are used for the data formats. We present some of them in Chapter 8. For the time being, we focus on the description of the communication procedures.

Description methods for communication protocols can be differentiated into constructive and descriptive methods [Gotz 92] (see Figure 7.3/1).

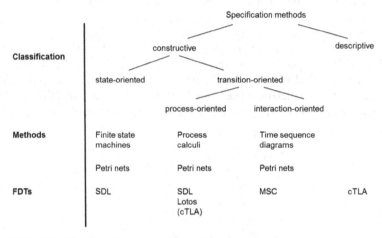

Figure 7.3/1: Classification of the description methods for communication protocols

Constructive methods

Constructive methods describe the protocol by means of an abstract model whose execution determines how the communicating entities behave. The description represents a quasi-implementation of the protocol on a more abstract level. Executable prototypes can be derived from the specification to validate the design. Examples of constructive description methods are finite state machines and labeled transition systems. The advantage of constructive methods is their direct support of subsequent protocol development stages. However, their drawback is that they do not allow explicit specification of certain properties, e.g., liveness and safety properties (see Section 7.8), the protocol should fulfill. These properties must be verified implicitly in the context of the applied semantic model.

Constructive methods can be further differentiated into state and transition-oriented description methods. *State-oriented description methods* focus on the representation of the states of an entity and the state transitions. The resulting representation is a behavior-oriented one (cp. Section 7.1). State-oriented descriptions are easy to produce, which is why they are preferentially used in practice. The *transition-oriented description methods*, in contrast, emphasize the representation of the transition sequences to be executed. States are not explicitly represented thereby; they are implicitly given through the execution sequence. The transition-oriented methods can be again differentiated into process and interaction-oriented methods. The *process-orientated methods* describe the execution order within an entity, while the *interaction-oriented methods* represent the interaction between two (or even several) entities (cp. Section 7.1). Transition-oriented descriptions are more challenging to develop in comparison with behavior-oriented ones, since it is in general substantially more complicated to derive the transition sequences from an informal protocol description [Boch 87]. The difficulty is in particular the detection of existing concurrent execution paths rather than the states themselves, which are usually given by state tables. In Figure 7.3/1 examples of different description methods and techniques are given for each approach. Some methods and techniques can contribute under more than one approach. We will refer to the respective description method when we introduce the methods below.

Descriptive methods
Descriptive methods specify the properties the protocol to be designed should meet using mathematical logics. They do not provide a model of the protocol. The advantage of descriptive methods is the explicit specification of desired protocol properties and their verification for appropriateness under complete abstraction of an implementation. This supports, in particular, the verification process. It is, however, not generally decidable whether a specification describes the desired protocol properties completely.

The deployment of descriptive methods has proved useful during the early design phase to formulate requirements on the protocol without already modeling the protocol behavior by a prototype and thus making design decisions [Herr 00]. Their continuous employment though is only efficient if the transition from the problem-oriented specification to the model and later implementation is supported by a unified technology and appropriate development tools, which are not sufficiently available so far. Descriptive methods need a high familiarity with the mathematical basics. Therefore they are less used for protocol development in practice.

We now introduce the most important methods for describing protocols.

7.4   Finite state machines

Finite state machines (FSMs) specify a protocol by describing the behavior of the peer protocol entities. In symmetric protocols only one entity has to be described, in asymmetric protocols both entities. Sometimes the behavior of the (N-1)-service provider is described by an additional automaton[2]. Finite state machines are a simple and natural model for the description of protocol entities because they permit one to directly represent the waiting of the entities for certain events (inputs), and their reaction to them (outputs) including the transition to a successor state.

A **finite state machine** is a quintuple $<S,I,O,T,s_0>$ with

   S – finite, non-empty set of *states*,
   I – finite, non-empty set of *inputs*,
   O – finite, non-empty set of *outputs*,
   $T \subseteq S \times (I \cup \{\tau\}) \times O \times S$ – a state *transition function*, and
   $s_0 \in S$ – *initial state* of the automata.

A transition $t \in T$ is defined by the quadruple $<s, i, o, s'>$ whereby $s \in S$ denotes the current state, $i \in I \cup \{\tau\}$ an input (event), $o \in O$ the associated output, and $s' \in S$ the successor state. The special event $\tau \notin I$ designates an empty input. It is used for modelling spontaneous transitions to describe internal events (cp. Section 1.2).

Finite state machines are usually represented by state transition diagrams. Other presentation forms are state tables and state transition matrices. Figure 7.4/1 shows the finite state machine for the receiver entity of the XDT protocol. State transition diagrams represent the states by labeled circles and the transitions by labeled, directed edges. The respective input/output events $i \in I$ and $o \in O$ are assigned in the form i/o to each edge. The state machine in Figure 7.4/1 deviates somewhat from the definition given above. It permits several outputs per input. This is a frequently used simplification to avoid too complex representations of the automaton. Moreover, the figure contains an empty output λ. This means that the automaton does not make an output on a given input for a defined finite time. The set of output events O' of the state machine represented in such a way is defined by $O' = \wp(O) \cup \{\lambda\}$, with $\wp(O)$ as power set of O. The state transition function T' is modified accordingly to $T' \subseteq S \times (I \cup \{\tau\}) \times O' \times S$.

---

[2] The terms finite state machine and automaton are used synonymously below.

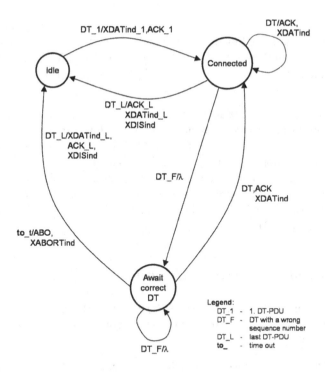

Figure 7.4/1: Simplified finite state machine of the XDT receiver entity

More complex protocols are often further divided into sub-automata. In order to describe the communication with the sub-automata there are two possibilities: asynchronous and synchronous coupling [Holz 91], [Holz 04] which model different communication paradigms. When asynchronous coupling is applied, the executions of the transitions in the sub-automata are not coupled with each other. The interactions (events, messages) among the sub-automata are exchanged via finite or infinite FIFO queues. The receiving automaton takes the first event and triggers the associated transition. This kind of coupling is closer to that applied in protocol implementations (see Section 13.3). Synchronous coupling, in contrast, bounds the execution of the related transitions in both automata to a synchronizing event which represents the output event of one automaton and the input event of the other. The execution of the transitions takes place simultaneously. All not-coupled transitions are executed concurrently. Synchronous coupling is more abstract. It supports a more comprehensive modeling of the interactions which has advantages for the verification.

Finite state machines only describe the functional protocol procedures, i.e., the control flow. Changes in the data structures, i.e., the data flow, cannot be represented. For example, if we wish to model the use of sequence numbers in the automaton of Figure 7.4/1 it would be necessary to introduce a separate state for each sequence number value. This soon makes the automaton very complex. Therefore, we simplified the automaton and waived the representation of the sequence numbers in Figure 7.4/1. The description of the XDT sender entity by a finite state machine would be almost impracticable for that reason.

Pros and cons

Finite state machines are an adequate and intuitive means for modelling the behavior of protocol entities. They are often used. However, finite state machines may soon become too complex, which is why they are only limitedly applied for protocol specifications; instead extended finite state machines (see below) are preferred. FSM representations are mostly used for illustrating single protocol procedures. Another important application area is the derivation of test cases. The basic test case derivation methods are based on FSM presentations of the protocol entities (see Section 14.3).

7.5   Extended finite state machines

Extended finite state machines (EFSMs) extend the FSM description by the use of variables to store context information. This significantly reduces the complexity of the automaton.

An **extended finite state machine** is a tuple $<S,C,I,O,T,s_0,c_0>$ with

S – finite, non-empty state of *states*,

$C = domain(v_1) \times \ldots \times domain(v_n)$ – non-empty set of contexts with $v_i \in V$, where V denotes a finite, non-empty set of variables and $domain(v_i)$ a non-empty, countable set of values - the range of v_i,

I – finite, non-empty set of *inputs*,

O – finite, non-empty set of *outputs*,

$T \subseteq S \times C \times (I \cup \{\tau\}) \times O \times S \times C$ – a *state transition function*,

$s_0 \in S$ – *initial state*, and

$c_0 \in C$ – *initial context of the automaton.*

A context C is given by the current values of the variables. A transition $t \in T$ is defined by the tuple $<s,c,i,o,s',c'>$, where $s \in S$ denotes the current state, $i \in I$ an input, $c \in C$ the context before executing the transition, $o \in O$ the associated output, $s' \in S$ the successor state, and $c' \in C$ the context after executing the transition. The empty transition τ is also used here to model spontaneous transitions. The states $s \in S$ are also called **major states**, accordingly the states characterized by $s \in S$ and $c \in C$ **minor states**.

Using EFSMs we can describe the sender entity of our XDT protocol, since the required context information on missing acknowledgements or required retransmissions of DT-PDUs can be stored in the variables now. Figure 7.5/1 depicts the automaton. We apply the same simplifications as in the last section. Again several outputs including the empty output are allowed. The set of outputs is defined as O' = $\wp(O) \cup \{\lambda\}$, with $\wp(O)$ - power set of O, and the state transition function accordingly by $T \subseteq S \times C \times (I \cup \{\tau\}) \times O' \times S \times C$. For the states *Await ACK*, *Connected*, and *go back N*, the variables are indicated which are relevant in this context. These are those variables whose value changes during transition. For example, the value of variable N is increased when a correct acknowledgement *ACK* arrives in state *Connected*.

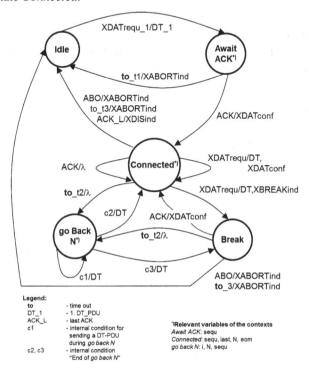

Legend:

to	- time out
DT_1	- 1. DT_PDU
ACK_L	- last ACK
c1	- internal condition for sending a DT-PDU during *go back N*
c2, c3	- internal condition "End of *go back N*"

")Relevant variables of the contexts
Await ACK: sequ
Connected: sequ, last, N, eom
go back N: i, N, sequ

Figure 7.5/1: Simplified extended finite state machine of the XDT sender entity

Pros and cons

Extended finite state machines are the most frequently used description method for communication protocols. The semantic models of SDL (and Estelle) as well as that of our model language are based on them. The most important advantages of extended finite state machines are the adequate modeling of the behavior of the protocol entities, as already discussed with FSMs, and the support of a transformation directly into an implementation (see Section 13.2). This may, however, also seduce one to write specifications that are too close to an implementation. The description of complex protocols remains problematical because the automata are difficult to understand and to use. Therefore, many formal description techniques support the decomposition of complex automata into sub-automata. Extended finite state machines support certain verification methods as well (see Section 11.3).

7.6   Petri nets

Petri nets are a frequently used method for the description of system proce-dures, in particular for the modeling of concurrent processes [Mura 89], [Hein 08]. They represent a more general variant of state-transition models. Petri nets com-bine a graphical representation with an analyzable mathematical formalism. For this reason, they are also suitable for the description of protocols.

Nets

A net is a directed graph with two disjoint sets of nodes: places and transitions (see Figure 7.6/1). The nodes are so connected that there is no arc between two nodes of the same kind.

A **net** is a triple $N = (P,T,F)$ with

P – finite, non-empty set of places,

T – finite, non-empty set of transitions and $P \cap T = \varnothing$, and

$F \subseteq (P \times T) \cup (T \times P)$ – a flow relation.

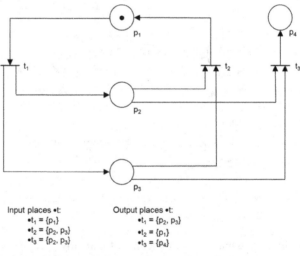

Input places •t:
  •t_1 = {p_1}
  •t_2 = {p_2, p_3}
  •t_3 = {p_2, p_3}

Output places •t:
  •t_1 = {p_2, p_3}
  •t_2 = {p_1}
  •t_3 = {p_4}

Initial marking m_0: $m_0(p_1)$ = 1, $m_0(p_2)$ = 0, $m_0(p_3)$ = 0, $m_0(p4)$ = 0

Figure 7.6/1: A net

Places describe states, conditions, or components of the system to be modeled. They are graphically represented by circles. **Transitions** refer to system activities (events, state transitions). They are drawn by boxes or bars. The flow relation is defined so that an arc always connects a place with a transition or vice versa, but never places or transitions among themselves.

The neighbor nodes of a node are differentiated into a pre- and a post-domain. If $x \in P \times T$ is a net node then $\cdot x$ denotes the *pre-domain* of x. This is the set of all nodes y from which an edge leads to x:

$\cdot x := \{y \mid (y,x) \in F\}$.

Accordingly the *post-domain* $x \cdot$ comprises the set of all nodes z to which an edge from x leads:

$x \cdot := \{z \mid (x,z) \in F\}$.

If x is a place, i.e., $x = p \in P$, then $\cdot p$ denotes the set of *pre-transitions* and $p \cdot$ the set of *post-transitions*. Accordingly $\cdot t$ refers to the set of *pre-places* or *input places* of t and $t \cdot$ to the set of *post-places* or *output places*. The input and output places represent pre- and post-conditions of the transition. Figure 7.6/1 indicates the input and output places of each transition.

Marking

The reaching of certain system states is expressed by tokens which circulate in the net. They are represented by black dots on the respective places (see Figure 7.6/1). The mapping $m: P \rightarrow Nat$ of the places on the set of the natural numbers is called the **marking** of P. The number of tokens on place p is described by $m(p)$. A marking indicates a system state. The marking of the initial state of the net is called the initial marking m_0. The initial marking of our example net in Figure 7.6/1 is m_0: $m_0(p_1) = 1$; $m_0(p_2) = 0$; $m_0(p_3) = 0$; $m_0(p_4) = 0$. A sequence of markings forms a token flow that reflects a course of changes in the system.

Petri nets

A **Petri net** or a **place/transition net** (*P/T-Net*) is a 5-tuple $N=(P,T,F,V,m_0)$ where

(P,T,F) is a net,

V – a mapping $V: F \rightarrow Nat$ that assigns to each arc $f \in F$ a number $V(f)$ denoting the number of tokens consumed from a place by a transition, or produced by a transition and put on each place, and

m_0 – the initial marking of P.

Petri nets with $V(f)=1$ are called ordinary Petri nets. They are the only kind considered here. An interesting point is that both ordinary and non-ordinary Petri nets have the same modeling power. They differ in the efficiency and convenience in modeling [Mura 89].

Execution of Petri nets

The behavior of a Petri net is described in terms of system states and their changes. System states are represented by the current marking indicating conditions which are fulfilled in the respective state. Changes of system states are modeled by the firing of transitions. A transition can fire, when the respective **pre-conditions** of the transition are fulfilled, i.e., all input places $p \in \cdot t$ contain a token, i.e., $m(p) \geq 1$. The transition is then called **enabled** concerning the marking m. When a transition fires, the marking changes ($m \text{ -}t\to m'$). How this is done in the various kinds of Petri nets is defined by the respective **firing rule**. In ordinary Petri nets the following firing rule is applied:

$$m'(p) := \begin{cases} m(p) - 1, & \textit{if } p \in \bullet t \textit{ and } p \notin t\bullet, \\ m(p) + 1, & \textit{if } p \notin \bullet t \textit{ and } p \in t\bullet, \\ m(p), & \textit{otherwise} \end{cases}$$

The firing of a transition t removes a token from each input place and adds one to each output place. All other places do not change their marking. A sequence of transitions $\delta = t_i \, t_{i+1} \ldots t_{i+n}$ which transfers the marking m into the marking m' ($m \text{ -}t\to m'$), is called a *firing sequence*. The reachability of a marking m' is expressed by the reachability relation $\xrightarrow{*}$:

$$m \xrightarrow{*} m' \Leftrightarrow \exists \delta \in T^* \colon m \xrightarrow{\delta} m'$$

where T^* denotes the set of all sequences of transitions in T. All markings that can be reached from a marking m form the *set of reachable markings* of m:

$$R_N(m) = \{m' \mid m \xrightarrow{*} m'\}$$

All markings which can be reached from the initial marking m_0 represent the *state space* of the modeled system.

A net structure in which two or more transitions share some input places is referred to as a **conflict**, *decision*, or *choice* depending on the application. Such a structure represents nondeterminism (cp. Section 1.2.4). It is indecisive but observable which transition will be selected. If a net unintentionally contains a conflict then it must be dissolved when the net structure is further refined. A conflict, however, can be deliberately integrated into a net to express nondeterministic behavior concerning a resource or to represent alternative operational sequences (see Figure 7.6/2). To decide conflicts additional information must be integrated into the net. In tools for net execution this is the responsibility of the applied scheduling strategy.

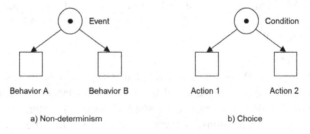

a) Non-determinism   b) Choice

Figure 7.6/2: Use of conflicts

Generation of Petri nets

There are two ways to develop a Petri net description of a protocol: either directly by describing the protocol by means of Petri nets or indirectly by deriving them from another formal description. The first approach is troublesome because many protocol details have to be mapped into an adequate Petri net representation. The second approach uses samples that map the elements of the formal description technique into the corresponding Petri net representation. Figure 7.6/3 gives some examples of such mapping samples for our model language. Note that in both cases the designer has the choice to represent the protocol either in a behavior- or a communication-oriented representation (cp. Section 7.1).

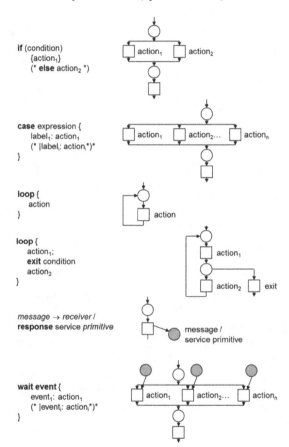

Figure 7.6/3: Petri net representation of selected elements of the model language

We show the Petri net representations of the XDT protocol parts *connect_s* and *connect_r* as examples (see Figure 7.6/4). The nets of both protocol parts have to be assembled to build up the Petri net for the connection set up. As interface to the other net, **fusion places** are used which are marked in grey. The Petri nets of the protocol parts are derived from the specifications in Section 2.3 according to the mapping samples given above. To illustrate the mapping the statements are assigned to the respective transitions. *Start* and *reset* a timer as well as *time-out* are represented as events. The modeling of the timer is not given here because it cannot be easily modeled in a place/transition net. The fusion places represent the PDUs *DT*, *ACK*, and *ABO*.

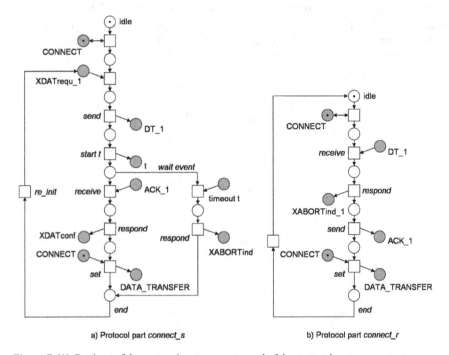

Figure 7.6/4: Petri net of the protocol part *connect_s* and of the protocol part *connect_r*

The resulting net, however, does not allow pursuing the token flow yet because the places representing service primitives are not connected to the environment which models the behavior of the service users. Their behavior can be derived from the Petri net of the service specification. Only thus can meaningful analyses be performed. We continue this discussion in Section 11.4, when we deal with protocol verification. In that section we will also present the merged net for the XDT connection set up.

Pros and cons

The advantage of Petri nets consists of the fact that they permit one to represent the control flow in protocols on a very abstract and detailed level. This allows various analyses to verify the protocol design (see Section 11.4). The protocol behavior can be easily comprehended by pursuing the token flow. Furthermore, both behavior- and communication-oriented descriptions are possible.

However, the use of Petri nets (in particular place/transition nets) for the specification of complex protocols causes similar problems to the use of finite state machines. The complexity of the nets is a main obstacle as well. Furthermore, it is unfavorable that important elements of the protocol description like the coding/ decoding of PDUs and service primitives, the adherence to certain conditions, such as the transmission sequence, the error handling and others, cannot be modeled at all or only with large difficulties. Therefore various extended Petri net variants have been used which are more expressive by using additional rules and attributes. Examples of the application of other networks to communication systems are given in [Bill 99], [Gord 00].

Due to the discrepancy between the high degree of abstraction and the tide of details which have to be considered when specifying complex protocols, Petri nets are rarely used for the specification of communication protocols in practice. They are mainly deployed for verification and performance analyses [Bill 99], [Baus 02] (see Chapters 11 and 12).

7.7   Process calculi

Process calculi (or *process algebras*) are algebraic-based approaches for the modeling of concurrent systems. They are also applied to the protocol field. Process calculi model the protocol behavior by means of interacting processes. Several notions of equivalence allow reasoning about the functional behavior of the system, e.g., to prove equivalences between specifications or to substitute components by equivalent ones (see Figure 7.7/1).

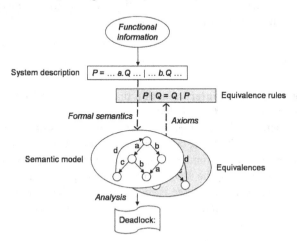

Figure 7.7/1: Basis concepts of process calculi (source [Herm 98])

Basic elements

Process calculi generalize the classic automata theory. They allow one to model concurrent systems by cooperating smaller components which can be composed to modular, hierarchical system structures. The system components are represented by **processes**, i.e., they enforce a process-oriented description (cp. Section 7.3). The modeling considers only their externally visible behavior, i.e., their interactions with the environment or with other processes. The basic elements of the description are actions and composition operators. **Actions** denote the interactions of the processes. They are considered to be atomic at the given abstraction level. The **composition operators** define how the processes are composed to build larger system components. This can be done by sequential or parallel composition. Further abstraction is achieved by hiding internal details of the composition. Process calculi possess a formal semantics which maps the system descriptions onto *Labeled Transition Systems* (LTS) (see Section 8.3.6). They define various equivalence relations to determine the equivalence between processes or specifications, respectively.

The most commonly used process calculi in *Protocol Engineering* is the **Calculus of Communicating Systems (CCS)** by Milner [Miln 89], which was used as the basis for the development of the formal description technique LOTOS (see Section 8.3). In CCS a system is described by its externally visible actions which express its behavior. An **action** $a \in Act$ denotes an atomic, synchronous interaction with another system or process in its environment. It represents a process activity or an external event. Actions are represented by **labels**. These are port names denoting the points of interaction. Usually the names of the activities or events appearing at the interaction points are used as labels. In contrast to finite state machines, process calculi do not distinguish explicitly between input and output events. Thus, the set of actions Act is defined by the set of labels L and the action τ:

$Act = L \cup \{\tau\}.$

The action τ denotes an **internal action** that is not visible externally. It can be used to model internal events (cp. Section 1.2.3).

The system behavior is described by a **behavior expression**. CCS distinguishes five basic expressions which can be composed to more complex expressions. These expressions are prefix, summation, composition, restriction, and relabeling. We adumbrate the principle for the XDT connection set up in the following. We confine ourselves here to the first three expressions. The other two are considered in the context of LOTOS in Section 8.3.

Prefix

The appearance of an action $a \in Act$ is described by a prefix

$B = a \,.\, B'$

where B and B' are behavior expressions. Action a transfers the system from behavior expression $B = a.B'$ to behavior expression B'. This represents a state transition. The states, however, are not represented explicitly in this notation. They can be derived implicitly from the action sequence.

We assume that S describes the (local) behavior at the *Sender*-SAP of the XDT service. Then

$S = XDATrequ . S'$ with $XDATrequ \in Act$

describes the occurrence of the *XDATrequ* primitive, while S' denotes the successor behaviour expression. S' is defined by

$S' = XDATconf . S''$

describing the occurrence of $XDATconf \in Act$. The behaviour expression for a successful connection set up can also be written as

$S = XDATrequ.XDATconf.S''$.

Since we do not consider the data transfer phase here, the connection set up is finished and the process may be activated again to set up another connection. This is expressed by recursion of the behaviour expression S:

$S = XDATrequ.XDATconf.S$.

Analogously, we can describe the behavior R at the *Receiver*-SAP:

$R = XDATind.R$

Summation

Summation expresses alternative behavior

$B = B_1 + B_2$.

It means that expression B behaves either like B_1 or like B_2. Using summation we can now describe both behavior alternatives at the XDT-*Sender*-SAP in one expression:

$S = XDATrequ.(XDATconf.S + XABORTind.S)$.

Composition

Composition is used to express concurrent behavior

$B = B_1 \mid B_2$.

It means that the behaviors B_1 and B_2 are executed concurrently. The expressions synchronize via common actions. The overall behavior is described by interleaving of the actions of both expressions (cp. Section 1.2.4).

Using the composition operator we can now describe the complete XDT service as

$XDT\_service = S \mid R.$

If we wish to express dependencies between actions of the two expressions, e.g., between interactions at both access points (cp. global behavior in Section 1.2.3), we have to introduce another behavior expression C:

$C = XDATrequ.XDATind.XDATconf.C + XDATrequ.XABORTind.C,$

which concatenates the other expressions through composition

$S \mid C \mid R.$

Such a behavior expression is called a **constraint**. It enforces the dependencies between the actions of the connected processes through the synchronization of the behavior expressions regarding the indicated common actions (see in addition also Section 8.3.2).

Behavior trees

Behavior expressions are graphically represented by **behavior trees**. A behavior tree is a transition-oriented representation of the expression execution which contains all possible sequences of actions. The edges correspond to actions, the nodes to states, which, however, are not explicitly named. The root of the tree is the initial state. Alternative behavior (summation) is represented by different branches (see Figure 7.7/2).

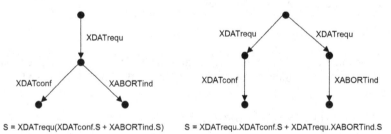

S = XDATrequ(XDATconf.S + XABORTind.S)   S = XDATrequ.XDATconf.S + XDATrequ.XABORTind.S

Figure 7.7/2: Behavior trees

Nondeterministic behavior is represented by separate branches for the same action which start at the same node as depicted in Figure 7.7/2b.

The behavior trees of the above introduced behavior expressions S, R, and $S|C|R$ are depicted in Figure 7.7/3. The points indicate that we only show a fragment of the tree here and that other actions follow in the states reached. If the inner structure of a (partial) tree is not of interest it can be replaced by a triangle as abbreviation, as in picture d).

Pros and cons

Process calculi permit an accurate and complete description of the interactions at service interfaces and in protocols. They support formal verification of the design (see Section 11.5.3) as well as the derivation of test cases (see Section 14.3.2). Similarly to Petri nets, important elements of the protocol description (coding/decoding of PDUs and service primitives, the adherence to certain conditions, error handling, and others) cannot be represented appropriately.

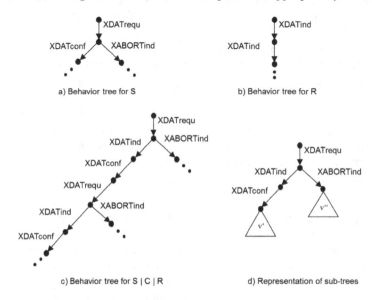

Figure 7.7/3: Behavior trees for the XDT service

The description is significantly more abstract than that of extended finite state machines. This may leave more freedom for the implementation, but relevant elements are not sufficiently represented at specification level as required for practical protocol development. The high abstraction degree leads inevitably to problems with user acceptance. Process calculi presuppose an appropriate algebraic training. For these reasons, algebraic process calculi are rarely used in practical protocol development. Their relevance lies in theoretical research.

7.8   Temporal logics

Temporal logics [Emer 90], [Mann 92], [Holz 04] are a special type of modal logics. They represent the most important descriptive specification method for communication protocols [Gotz 92], [Herr 00]. Temporal logics provide a formal system for describing systems with reference to the time in an abstract sense, like "before" or "after", to represent desired properties as well as causal and temporal dependencies between them. The system to be modeled is thereby described by (infinitely) long sequences of moments in time according to the applied notion of time. These moments represent system states. Absolute time is not of interest here, only the temporal relation in which things happen. In contrast to constructive techniques like finite state machines and Petri nets, which model the system behavior, temporal logics formulate assertions on the temporal behavior of the system in question, which can be true or false, allowing one thus, to reason about how the truth values of these assertions change over time. Adherence to these properties in the designed system can be verified by deductive verification and model checking (see Chapter 11).

Assertions are expressed by formulas using propositional logic combined with modal operators which express changes over time. A formula ϕ is *satisfied* in a model σ (written $\sigma \vDash \phi$), iff[3] it is true for some states of σ. It is said to be *valid* (written $\vDash \phi$), iff it is true for the entire behavior of the system. Temporal logics are particularly suitable for the description of the properties of concurrent, nondeterministic, and/or continuously operating systems, such as distributed systems, communication protocols, and hardware designs.

The correctness properties of interest in distributed system design are safety and liveness properties:

- **Safety properties** are system properties which describe expected, wanted behavior, i.e., if something happens then it is a desired behavior. They formulate the conditions that are needed to avoid unwanted (bad) system behavior and consequently the system may not violate the specified behavior. Note that safety properties are already fulfilled if nothing happens. Safety properties in the XDT design are the constraints that no data unit passed to the service provider will get lost and that they will be delivered to the receiver in the order they were sent.

- **Liveness properties** ensure that the specified events eventually occur and the desired states are reached. They describe the expected (good) system properties that consequently the system must satisfy. A liveness property of the XDT example is that after a successful connection set up the data transfer phase will be reached.

A variety of temporal logics has been proposed. They differ in their expressiveness on the time relations, e.g., past or future, they permit one to describe. There are different classifications as well. Generally temporal logics are divided into linear-time and branching-time temporal logics [Clar 00]. **Linear-time temporal logics** assume a linear course of time, i.e., there is always only one possible future

---

[3] iff – *if and only if*

moment. A representative of linear-time logics is *Linear Temporal Logic* (LTL). They are mainly applied in software verification. **Branching-time temporal logics** consider different paths from a given state, i.e., time may split into different courses representing alternative future developments. The best known example of a branching-time temporal logic is the *Computational Tree Logic* (CTL). Other classifications distinguish between the use of past- and future-tense operators, between the use of points in time or intervals, and between discrete and continuous time. Introductions to the different kinds of temporal logics and their application are given, among others, in [Emer 90], and [Clar 00].

We present a simple LTL as an example. This LTL permits statements about the present and the future. It uses the following propositional operators for statements about the present: negation ($\neg$), conjunction ($\wedge$), disjunction ($\vee$), implication ($\Rightarrow$), and logical equivalence ($\equiv$). Statements on the future are represented by the following temporal operators, where p denotes an atomic statement:

- $\square$ – **henceforth** (also *always*); $\square p$ means that statement p is true now and in future, e.g.,

  $\square(S.XDATrequ\_1 \Rightarrow phase \equiv CONNECT)$[4]

  i.e., the first *XDATrequ* at the XDT-*Sender*-SAP S can only be accepted in the CONNECT phase.

- $\Diamond$ – **eventually** (also *sometime*); $\Diamond p$ means that p is true or will be eventually true in future, e.g.,

  $\square(S.XDATrequ \Rightarrow \Diamond R.XDATind)$

  i.e., after *XDATrequ* at the XDT-*Sender*-SAP S follows eventually an *XDATind* at the *Receiver*-SAP R.

- $\bigcirc$ – **next** (also *nexttime*); $\bigcirc p$ means that if there is a next state then p is true in this state, e.g.,

  $\square(phase \equiv DATA\ TRANSFER \wedge S.XABORTind \Rightarrow \bigcirc(phase \equiv CONNECT))$

  i.e., if the transmission is cancelled then the XDT protocol returns to the CONNECT phase.

- U – **until**; p U q means that q eventually becomes true and until then p holds, e.g.,

---

[4] The letters S and R stand for *Sender*- and *Receiver*-SAP, respectively.

$\square(phase \equiv DATA\_TRANSFER$ U $(S.XDISind \lor S.XABORT))$

i.e., XDT remains in the DATA TRANSFER phase until the connection is released or the transmission is aborted, respectively.

- W – **unless**; p W q means that p holds until q becomes true, otherwise p always holds, e.g.,

$\square(S.XDATrequ \Rightarrow \Diamond(S.XDATconf$ W $state \equiv break)$

i.e., each *XDATrequ* at the XDT-*Sender*-SAP is eventually followed by an *XDATconf* primitive unless a break is signaled.

Figure 7.8/1 illustrates graphically the meaning of the different operators. White circles represent arbitrary states; black circles indicate states in which p is true, and grey ones states in which q is true.

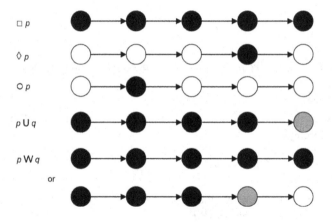

Figure 7.8/1: Intuitive meaning of the LTL operators

Next we present as an example the specification of the XDT service (cp. Section 1.3) in this temporal logic. As above, the letters S and R stand for *Sender*- and *Receiver*-SAP, respectively. The variable *phase* indicates the actual protocol phase (CONNECT or DATA TRANSFER), the variable *state* stands accordingly for the states of the service provider: *break* for break, *eom* for transmitting the last data unit, and *abort* for abortion of the transmission.

(1) $\square$ ((S.XDATrequ $\land$ S.XDATrequ.sequ $\equiv$ 1) $\Rightarrow phase \equiv$ CONNECT)

(2) $\square$ (*phase* $\equiv$ CONNECT $\Rightarrow \neg$ (S.XBREAKind $\lor$ S.XDISind $\lor$ R.XDISind))

(3) $\square$ ((S.XDATrequ $\land$ S.XDATrequ.sequ $\equiv$ 1)

$\Rightarrow \Diamond$ (S.XDATconf $\lor$ S.XABORTind))

(4) □ (S.XDATconf ⇒ *phase* ≡ (DATA_TRANSFER U(S.XDISind ∨ *state* ≡ abort)))

(5) □ ((S.XDATrequ ∧ S.XDATrequ.sequ ≡ 1)

$$⇒ ◇ (R.XDATind ∨ S.XABORTind))$$

(6) □ (R.XDATind ⇒ (*phase* ≡ DATA_TRANSFER U (R.XDISind ∨ *state* ≡ abort)))

(7) □ (*phase* ≡ DATA_TRANSFER ⇒ ¬ (S.XDATrequ ∧ S.XDATrequ.sequ ≡ 1))

(8) □ ((S.XDATrequ ∧ *phase* ≡ DATA TRANSFER)

$$⇒ ◇ (S.XDATconf ∨ S.XBREAKind ∨ S.XABORTind))$$

(9) □ ((S.XDATrequ ∧ *phase* ≡ DATA TRANSFER)

$$⇒ ◇ (R.XDATind ∨ S.XABORTind))$$

(10) □ (S.XBREAKind ⇒ (*state* ≡ break U (S.XDATconf ∨ *state* ≡ abort)))

(11) □ (S.XDATconf ⇒ (◇ (S.XDATrequ ∧

S.XDATrequ.sequ ≡ S.XDATconf.sequ + 1) ∨ ◇ *state* ≡ abort))

(12) □ ((S.XDATrequ ∧ XDATrequ.eom) ⇒ ◇ *state* ≡ eom)

(13) □ (*state* ≡ eom ⇒ ◇ (R.XDISind ∨ *state* ≡ abort))

(14) □ ((S.XDATconf ∧ *state* ≡ eom) ⇒ ◇ (S.XDISind ∨ *state* ≡ abort))

(15) □ ((S.XDISind ∧ R.XDISind) ⇒ ◇ *phase* ≡ CONNECT)

(16) □ (*state* ≡ abort ⇒ ◇ (S.XABORTind ∧ R.XABORTind ∧ phase ≡ CONNECT))

The specification contains safety and liveness properties. Statements (1), (2), (7) and (10) are safety properties which demand that the connection set up can only be initiated in the CONNECT phase and that the data units are delivered in order. The other properties are liveness properties which describe the protocol progress.

Pros and cons

The advantage of the use of temporal logics for describing communication protocols consists above all of the fact that the desired safety and liveness properties can be explicitly specified. The general validity of the properties in the designed system can be formally proven by deductive verification or model checking. The application of temporal logics requires, however, unless appropriate previous knowledge exists, a high learning expenditure. Therefore, their application in protocol development is limited. In addition, there is a lack of tools to support the transition from the abstract specification into an implementation.

For this reason, it is recommended to use temporal logics complementarily to constructive techniques, e.g., during the early design to define desired properties without anticipating design decisions by the modeling process [Gotz 92], [Herr 00]. In order to support a uniform development process, descriptive and constructive methods are combined. An example of this is the Hennessy-Milner logic [Henn 85] which combines a modal logic with the algebraic CCS calculus (cp. Section 7.7). Other approaches combine descriptive and constructive elements into a description technique, such as TLA (*Temporal Logic of Actions*) [Lamp 94] and cTLA (*compositional* TLA) (see Section 8.4). Another way to improve the applicability of descriptive techniques is the framework approach developed in [Herr 00]. This framework consists of a set of specification modules and theorems for transport protocols. The modules describe basic service and protocol mechanisms. The theorems state how service interactions are provided by the protocol mechanisms. The validity of the theorems is proven. More complex service and protocol specifications can be developed by composing the modules. Verification of whether a protocol provides the desired service essentially reduces then to a consistency proof of the associated theorems of the framework.

7.9   Hybrid methods

Comparing the presented methods it is obvious that none of them fully meets all the demands of protocol description as discussed at the beginning of this chapter. This limits their applicability. This realization has led to the development of hybrid methods which combine different description methods to profit from their advantages and to compensate for their shortcomings. Strictly speaking, all formal description techniques used today are more or less hybrid approaches. The specification language SDL (see Section 8.1) is an example of this. It combines extended finite state machines with programming language concepts and includes the data description notation ASN.1 (see Section 8.5). In the literature (see [FORTE], [SDL Forum]) further approaches are presented, e.g., the combination of formal description techniques with Petri nets. The complexity of the communication protocols and the diversity of their mechanisms can hardly be handled with homogeneous methods. The combined application of different description methods is therefore essential for practical protocol development.

Further reading

The summary of description levels and principles given at the beginning of this chapter extracts facts which are contained in many publications on protocols and their description. Besides the cited works we recommend the proceedings of the FORTE conference series [FORTE] including its predecessor PSTV (*Protocol Specification, Testing, and Verification*) for further studies.

More information about finite state machines can be found in standard text books giving an introduction to automata theory, such as [Ande 06], [Hopc 07].

Introductions to Petri nets are given among others in [Gira 01] as well as in the cited tutorials of Murata [Mura 89] and Heiner et al. [Hein 08]. Although the latter is devoted to biochemical networks it describes basic Petri net principles which are also relevant for protocol description.

The most authentic introduction to CCS remains of course the book of Milner [Miln 89]. A comprehensive description of the fundamentals of algebraic specifications can be found in the book of Bowman and Gomez [Bowm 06].

More insight into the fundamentals of temporal logics are contained in the book of Kröger and Merz [Krög 07] as well as in the cited books and tutorials [Emer 90], [Clar 00], and [Gotz 92].

Exercises
(1) Explain the relationship and the differences between the service and the protocol specifications. For what purposes are they needed?
(2) Explain why informal descriptions are less suited for protocol descriptions than formal ones?
(3) What characterizes a formal description technique? Which are the most important requirements imposed on on formal description techniques?
(4) Describe the advantages and the disadvantages of behavior and communication-oriented protocol descriptions.
(5) What characterizes constructive description methods? What variants exist? Give examples of each variant.
(6) What characterizes descriptive methods? Discuss the advantages and disadvantages compared to constructive methods.
(7) What are the most important description methods for communication protocols?
(8) What characterizes a protocol description using finite state machines? What kind of description principle is supported? What are the advantages and shortcomings of this description method?
(9) Discuss the difference between finite state machines and extended finite state machines.
(10) Modify the FSM and EFSM descriptions of the XDT entities in Figures 7.4/1 and 7.5/1 to integrate into XDT an explicit connection set up as described in exercise (11) of Chapter 2.
(11) Change the FSM presentation of the XDT receiver entity (cp. Figures 7.4/1) to integrate into XDT the data delivery regulation described in exercise (13) of Chapter 2.
(12) Modify the FSM and EFSM descriptions of the XDT entities in Figures 7.4/1 and 7.5/1 to integrate into XDT the explicit connection release described in exercise (15) of Chapter 5.
(13) In task (6) of Chapter 5 we replaced the *go back N* procedure by *selective repeat*. Change accordingly both automata representations of the XDT entities for the use of *selective repeat* instead of *go back N*.
(14) What characterizes a protocol description using Petri nets? What kind of description principle is supported? What are the advantages and shortcomings of this description method?
(15) Introduce the protocol changes of exercises (10) and (11) into the Petri nets of Figure 7.6/4. Modeling of the environment is not yet required in this exercise.

(16) What characterizes a description using CCS? What kind of description principle is supported? What are the advantages and shortcomings of this description method?

(17) Describe the services related to the protocol changes of exercises (10) and (11) by means of behavior trees.

(18) What characterizes a protocol design using temporal logics? What kind of description principle is supported? What are the advantages and shortcomings of this description method?

(19) Explain what is expressed by safety properties. Give some examples from the protocol field.

(20) Explain what is expressed by liveness properties. Give some examples from the protocol field.

(21) Describe the services related to the protocol changes of exercises (10) and (11) using the simple temporal logics of Section 7.8. Take the service specification of the same section as a basis. Indicate for each property whether it is a safety or liveness property.

8 Formal description techniques

The description methods introduced in the preceding chapter form the basis for the development of specification languages or formal description techniques. They are applied as semantic models for these techniques. In contrast to the description methods, **formal description techniques (FDTs)** permit an (almost) complete description of services, protocols, and distributed systems. The requirements on the design of formal description techniques resemble at first glance those of programming language design. Important requirements are a *high expressiveness*, i.e., the description technique should be able to represent all relevant elements of a service and a protocol, a *reasonable level of abstraction* to make no reference to possible implementations, the *presence of suitable structuring features* to promote the understanding and handling of the specification in the further development steps, and the *suitability of the language features* such that they do not limit or inadequately affect further development stages. Unlike programming languages, formal description techniques demand a *formally defined syntax and semantics*. The latter represents the crucial difference. It is required to ensure the unique interpretation of the formal specifications.

In the last 30 years mainly three formal description techniques have been deployed and fostered for the description of communication protocols: **Estelle, LOTOS,** and **SDL**. The first two languages were standardized by the *International Organization for Standardization* (ISO). Their development traces back to the foundation of an ad hoc group for formal description techniques within the WG1 of the ISO TC 97/SC 16 at the beginning of the 1980s. This ad hoc group was split into three sub-groups. Sub-group A dealt with architectural concepts to support the work of the other two sub-groups. Sub-group B was devoted to description techniques on the basis of extended finite state machines, while sub-group C developed algebraic-based description techniques. The work of sub-groups B and C led to the definition of the formal description techniques Estelle and LOTOS. In the mid-1980s SDL joined these languages; it had been developed in the 1970s, but was not primarily designed for describing protocols. These three languages formed *the* formal description techniques in a narrow sense for a long time. The situation has changed since the end of the last century. Only SDL has found a broad application in practice. Estelle disappeared and is not used any more. LOTOS found only theoretical importance. Another reason for this situation is the appearance of **UML** (*Unified Modeling Language*) which is a popular modeling technique in software engineering. Although UML is not a formal description technique in the sense defined above, it provides features for describing protocols and is widely deployed for that purpose.

Furthermore, the deployment of formal description techniques also inspired the application of techniques which complement the formal description techniques.

The most important ones are the abstract syntax notation **ASN.1** for data format description and **MSC** (*Message Sequence Charts*) for the graphical representation of protocol sequences.

In this chapter we introduce the principles of the most important formal description techniques for communication services and protocols. We consider the basic approaches: EFSM-based description, communication-oriented description, algebraic specification, and descriptive specification as well as the description of data formats. Each of these approaches represents not only a different way to describe services and protocols; they also represent different thinking models which shape the whole development process.

We introduce for each approach an example language: SDL for EFSM-based description, MSC for communication-oriented description, LOTOS for algebraic description, cTLA (*compositional* TLA) for descriptive specification, and ASN.1 for data formats. Finally we give a short overview of UML 2 features for protocol description. The introductions are confined to the protocol relevant features of the languages to give the reader an insight into the language approach and to allow him/her to understand the subsequent example. Readers with a deeper interest in the languages are referred to the standards and the indicated references. The introductions follow the same structure. They begin with a short overview of the basic language concepts, followed by an introduction to the most important language features and to the respective formal semantics after that. Next a complete or partial description of the XDT service and protocol is given as an example. This is to give the opportunity to the reader to compare the expressiveness of the various description techniques with one another. Especially the service description reveals large differences between the considered techniques. A final discussion of the pros and cons of the applicability of the techniques concludes the overview.

8.1   EFSM-based description – Example: SDL

SDL (*Specification and Description Language*) [ITU-T 100] is the formal description technique of the *International Telecommunications Union–Telecommunication Standardization Sector* (ITU-T) (formerly *Comité Consultatif International Téléphonique et Télégraphique* (CCITT)). The development of SDL began already at the beginning of the 1970s. It was originally developed for the specification of telecommunication systems, but later it was successfully applied to the description of protocols. The language definition has been continuously developed in so-called study periods of the ITU-T Study Group 10. Every four years till 2000 a new version of the language was released. Language versions with important extensions and changes were the versions SDL'88, SDL'92, and the current version SDL-2000, which was revised in 2006. A new version SDL-2010 is under discussion. The public forum to promote SDL is the **SDL Forum Society** (http://www.sdl-forum.org/). It is a non-profit organization to provide and disseminate information on the development and use of SDL. It runs several conferences, among them the SDL forum [SDL Forum]. Nowadays the SDL forum regards itself as a forum that also relates to other languages, such as ASN.1, MSC, TTCN, and UML, which we consider later in this chapter and book. SDL is the only of the three traditional, standardized formal description techniques for which commercial tools have been developed. In the meantime SDL gained strong competition with UML. SDL tries to meet the challenge by the unification of language concepts with UML and by the definition of a UML profile for SDL in the standard Z.109 to promote the use of SDL under UML (see Section 8.6 for this).

The following introduction refers to the current language version SDL-2000 including the revisions of 2006. SDL-2000 contains a sequence of fundamental changes in relation to the previous version SDL'96. These removed poorly used constructs, harmonized the remaining language elements, and introduced a number of new concepts. Important changes are the introduction of the agent concept, the integration of signal routes into the channel concept, and the replacement of the *service*-construct by the concept of state aggregation. Further extensions concern the interface descriptions, the exception handling, composite states, and an improved integration of ASN.1. Moreover, a new formal semantics definition was introduced. For the sake of brevity, it is not possible to give a comprehensive representation of all language concepts of SDL-2000 here, in particular also due to the fact that SDL was not exclusively designed for the description of protocols. We confine ourselves therefore to those concepts which are relevant for the protocol description. The differences to the preceding language versions are not represented either (see for this [Reed 01]). A short overview of the development of the language in the different language versions can be found on the above mentioned web page of the SDL Forum Society.

8.1.1 Basic Concepts

Notations

SDL provides two notations: a graphical and a textual one. They are both based on the same semantic model. The graphical notation SDL/GR (*Graphical Representation*) is the preferred representation. It provides graphical elements for most important language concepts. The graphical representation is supplemented by textual notations for those language elements for which a graphic representation is not appropriate. The predominantly graphic representation of SDL specifications forms the basis for the success and the high acceptance of the language. The later-developed SDL/PR (*Phrase Representation*) provides a purely textual representation. It is mainly used for compiler development. All language elements of SDL/GR that are represented textually form a subset of SDL/PR (see Figure 8.1/1). Both notations can be transferred automatically into one another. Starting from 2002 the Z.100-Standard contains only the graphic version. Thus today, SDL is primarily defined as a graphical language.

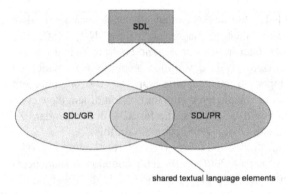

Figure 8.1/1: Relation between the two SDL notations

Agents

The basic concept of an SDL specification is the agent concept introduced with SDL-2000. **Agents** describe active components of the system to be specified. An agent represents an extended finite state machine. It can contain further agents, which can also be created dynamically. There exist two basic kinds of agents: **blocks** and **processes** (see Figure 8.1/2).

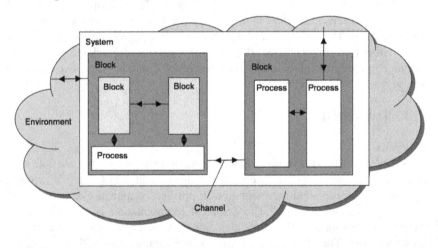

Figure 8.1/2: Agents in an SDL notations

Blocks and processes differ by the execution pattern applied by the contained agents. A block can contain both blocks and processes; a process only processes. In a block the contained agents and the state machine of the container block are executed concurrently, while processes interpret them alternating with each other and with the state machine of the containing process instance, if any. Therefore, only one transition is active in processes at each moment. Its execution cannot be interrupted.

The outermost block of a specification is called the **system**. It describes the interaction with the environment.

Each agent possesses an identifier and a lifetime. Further an infinite input queue is assigned to each agent to buffer incoming **stimuli**. These are events that trigger the firing of a transition which transfers the agent into a new state. A transition is always triggered by the first stimulus in the queue.

Communication

SDL-2000 distinguishes three basic types of communication:

- asynchronous message exchange,
- remote procedure call, and
- shared variables.

Asynchronous message exchange is the most important form of interaction between agents. Remote procedure calls correspond to the interaction paradigm of client/server applications. Shared variables permit a read only access to a remote variable.

Asynchronous message exchange uses signals to transport user data. A **signal** has a name and contains an implicit sender identification. Signals are exchanged via channels. A **channel** is a uni- or bi-directional communication path between two agents which ensures a reliable, order-preserving transmission of the signals. The transmission in a channel can be either delayed or delay-free. The end points of the channels are gates. A **gate** marks external communication points of an agent. SDL distinguishes explicit gates, which have a name, and implicit gates.

Composite states and state aggregation

Apart from structuring a specification by agents, SDL-2000 offers the possibility, following UML, to structure the description of a state machine in a hierarchical manner, i.e., a state is described by another state machine. There are two concepts: composite states and state aggregation. **Composite states** allow the nesting of states. The agent can be in more than one (sub-states); exactly one transition is always executed. All states have a common input queue. A **state aggregation** partitions the state space of the agent. Each partition handles a different set of input stimuli. Enabled transitions are executed in an interleaved manner.

Exceptions

SDL-2000 introduced the concept of exception handling, which is also very useful for describing protocols, e.g., to describe error cases. An **exception** can be triggered explicitly or implicitly. In this case it interrupts the normal control flow and assigns the exception to the next **exception handler** which reacts to this situation. The exception handler is described explicitly. Exception handlers can be assigned to nearly all elements of the behavior description. After handling the exception the execution returns to the place of the interruption, unless the exception handler terminates the system.

Object-Orientation

SDL is an object-oriented language that is based on the definition of classes and the creation of objects from them. For historical reasons, classes are called **types** in SDL and objects **instances** of a type. All instance definitions are based on types. There are agent types, composite state types, signal types, simple data types, and others. A system, a block, a process, a signal etc. is then an instance of the respective type. If not indicated otherwise we refer to instances, when we use these terms in the following. Types can be specialized to derive sub-types. They can be defined by new definitions or by means of redefinitions.

8.1.2 Language Elements

In this section we introduce those elements of SDL needed to describe services and protocols. In part they go back to SDL'88. Our introduction is limited to SDL/GR. The graphical language symbols are usually depicted at left in the sequel. We begin with the structural elements of the language. Data type definitions and object orientation are considered afterwards.

8.1.2.1 Agents

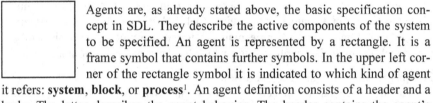

Agents are, as already stated above, the basic specification concept in SDL. They describe the active components of the system to be specified. An agent is represented by a rectangle. It is a frame symbol that contains further symbols. In the upper left corner of the rectangle symbol it is indicated to which kind of agent it refers: **system**, **block**, or **process**[1]. An agent definition consists of a header and a body. The latter describes the agent behavior. The header contains the agent's name, the number of possible agent instances, and the formal parameters. The number of possible agent instances consists of the number of instances which are created during system initialization and the maximum number of instances. Both parameters are optional. The associated default values are: 1 and unlimited. These parameters are given after the agent name, e.g.,

Formal parameters, if available, are given after this in the usual form by a name and the respective data type.

The agent description consists of several parts which can be optionally contained. They can be summarized into three main parts:

---

[1] Terminals are represented either by capital or small letters.

- declarations,
- behavior description, and
- internal structure.

Declarations

Declarations introduce the elements needed in the respective agent, e.g., signals, variable, timers, procedures, exceptions, and others. We describe them below. Declarations do not possess their own graphical symbol. They are textually represented. For this, the **text-symbol** depicted at left is used (see Figure 8.1/3). Variable declarations define special visibility rules (see below).

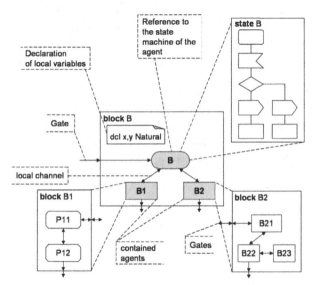

Figure 8.1/3: Example of an agent definition

Behavior description

The behavior of an agent is described by an extended finite state machine which is directly integrated in the agent definition if the agent does not contain further agents (see below). Otherwise the state machine is described separately. One refers to this description by means of the left depicted state symbol which contains the name of the agent (see Figure 8.1/3).

Internal structure

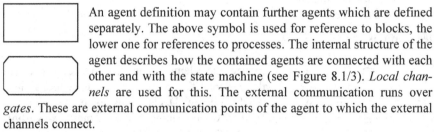

An agent definition may contain further agents which are defined separately. The above symbol is used for reference to blocks, the lower one for references to processes. The internal structure of the agent describes how the contained agents are connected with each other and with the state machine (see Figure 8.1/3). *Local channels* are used for this. The external communication runs over *gates*. These are external communication points of the agent to which the external channels connect.

The principle of references and contained agents, which are described in separate diagrams, results in a hierarchical description structure. The frame of the description is the **system**-diagram which describes the interaction with the environment. The system-diagram contains one or more block-diagrams, which further subdivide accordingly. Figure 8.1/4 shows an example of a possible configuration.

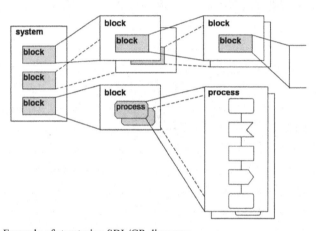

Figure 8.1/4: Example of structuring SDL/GR diagrams

Lifetime of an agent

An agent exists from its generation by the container agent till its termination. Both points are marked in the description by the *start-* and *stop-*symbols.

The **start-symbol** refers to the starting point of the interpretation of an agent description. It is not a state of the state machine. The start implies the assignment of the actual parameters of the agent instance to the formal ones, the creation and initialization of the variables, and the transfer to the initial state of the agent. An agent can only contain one *start*-symbol.

The **stop-symbol** marks the termination of the agent. It can be contained several times in an agent definition. A *stop* implies that all stimuli in the input queue are discarded and that the agent is transferred into an implicit *stop* state. The agent remains in this state until all contained agents are terminated. In the stop state no further stimuli are accepted except the access to global variables via implicit remote procedure calls. When all contained agents are terminated, the agent terminates too.

Agent instances can be dynamically created by means of the **create-symbol**. They are created in the agent executing the *create*-statement. This implies the assignment of the indicated actual parameters and the creation of the internal structure of the agent. If the maximum number of defined instances is reached no further agent is instantiated.

8.1.2.2 Variables

Variables can be declared in agents to store data. A **variable declaration** is represented in a *text*-symbol starting with the terminal **dcl**. It follows familiar structures. An initialization of the variables is possible, e.g.,

> **dcl** i,j Integer;
>   n Integer:= 0;
>   **exported** class Integer;

Variables are distinguished concerning access and visibility into private, local, and exported ones.

Private variables are visible only within the state machine of an agent. They cannot be accessed by other agents.

Local variables are visible to the agent's state machine and all contained agents. They can access these variables. In *blocks* local variables are administered by the state machine of the block. Access by contained agents to these variables is mapped on implicit *get*- and *set-remote*-procedures. Simultaneously occurring *remote*-procedure calls are sequenced by the input queue of the agent. In *processes* access collisions are avoided by the alternating execution of the transitions of the contained processes.

Exported variables are public variables which provide read access to other agents. They represent an abbreviation of a signal exchange between agents. A variable is marked as public if the attribute **exported** is indicated in its declaration, e.g.,

> **dcl exported** ack Boolean.

An agent that will access this variable must introduce it by a *remote*-declaration, e.g.,

> **dcl remote** ack Boolean.

The remote variable is made visible by the possessing agent through the **export-statement**, e.g.,

export ack.

In order to access the variable in the importing agent an **import-statement** is required, e.g.,

import ack.

In the **import**-statement additional constraints concerning the communication path can be indicated.

Address information

Each agent possesses four anonymous variables of the pre-defined sort *Pid* (*Process Identity*). They store address information. These variables are *self, parent, offspring,* and *sender*. The address information is assigned implicitly during agent creation. They can be accessed by other agents:

- **self** – address of this agent instance,
- **parent** – address of the creating agent instance. The *Pid*-value is zero if the agent was created during system initialization,
- **offspring** – address of the last agent instance created by this instance. The *Pid*-value is zero if no agent was created
- **sender** – address of the agent that sent the last consumed signal. The *Pid*-value is zero if no signal has been received.

8.1.2.3 State machine

The behavior of an agent may be described by an extended finite state machine, for short state machine. SDL provides various constructs to describe the operation sequences of the state machine. The most important ones are introduced here. In Figure 8.1/5 we give a final example of how they are used to describe a transition.

States and transitions

The state in which the transition is triggered is described by the **state-symbol**. It can occur several times in the description. This allows structuring the descriptions of the state machine not only by states, but also by signals.

The *state*-symbol contains the name of the state. Several names may be indicated if they possess the same follow-on behavior. If the described follow-on behavior refers to all or almost all states then the "*"- notation may be used as a shortcut. The states which are not concerned are listed after the "*"-symbol in square brackets [...].

A transition is fired by a stimulus in the input queue of the agent. We consider this in more detail later. The expected stimulus is in-indicated in the **input-symbol**. The "*"-notation may also be used here to denote all stimuli of the agent.

The firing of a transition may be predicated on an additional con-dition. This **enabling-condition** is placed after the *input*-symbol. The transition is only fired if in addition to the expected stimulus also the *enabling*-condition is fulfilled. Otherwise the input event is "saved" (see below). The associated transition is fired as soon as the *enabling*-condition be-comes true. If only an *enabling*-condition and no input event is indicated one speaks of a **continuous signal** (see also below).

The sending of a message or other output events are represented by means of the **output-symbol** which contains similarly to the *input*-symbol the output event. In addition, a specification of the receiver is required, which we explain when speaking about the communication principles. The *output*-symbol like the other following statements is executed dur-ing transition execution.

There are no special graphical symbols for describing local ac-tions of the agent (cp. Section 2.2.4), such as assignments to vari-ables and other things. Local actions must be included in the **task-symbol**. These may be sequences of simple statements, e.g., value assignments, compound statements, and informal text. Compound statements subsume several statements represented in the SDL/PR notation, e.g., the **import-**, **export-**, **if-**, **de-cision-**, **loop-**, **break-**, and **timer-**statements. Informal text is not subject to the SDL semantics. It can be replaced in a later refinement phase of the formal de-scriptions.

Time and time surveillance

Time is expressed indirectly. SDL assumes continuously progressing time. To handle time a predefined sort *time* is defined. A moment in the future is expressed by the operator **now** for the actual time plus the time units in the future, e.g. **now**+10. The result is a value of sort *time*.

Time surveillance is performed by means of timers which must be declared in a *text*-symbol, e.g.,

timer t1

It is possible to specify an upper bound, e.g., t:=100. Time units are not explic-itly indicated. They have to be defined in the context of the application. A timer is activated and deactivated with a **set-** and a **reset-statement**, respectively, which are also included in a *task*-symbol. It contains two parameters: the time-out and the name of the timer. The time-out value is indicated by means of the **now**-operator, e.g.,

In case of a time-out a *timer signal* is put in the input queue of the agent, which handles it like the other stimuli. The timer signal is represented by an *input*-symbol containing the name of the timer, e.g.,

> t

Note that the timer signal may be delayed in the input queue because it already contains other signals which are handled first. Therefore timers must be reset explicitly when they are not needed any more, to avoid unwanted side effects. The **reset**-statement removes the timer signals from the input queue. Furthermore, there is a Boolean operator to check whether a timer is active, i.e., whether it has been started

active(t)

Branching

Alternative behavior can be expressed by means of the **decision-statement**. Simple or multiple branches are possible. The branching condition is interpreted as a question which can be formulated either by a Boolean expression or informally. The possible answers are indicated at the branches. The interpretation of the question permits only the indicated answers, i.e., on such alternative must always become true.

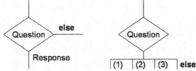

Otherwise the specification is no longer interpretable. To avoid this, an **else**-branch must be introduced which is selected if none of the indicated answers applies. The **else**-branch can be omitted if the keyword **any** is used in the question. In this case one of the indicated answers is selected. Thus **any** is a way to express nondeterminism in the specification.

In the graphical representation branches are reunited at the end of alternative paths. If this leads to complex representations parts of the description can be separated using *labels* and the **break-statement**. The break is carried out by the **break**-statement, which is represented in a *task*-symbol, e.g.,

> **break** *label*

The **break**-statement causes the interpretation of the specification to be continued at the labeled statement. The interpretation can also be continued at another label when using the **join-statement**, which corresponds to a *goto* in programming languages, e.g.,

> **join** *label*

End point of a transition

The end point of a transition is indicated by the follow-up state depicted by the **nextstate-symbol**, left. It contains the name of the next state (see Figure 8.1/5). In case the transition returns to the starting state, this can be indicated by a "-" in the *nextstate*-symbol. Alternatively, the *stop*-symbol may be indicated instead which transfers the agent into the implicit stop state as described above.

The *nextstate*-symbol may occur several times in alternative statements in a transition. The follow-up state is then only determined during the execution of the transition.

text — Like in any language, statements can be commented. This can be done by the symbol shown at left which is connected to the respective graphical symbol.

Describing a transition

We now know all the symbols and statements needed to describe a transition. The principle is exemplarily shown in Figure 8.1/5. The description begins with the starting state. Then the inputs expected in this state are indicated. There are also timer signals and continuous signals to represent spontaneous transitions (see below). The inputs can be bound to additional conditions. For each event, a reaction is given by means of the statements introduced above. Each of the reactions and thus the transitions is completed by a *nextstate*-symbol.

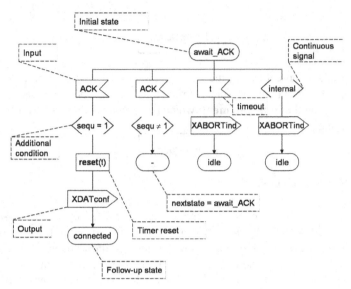

Figure 8.1/5: Principle of the description of a transition in SDL

8.1.2.4 Procedures

Procedures are a further structuring element in an SDL description. A procedure is a parameterized piece of code that can be activated from different parts of an agent. It is local to the agent in which it is declared. The agent instance must contain a reference to the procedure. For this, the **procedure-symbol** is used. Procedures also contain states and transitions. They define their own visibility scope for variables, data types, states, and labels. Names of variables, data types, etc. which are declared outside the procedure remain valid, unless they are replaced by a local declaration.

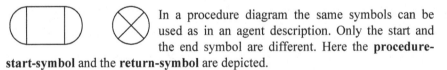

Procedures are described in a procedure diagram which has a similar structure to the agent diagrams. After the keyword **procedure** and the name of the procedure the formal parameters can be indicated by their name and type. There are two kinds of parameters: **in**- and **in/out**-parameters. The keyword **in** refers to parameters that are handed over according to the *call by value* principle, **in/out** accordingly parameters which follow the *call by reference* principle.

In a procedure diagram the same symbols can be used as in an agent description. Only the start and the end symbol are different. Here the **procedure-start-symbol** and the **return-symbol** are depicted.

To activate a procedure the **procedure-call-symbol** has to be used. It contains the name of the procedure and in parentheses the actual parameters.

Like functions in high-level programming languages, procedures may return a value. The type of the return value is indicated in the procedure declaration by means of **returns**, e.g.,

returns Integer.

The procedure is called in an expression in a *task*-symbol using the keyword **call**, e.g.,

call fak(n).

An agent can make its procedures accessible also to other procedures. **Remote procedures** are marked by the keyword **remote** in their declaration. The calling agent refers to them with the *procedure*-symbol. The communication between the calling and the server agent is bi-directional. The communication path between the two agents can be specified explicitly. After calling a remote procedure the calling agent is blocked until the results of the procedure execution are conveyed.

8.1.2.5 Stimuli

Each agent possesses an input queue following the *first-in first-out* principle (FIFO). The queue stores the incoming stimuli which can trigger transitions. Stimuli are signals including the timer signal.

Signals

Agents communicate asynchronously by exchanging signals, which may contain data. The signals must be explicitly introduced in a **signal declaration** placed in a *text*-symbol. If data are contained the data type must be indicated. The data themselves can be directly indicated in the *output*-symbol. The *input*-symbol contains the names of the respective variables which receive the values (see Figure 8.1/6).

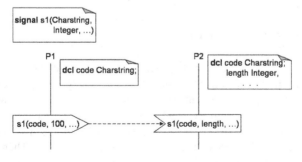

Figure 8.1/6: Exchange of signals

The data types and the order of the data and variables must match in both signals. It is also possible to omit parameters. In this case the respective values are not transferred or get lost.

Reading out the input queue

The entries of the input queue are read out according to the FIFO principle (see Figure 8.1/7). The agent always takes the first signal out of the queue. If this signal is expected in the reached state then the associated transition is executed. Otherwise the signal is discarded. In the follow-up state this procedure is repeated. If there are still signals in the queue which belong to the predecessor state then they are discarded as long as a signal appears that is expected in the current state.

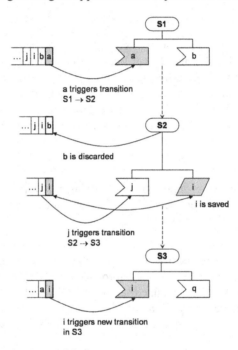

Figure 8.1/7: Reading signals out of the input queue

Saving signals in the input queue

Sometimes it can be necessary that signals are not discarded but remain in the input queue. Here SDL provides a special mechanism: the **save-symbol**. It causes a signal (e.g., the timer event *t* in Figure 8.1/8) not to be removed from the input queue if it is not expected in the given state. It is only read out in the successor state, unless it is saved again. If several events have to be saved the "*"-notation can be applied. Thereby all events are left in the queue which are not explicitly specified as inputs for this state.

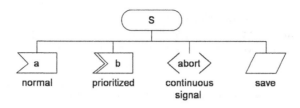

Figure 8.1/8: Input variants

Other input variants

The order in which signals are read out of the input queue can be changed by a **prioritized input** (see Figure 8.1/8). The indicated signals are picked out first, even if they are placed behind other expected signals.

As already explained above a transition can also be fired by a **continuous signal** which is represented by a condition without an input event (see Figure 8.1/8). Continuous signals possess a lower priority than normal signals for triggering transitions, i.e., a transition is only fired by a continuous signal if none of the other specified input signals is in the input queue.

Spontaneous transitions

Nondeterministic behavior can be represented by means of spontaneous transitions (cp. Section 1.2.3). These are *input*-symbols containing the keyword **none** (see Figure 8.1/9). The activation of a spontaneous transition is independent of the presence of a signal in the input queue of the agent. No priority exists between normal and spontaneous transitions.

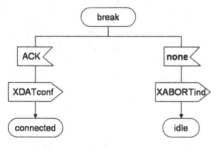

Figure 8.1/9: Spontaneous transition

Sending of signals

The sending of signals requires information about the receiver. Signals which cannot be assigned to a receiver instance are removed. The specification of the receiver agents can be done indirectly or directly. If the communication path is clearly recognizable from the channel route (see below) no further information has to be given. Otherwise address information has to be supplemented in the *output-*symbol. SDL offers several possibilities for this:

- **to** *receiver*

The receiver can thereby be specified either by a *Pid* expression which supplies the address of the agent instance as value, e.g.

or by the name of the receiving agent. In the latter case the set of all instances of this agent is referred to. The signal is assigned arbitrarily to one of these instances.

- **via [all]** *paths*

The receiving agent instance is determined by the path, i.e., by the channel that leads to this agent, e.g.,

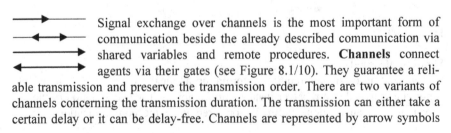

The keyword **all** indicates that the signal is sent out over all specified paths in the order of their listing.

8.1.2.6   Gates

Gates refer to external communication interfaces of the agents to which the channels are attached. These interfaces can be uni- or bidirectional. A gate possesses a name. Restrictive conditions can be formulated for the gates using **signal lists**, which are represented by square brackets. Signal lists contain the signals which are accepted and allowed to be sent at a gate. The first signal list specifies the input signals, the second one the output signals (see Figure 8.1/10). Channels attached to these gates must fulfill these constraints. Furthermore, SDL also permits the possibility of implicit gates that are not referred to by a name. The exchanged signals are declared in a *text*-symbol in the agent.

8.1.2.7   Channels

Signal exchange over channels is the most important form of communication beside the already described communication via shared variables and remote procedures. **Channels** connect agents via their gates (see Figure 8.1/10). They guarantee a reliable transmission and preserve the transmission order. There are two variants of channels concerning the transmission duration. The transmission can either take a certain delay or it can be delay-free. Channels are represented by arrow symbols which are drawn from gate to gate. Delaying channels are represented by the two upper arrow symbols, depending on the use of uni- or bidirectional communication. Delay-free channels use the lower arrows.

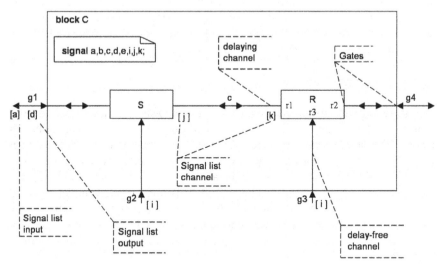

Figure 8.1/10: Channels and gates

8.1.2.8 Composite states

Apart from structuring of agents into sub-agents, SDL-2000 also provides the possibility of nesting the states of the agent's state machine in a hierarchical way (cp. Section 7.4). This can be done using composite states. A **composite state** is a state the behavior of which is described by a separate state machine (see Figure 8.1/11). A sub-state in this state machine can again be described by a composite state. As a consequence, the agent may be in more than one state simultaneously.

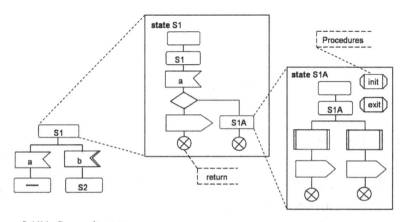

Figure 8.1/11: Composite states

The state machine of the agent is the highest machine in the hierarchy. Contrary to the structuring of an agent into sub-agents, there is only one input queue, that of the agent. Always only one transition can be executed. Internal transitions, i.e., transitions in the state machine of the composite state, have priority over external transitions if they expect the same triggering signals. Special procedures can be defined for the initialization and completion of composite states which are called implicitly when entering and leaving the composite state.

8.1.2.9 State aggregation

A **state aggregation** is a partitioning of a composite state into multiple composite states (see Figure 8.1/12). The state partitions are static and cannot be addressed. The input signal sets of the state partitions must be disjoint. The transitions of the different partitions are executed in an interleaved manner. At any given time each partition of a state aggregation is in one of the states of that partition, or (for one of the partitions only) in a transition, or has completed and is waiting for other partitions to complete. Each transition runs to completion. State aggregations generalize the service concept contained in earlier SDL versions. Their application is useful if concurrent behavior has to be expressed in a composite state.

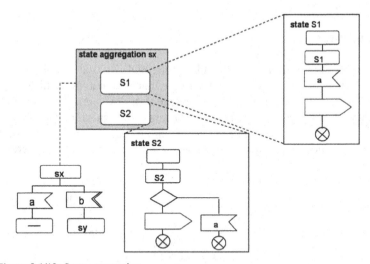

Figure 8.1/12: State aggregation

8.1.2.10 Exceptions

SDL-2000 provides constructs to specify the reaction to unexpected behavior, e.g., errors (see Figure 8.1/13). This can be done by means of exceptions. They must be defined in a *text*-symbol, e.g.,

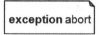

An exception (instance) can be triggered implicitly or explicitly. Implicit exceptions are triggered by the underlying system. These are pre-defined exceptions. Explicit exceptions are initiated by means of the *raise*-symbol (see below) which contains the exception's name. Exceptions can be assigned to all elements of the behavior description, e.g., agents, states, transitions, operations, and procedures. When an exception occurs, the normal control flow is interrupted and branches to the next exception handler. If an exception cannot be handled in a procedure or compound statement the control returns to the next call level. As a consequence, if an exception cannot be handled within an agent the further execution of the system is undefined.

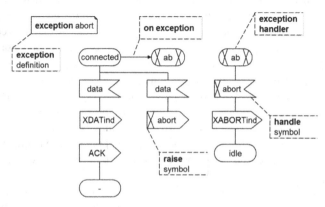

Figure 8.1/13: Exception handling

The reaction to an exception is described in the **exception handler** that is assigned to an element of the behavior description by an **on exception-symbol** indicated below the *exception handler*-symbol. The latter is represented by an arrow which connects the respective symbol with the *exception handler*-symbol. With *on exception*, the reaction on the exception is described. An exception handler is said to be active whenever it is able to react to an exception. Several exception handlers may be active at the same time.

The exception handling begins with the **handle-symbol** which contains the name of the respective exception followed by the handle transition that describes the reaction. It consumes the exception (instance) and makes the related information available to the agent or procedure.

An exception (instance) is created using the **raise-symbol** in the behavior description, i.e., in a transition. The *raise*-symbol branches to the next possible exception handler. Actual parameters may be assigned to the exception.

8.1.2.11 Object orientation

SDL-2000 is a completely type-oriented language. An agent definition is explicitly or implicitly derived from an agent type. Agent definitions which are not type based are transformed implicitly into an agent type definition and an agent definition which is based on this type.

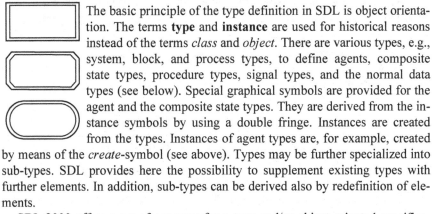

The basic principle of the type definition in SDL is object orientation. The terms **type** and **instance** are used for historical reasons instead of the terms *class* and *object*. There are various types, e.g., system, block, and process types, to define agents, composite state types, procedure types, signal types, and the normal data types (see below). Special graphical symbols are provided for the agent and the composite state types. They are derived from the instance symbols by using a double fringe. Instances are created from the types. Instances of agent types are, for example, created by means of the *create*-symbol (see above). Types may be further specialized into sub-types. SDL provides here the possibility to supplement existing types with further elements. In addition, sub-types can be derived also by redefinition of elements.

SDL-2000 offers a set of concepts for a type and/or object oriented specification. We do not enlarge on this further here, since it does not change anything in the basic principle of describing protocols with SDL. Because protocol specifications only describe the demanded external behavior of the protocol entities their implementations need not necessarily be object-oriented, even if the specification is object-oriented.

8.1.2.12 Data type definitions

The SDL data type concept is based on the abstract data type approach. Two kinds of data types are principally distinguished:

- value types, and
- object types.

Value types correspond to conventional data types, familiar from high-level programming languages. Object types define pointers which refer to values. These references are local to the respective agent. A transformation between the two kinds of types is possible.

Alternatively SDL permits the use of ASN.1 (see Section 8.5) for the description of data formats. ASN.1 definitions can be inserted into SDL specifications in *text*-symbols. They are mapped onto SDL data types. The rules for this mapping are described in the ITU-T recommendation Z.105 [ITU-T 105]. Since we introduce ASN.1 separately in Section 8.5, we do not expand on it further here.

Data type definitions

The basic form of a data type definition in SDL is represented in Figure 8.1/14 for the *value type* definition. An *object type* definition has a syntactically similar form. A data type definition consists of the definition of the set of values which belong to this data type – the *sort* – and the definition of the operations and methods to manipulate the values. A description of the semantic properties of the operations by means of axioms is not contained any more since SDL-2000. For each *object type* definition, the operations *Make* and *Null* for the creation of the data structure and the null pointer are defined implicitly.

value type Boolean
   literals true, false
   operators not: Boolean $\rightarrow$ Boolean
           and: Boolean,Boolean $\rightarrow$ Boolean
           or: Boolean,Boolean $\rightarrow$ Boolean

          . . .

endvalue type Boolean

Figure 8.1/14: Value type definition

The set of values of a data type can be defined by enumeration or derived from other sorts. SDL offers three constructors for this: **literals**, **struct**, and **choice**.

Literals and synonyms

Literals are constants with an implicitly defined value. They must be introduced by enumerating by means of **literals**, e.g.,

literals true, false;
literals 0, 1;

A set of operations is implicitly defined over the enumerated values, such as *first*, *last*, *succ*, *pred*, and others. There is further the possibility to introduce synonymous names for constants. They are declared with the keyword **synonym**:

synonym pi Real 3,14;

Besides sub-range types, so-called *syntypes* can be defined which cover a subset of a sort. The range limit (*constraint*) is indicated after **constants**. *Syntypes* have the same properties as the basic type, but now the affiliation to the subset is proved, e.g.,

syntype Nat = Integer **constants** >= 0 **endsyntype**.

Structures

Compound data types are represented by structures which are defined using the **struct**-constructor in the familiar way, e.g.,

value type ABO_type
   struct
   code: Bitstring default '1101'B,
   conn: Bitstring,
   reason: error
  endvalue type.

The field elements can be supplemented by **optional** and **default** if the element can be contained optionally and/or an initial value is assigned. Apart from the operation *make*, three further operations are implicitly defined for structures: *modify* for inscribing values, *extract* for reading out values, and *present* for testing the presence of a field element. The latter can be accessed by "!", e.g.,

dcl ABO ABO_type;
  . . .
ABO!reason:=2;

A further possibility for assigning values to a structure is the use of the parentheses (. and .), e.g.,

ABO:= (. '1101'B,'1'B,0 .);

Choice

The **choice**-constructor defines a data type consisting of several alternatives. Exactly one alternative applies in each case, e.g.,

XDT-pdu_type ::= **choice**{
                dt   dt_type,
                ack ack_type,
                abo abo_type
                }.

This data type has been introduced for compatibility reasons with ASN.1which uses the same type (see Section 8.5.3).

Parameterized data types

Data types can be parameterized, e.g.,

object type queue<**type** element>
  operators make(element) → queue

```
    methods enter: element,queue → queue
            remove: queue → element
            IsEmpty: queue → Bool
endobject type.
```

The concrete data type is derived by inheritance (see below) from the above definition:

```
object type in_queue inherits queue <XDT-pdu_type>;
dcl input in_queue;
make(20);
input.enter(ABO)
```

Specialization

Data types can be specialized in order to derive further (sub-)types. Specialization is based on inheritance (**inherits**). It defines a new data type that is different from the basic type. The new type takes over all literals and the indicated operators. The literals and operators may be renamed, e.g.,

```
value type bit
    inherits Boolean
        literals 1 = true, 0 = false;
        operators ("not","and","or")
    adding
        operators xor: bit,bit → bit
endnewtype bit;
```

There are two possibilities to specialize a data type: **adding** new elements and the redefinition of elements of the basis type. New literals and operators are introduced after adding. Elements which can be redefined must be marked in the basis type by **virtual**, the redefined elements accordingly by **redefined**.

Any

Each value and object type is directly or indirectly a sub-type of the object type *Any*. This type can be used in variable, type, operator, and method definitions to indicate that here values of any type are allowed.

Predefined data types

Frequently used data types and operations are standardized for use in each SDL specification. These data types and operations are defined in the package *Predefined* (see also Section 8.1.2.14). These are data types familiar from other languages, such as *Boolean, Integer, Natural, Real, Character, Characterstring, Bit, Bitstring, Octet,* and *Octetstring*. Further SDL-specific data types are defined, which we mentioned in part already:

- *Pid*
  Pid (*Process Identity*) denotes references to agent instances (cp. Section 8.1. 2.2). *Pid* values are stored in the above introduced variables **self**, **parent**, **offspring**, and **sender**. A *Pid* literal is *Null*.
- *Time*
  The type *Time* supports the definition of time limits for setting timers.
- *Duration*
  Duration allows the definition of time intervals which can also be used when setting timers.

Furthermore, parameterized compound data types are defined, such as *String*, *Powerset*, *Array*, and *Vector*. In addition, the package *Predefined* contains the definition of a number of frequently appearing exceptions, e.g., *OutOfRange*, *InvalidReference*, *UndefinedField*, *DivisionByZero*, and others.

8.1.2.13 Structure of an SDL specification

An SDL specification, as presented in Figure 8.1/4, consists of a sequence of SDL diagrams. The starting point is the *system*-diagram which forms the framework of the description. SDL permits that a specification does not contain a *system*-agent. In this case the specification serves the provision of definitions which can be used in other specifications. Such referenced definitions must be summarized in a **package-definition**. Such definitions can be data type definitions, signal lists, exceptions, agent type definitions, procedure declarations, and others. Packages can contain further *package*-definitions.

The use of a package in an SDL specification must be declared through a **use-statement** which prepends the specification in a *text*-symbol, e.g.,

use Serv_Def
Prot_Def

Each SDL specification implicitly contains a *use*-statement *Predefined*. It integrates the package *Predefined* that contains predefined data types and exceptions. These definitions are specified in appendix D of the SDL standard.

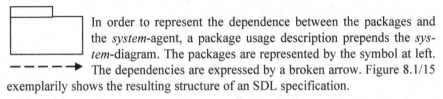 In order to represent the dependence between the packages and the *system*-agent, a package usage description prepends the *system*-diagram. The packages are represented by the symbol at left. The dependencies are expressed by a broken arrow. Figure 8.1/15 exemplarily shows the resulting structure of an SDL specification.

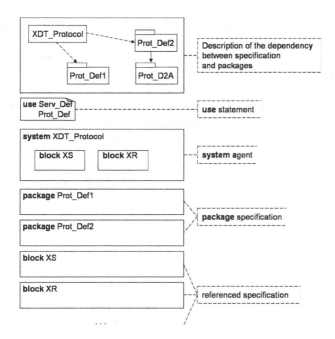

Figure 8.1/15: Structure of an SDL specification

8.1.3 Semantics

With SDL-2000, a new formal semantics has been introduced for SDL. The previous formal semantics was based on a combination of the languages Meta IV and CSP (*Communicating Sequential Processes*). The semantics description comprised approx. 500 pages and required an extensive knowledge of Meta IV. This proved impracticable and led to the development of a new, more easily usable formal semantics [Esch 00]. It is described in part 1 of appendix F of the Z.100 standards [ITU-T 100F].

The formal semantics is defined for a core language only, in order to be able to control the variety of language constructs in the formal definition. This core language is described by an operational semantics. It consists of a static and dynamic semantics. The **static semantics** defines the semantic rules to write a syntactically correct specification. The **dynamic semantics** defines the set of computations associated with a specification. It can only be applied to a syntactically correct specification.

Static semantics

The static semantics comprises the grammar, the well-formedness conditions, and the transformation rules (see Figure 8.1/16). To define the formal semantics a syntactically correct SDL specification is presumed which is represented as an abstract syntax tree. The set of syntactically correct specifications is determined by the *grammar* which is defined in Backus-Naur Form (BNF). To obtain the abstract grammar from the concrete grammar irrelevant details, such as separators and lexical rules, are removed. The *well-formedness conditions* define which specifications are correct with respect to context information, e.g., which names are allowed to be used at a given place or which kind of values can be assigned to variables. Well-formedness conditions are defined in terms of the first-order predicate calculus (PC1). Further *transformation rules* are applied to replace certain language elements of the concrete grammar by other language elements. This is done to keep the core concepts small. The transformation rules are formally expressed by rewrite rules.

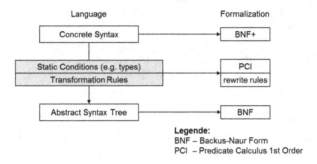

Figure 8.1/16: Static semantics of SDL (Source [ITU-T 100F])

Dynamic semantics

The dynamic semantics of SDL is described by Abstract State Machines (ASMs) [Börg 05]. These are generalized finite state machines. The interpretation of the dynamic semantics starts with the abstract syntax tree from which a behavior model for SDL specifications, the *SDL Abstract Machine* (SAM) is derived (see Figure 8.1/17). The behavioral parts of SDL are mapped by an abstract compiler to abstract code (*denotational semantics*). The initialization defines the initial system structure (*operational semantics*). The semantics of the data is separated by an interface. This allows exchanging the built-in data model without affecting the rest of the semantics.

The *dynamic semantics* associates a particular distributed real-time ASM with each SDL specification. This distributed real-time ASM consists of a set of autonomous agents which cooperatively perform concurrent machine runs. The behavior of an agent represents a transition rule. The cooperative execution defines the set of possible machine runs.

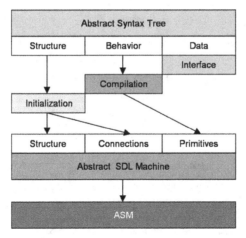

Figure 8.1/17: Dynamic semantics of SDL (source [ITU-T 100F])

8.1.4   Example

Finally we present, as initially announced, the SDL specification of the XDT protocol. The description comprises the service and the protocol specification. They are each described by a *block*-agent, which are subsumed by the *system*-agent *xdt*. The protocol specification is confined for complexity reasons to the representation of the (virtual) communication between the protocol entities, which corresponds to the representation in Section 2.3. This also applies to the following specifications using the other description techniques.

In contrast to other formal description techniques, there are recommendations for how to apply SDL. They are contained in the **SDL Methodology Guidelines** in supplement I of the ITU-T recommendation Z.100 [ITU-T 100]. These recommendations are based on experience in using SDL. The *SDL Methodology Guidelines* also contain recommendations for the structuring of service and protocol specifications which we follow here.

Service specification

The structure of the XDT SDL service specification, given below, differs from the service specification introduced in Section 1.3 by the fact that the two processes *sender* and *receiver*, which describe the local behavior at the service access points, are connected by a channel. The latter serves for describing the interaction between the processes to express the global dependencies between the service primitives at both sides. (This corresponds in principle to a simplified protocol.) For describing the interaction between the processes, we use the signals *data*, *ack*, and *eom* which correspond to the internal events in the service specification in Section 1.3. Note that the abandonment of the connection set up and of the transmission is described by the spontaneous transition **none**.

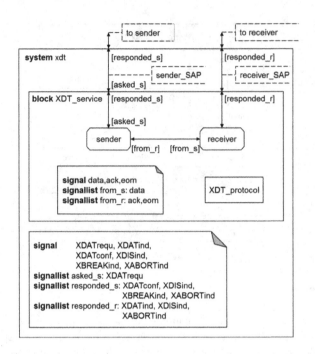

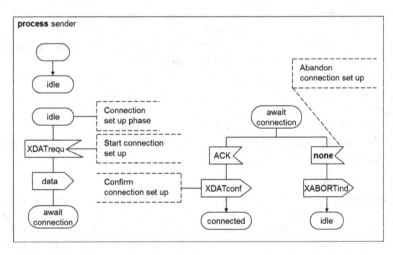

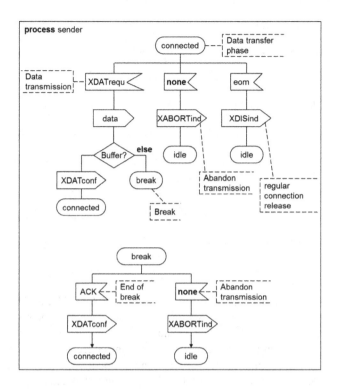

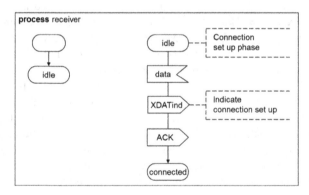

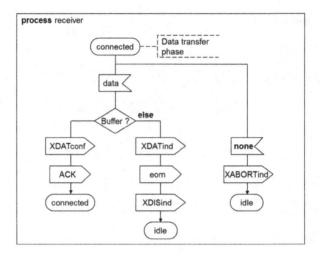

Protocol specification

The SDL XDT protocol specification is represented by a *block*-agent in which the protocol entities are described by processes. Since we waive the representation of the Y-layer, there is a difference to the *SDL Methodology Guidelines* which recommend a structuring principle similar to that introduced in Chapters 2 and 3: one process for the communication between the protocol entities and one process for the mapping of the interactions on the (N-1)-service. The latter process, which corresponds to the SAP handler in Section 3.3, is not contained in the following specification. Exactly speaking, we could even directly integrate the protocol procedures into the upper *block* agent. We forego this to leave this extension open. Note further that for space reasons the specification does not contain all procedures. Another difference to the representation in Section 2.3 is that no protocol parts are used here. All operational sequences in the protocol entities are represented by one extended finite state machine only. The concurrency between the protocol parts *transfer_s* and *ack_handler* is described by different transitions in the state *connect* which are executed alternately according to the respective top event in the input queue. For describing the abandonment of the transmission at sender side, we apply the exception *abort*, which is triggered when an *ABO*-PDU occurs or the activity timer *t1* triggers a time-out. In the receiver entity the abandonment is represented as a reaction to a time-out.

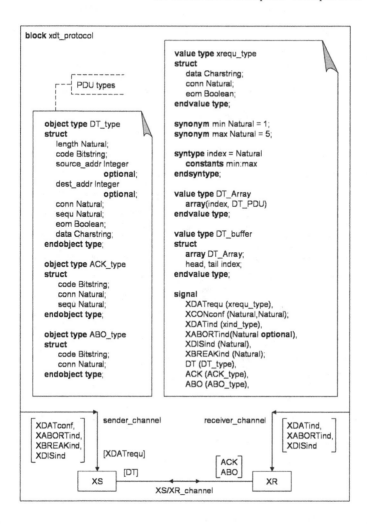

block xdt_protocol

PDU types

object type DT_type
struct
 length Natural;
 code Bitstring;
 source_addr Integer
  optional;
 dest_addr Integer
  optional;
 conn Natural;
 sequ Natural;
 eom Boolean;
 data Charstring;
endobject type;

object type ACK_type
struct
 code Bitstring;
 conn Natural;
 sequ Natural;
endobject type;

object type ABO_type
struct
 code Bitstring;
 conn Natural;
endobject type;

value type xrequ_type
struct
 data Charstring;
 conn Natural;
 eom Boolean;
endvalue type;

synonym min Natural = 1;
synonym max Natural = 5;

syntype index = Natural
 constants min:max
endsyntype;

value type DT_Array
 array(index, DT_PDU)
endvalue type;

value type DT_buffer
struct
 array DT_Array;
 head, tail index;
endvalue type;

signal
 XDATrequ (xrequ_type),
 XCONconf (Natural,Natural);
 XDATind (xind_type),
 XABORTind(Natural **optional**),
 XDISind (Natural),
 XBREAKind (Natural);
 DT (DT_type),
 ACK (ACK_type),
 ABO (ABO_type),

⎡XDATconf,⎤   sender_channel   receiver_channel   ⎡XDATind,⎤
⎢XABORTind,⎥   ⎢XABORTind,⎥
⎢XBREAKind,⎥   ⎣XDISind⎦
⎣XDISind⎦   [XDATrequ]

                                            ⎡ACK⎤
                                            ⎣ABO⎦
  XS   [DT]   XR
         XS/XR_channel

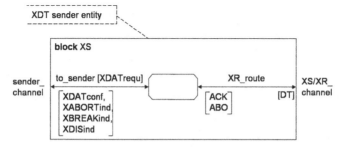

XDT sender entity

block XS

sender_   to_sender [XDATrequ]   XR_route   XS/XR_
channel   channel
         ⎡XDATconf,⎤   ⎡ACK⎤   [DT]
         ⎢XABORTind,⎥   ⎣ABO⎦
         ⎢XBREAKind,⎥
         ⎣XDISind⎦

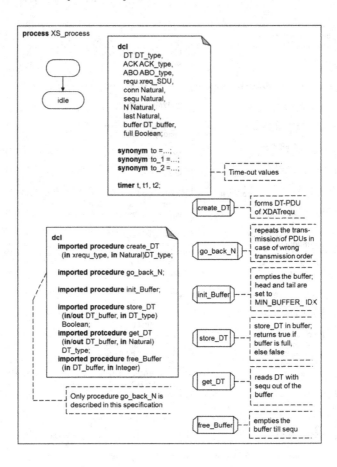

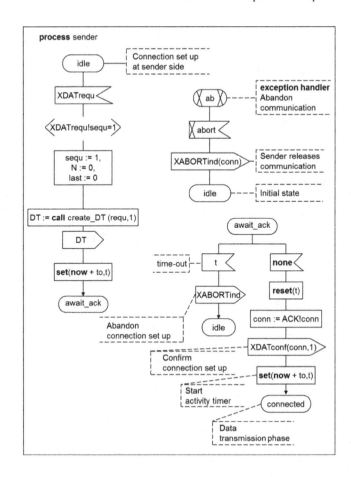

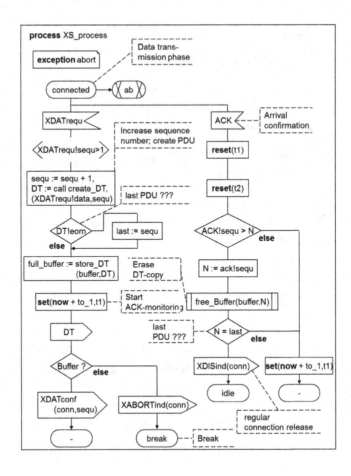

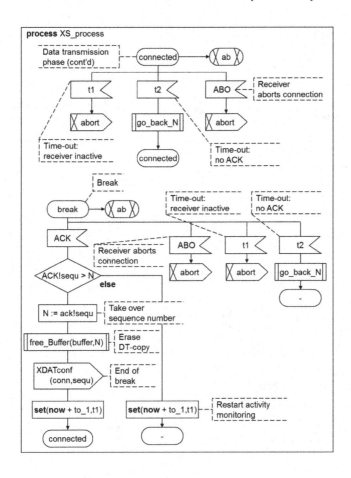

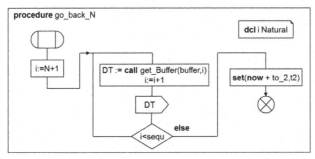

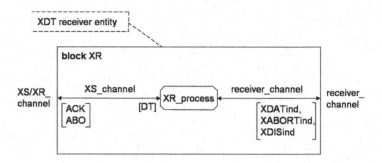

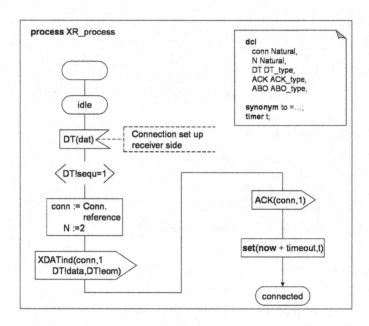

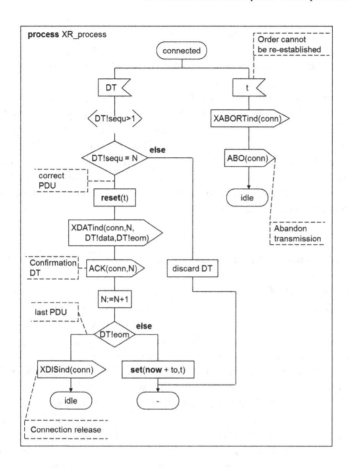

8.1.5 Applicability

SDL is a formal description technique that has been successfully deployed for describing protocols in practice. It combines the familiar EFSM method with a graphical representation that helps one to easily learn and apply the language. Especially, the graphical representation makes the application of SDL attractive for many users. However, SDL was not especially designed for describing protocols. Thus, it also contains a couple of features, e.g., object orientation, which are not primarily required for describing protocols. As an EFSM-based language SDL does not allow one to directly represent the protocol flow. To remedy this Message Sequence Charts (MSC) were developed which we introduce in the next chapter. SDL does not directly support verification. For this, the specifications have to be transferred into other representations. There are tools that support such transformations.

Meanwhile, SDL has become a pretty complex language that is difficult to maintain. Full tool support for SDL is costly to implement. Therefore, only subsets of SDL are currently supported by tools. These SDL subsets are called *SDL profiles*. They cover a wide range of applications and have proved sufficient in practice. An overview of available tools can be found on the web site of the SDL Forum Society.

A decisive factor for the success of SDL is its standardization by the International Telecommunication Union (ITU), which continuously develops the language further and adapts it to new requirements, as well as its support by the SDL Forum which organizes the user community. Thus SDL is a living language. The language though is losing importance with the emergence of UML. The SDL community has tried to cope with this by approaching the UML methodology. An SDL-UML profile was designed to use the SDL methodology in the context of UML. We enlarge on it in Section 8.6.

8.2   Communication-oriented description – Example: MSC

Message Sequence Charts (MSC) is a specification language of the ITU-T for the representation/visualization of interactions between independent message-passing system components. A message sequence chart describes a selected interaction scenario. MSC can be deployed in various engineering phases, e.g., for overview specifications, requirement specifications, documentations, and test case descriptions. Originally MSC was not designed as a formal description technique. It aimed at the visualization of interaction scenarios. The principle of message sequence charts goes back to a suggestion of Rudolph and Grabowski, which was based on OSI time sequence diagrams (cp. Section 1.1) and ISDN information flow diagrams. MSC was standardized between 1989 and 1992 by the International Telecommunication Union in the recommendation Z.120 [ITU-T 120]. This version was called MSC '92. In the following ITU-T study periods the language was developed further and the versions MSC '96 and MSC-2000 were defined. The latter is the current version. With the version '96, a formal semantics was defined based on process calculi. It is contained in annex B of the Z.120-Standards (see also [Mauw 96, 99]). Thus, MSC changed into a self-contained formal description technique. In the same version MSC was extended by means for combining message sequence charts to build complete specifications. This structuring concept is called *High-level MSC* (HMSC). In MSC-2000 data types, remote method calls, and object orientation were added. The concept of time was extended. Apart from absolute time, relative time was introduced.

MSC is not bound to a particular specification language. It is frequently used in connection with SDL, which substantially contributed to its high acceptance. The transformation of MSC into SDL representations and vice versa is supported by tools. The basic principles of the MSC representation, also called *Basic MSC*, are very simple. It spread fast and attained large popularity. UML 2 adopted the MSC representation principle for its sequence diagrams.

In the following introduction we confine ourselves to a description of *Basic MSC* and some additional structuring concepts. A goal of this short introduction is to present the principles of this frequently used graphic description of communication procedures.

8.2.1 Basic concepts

Notation forms

MSC is a graphical scenario language which possesses like SDL a graphical and a textual notation form: MSC/GR and MSC/PR. The graphical notation form represents the notation relevant for practical applications. The textual form mainly serves as a representation format for tools. The graphic notation can be automatically transferred into the textual one. We consider here only the graphical notation.

Message sequence chart

The basic element of the description is the *message sequence chart*, also called an MSC diagram. It describes the interactions between two or several system components, the instances, as well as with the environment. A message sequence chart is limited by a frame that represents the environment. An instance, e.g., an agent in SDL, is represented by a vertical axis (see Figure 8.2/1). The instances interact between each other and/or with the environment by the exchange of **messages**. These are represented by horizontal arrows with the name of the respective message. Sending and receiving a message are different events which occur at the respective axis. The interactions are asynchronous. The send event always precedes the receive event.

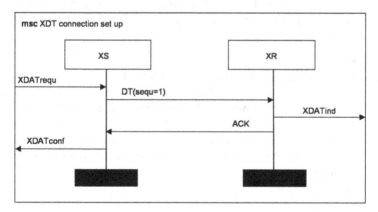

Figure 8.2/1: Message sequence chart for a (successful) XDT connection set up

Figure 8.2/1 shows a message sequence chart for the XDT connection set up. It contains two instance axes for the protocol entities *XS* and *XR*. The service primitives describe the communication with the environment, in this case with the XDT service users. It is assumed that the environment is able to send and/or receive messages to/from the chart. The behavior of the environment is nondeterministic, but it is additionally presupposed that the communication with the environment follows the interaction sequence specified in the message sequence chart.

There is no global time scale in a message sequence chart. Concerning time, it is assumed that it progresses along each instance axis from top to bottom except in **coregions** which describe concurrent behavior. The events occurring in the instances are arranged in the order of the message exchange. A message must always be sent first, before an acknowledgment can be received, but this is not expressed in the time axis. A message sequence chart describes a partial order over the events which has to be preserved.

MSC provides further constructs needed for describing the interaction/communication flow between the instances, such as system states, timers, gates, actions, process creation, and process termination. In addition, there is the possibility to combine partial sequences by means of so-called inline expressions in order to represent alternatives, options, loops, exceptions, and concurrency.

Data definitions

Starting from MSC-2000 there is the possibility to declare data for use in messages, actions, or timers, or as parameters. MSC has no data description of its own. It permits the use of the data notation preferred by the user. The semantics of the data notation used is linked by interface modules with the MSC description.

8.2.2 Language constructs

MSC achieved considerable complexity with the extensions introduced in the different language versions. They cover a broad range of applications. Not all language concepts are relevant for protocols. We consider here those elements which are relevant for protocol description.

Basic MSC

mscdocument *name*

The **MSC document** forms the frame of a description in MSC. It is represented by a frame symbol followed by further MSC diagrams. The MSC document contains the name of the document and describes the structure of the specification. The name can optionally refer to an SDL specification (if the document is provided for such a specification). Moreover, it can contain inheritance clauses, message and timer declarations as well as the interface module for the data description.

msc *name*

A **message sequence chart** is also represented by a frame. It forms the environment of the interaction sequence in question. Each message sequence chart has a name which is indicated after the keyword **msc**. After the keyword **inst** the instances in question can be listed. In addition, the associated SDL agent (*system*, *block*, or *process*) can be indicated for each instance, e.g.,

   msc connection establishment **inst** *XS*: *process*, *XR*: *process*.

A message sequence chart consists of interacting instances. An **instance** represents a communication partner. It is represented by a vertical axis along which time progresses from top to bottom (see Figure 8.2/2). A message sequence chart can contain more than two axes. This is very useful for protocol descriptions because it allows representing protocol sequences over several layers.

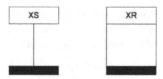

Figure 8.2/2: Representation forms of instances

There are two representational forms for instance axes: the line and column. We mostly use the line representation here. The axis is limited by a head and an end symbol that mark the beginning and the end of the description (but not the creation and/or termination of the instance). Along the axis, the interactions between the instances are indicated. For this, the following constructs are available: sending and receiving of messages, actions, local and common conditions, timers, process creation, and stop.

Messages are represented by horizontal arrows with the name of the message. Parameters may follow the name. It is also possible to specify data bindings, e.g., that the sequence number of the first PDU has to be equal to 1 (cp. Figure 8.2/1).

Arrows which end at the instance axis mark inputs, outgoing arrows accordingly outputs. The arrows go from the instance axis that sends the messages to the axis of the instance that receives them. The arrows may also contain a drop directed downwards to represent the consumption of time, a overtaking, or a crossing of messages (see Figure 8.2/3).

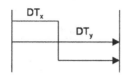

Figure 8.2/3: Overtaking of messages

When the instances interact with the environment, the arrows begin and/or end at the chart frame. The interfaces with the environment are described by **gates** which can be named explicitly or implicitly. Gates are used when references to the message sequence chart are put in a wider context with other charts. We do not consider this further here.

Furthermore, the **loss** and the **finding of a message** can be represented. A message loss is represented by the upper symbol at left, where the arrow must begin at an instance axis. The "finding of a message" is described similarly by the lower symbol. Here the arrow must end at an instance axis. This symbol can be, for instance, used to represent a late arrival of a message.

Sending and receiving of messages are asynchronous events. MSC defines the following **time relation**. A message sequence chart defines a partial ordering over the events to be described. It supposes a global clock for each message sequence chart. Along each instance axis the time is progressing downwards without assuming a concrete time scale. If no coregions or inline expressions are used a total time ordering of events is assumed along each instance axis. Events of different instances are either ordered via messages, i.e., a message must first be sent before it is consumed, or by the generalized ordering mechanism. The latter can be used for an explicit ordering of events in different instances (even in different sequence charts). Other ordering relations are not defined. For example, the following ordering relations can be derived from the message sequence charts in Figure 8.2/4, where $in(m_i)$ and $out(m_j)$ label message inputs and outputs, respectively:

out($m2$) < in($m2$), out($m4$) < in($m4$), in($m1$) < out($m2$) < in($m4$) < out($m5$), in($m2$) < out($m3$) < out($m4$) including the transitive closure.

The partial ordering can be described, without explicitly representing the transitive closure, by a connectivity graph (see Figure 8.2/4)

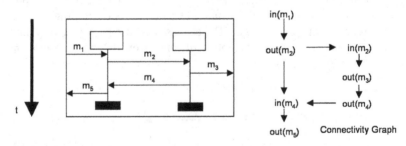

Figure 8.2/4: Example message sequence chart with its associated connectivity graph

Conditions are used to represent system states and guards. System states are differentiated into global states, which apply to all instances (*shared all*), shared states, which are only shared by some instances, and local states, which belong to a single instance. Global and shared states may therefore be contained in different message sequence charts. They refer to states at which message sequence charts end and others begin. Figure 8.2/5 refines the message sequence chart from Figure

8.2/1 for the XDT connection set up by the introduction of the global states IDLE and CONNECTED.

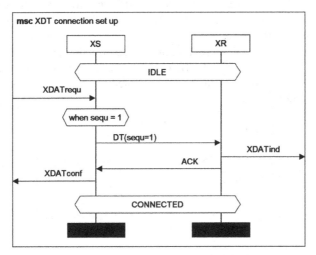

Figure 8.2/5: MSC diagram for the XDT connection set up with states and preconditions

Guards describe preconditions which must additionally be fulfilled to trigger a transition (cp. Section 1.2). The respective condition is indicated after the keyword **when** (see Figure 8.2/5). A guard is only valid within a chart. It can refer to one or more instances.

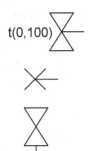

MSC provides **timers** with the well-known functionality (*start, stop, time-out*) for time control. A timer is represented by an hourglass symbol. The symbols for start, stop, and time-out are given at left. Beyond that there are still further representational variants. The time control can be extended over several MSC diagrams, i.e., the timer can be started in one chart, while it is stopped in another and/or a time-out is indicated. Timer events can be interconnected by a vertical line if they refer to the same timer. Optionally, a name and a time interval can be assigned to a timer. The time interval is described by its lower and upper limits. The latter may be infinite (**inf**).

Apart from absolute time, MSC also supports relative time. It can be used for time stamps or for the definition of time constraints, e.g., execution intervals of partial sequences for performance modeling.

Local **actions,** e.g., for handling arrived messages or reacting to a time-out, are represented in an *action*-symbol as in SDL. Informally described actions are set in quotation marks.

Similarly to SDL, instances can be created and terminated dynamically, whereby an instance can be only created by another instance (see Figure 8.2/6). The **creation of an instance** by means of a *create*-statement is represented as in SDL by a dashed arrow. An instance can be created only once in a message sequence chart. Several *create*-statements with the same instance name are not allowed. The *create*-statement is executed immediately. Before the instance creation no messages may take reference to this process instance. A created instance terminates itself. For this, the *stop*-symbol is used.

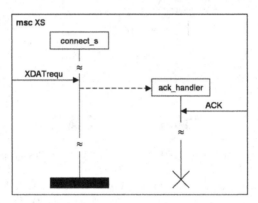

Figure 8.2/6: Creation and stop of an instance

The representation of interactions, as it has been described so far, defines a firm order for the message exchange. In order to describe nondeterministic occurrences of interactions, **coregions** can be used. In a coregion the firm temporal succession of the events connected with the instance axis is suspended, i.e., there is no defined order in which the indicated events occur. Only the sending and receiving of messages as well as a time-out are allowed as events. Figure 8.2/7 shows the integration of coregions into the representation of an instance.

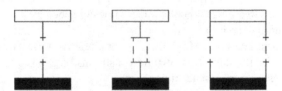

Figure 8.2/7: Representation variants of coregions

Decomposition

The description of an instance in a message sequence chart can be refined by another chart. This principle is called *decomposition*. It is a means for structuring the description to introduce several representation levels. An instance which is refined in another sequence chart is marked by **decomposed as** plus the name of this chart (see Figure 8.2/8).

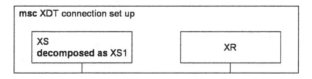

Figure 8.2/8: Decomposition

In Figure 8.2/8 the sender instance is refined by the sequence chart *XS1* (not represented here). The refined chart may not change the outside communication behavior of the superior chart, i.e., it must be mapped on this communication behavior. Therefore all messages to the environment must correspond to messages in the superior chart. There are no restrictions concerning the refinement of actions and conditions. In the refined chart also several instances may exist.

Inline expressions

Inline expressions allow combining partial procedures or sequence charts to describe more complex interactions. The following expressions are defined:

- **loop** for loops,
- **opt** for the optional execution of an interaction sequence,
- **exc** for exception handling,
- **alt** for describing alternative behavior, and
- **par** for the parallel execution of interaction sequences.

Inline expressions are represented by a special symbol in the left upper corner that contains the keyword of the expression (see Figure 8.2/9). For loops, the execution interval is indicated additionally. In expressions with several alternatives (**alt, par**) the different alternatives are separated by dashed lines. Figure 8.2/9 shows as an example how both outcomes of the XDT connection establishment can be represented in one message sequence chart using an alternative. The execution of alternatives may also be dependent on preconditions. In addition, an alternative can be described by means of **otherwise** which is performed if none of the other preconditions is fulfilled. The inline expression **opt** (*option*) represents a special case of the alternative with only one execution variant. It is only executed if the precondition is fulfilled. Exceptions can be described by **exc** (*exception*). If an exception occurs the statements in the **exc**-expression are executed. After that the chart terminates.

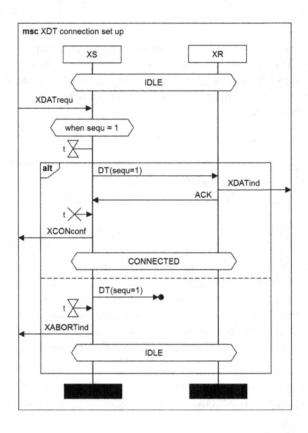

Figure 8.2/9: Message sequence chart for the XDT connection set up

High-level MSC

With the extension to **High-level MSC (HMSC)**, MSC provides means to combine message sequence charts in order to produce more complex and/or complete descriptions of a system. Thus, the use of MSC is not confined to the description of selected communication sequences any more, as it was the intention of the original version.

In order to be able to combine various charts the concept of a reference to a message sequence chart was introduced. A reference is represented by the symbol indicated at left. References may be part of other charts as Figure 8.2/10 shows.

connection set up

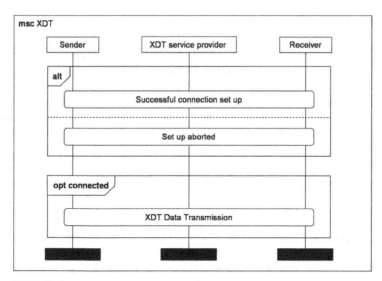

Figure 8.2/10: References to message sequence charts

A high-level MSC description begins and ends with a *start-* and a *stop-* symbol, respectively. Further composition elements are conditions, interconnection points, and parallel frames. These elements are interconnected by flow lines to indicate the execution sequence of the message sequence charts. Loops can also be represented. Figure 8.2/11 shows an example for a simplified representation of the XDT service usage with references to the charts for successful and abandoned connection establishment as well as for data transmission. The conditions refer to the states *Idle* and *Connected*. An aborted connection set up leads back to the initial state *Idle*.

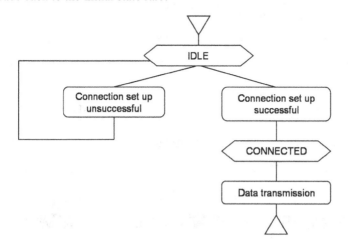

Figure 8.2/11: High-level MSC description for the XDT service

8.2.3 Example

Finally we demonstrate the use of MSC again with the XDT protocol. Since an individual message sequence chart permits one to describe only a selected communication sequence, the service and the protocol specification have another character here than in specifications with other formal description techniques. Although the introduction of High-level MSC and inline expressions give the opportunity to combine communication sequences, it is nevertheless necessary to describe all conceivable communication sequences for a complete MSC specification. For XDT, this leads already to a quite extensive specification. Therefore, we confine ourselves to the representation of some selected sequences to demonstrate the principle.

Service specification

We first present the diagrams of the XDT service specification. They show the various interactions at the XDT service interface for connection establishment, for normal data transmission, for data transmission with break, and for connection release. We use the column notation for the service provider to symbolize the complexity of the internal operational sequences. The represented states of the service provider are the states IDLE and CONNECTED (cp. Figure 1.3/3). The possibility to consider several instances in a message sequence chart allows representing both the local behavior at both service access points and the causal dependencies between them (cp. Sections 1.2 and 1.3).

The first chart shows the connection establishment. The two possible outcomes (set up or abandonment) are represented using the **alt**-expression. In the subsequent message sequence charts the possibility that at each time the transmission can be aborted is described by means of an exception **exc**.

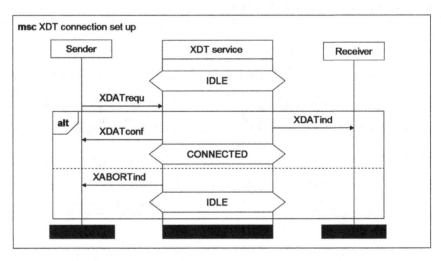

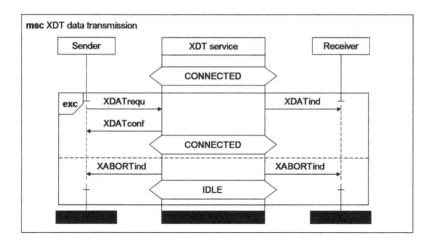

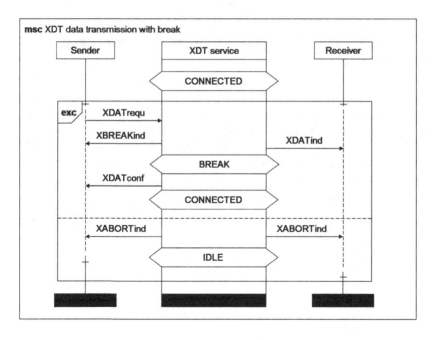

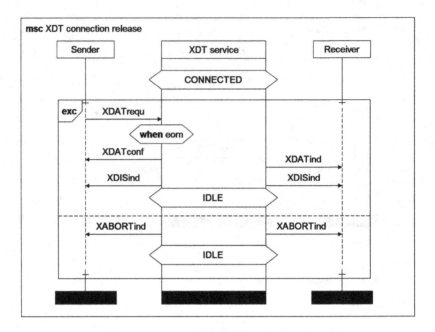

Protocol specification

We present two message sequence charts of the XDT protocol specification. The first chart shows the successful connection establishment, where also the interactions with the underlying *Y*-layer (cp. Section 3.3) are considered. All instances are represented in the axis notation.

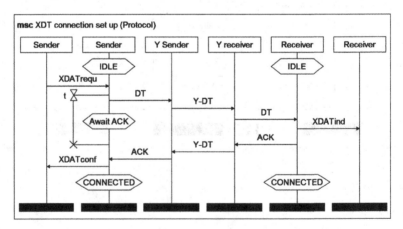

The second MSC diagram shows a slightly simplified representation of the data transmission with a break. It contains the four instances of the service users and the protocol entities. The possibility of a break is here represented as option (**opt**). The indices at the *DT*- and *ACK*-PDU indicate that also an *ACK* of a preceding *DT*

can clear the buffer space and terminate the break. Note that the message sequence chart does not contain timers. This as well as the possibility of the arrival of further *ACK*s can make very quickly the diagram quite complex.

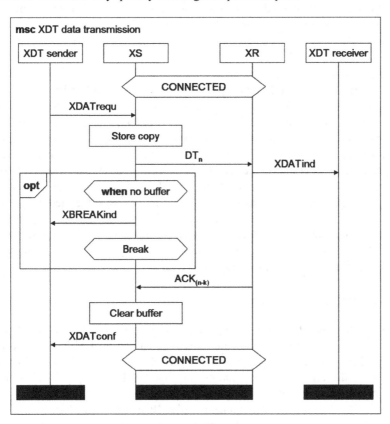

8.2.4 Applicability

MSC is a very popular means for describing communication scenarios in protocols and distributed systems. The reason for this popularity is the simple graphical representation. MSC provides the protocol engineer with a description form to directly represent the interactions between the communicating entities when reasoning about protocol procedures. Thus, it is an ideal supplement to the (E)FSM-based description techniques like SDL that do not directly represent the communication flow. MSC is more a scenario language rather than a real formal description technique, although it supports complete specifications. It is especially convenient for representing selected communication sequences as needed during protocol design and documentation. The language is less practical for elaborating complete specifications of complex systems because all conceivable sequences have to be represented. This may lead to very complex specifications which are difficult to handle. High-level MSC mitigates this problem, but nevertheless the advantage is not that large compared to other description techniques. MSC is like SDL also supported by various tools for developing and validating message sequence charts. Finally it must be mentioned that due to the success and broad acceptance of MSC it has been incorporated into UML 2 as *sequence diagrams* (see Section 8.6 for this).

8.3   Algebraic-based description – Example: LOTOS

The formal description technique **LOTOS** (*Language of Temporal Ordering Specification*) is our representative of algebraic description techniques. It is based on the CCS calculi of MILNER (cp. Section 7.7). LOTOS was standardized by ISO [ISO 8807]. A graphical variant GLOTOS as well as an enhanced version E-LOTOS to support real-time applications were defined later, but they did not find broad acceptance. The significance of LOTOS derives from the theoretical foundations for concurrent systems, which are still relevant today [Bowm 06]. For that reason, it is worthwhile to consider the basic principles of LOTOS in the context of this chapter because the language presents an entirely different approach to the description of protocols than we have seen so far.

8.3.1   Basic concepts

LOTOS consists of two parts: the behavior description and the data description. The behavior description relies on the process calculi CCS of Milner (cp. Section 7.7) and CSP (*Communicating Sequential Processes*) of Hoare [Hoar 85]. For data description, the algebraic specification language ACT ONE [Ehri 85] is used. These two parts results in two language levels. The behavior description, which only describes the process interactions, is called **Basic LOTOS**. *Basic LOTOS* and *ACT ONE* combined form **Full LOTOS** which describes both the process interactions and the data exchange.

Processes

The basic concept of description in LOTOS is the process. A **process** is described by its externally visible behavior, i.e., its interactions with the environment (see Figure 8.3/1). A process can consist of several sub-processes, which again can contain further sub-processes. Thus, a hierarchy of process definitions develops.

Actions

Interactions between the processes are described by **actions** which designate events. Actions take place at special points of interaction, the **gates**. The interaction is atomic and synchronous (*rendezvous principle*). *Basic* LOTOS describes only the synchronization between processes. Therefore, gate and action names coincide. Figure 8.3/1 shows the principle for an example process *PQ* which interacts with the environment over the actions *a*, *b*, and *c*. The process *PQ* consists of the two sub-processes *P* and *Q* which communicate with each other using action *d*.

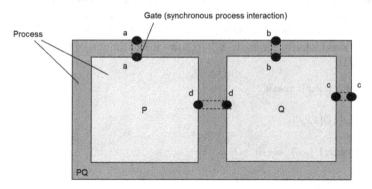

Figure 8.3/1: Process interactions in LOTOS

Behavior expressions

The observable behavior of a process is described in **behavior expressions**. Graphically, behavior expressions are represented by means of behavior trees (cp. Section 7.7) (see Figure 8.3/2). Sub-trees can be replaced by a triangle if they are defined elsewhere or if their structure is not relevant for the current representation.

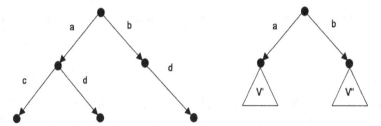

Figure 8.3/2: Behavior trees

8.3.2 Basic LOTOS

Basic LOTOS represents the kernel language. It is confined to the description of the processes and their interactions. The set of observable interactions is finite. This is due to the fact that the actions coincide with the names of the gates, whose number is finite.

Processes

A *process definition* has the following general structure:

process *identifier* [*gate list*]: *functionality*:=
    behavior expression
endproc

The *identifier* denotes the name of the process. The *gate list* refers to the process gates and thus to the externally visible actions. *Functionality* indicates whether a process runs into a deadlock (**noexit**) or terminates properly (**exit**). The observable behavior of the process is described by the *behavior expression*. If the behavior expression contains further sub-processes their definition is included after the keyword **where**. Example 8.3/1 shows the definition of the process *PQ* of Figure 8.3/1.

process *PQ* [*a,b,c*]: **noexit** :=

   . . .

P[*a,d*] | [*d*] | Q[*b,c,d*]
   where
      process P [*a,d*]: **noexit** :=

      . . .

      endproc (* P *)
      process Q [*b,c,d*]: **noexit** :=

      . . .

      endproc (* Q *)
   endproc (* PQ *)

Example 8.3/1: Definition of the process *PQ*

Behavior description

Basic LOTOS provides various language elements for describing the process behavior.

Inactive behavior

Inactivity of a process is represented by **stop.** It describes situations, in which processes are no longer able to interact with their environment, i.e., they are in a deadlock. Processes that end with **stop** have the functionality **noexit**. In the behavior tree representation **stop** represents a leaf node. Note that this is an important difference to others FDTs. LOTOS explicitly describes deadlocks!

Action prefix

The action prefix which corresponds to the prefix in CCS (cp. Section 7.7) is used to describe the sequencing of actions.

   a;B

is a behavior expression that will perform action $a \in Act \cup \{i\}$ and then behaves like *B*. In this way sequential behavior can be specified, e.g.,

   *a;b;c;***stop.**

Apart from visible actions, $a \in Act \cup \{i\}$ also includes the **internal action** *i* which cannot be observed from the outside. It models an internal event of the process, e.g., a failure of the communication connection or a time-out (cp. Section 1.2.3).

Alternative behavior

Alternative behavior of a process can be described by the *choice*-operator [], which corresponds to summation in CCS. If B_1 and B_2 are two behavior expressions then

B_1 [] B_2

describes two possible behaviours of the process, e.g.,

a;(*c*;**stop**[]*d*;**stop**).

The selection of the behavior depends on the occurrence of the events. Figure 8.3/3 shows the associated behavior tree.

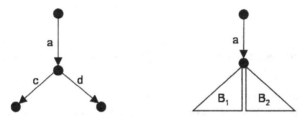

Figure 8.3/3: Choice

Nondeterministic behavior can be expressed likewise (see Figure 8.3/4), e.g.,

a;*e*;*c*
[] *a*;*d*;*e*.

Nondeterministic behavior can also be expressed using the internal action *i*, whose occurrence triggers an alternative behavior to the expected visible interaction, e.g.,

a;*b*;*c*
[] *i*;*e*;**stop**.

Figure 8.3/4: Nondeterministic behavior

Recursion

The language elements introduced so far permit only the description of finite behavior. A LOTOS specification though generally describes infinite behavior. This is achieved by a **recursive invocation of processes** in process definitions, e.g.,

process $R[a,b,c]$: **exit**:=
  $a;b;R[a,b,c]$
  [] c; **exit**
endproc

If a process ends with **stop** it cannot be invoked recursively. This is only possible if the process terminates successfully. The **successful termination of a process** is represented by **exit**, e.g.,

process S[a,b,c,]: **exit**:=
  a;b;c;**exit**
endproc

A successful process termination must be specified by the functionality **exit** in the head of the process definition.

Sequential composition

The action prefix describes action sequencing within a behavior expression. To describe sequencing between behaviors sequential composition has to be applied. LOTOS offers two operators for this. The *enabling*-construct

$B_1 >> B_2$

expresses that the behavior expression B_2 will only be activated if B_1 terminates successfully. For example, we can describe the succession of protocol phases by means of the *enabling*-construct:

Connection establishment >> Data transmission >> Connection release.

The second operator, the *disabling*-construct, describes the disabling of a normal behavior B_1 by an exceptional behavior B_2

B_1 [> B_2.

The *disabling*-construct [> means that the execution of B_1 is aborted when the triggering event B_2 occurs. Subsequently, the behaviour expression behaves as B_2. If B_1 terminates successfully it cannot be disabled by B_2 any more. We can use the *disabling*-construct to express that a protocol phase can be interrupted because the connection is aborted, e.g.,

(Connection establishment >> Data transmission) [> Connection abandonment

Parallel composition
Concurrent behavior can be described through parallel composition, which corresponds to composition in CCS. LOTOS distinguishes three forms of parallel composition which differ in their level of synchronization.

General parallel operator
The general parallel operator

$B_1 |[a_1, ... ,a_n]| B_2$

describes the composition of two behavior expressions B_1 and B_2 which synchronize with respect to the events $a_1, ..., a_n$ indicated in the square brackets. The behavior expression

$P[a,d] |[d]| Q[b,c,d]$

describes the parallel composition of process P and Q of Figure 8.3/1. The two processes synchronize with respect to d. The actions a and/or b, c are interactions of the processes P and/or Q with the environment. Parallel compositions can be interpreted by either interleaving or true concurrency semantics (cp. Section 1.2.4). The standard interpretation is interleaving (see [Bowm 06] for this).

Full synchronization
If B_1 and B_2 synchronize with respect to all events one speaks of full synchronization

$B_1 || B_2$.

Note that parallel composition can be represented alternatively by means of the action prefix and the *choice*-operator. Example 8.3/2 shows this for full synchronization. Since the event d is not expected in process U, the alternative $w;v;$**exit** in V will not be executed so the process UV behaves as the expression indicated at bottom right.

process $UV[a,b,c,d]$: **exit** :=
    $U[a,b,c] || V[a,b,c,d]$
    where
        process $U[t,u,v]$: **exit** :=
        $t;u;$**exit** [] $v;$**exit**
        endproc (* U *)
        process $V[t,u,v,w]$: **exit** :=
        $t;u;$**exit** [] $w;v;$**exit** [] $v;$**exit**
        endproc (* V *)
endproc (* UV *)   ➔   corresponds to $a;b;$**exit** [] $c;$**exit**

Example 8.3/2: Alternative representation of full synchronization

Independent parallelism

The case that two behavior expressions B_1 and B_2 do not synchronize with respect to any action is called *independent parallelism*

$B_1 \parallel B_2$.

The behaviors evolve concurrently. They only interact with the environment. Example 8.3/3 shows again the alternative representation using action prefix and *choice*-operator. The resulting behavior expression contains the possible interleaving sequences (cp. Section 1.2.4)

process *UV*[*a,b,c,d*]: **exit** :=
   U[*a,b,c,d*] ||| V[*d*]
   where
      process *U*[*t,u,v,w*]: **exit** :=
         *t;u;***exit** [] *v;w;***exit**
      endproc (* U *)
      process *V*[*w*]: **exit** :=
         *w;***exit**
      endproc (* V *)
endproc (* UV *)
→corresponds to *d;*(*a;b;***exit** [] *c;d;***exit**) [] *c;d;d;***exit** [] *a;*(*b;d;***exit** [] *d;b;***exit**)

Example 8.3/3: Alternative representations of independent parallelism

If sequential and parallel compositions are combined attention must be paid to the fact that parallel composition only terminates after all sub-processes have terminated successfully. Accordingly, *B* is never reached in the following behavior expression

(*a;b;***exit** |[*b*]| *b;c;***stop**) >> *B*

because sub-process *b;c;***stop** runs into a deadlock.

Multi-way synchronization

Parallel composition can also be applied to several behavior expressions and/or processes simultaneously, if they synchronize with respect to the same action, e.g.,

P[*a,b*] |[*b*]| *Q*[*b,c*] |[*b*]| *R*[*b,d*].

Action *b* can only be performed if the processes *P*, *Q*, and *R* all participate.

Hiding

So far we have assumed that the synchronizing actions of parallel behavior expressions are visible to the environment. Sometimes it is appropriate to consider the communication between two behavior expressions and/or sub-processes as internal and hide it from the environment. This concept is called **hiding**. It corresponds to restriction in CCS. To hide interactions the *hide*-construct **hide** x **in** must be used. Now the internal communication between P and Q of Figure 8.3/1 can be described as follows:

process *PQ*[*a,b,c*]: **exit**:=
hide *d* **in**
  P[*a,d*] |[*d*]| Q[*b,c,d*]
  where
    . . .
endproc

Note that d does not appear as an action of *PQ* because it is no longer visible to the environment. Example 8.3/4 shows the complete description of the process *PQ* at the end of our introduction to *Basic* LOTOS.

process *PQ*[*a,b,c*]: **exit** :=
hide *d* **in**
  P[*a,d*] |[*d*]| Q[*b,c,d*]
  where
    process *P*[*a,d*]: **exit** :=
      *a;d;***exit**
    endproc (* P *)
    process Q[*b,c,d*]: **exit** :=
      *d;b;c;***exit**
    endproc (* Q *)
  endproc (* PQ *)

Example 8.3/4: Complete specification of process *PQ*

8.3.3 Data type definition

Before coming to *Full* LOTOS we have to consider how data types are represented in LOTOS. In the original LOTOS definition the algebraic data description language ACT ONE [Ehri 85] was used for specifying data formats. ACT ONE is an abstract data type language which supports an implementation-independent representation of data formats. The use of ACT ONE has proved cumbersome though, and is considered to be a hindrance to the broader use of LOTOS. In E-LOTOS another data language was introduced. Since we do not consider E-LOTOS [ISO 15437], we sketch the principles of the original LOTOS data description here, which more or less shaped the use of LOTOS in the protocol field.

Basic types

In LOTOS all data types including the elementary ones must be defined. Frequently used data types can be included in a standard library. Their use must be indicated in the *library*-reference at the beginning of the specification, e.g.,

library
Boolean, Character, NaturalNumber
endlib.

Data type definition

A data type definition consists of two parts: the description of the signature and the definition of semantic properties. The **signature** refers to the sort and operators of the data type. The **sorts** denote the sets of values that form the data type. The **operations** define mapping rules between sorts. Each operation possesses a domain, which comprises zero or several sorts, and a range of values, which consist of exactly one sort.

Example 8.3/5 shows examples of type definitions. The elements of a sort are called as *terms*. Accordingly the terms of sort *s* are referred to as *s-terms*, e.g., bool-terms.

Operations with *n* arguments are called *n*-ary operations. The operations *not* and *succ* in Example 8.3/5 are accordingly unary operations. Constants like *true* and *false* are operations without an argument or null-ary operations.

The sort of the left- and right-hand sides of the equations is indicated after **of-sort**.

type *Boolean* **is**
sorts *Bool*
opns
    true,false: $\rightarrow$ *Bool*
    not: *Bool* $\rightarrow$ *Bool*
eqns
    ofsort Bool
        not(*true*) = *false*;
        not(*false*) = *true*;
endtype

type *Nat_Numbers* **is**
sorts *Nat*
opns
    0:        $\rightarrow$ *Nat*
    succ: *Nat* $\rightarrow$ *Nat*
endtype

Example 8.3/5: Data type definitions

The signature defines the syntax of the data type. The semantic properties of the operations are described by additional **equations**, which directly follow the definition of the operations (see Example 8.3/5). The equations define which terms are equal, e.g., *not*(*true*) = *false*.

Extension and combination

New data types can be derived by extension from existing data types using other sorts and operations. Example 8.3/6 shows an extension of the data type *Nat_Numbers*. The type definition contains only the extensions. The definitions of the basis type are inherited by the new type. The underscore symbols indicate an infix operator. The **forall**-construct in the **eqns**-part defines free variables of a certain sort which are used in the following equations.

type *Extended_Nat_Numbers* **is** *Nat_Numbers*;
opns
   _+_ : *Nat,Nat* → *Nat*
eqns forall *x,y*: *Nat*
    ofsort *Nat*
      x+0=*x*
      x+*succ*(*y*)=*succ*(*x*+*y*);
endtype

Example 8.3/6: Extension of a data type

Complex data types can also be defined by the **combination** of several already existing types. Example 8.3/7 shows the definition of a queue type using the data types *NaturalNumber* and *Boolean*.

type *Nat_queue* **is** *NaturalNumber*, *Boolean*
sorts *Queue*
opns
   create: → *Queue*
   enter: *Nat,Queue*   → *Queue*
   first: *Queue*   → *Nat*
   isEmpty: *Queue*   → *Bool*
eqns forall *x,y*: *Nat,q*: *Queue*
   ofsort *Bool*
     isEmpty(*create*) = *true*;
     isEmpty(*enter*(*x,q*)) = *false*;
   ofsort *Nat*
     first(*enter*(*x,create*)) = *x*;
     first(*enter*(*x,enter*(*y,q*))) = *first*(*enter*(*y,q*))
endtype

Example 8.3/7: Combinations of data type definitions

Parameterization

Data type definitions can be parameterized. A parameterization is possible for sorts (denoted by **formalsorts** in the specification), operations (**formalopns**), and equations. Example 8.3/8 shows this for the above queue type definition. The data type definition must be updated when it is applied. That happens in a separate actualization definition (see Example 8.3/8). The formal sorts and operations are replaced by actual parameters similarly to parameter transfer in procedures.

type *Generic_queue* **is** *Boolean*
formalsorts *Element*
sorts *Queue*
opns
   create: → *Queue*
   enter: *Element,Queue*   → *Queue*
   first: *Queue*   → *Element*
   isEmpty: *Queue*   → *Bool*
eqns forall *x,y*: *Element,q*: *Queue*
  ofsort *Bool*
    isEmpty(*create*) = *true*;
    isEmpty(*enter*(x,q)) = *false*;
  ofsort *Element*
    first(*enter*(x,*create*)) = x;
    first(*enter*(x,*enter*(y,q))) = *first*(*enter*(y,q))
endtype

type *Nat_queue* **is** *Generic_queue* **actualizedby** *Nat_Number* **using**
sortnames
   Nat **for** *Element*
endtype

Example 8.3/8: Parameterized data type definitions with actualization

Renaming

A further possibility for introducing new contextual types is renaming. The new data type is completely independent. Beside the type also the sort and operation names are changed. Names which are not changed apply invariably in the new type definition (see Example 8.3/9). Renaming is frequently used in connection with extension by first introducing a new type through renaming and then extending it. Thus, conflicts with the basis type are avoided.

The renaming in Example 8.3/9 introduces the new type *Generic_connection* with the new sort *Channel*, the formal sort *Object* as well as the operations *send*, *receive*, *create*, and *isEmpty*. The operations *create* and *isEmpty* are defined likewise over the sorts *Channel* and *Object* (*operation overloading*).

type *Generic_connection* **is** *Generic_queue* **renamedby**
sortnames
   Channel **for** *Queue*
   Object **for** *Element*
opnnames
   send **for** *enter*
   receive **for** *first*
endtype

Example 8.3/9: Renaming

8.3.4 Full LOTOS

Full LOTOS extends the description of process synchronization in *Basic* LO-
TOS by data which are exchanged at the gates. The data types are defined as described in the previous section. The set of observable events in a *Full* LOTOS
specification is usually infinite, since the values ranges of the data are often infinite.

Structured events
Full LOTOS applies the concept of structured events to describe interactions. A
structured event consists of the gate name that refers to the interaction point and
a list of interaction parameters, the **event offers**. Two kinds of offers are distinguished: value offers and variable offers.

Value offers denote a concrete value. They are represented by an exclamation
mark followed by a value or a term, e.g.,

   $!0$, $!true$, $!(2+7)$, $!(x+y)$, $!ident$.

Variable offers describe a range of values. They generally possess the form
$?x: t$, where x denotes a variable of the sort t, e.g.,

   $?x: Bool$, $?A: Nat$

There are three different types of interactions: value matching, value passing,
and value generation (see Table 8.3/1).
Value matching describes synchronization with agreement of the expected
values, otherwise a deadlock occurs. For example, in a process A with $g!false$; *error* the process *error* will only be activated if process B offers a value offer *false*
at gate g.

	Process A	Process B	Synchronization condition	Effect
Value matching	$g!E_1$	$g!E_2$	$value(E_1) = value(E_2)$	Synchronization
Value passing	$g!E_1$	$g?x:t$	$value(E_1) \in domain(t)$	after Synchronization $x = value(E_1)$
Value generation	$g?x:t$	$g?y:u$	$t = u$ $v \in domain(t)$	after Synchronization $x = y = v$ for $v \in domain(t)$

Table 8.3/1: Interaction types of structured events

Value passing describes the passing of a value between two processes. Process A hands a value $g!E_1$ to process B ($g?x:t$). Thereafter the variable x in B possesses the value of E_1.

In **value generation** a value from the value range is handed over to a variable of the other process. Both variables participating in the synchronization have thereafter the same value ($x = y$). For example, during a synchronization of the processes A ($g!$ x: *Bool*) and B ($g?$ y: *Bool*) either *true* or *false* is handed over. Value generation is used to describe the exchange of values not known a priori (e.g., addresses, connection references).

The value range of variables in variable offers can be limited by means of the **selection predicate**, e.g.,

$(g?x: Nat[x < 5];B) \parallel (g?y: Nat[y > 2];C)$

In this case an interaction only takes place if x offers the values 3 or 4. This can, for instance, be used to describe negotiations between protocol entities.

Conditional behavior

Full LOTOS, like other FDTs, offers the possibility of predicating behavior on conditions. These conditions, called **guards,** precede the behavior expression, e.g.,

$[x>0] \rightarrow sap!x; B;$

If the condition holds then the behavior B is expected, otherwise a deadlock **(stop)** occurs. In the conditions variables can be used. For example, a case selection can be represented using guards and the *choice*-construct as follows:

[*x*>=0]→ *sap*!*x*; *process1*

[][x < 0]→ *sap*!-1; **stop**.

Parameterized processes

Processes can be parameterized in *Full* LOTOS. The data parameters are enclosed in parentheses and positioned between gate list and functionality (see Example 8.3/10).

> **process** *range*[*inp,outp*](*min,max*: *Nat*): **exit** :=
>> *inp* ?*x*: *Nat*;
>> ([(*x*<*min*) or (*x*>*max*)] → *outp*!*false*; **exit**
>> [] [(*x*>=*min*) and (*x*=<*max*)] → *outp*!*true*; **exit**
>>)
> **endproc**

Example 8.3/10: Parameterized process

When the process is activated, the actual parameters substitute the formal ones, e.g.,

> *range*[*input,output*](0,100).

The actual parameters are value expressions of the same sort. They substitute the formal parameters of the process according to the *call by value* principle. If the values of the parameters have to be changed then this can only take place via a recursive process invocation, e.g.,

> **process** *range*[*inp,outp*](*min,max*: Nat): **exit**:=
>> …
>> *range*[*inp,outp*](*min*+10,*max*+10)
>> …
> **endproc** (* range *)

Parameterized exit

Full LOTOS permits values to be handed over to another process when a process terminates successfully. The parameters to be handed over are listed as value expressions after **exit**, e.g.,

> **exit**(*x*+*y*+3, **any** *Bool*, **any** *Nat*).

The **any**-construct indicates that any value of the sort can be handed over. The *exit*-construct of *Basic* LOTOS is a special case of parameterized exit without parameter list.

Using a parameterized exit the process *range* of Example 8.3/10 can be simplified (see Example 8.3/11).

> **process** *range* [*inp*](*min,max*: *Nat*): **exit**(*Bool*):=
>   *inp* ?x: *Nat*;
>   ([(x < *min*) or (x > *max*)] → **exit**(*false*)
>   [] [(x >= *min*) and (x =< *max*)] → **exit**(*true*)
>   )
> **endproc**

Example 8.3/11: Parameterized exit

Parameterized sequential composition

Parameterized exit is used in the generalized form of sequential composition: *parameterized sequential composition*. The values passed to the follow-up process are indicated in the *accept*-construct which follows the *enabling*-construct, e.g.,

> *range*[*input*](0,100) >> **accept** b: *Bool* **in** ([b=*true*] → ...
>   [] [b=*false*] → ...
>   ) .

It is demanded that the functionality of the process before the *enabling*-construct corresponds to that of the *accept*-parameter list.

The **functionality** *func* of a process or behavior expression that does not have a linear structure must be derived by rules. The functionality of a process is determined by the functionality of its behavior expression. These rules are summarized in Table 8.3/2.

Local variable definitions

To make the representation more readable and compact it is possible to introduce local names for value expressions. This can be done in the following form:

> **let** $x_1{:}t_1{=}E_1, \ldots ,x_n{:}t_n{=}E_n$ **in** B,

e.g.,

> **let** $x{:}Nat{=}a{+}b{+}c, y{:}Nat{=}a{*}b{*}c$ **in** ([p>=0]→g!x [] [p<0]→g!y).

These names represent local variables whose use, however, is restricted. They cannot be modified by value assignments as in other languages. The only possibility to pass their values to another process is the invocation of the processes within the *let*-construct or a parameterized exit.

Operator	Conditions	Functionality
stop	-	noexit
exit	-	$\diamondsuit$
exit $(v_1 \ldots v_n)$	$sort(v_1) = s_1, \ldots, sort(v_n) = s_n$	$<s_1, \ldots, s_n>$
$a;B$	-	$func(B)$
$B_1 \, [] \, B_2$	$func(B_1) = func(B_2)$	$func(B_1)$
	$func(B_1) = $ **noexit**	$func(B_2)$
	$func(B_2) = $ **noexit**	$func(B_1)$
	otherwise	not permitted
$B_1 >> B_2$	-	$func(B_2)$
$B_1 \, [> \, B_2$	as $B_1 \, [] \, B_2$	like $B_1 \, [] \, B_2$
$B_1 \, parop \, B_2$ [2]	$func(B_1) = func(B_2)$	$func(B_1)$
	$func(B_1) = $ **noexit**	**noexit**
	$func(B_2) = $ **noexit**	**noexit**
	otherwise	not permitted

Table 8.3/2: Rules for determining the functionality of a process or behaviour expression

Generalized choice and parallel composition
Full LOTOS offers two further constructs for a more compact representation: generalized choice and generalized parallel composition.

Generalized choice
Generalized choice subsumes identical behavior expressions. There are two possibilities:

(1) *Choice between gates*

choice g **in** $[g_1, \ldots, g_n] \, [] \, B[g]$

e.g.,

choice g **in** $[a,b]$, h **in** $[c,e]$ process$[g,h]$

---

[2] *parop*: $||, |[\ldots]|, |||$

as abbreviation for

> process[*a,c*]
> [] process[*a,e*]
> [] process[*b,c*]
> [] process[*b,e*].

(2) *Choice between values*

> **choice** $x_1:t_1,...,x_n:t_n$ [] $B(x_1,...,x_n)$,

e.g.,

> **choice** $x:Nat$ [] $B(x)$.

This defines a choice over the *Nat* value range for *B*, i.e., *x* may be any value of *Nat*.

Generalized parallel composition
Generalized parallel composition has a similar syntactical structure, but it exclusively refers to gates

> **par** g **in** $[g_1,...,g_n]$ *parop* $B[g]$,

where *parop* stands for one of the parallel operators ||, ||| or |[...]| . For example, the composition

> **par** g **in** $[a,b,c]$ |[*f*]| $B[f,g]$

stands for

> $B[f,a]$ |[*f*]| $B[f,b]$ |[*f*]| $B[f,c]$.

8.3.5 Structure of a LOTOS specification

After introducing the basics of the two language variants we finally consider the structure of a LOTOS specification. The frame of a LOTOS specification is defined by the process **specification** which contains the complete protocol and/or system description. The syntax of the frame process is very similar to that of the **process** definition as the following example shows:

> **specification** $S[a,b,c]$: **noexit**
> **library** *Boolean, ...* **endlib**
> **type** *x-type* **is**   . . .
>   **sorts** *x-sort*
>   **opns** $x\text{-}Op$: $x\text{-}sort \rightarrow x\text{-}sort$
> **endtype**

behaviour
hide *d* **in**
  $P[a,d]$ | [*d*] | $Q[b,c,d]$
  where
    process *P*

    . . .

    endproc (* P *)
    process *Q*

    . . .

    endproc (* Q *)
endspec (*S *)

The process **specification** differs from a normal process definition through the behavior expression which describes the global behavior of the system. It begins with the keyword **behaviour** instead of the sign ":=". In addition, the process **specification** may contain a *library*-reference to pre-defined data type definitions. All definitions (processes, data types) in **specification** are global, i.e., they apply to all included processes. Definitions in a process definition apply only locally within the respective process.

8.3.6 Formal semantics

Different semantic models have been associated with LOTOS, such as trace semantics, labeled transition systems, event structure semantics, or trace-refusal semantics. Labeled transition systems is the semantic model used as formal semantics in the LOTOS standard [ISO 8807]. It represents the standard semantics of LOTOS and is considered here. Comprehensive introductions to the other semantic models can be found in [Bowm 06].

Labeled transition systems
Labeled transition systems (LTS) model systems as behavior trees (cp. Section 7.7), solely in terms of sequence and choice. Sequences denote sequences of arcs, choices branching nodes, respectively. The nodes represent the states, which are not named. The arcs represent the transitions, and the triggering actions including the internal action are the labels assigned to the transitions. Unlike finite state machines, labeled transition systems do not distinguish between input and output.

Formally, a **labeled transition system** is defined as a quadruple $<S,Act,T,s_0>$ with
S – non-empty set of states,
Act – set of observable actions,
T – set of transition relations with $T = \{-a \rightarrow \subseteq S \times S \mid a \in Act \cup \{\tau\}\}$,
$s_0 \in S$ – initial state.

Pure LTS describe the semantics of *Basic* LOTOS. The rules of the operational semantics to interpret a LOTOS specification are not given here. Important rules are described in [Bowm 06]. Some examples are given below.

Structured labeled transition systems

Labeled transition systems model process behavior as it can be described in *Basic* LOTOS, i.e., only the interactions without data exchange. In order to model also the data exchange at the gates an extended semantic model is needed that combines labeled transition systems with many-sorted algebras. This model is called structured labeled transition system and is the semantic model of *Full* LOTOS.

A **structured labeled transition system** (SLTS) is a quintuple $<S, L \cup \{i\}, A, T, s_0>$ with

S – non-empty set of states,

L – non-empty set of labels or gates,

$i \notin L$ – internal event,

$A = <D,O>$ – many-sorted algebra with

   D – set of sorts and

   O – set of operations,

$T=\{t \mid t = s \text{ -}<e,c>\text{→}s'\}$ – set of transitions, where

   • $s, s' \in S$,

   • e – structured event of the form $g\alpha_1, ...\alpha_n$ with $g \in L$ and $\alpha_i \in D$,

   • c – condition for e,

$s_0 \in S$ – initial state.

A structured labeled transition system is a special case of a labeled transition system in which the actions are represented by structured events consisting of a label or gate followed by the data value. The latter represents the result of the action.

Formal interpretation of LOTOS specifications

Before a LOTOS specification can be interpreted as a labeled transition system, the LOTOS specification must be transformed. This transformation consists of two steps: the static semantics phase and the dynamic semantics phase.

The **static semantics phase** proves the static semantics requirements and transforms the LOTOS specification into an abstract syntax structure, the canonical LOTOS specification. The *static semantics requirements* comprise all rules concerning the use of the LOTOS language elements that cannot be derived solely from the syntax definition. The *canonical LOTOS specification* (CLS) is the result of the application of a partial syntax transformation function, the *flattening function*, which transfers all data structures to a global definition level, removes all nested process definitions, and defines all identifiers globally unambiguously. The transformation is partial because only LOTOS specifications that fulfill the static semantics requirements are mapped into the canonical form. The result of a transformation of a LOTOS specification which breaks this requirement is not defined. The canonical LOTOS specification consists of two parts: the *algebraic specification AS* for the data types and the flattened *behavior specification BS*.

In the **dynamic semantics phase** the canonical LOTOS specification is interpreted as a structured labeled transition system. For this purpose, the canonical LOTOS specification is transformed into a class of structured labeled transition systems that defines a structured labeled transition system for each substitution of the formal parameters of the specification by current actual ones.

The interpretation of dynamic semantics is divided into the interpretation of the data type part *AS* and the behavior part *BS*. The interpretation of the formal model of the LOTOS data types *AS* is a particular many-sorted algebra $Q(AS)$, the *quotient term algebra* of *AS*, which is used for the interpretation of the behavior part *BS* in the following. The interpretation of the behavior part is a class of structured labeled transition systems over the quotient term algebra $Q(AS)$ or more exactly a function with that class as its range of values. This function maps each correct substitution of the formal specification parameters by actual parameters into a structured labeled transition system which serves as model for the dynamic behavior of the respective instance of the LOTOS specification. We demonstrate the mapping for simplicity reasons for some rules for *Basic* LOTOS using the operational style of [Herm 98]. It associates with every valid LOTOS expression P a tuple $(P, -a\rightarrow)$, where P denotes the initial state and $-a\rightarrow \subseteq S \times S \mid a \in Act \cup \{\tau\}$ represents a possible transition between states. Further A denotes the synchronization set in parallel composition, i.e., $P|[A]|Q$. We list subsequently the inference rules for prefix, choice, hiding, and variants of parallel composition as examples.

> $a; P\text{-}a\rightarrow P$
> *if* $P\text{-}a\rightarrow P'$ *then* $P[]Q \text{-}a\rightarrow P'$
> *if* $Q\text{-}a\rightarrow Q'$ *then* $P[]Q \text{-}a\rightarrow Q'$
> *if* $P\text{-}a\rightarrow P'$ *and* $a \in A$ *then* **hide** A **in** P - i → **hide** A **in** P'
> *if* $P\text{-}a\rightarrow P'$ *and* $a \notin A$ *then* **hide** A **in** P -a→ **hide** A **in** P'
> *if* $P\text{-}a\rightarrow P'$ *and* $a \notin A$ *then* $P|[A]|Q$ -a→ $P'|[A]|Q$
> *if* $Q\text{-}a\rightarrow Q'$ *and* $a \notin A$ *then* $P|[A]|Q$ -a→ $P|[A]|Q'$
> *if* $P\text{-}a\rightarrow P'$ *and* $Q\text{-}a\rightarrow Q'$ *and* $a \in A$ *then* $P|[A]|Q$ -a→ $P'|[A]|Q'$
> *if* $P\text{-}a\rightarrow P'$ *and* $P=P_1 ||| P_2$ *then* $P_1 ||| P_2$ -a→ P'

A complete list of the interference rules is contained in [ISO8807].

8.3.7 E-LOTOS

LOTOS was revised in the second half of the 1990s. The standardization process was finished in 2001 (see [ISO 15437]). A number of new features were added, such as a new data language, time, imperative features (assignments, loops), generalized parallel and disabling constructs, exception handling and others. E-LOTOS maintains compatibility with LOTOS, but in principle it is a completely new language. In the protocol field E-LOTOS has not been applied broadly. Therefore it not considered further here.

8.3.8 Specification styles

Before considering our example specification we have to address the specification styles developed for LOTOS [Viss 88]. These give a good impression of how LOTOS specifications look. Specification styles define a coordinated procedure for the elaboration of a specification in order to emphasize certain characteristics of the system to be described. For LOTOS, mainly four specification styles were proposed: the monolithic, constraint-oriented, state-oriented, and resource-oriented styles. The first two styles aim at system design. They reflect above all the functional behavior of the system. The other two styles are more implementation-oriented. They represent internal interrelations of the system.

Monolithic style

The monolithic style describes the behavior of the system through one process. There is no reference to the local origins of the actions or to the internal structure of the system. Only the action prefix and the *choice*-construct are allowed in the specification. Cyclic behavior is expressed through recursive process invocations. Example 8.3/12 describes the (successful) XDT connection set up in the monolithic style. Note that the entire behavior at the service interface is described by this process. Gate *S* represents the sender SAP, gate *R* the receiver SAP.

> **process** *XDT_connect* [*S,R*]: **exit**:=
>   *S!XDATrequ*; *R!XDATind*; *S!XDATconf*; **exit**
> **endproc**

Example 8.3/12: Monolithic style

Each LOTOS specification can be translated into a monolithic representation (cp. Examples 8.3/2 and 8.3/3 for this). The monolithic style is recommended as an initial step for the development of a specification. Its use for the description of more complex systems is less appropriate due to the lack of internal structure.

Constraint-oriented style

The constraint-oriented style describes the behavior of the system by several sub-processes which are related to each other by means of parallel composition and a constraint (cp. Section 7.7). Here independent parallelism (interleaving) denotes an OR operation to represent alternative behavior and synchronizing parallelism an AND operation to express existing dependencies. The constraint-oriented style supports separation of local and remote constraints. It is particularly recommended therefore for the early design phase, e.g., for the service specification. Example 8.3/13 contains the constraint oriented variant of the successful XDT connection set up of Example 8.3/12. The two processes *local_S* and *local_R* describe the local behavior at the respective service access points S and R. The process *global_SR* specifies global dependencies between the two processes.

process *XDT_connect[S,R]*: **exit** :=
   (*local_S[S]* ||| *local_R[R]*)
   |||
   (*global_SR[S,R]*)
   where
      process *local_S[S]*:**exit** :=
      S!XDATrequ; *S!XDATconf*; **exit**
   endproc
      process *local_R[R]*: **exit**:=
      R!XDATind; **exit**
   endproc
   process *global_SR[S,R]*: **exit** :=
      S!XDATrequ; *R!XDATind*; *S!XDATconf*; **exit**
   endproc
endproc

Example 8.3/13: Constraint-oriented style

State-oriented style
   The state-oriented style supports the explicit representation of system states, which is unusual in LOTOS specifications, including the events that trigger the transitions. The state-oriented representation is applied as a preliminary step for transferring the specification into an implementation specification. Example 8.3/14) shows the XDT connection set up in this style.

type *StateType* **is** *Boolean*
sorts *State*
opns *open*: →*State*
   remote: →*State*
   closed: →*State*
   _==_: *State, State*: →*Bool*
endtype

process XDT_*connect[S,R]* (*st*: *State*): **exit**:=
   [*st* == *closed*] → *S!XDATrequ*; XDT_*connect[S,R](remote)*; **exit**
   [] [*st* == *remote*] → *R!XDATind*; XDT_*connect[S,R](open)*; **exit**
   [] [*st* == *open*] → *S!XDATconf*; **exit**
endproc

Example 8.3/14: State-oriented style

   The state-oriented style, like the monolithic style, describes the behavior of the system by only one process. It also allows solely the use of the action prefix and the *choice*-construct. The system states are introduced by a data type definition.

The description lists the states and the actions which trigger the transitions, as is typical for state-oriented description. Since labeled transition systems permit only one interaction per state with the environment, only one action can occur in each state. The transition to the new state is represented by a recursive invocation of the process, where the new state is handed over as parameter.

We present still another example of the state-oriented representation: the modeling of a timer. Time is not contained in LOTOS. Example 8.3/15 shows how to model timers in a specification. Another example of timer modeling is given in Section 8.3.9 when we describe the XDT protocol in LOTOS.

type *TimerType* **is** *Boolean*
sorts T_*msg*,T_*state*
opns *start*: → T_*msg*
     stop: → T_*msg*
     timeout: → T_*msg*
     waiting:→ T_*state*
     running: → T_*state*
     _==_: T_*state*,T_*state* → *Bool*
eqns ofsort Bool
     waiting == *waiting* = *true*;
     waiting == *running* = *false*;
     running == *waiting* = *false*;
     running == *running* = *true*;
endtype (* TimerMsgType *)

process *timer*[T](*st*:T_*state*): **exit**:=
     [*st* == *waiting*] → T!*start*; *Timer*[T](*running*)
     [] [*st* == *running*] →T!*stop*; *Timer*[T](*waiting*)
     [] *i*; T!*timeout*; **exit**
endproc (* timer *)

Example 8.3/15: Modeling of a timer in the state-oriented style

Resource-oriented style

The resource-oriented style supports likewise an implementation-oriented representation that describes both the behavior observable from the environment and interactions between system components. It refines the constraint-oriented representation by an internal structuring which permits it to identify the system components – the **abstract resources** – and their interfaces. Each resource is defined by their internal and external interactions. The resources are implemented separately and can consequently be described in another style, e.g., monolithic or state-oriented. The internal communication uses internal gates (*hidden gates*). The observable (external) behavior of the system is represented by parallel composition of the abstract resources. The resource-oriented description can be gradually refined until the specified resources can be mapped onto pre-defined implementation structures.

Finally example 8.4/16 shows the modeling of the successful XDT connection establishment in the resource oriented representation[3]. In contrast to the constraint-oriented description, the global behavior between the two service access points is now enforced by the use of the internal gate *SR* through which the processes *Sender* and *Receiver* synchronize. Another variant would be the introduction of a further process *Association* as in the constraint-oriented variant which connects the two processes Sender and *Receiver* and thus models the behavior of the service provider. This variant would be useful for a complete description of the XDT service specification.

process XDT_*connect*[*S,R*]: **exit**:=
hide *SR* **in**
   Sender[*S,SR*] | [*SR*] | *Receiver*[*SR,R*]
where
   process *Sender*[*S,SR*]: **exit**:=
      S!XDATrequ; *SR!XDATrequ*; *S!XDATconf*; **exit**
   endproc
   process *Receiver*[*SR,R*]: **exit**:=
      SR!XDATrequ; *R!XDATind*; **exit**
   endproc
endproc

Example 8.3/16: Resource-oriented style

8.3.9 Example

We conclude the introduction to LOTOS with a specification of the XDT protocol in *Full* LOTOS as we did for SDL and MSC. The description comprises the service and the protocol specification, where we consider in the protocol specification as in the SDL specification only the virtual communication between the protocol entities.

Service specification

The XDT service specification describes the behavior at the service interface with the service access points *Sender_SAP* and *Receiver_SAP*, for short *S* and *R*. The specification uses the resource-oriented style because it allows a more detailed representation of the causal dependencies between the interactions at the service access points.

---

[3] The resource-oriented style is actually not used for the service specification because the protocol only determines the implementation of the service. We use this style here to demonstrate all specification styles using the same example.

The specification consists of three main processes: *sender*, *association*, and receiver (see Figure 8.3/5). They are linked as follows:

sender[S,SA] |[SA]| association[SA,RA] |[RA]| receiver[R,RA].

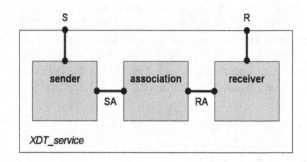

Figure 8.3/5: Structure of the LOTOS XDT service specification

The processes *sender* and *receiver* describe the exchange of the service primitives at the gates *S* and *R*. They contain two sub-processes CONNECT and DATA TRANSFER which represent the protocol phases. The latter are described monolithically. The process *association* has a similar function to the *cause*-statement in our model language (cp. Section 1.3). It connects the two service access points and transfers the data of the *XDATrequ* primitive from the sender to the receiver, where they are passed to the receiver by an *XDATind* primitive. The process *association* is connected with the processes *sender* and *receiver* by the non-visible gates *SA* and *RA*. It is also specified monolithically.

Two data types are introduced: *DataType* and *SPType*. The type *DataType* describes placeholders for the user data transferred by the XDT service. *SPType* defines the service primitives and functions for their handling. Moreover, the data types *Boolean* and *NaturalNumber* are used from the standard library. We extend the data type *NaturalNumber* by the relations = and >. Additionally, we introduce the constants 1 and 2 for use as sequence numbers as in the other specifications. We need this extension though only in the protocol specification.

The LOTOS XDT service and protocol specification differ in still another aspect from the XDT specifications in other FDTs presented in this book. The specifications describe not only the expected events at each interaction point but also reactions to unexpected events. For this, identification functions are introduced, e.g., *IsXDATrequ*, *IsXDATind* etc. which deliver the value *true* if the expected event occurs. This representation increases the robustness of the specification because it avoids deadlocks concerning unexpected events.

specification XDT-Service[S,R]: **noexit**
library
    Boolean, NaturalNumber
endlib
                                                (* DATA TYPE DEFINITION *)
type Ext_Nat **is** NaturalNumber
opns 1: $\rightarrow$ Nat
       2: $\rightarrow$ Nat
      _==_ : Nat,Nat $\rightarrow$ Bool
      _>_   : Nat,Nat $\rightarrow$ Bool
eqns forall a, b: Nat
ofsort Bool

a	==	a	= true;
succ(a)	==	0	= false;
0	==	succ(a)	= false;
succ(a)	==	succ(b)	= a == b;
a	>	a	= false;
succ(a)	>	0	= true;
0	>	succ(a)	= false;
succ(a)	>	succ(b)	= a > b;

endtype (* Ext_Nat *)

type DataType **is**   (* Place holder for user data   *)
sorts Data
opns data1,data2,data3 : $\rightarrow$ Data
      data   : $\rightarrow$ Data
endtype (* DataType *)

type SPType **is** DataType,Boolean,NaturalNumber   (* XDT service primitives   *)
sorts X_sp
opns XDATrequ   : Nat,Nat,Bool,Data $\rightarrow$ X_sp
      XDATind   : Nat,Nat,Bool,Data $\rightarrow$ X_sp
      XDATconf   : Nat,Nat $\rightarrow$ X_sp
      XABORTind   : Nat $\rightarrow$ X_sp
      XBREAKind   : Nat $\rightarrow$ X_sp
      XDISind   : Nat $\rightarrow$ X_sp
      transport   : X_sp $\rightarrow$ X_sp
                           (* Transport/Conversion XDATrequ $\rightarrow$ XDATind   *)
      map   : X_sp $\rightarrow$ Nat
                           (* Mapping service primitive $\rightarrow$ natural number   *)

IsXDATrequ   : X_sp → Bool
                  (* Identification function, which delivers *true* if   *)
                  (* the service primitive is XDATrequ   *)
IsXDATind   : X_sp → Bool
                  (*Identification function for XDATind   *)
CONN   : X_sp → Nat
                  (* Function for accessing parameter *conn*   *)
DATA   : X_sp → Data
                  (* Function for accessing the data part   *)
EOM   : X_sp → Bool
                  (* Function for accessing the parameter *eom*   *)

eqns forall c: Nat, d: Data, e: Bool, s: X_sp
ofsort X_sp
  transport(XDATrequ(c,d,b))   = XDATind(c,d,b);
ofsort Nat
  map(XDATrequ(c,s,e,d))   = 0;
  map(XDATind(c,s,e,d))   = succ(0);
  map(XDATconf(c,s))   = succ(succ(0));
  map(XABORTind(c))   = succ(succ(succ(0)));
  map(XBREAKind(c))   = succ(succ(succ(succ(0))));
  map(XDISind(c))   = succ(succ(succ(succ(succ(0)))));
ofsort Bool
  EOM(XDATrequ(c,s,e,d))   = e;
  EOM(XDATind(c,s,e,d))   = e;
  IsXDATrequ(s)   = map(s) == 0;
  IsXDATind(s)   = map(s) == succ(0);
ofsort Data
  DATA(XDATrequ(c,s,e,d))   = d;
  DATA(XDATind(c,s,e,d))   = d;
ofsort Nat
  CONN(XDATrequ(c,s,e,d))   = c;
  CONN(XDATind(c,s,e,d))   = c;
endtype (* SPType *)
                              (* BEHAVIOR AT THE SERVICE INTERFACE *)
behaviour
  hide SA,RA **in**
    sender[S,SA] |[SA]| association [SA,RA] |[RA]| receiver[R,RA]
  where
    process sender[u,v]: **exit**:=   (* Behavior at Sender-SAP   *)
    CONNECT[u,v](0) >> **accept** conn: Nat **in**
                              DATA_TRANSFER[u,v](conn,2,eom,false)

where
   process CONNECT[u,v](conn:Nat): **exit**(Nat):=   (* Connection set up *)
   u?sp:X_sp; ([IsXDATrequ(sp)]
                 → (v!sp   (* XDATrequ to *association* *)
                      u!XDATconf(conn,1); (* Set up confirmed *)
                      exit(conn)
                  [] u!XABORTind(conn);
                      (* Abandon connection set up   *)
                      CONNECT[u,v](0)
)
             [] [not(IsXDATrequ(sp))] → CONNECT[u,v](0)
                         (* ignore other events *)
)
   endproc (* CONNECT *)

   process DATA_TRANSFER[u,v](conn,sequ:Nat;eom,break:Bool): **exit**:=
                              (* Data transmission *)
    [(not(break)) and (not(eom))]
      → u?sp:X_sp;
        ([IsXDATrequ(sp)]→
           (v!sp   (* XDATrequ to *association* *)
            u!XDATconf(conn,sequ)
            DATA_TRANSFER[u](conn,succ(sequ),EOM(sp),false)
                      (* Data transmission *)
)
          [] [not(IsXDATrequ(sp))] → DATA_TRANSFER[u,v](conn,sequ,
                                 eom,break)
                        (* ignore other events *)
)
    [] v?XBREAKind(conn);   (* Break   *)
      u!XBREAKind(conn);
      DATA_TRANSFER[u,v](conn,sequ,EOM(sp),true)
    [] [break] →u!XDATconf(conn,sequ);   (* End of break   *)
          DATA_TRANSFER[u,v](conn,succ(sequ),EOM(sp),false)
    [] [(not(break)) and eom] → u!XDISind(conn); (* Regular connect. release*)
                      CONNECT[u,v](0)
    [] v?XABORTind(conn)   (*Abandon connection   *)
      u!XABORTind(conn);
      CONNECT[u,v](0)
   endproc (* DATA_TRANSFER *)
endproc (* sender *)

process receiver[v,u]: **noexit**:=   (* BEHAVIOR AT RECEIVER-SAP   *)
CONNECT[v,u] >> **accept** conn:Nat **in** DATA_TRANSFER[v,u](conn)
where
  process CONNECT[v,u]: **exit**(Nat):=   (* Connection set up *)
  v?sp:X_sp;
  ([IsXDATind(sp)] → u!sp   (* XDATind_1   *)
                    DATA_TRANSFER[u](CONN(sp))
                                                          (* Connection set up *)
  [] [not(IsXDATind(sp))]→ CONNECT[v,u]   (* ignore other events *)
)
  endproc (* CONNECT *)

  process DATA_TRANSFER[v,u](conn: Nat): **noexit**:= (* Data transmission *)
  v?sp:X_sp;
  ([IsXDATind(sp)]
          → ([EOM(sp)] →u!sp   (* XDATind to receiver *)
                        u!XDISind(conn);   (* Regular conn. release *)
                        CONNECT[v,u]
          [] [not(EOM(sp))] → u!sp   (* XDATind to receiver *)
                        DATA_TRANSFER[v,u] (conn)
                                                          (* continue data transfer *)
)
  [] IsXABORT(sp));   (* Abandon transmission *)
     CONNECT[v,u](0)
  [] [not(IsXDATind(sp) or IsXABORT(sp))]
          → DATA_TRANSFER[v,u] (conn: Nat)   (* ignore other events   *)
)
  endproc (* DATA_TRANSFER *)
endproc (* receiver *)

process association[s,r]: **noexit**:=   (* BEHAVIOR TRANSPORT MEDIUM *)
s?sp: X_sp; ([IsXDATrequ(sp)]
          → (r!transport(sp);   (* Forwarding XDATrequ to *R*   *)
              association[s,r]
)
          [] [not(IsXDATrequ(sp))] →association[s,r] (* ignore other events *)
)
[] *i*; s!XBREAKind(conn); association[s,r]   (* Internal event: *break*   *)
[] *i*; s!XABORTind(conn);   (* Internal event: *abort*   *)
   r!XABORTind(conn); association[s,r]
[] s?sp: X_sp; association[s,r]   (* ignore other primitives at *S* *)
  endproc (* association *)
endspec (* XDT-Service *)

Protocol specification
The protocol specification adds three new data type definitions: *PduType*, *BufferType*, and *TimerMsgType*. The XDT PDUs are specified in the data type *PduType*, while the data type *BufferType* describes the buffer for the *DT*-copies and the associated operations. The last data type *TimerMsgType* defines timer events. Moreover, we introduce the signals *ack_N*, *go_back_N*, *abort*, and *end* for internal communication between the processes *transfer_s* and *ack_handler* at sender side.

specification XDT-Protocol[S,R]: **noexit**
library
    Boolean,Nat_Number
endlib
type Ext_Nat **is** NaturalNumber   (* analogous to service specification *)
   . . .
endtype (* Ext_Nat *)
type DataType **is**   (* analogous to service specification *)
   . . .
endtype (* DataType *)
type SpType **is** DataType,Boolean,NaturalNumber
                             (* analogous to service specification *)

   . . .
endtype (* SpType *)

type PduType **is** DataType,Boolean,NaturalNumber   (* XDT PDUs *)
sorts X_pdu
opns

DT	: Nat,Ext_Nat,Bool,Data	→ X_pdu
ACK	: Nat,Ext_Nat	→ X_pdu
ABO	: Nat	→ X_pdu
map	: X_pdu	→ Nat
IsDT	: X_pdu	→ Bool
IsACK	: X_pdu	→ Bool
IsABO	: X_pdu	→ Bool
SEQU	: X_pdu	→ Nat
EOM	: X_pdu	→ Bool
generate_conn:		→ Nat
CONN	: X_pdu	→ Nat
DATA	: X_pdu	→ Data

eqns forall c,n:Nat, e:Bool, d:Data, p:X_pdu
ofsort Nat
    map(DT(c,n,e,d))   = 0;
    map(ACK(c,n))   = succ(0);
    map(ABO(c))   = succ(succ(0));
    SEQU(DT(c,n,e,d)) = n;

```
     SEQU(ACK(c,n))      = n;
     CONN(DT(c,n,e,d))   = c;
     CONN(ACK(c,n))      = c;
ofsort Data
     DATA(DT(c,n,e,d))   = d;
ofsort Bool
     EOM(DT(c,n,e,d))    = e;
     IsDT(p)             = map(p) == 0;
     IsACK(p)            = map(p) == succ(0);
     IsABO(p)            = map(p) == succ(succ(0));
endtype (* PduType *)
```

```
type SignalType is
sorts X_signal
opns
     ack_N:          → X_signal
     go_back_N:      → X_signal
     abort :         → X_signal
     end   :         → X_signal
endtype (* SignalType *)
```

The buffer for the *DT* copies is defined by the data type *BufferType*. It defines the operations for storing and removing the *DT* PDUs as well as for querying the current allocation. The buffer contains maximally five *DT* PDUs.

```
type BufferType is PduType,Boolean,NaturalNumber
sorts X_buffer
opns empty     :                        → X_buffer
     put       : X_buffer,Nat,X_pdu     → X_buffer
     get       : X_buffer,Nat           → X_pdu
     remove    : X_buffer,Nat           → X_buffer
     size      : X_buffer               → Nat
     IsEMPTY   : X_buffer               → Bool
     IsFULL    : X_buffer               → Bool
     maxbuffer :                        → Nat
eqns forall p: X_pdu, b: X_buffer, n, k: Nat
ofsort X_buffer
     remove(empty,k)                    = empty;
     get(empty,k)                       = empty
ofsort X_pdu
     get(empty,k)                       = 0;
     n == k    ⇒ get(put(b,n,p),k)      = p
ofsort Nat
     size(empty)                        = 0;
```

size(put(b,n,p))	= succ(size(b));
size(get(b,k))	= pred(size(b))

ofsort Bool

IsEMPTY(empty)	= true;
IsEMPTY(put(b,n,p))	= false;
IsFULL(b)	= size(b) == maxbuffer

endtype (* BufferType *)

Time cannot be directly represented in LOTOS as we already discussed above. The basic functionality of a timer (*start, stop, time-out*) can be modeled, however. For this purpose, we introduce the type *TimerMsgType* which describes the well-known timer functions. The timer process is described further below.

type TimerType **is** Boolean
sorts T_event
opns start   :   → T_event
       stop   :   → T_event
       timeout :   → T_event
       _==_   : T_event,T_event → Bool
eqns
  ofsort Bool
  start == start   = true;
  start == stop   = false;
  stop == start   = false;
  stop == stop   = true;
endtype (* TimerMsgType *)

The LOTOS specification of the XDT protocol follows the structure of the reference specification in Section 2.3. It is written in the resource-oriented style. The specification is divided into the three processes *sender, medium,* and *receiver* (see Figure 8.3/6) that are connected by the internal gates *SM* and *RM*:

hide SM,RM **in**
    sender[S,SM] |[SM]| medium[SM,RM] |[RM]| receiver[RM,R]

The **process** *sender* with gate *S* to the service user describes the sender behavior, the process *receiver* with gate *R* correspondingly the *receiver* behavior. The process *medium* models the communication between the entities. The processes *sender* and *receiver* subdivide according to the XDT phases into the sub-processes CONNECT and DATA_TRANSFER which are successively activated

CONNECT[u,v] >> DATA_TRANSFER[u,v].

The processes CONNECT and DATA_TRANSFER contain further processes. Figure 8.3/6 shows the process structure for the two protocol phases. We discuss these processes directly before their description.

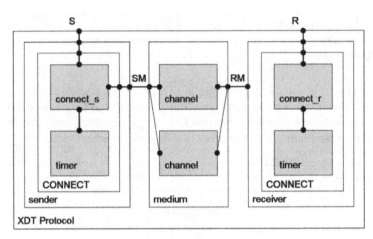

a) Process structure of the CONNECT phase

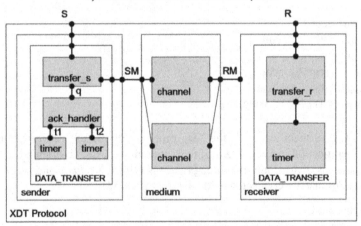

b) Process structure of the DATA_TRANSFER phase

Figure 8.3/6: Process structure of the LOTOS XDT protocol specification

behaviour   (* Protocol behavior *)
   hide SM,RM **in**
    sender[S,SM] |[SM]| medium[SM,RM] |[RM]| receiver[RM,R]
   where
    process sender[u,v]: **noexit**:=
     CONNECT[u,v] >> **accept** conn: Nat **in**
                    DATA_TRANSFER[u,v](conn,2,eom,empty)

where
  process CONNECT[u,v]: **exit**(Nat):=   (* Connection set up   *)
  hide t **in**
  connect_s[u,v,t] | [t] | timer[t]
  where
    process connect_s[u,v,T]:**exit**(Nat):=   (* SET UP AT SENDER *)
    u?sp: X_sp;
    ([IsXDATrequ(sp)] → v!DT(0,1,EOM(sp),DATA(sp));
                   T!start;   (* Timer ACK monitoring *)
                   wait[u,v,T]
                       >> **accept** conn: Nat **in exit**(conn)
    [] [not(IsXDATrequ(sp))] → CONNECT[u,v,T]
                         (* Ignore other primitives *)
    [] v?pdu:X_pdu;CONNECT[u,v,T]   (* Ignore other PDUs   *)
)
    where
      process wait[u,v,T]: **exit**(Nat):=   (* Waiting for ACK   *)
      v?pdu: X_pdu;
      ([IsACK(pdu)] → ([SEQU(pdu)==1]   (* ACK.sequ = 1   *)
                       →T!stop;
                       u!DATconf(CONN(pdu),1);
                            (* Confirm set up   *)
                       exit(conn)
                       [][not(SEQU(pdu)==1)] → wait[u,v,T]
                            (* ACK.sequ ≠ 1 *)
)
      [] [not(IsACK(pdu))] → wait[u,v,T]
)
      [] T!timeout;   (* no connection set up *)
      u!XABORTind(0);
      connect_s[u,v,T]
    endproc (* wait *)
  endproc (* connect_s *)

  process timer[T]: **noexit**:=   (* Timer modeling   *)
    waiting[T]
    where
      process waiting[T]: **noexit**:=
      T?m: T_event;
      ([m == start] → running[T]
      [] [not(m == start)] → waiting[T]
)
    endproc (* waiting *)

```
process running[T]: noexit:=
  T?m:T_event;
  (  [m == stop] → waiting[T]
     [][not(m == stop)] → running[T]
  )
  [] i;T!timeout;waiting[T]
  endproc (* running *)
endproc (* timer *)
endproc (* CONNECT *)
```

The process DATA_TRANSFER consists at sender side of the processes *transfer_s*, *ack_handler*, and *timer*. The processes *transfer_s* and *ack_handler* have the same tasks as in the reference specification in Section 2.3. Since there are no shared variables in LOTOS, all actions over the *DT*-PDU-buffer are included in process *transfer_s*, in contrast to the reference specification. For this, the processes exchange the signals *ack_N*, *go_back_N*, *abort*, and *end* via the internal gate *Q*.

```
process DATA_TRANSFER[u,v](conn,sequ:Nat,eom:Bool,b:X_buffer):
                                                        noexit:=
hide q,t1,t2 in
  transfer_s[u,v,I](conn,sequ,eom,b)|[q]|
      ack_handler[u,v,q,t1,t2](conn,sequ,0,eom) |[t1]| timer[t1] |[t2]| timer[t2]
where
  process transfer_s[u,v,q] (conn,sequ:Nat;eom:Bool;b:X_buffer):exit:=
  [(not(IsFULL(b)))]→ u?sp: X_sp;
    (  [IsXDATrequ(sp)]
        → v!DT(CONN(sp),sequ,EOM(sp),DATA(sp));  (* Sending DT *)
          [EOM(sp)] → q!sequ;
                      (* Sequence number of last DT to ack_handler *)
          (  [not(succ(size(b)) = maxbuffer)]
              →  u!XDATconf(conn,sequ);   (* Confirmation sending*)
                transfer_s[u,v,q](conn,succ(sequ),EOM(sp),
                                  put(b,succ(size(b)),DT(CONN(sp),
                                    sequ,EOM(sp),DATA(sp))))
          [] [succ(size(b)) = maxbuffer]
              → u!XBREAKind(conn)                       (* Break *)
                transfer_s[u,v,q] (conn,succ(sequ),EOM(sp),
                                  put(b,succ(size(b)),DT(CONN(sp),
                                    sequ,EOM(sp),DATA(sp))))
          )
       [][not(IsXDATrequ(sp))] → transfer_s[u,v,q](conn,sequ,eom,b)
    )
  [] q?s: X_signal;
    (  [s = ack_N] → q?n: Nat;                  (* ACK received      *)
```

                    [IsFULL(b)] → u!XDATconf(conn,sequ)
                                        (* Break terminated   *)
                        remove(b,n)   (* Remove DT copy   *)
  [] [s = go_back_N] → q?N: Nat;   (* *go back N*   *)
                    resend_DT[P](N,sequ,b)
  [] [s = abort] → **exit**   (* Abandon transmission *)
  [] [s = end] → **exit**   (* Connection released   *)
)
  where
    process resend_DT[P](N,sequ:Nat,b:X_buffer): **exit**:=   (* *go back N* *)
      [not(N > sequ)] →P!get(b,N);
                        resend_DT[P](succ(N),sequ,b)
  [][N > sequ] → **exit**
  endproc (* resend_DT *)
endproc (* transfer_s *)

process ack_handler[u,v,q,t1,t2](conn,last,N:Nat,eom:Bool):**noexit**:=
  t1(waiting)!start;   (* Start activity timer *)
  t2(waiting)!start;   (* Start timer ACK monitoring *)
  v?pdu:X_pdu;
  ([IsACK(pdu)]
      → ([SEQU(pdu) > N]
          → (t2!stop;   (* correct ACK   *)
            q!ack_N   (* ACK number to *transfer_s* *)
                    q!SEQU(pdu)-N
          ([eom and (SEQU(pdu) = last)]
                    → u!XDISind(conn); (* reg. connection release *)
                    q!end;
                    sender[u,v]
          [][not(eom and SEQU(pdu) = last)]
                    →T!start;
                    ack_handler[u,v,q,t1,t2](conn,last,SEQU(pdu),eom)
)
        [][not(SEQU(pdu) > N)] →
                        ack_handler[u,v,q,t1,t2](conn,last,N,eom)
)
    [] [IsABO(pdu)] → u!XABORTind(conn); (* Abandon transmission *)
                    q!abort;   (* *abort* signal to *transfer_s*   *)
                    sender[u,v]
)
  [] q?last;   (* Hand over sequence number of last DT *)
  ack_handler[u,v,q,t1,t2](conn,last,N,true)
  [] t2!timeout;   (* no correct ACK   *)
  q!go_back_N;   (* *go back N* signal to *transfer_s* *)

```
            q!N;
            ack_handler[u,v,q,t1,t2](conn,last,N,eom)
        [] t1!timeout;                              (* Receiver inactive  *)
            u!XABORTind(conn);           (* Sender aborts transmission   *)
            q!abort;                     (* Abort signal to transfer_s   *)
            sender[u,v]
        endproc (* ack_handler *)


        process timer[T]: noexit:= (* see CONNECT *) endproc      (* timer *)
      endproc (* DATA_TRANSFER *)
    endproc (* sender *)
```

The process **medium** models the transmission. It consists of two channels with opposite directions. During the transmission PDUs may be lost.

```
    process medium[s,r]: noexit:=
      channel[s,r] ||| channel[r,s]
      where
        process channel[s1,s2]: noexit:=
          s1?pdu:X_pdu;
          (   s2!pdu;channel[s1,s2]                      (* Sending PDU  *)
          [] i;channel[s1,s2]                            (* PDU loss     *)
          )
        endproc (* channel *)
    endproc (* medium *)
```

The process **receiver** corresponds in its structure also to the reference specification. It consists of two processes CONNECT and DATA_TRANSFER for the protocol phases between which the variables *conn* and *eom* are exchanged.

```
    process receiver[v,u]:noexit:=
    CONNECT[v,u] >> accept conn: Nat in T!start;
                                DATA_TRANSFER[v,u](conn,2)
    where
      process CONNECT[v,u]: exit(Nat):=
      hide t in
        connect_r[v,u,t] | [t] | timer[t]
      where
        process connect_r[v,u,T]: exit(Nat):=      (* CONN. SET UP RECEIVER *)
        v?pdu:X_pdu;
        (  [IsDT(pdu)] → (  [SEQU(pdu) == 1)]
                         → let conn: Nat=generate_conn in
                            (u!XDATind(conn,1,EOM(pdu),DATA(pdu));
                                (* Indication of new connection*)
                            v!ACK(conn,1);      (* ACK_1 to sender *)
```

```
                              exit(conn)
                              )
                    [][not(SEQU(pdu) == 1)] → connect_r[v,u,T]
                    )
        [][not(IsDT(pdu))] → connect_r[v,u,T]          (* Ignore other PDUs *)
        )
        endproc (* connect_r *)


        process timer[T]: noexit:= (* see sender/ CONNECT *) endproc
        endproc (* CONNECT *)

        process DATA_TRANSFER[v,u](conn,sequ:Nat):noexit:=
        hide t in
        transfer_r[v,u,t](conn,sequ) |[t]| timer[t]
        where
          process transfer_r[v,u,T](conn,sequ:Nat)
            P?pdu:X_pdu;                          (* Waiting for DT    *)
            (  [IsDT(pdu)]
                  → (  [SEQU(pdu) == sequ]        (* Correct DT        *)
                      → T!stop;
                        u!XDATind(conn,sequ,EOM(pdu),DATA(pdu));
                        v!ACK(conn,sequ);
                        (  [EOM(pdu)] → u!XDISind(conn)
                                        receiver[v,u]
                                              (* reg. connection release*)
                          [][not(EOM(pdu))]
                                        → T!start;
                                          transfer_r[v,u,T](conn,succ(sequ))
                        )
                     [][not(SEQU(pdu) == sequ)]
                          → DATA_TRANSFER[v,u](conn,sequ)
                    )
               [][not(IsDT(pdu))] → DATA_TRANSFER[v,u](conn,sequ)
            )
            []T!timeout;                          (* Order not re-established   *)
            u!XABORTind(conn);                    (*Abandon of the connection *)
            v!ABO(conn);
            receiver[v,u]
          endproc (* transfer_r *)

        process timer[T]: noexit:= (* see sender/CONNECT *) endproc
        endproc (* DATA_TRANSFER *)
     endproc (* receiver *)
  endspec (* XDT Protocol *)
```

8.3.10 Applicability

LOTOS is the only algebraic specification technique that was developed specifically for the description of protocols and distributed systems. It has achieved therefore a corresponding popularity in algebraic-minded communities, also because of its usefulness for verification and testing as we will see later. The FDT LOTOS is characterized by a relatively small and expressive set of operators that allows describing many basic features of protocols and distributed systems in a very concise manner. This is appropriate for algebraic validations and other analyses. It also leaves much freedom to the implementer.

The resulting specifications though are quite abstract. This is acceptable for small example protocols (see [Bowm 06]), but when applying LOTOS to realistic, complex protocols these abstract specifications very soon become difficult to read, to understand, and to handle. The specification of the still relatively small XDT protocol demonstrates this. Although LOTOS supports a transition-oriented specification style (cp. Section 7.3) the protocol flow is difficult to derive. There are several reasons for this. The nested process structure of the specification "blankets" the proper protocol flow. In addition, LOTOS specifications do not contain those features which protocol engineers like to have in a specification: explicit state and interaction representations, respectively. Moreover, LOTOS does not provide appropriate means for representing timers, local actions, and the data formats of service primitives and protocol data units. Especially the latter has proved impracticable for the original LOTOS definition. Therefore, complex specifications become difficult to handle. Admittedly, several case studies about successful applications of LOTOS in practice have been reported in the literature [FORTE], but mostly these studies were performed by specialists. In practical protocol developments LOTOS has attained little relevance. Its main application has been in theoretical research. LOTOS and the related process calculi represent powerful and compact means for abstract reasoning on concurrent systems, but for real protocol developments with all their complex relations and detailed dependencies it is less suited.

8.4   Descriptive specification – Example: cTLA

After looking at different constructive techniques we now briefly give an example of a more descriptive language: **cTLA** (*compositional Temporal Logic of Actions*) which goes back to Herrmann [Herr 00]. cTLA is a variant of Lamport's *Temporal Logic of Actions* (TLA) [Lamp 94]. It is a descriptive specification technique that is extended by elements of imperative programming languages. Therefore it is more a hybrid concept rather than a pure descriptive language. In contrast to other formal description techniques introduced in this chapter, cTLA was designed with the objective of explicit verification support. A cTLA specification is composed of processes which can be used to describe service and protocol features and functions. These processes can be combined with other processes to model more complex service and protocol behavior. With each of these definitions, a set of constraints or desirable properties is specified which have to be fulfilled by the protocol. The preservation of these constraints in the composition can be proved formally.

8.4.1 Basic concepts

cTLA describes state transition systems in a process-like specification style (cp. Section 7.3). Processes are distinguished into simple and compositional processes.

Simple process
A simple process serves for modeling single system resources or constraints. Its structure is defined in a process type definition in a programming language-like syntax (see Examples 8.4/1). The process header contains the name of the process and a list of process parameters. The parameters enable one to create several instances of the process type. As in programming languages, first local constants and variables are defined. The variables declared determine the state space of the process. After the keyword **INIT** the initial state of the process is specified. The operator ≙ is used for this as well as for other definitions. The action definition part begins with the keyword **ACTIONS**. It defines the actions which belong to this process. An action is a predicate about a pair of the current state of a variable and its next state. The latter is referenced by primed variable identifiers, e.g., *channel'*. The actions model the set of possible state transitions of the process. Actions may have parameters to describe data transfer between processes.

> **PROCESS** communicate(pdu_type: ANY)
> **CONSTANTS** FREE ∈ pdu_type
> **BODY**
>   **VARIABLES** channel: pdu_type
>   **INIT** ≙ channel = FREE
>   **ACTIONS**
>   send(sd: pdu_type) ≙ channel = FREE ∧ channel' = sd;
>   receive(rd: pdu_type) ≙ channel ≠ FREE ∧ channel = rd ∧ channel' = FREE;
> **END**

Example 8.4/1: Simple process for sending and receiving PDUs

Example 8.4/1 defines a process *communication* with actions for sending and receiving PDUs. The medium is modeled by the variable *channel* which is of *pdu_type*. In the initial state this variable is set to FREE indicating that the channel is free. When a PDU is sent, the channel must be free. After execution the channel contains the PDU.

PROCESS timer
BODY
   VARIABLES
     state: {"idle","active"}
     t,ti: natural
   INIT $\triangleq$ state = "idle" $\wedge$ t = 0;
   ACTIONS
     start(tov: natural) $\triangleq$ state = "idle" $\wedge$ state' = "active" $\wedge$ ti'=tov;

     reset $\triangleq$ state = "active" $\wedge$ state' = "idle" $\wedge$ t' = 0;

     time-out(to: bool) $\triangleq$ state = "active" $\wedge$ t $\geq$ ti $\wedge$ state' = "idle" $\wedge$ to = true $\wedge$ t' = 0;

     tick $\triangleq$ state = "active" $\wedge$ t' = t+1 $\wedge$ state' = state;

END

Example 8.4/2: Timer process

Example 8.4/2 contains the definition of a timer process with the operations we introduced in Section 2.2.4. The respective actions do not describe the procedures themselves. They formulate conditions that have to be fulfilled when the actions are executed. The additional action *tick* was introduced to express the progress of time. Note that parameters are not variables but only placeholders for values, e.g., to = true. Here no primed variable is used because it does not indicate a new state.

Compositional processes

Compositional cTLA processes are used to describe the behavior of systems and sub-systems as compositions of cTLA processes that cooperate by means of synchronously executed process actions. The processes which compose the compositional process are listed after **PROCESSES**. For each process, an instantiation is created which is represented by a name. Example 8.4/3 shows a fragment of the compositional process *connect_s* for setting up an XDT connection. The complete process is given in Section 8.4.4. We assume in this example that a data type definition for the *DT*-PDU is imported from another process definition.

In the action part **ACTIONS** of the compositional process definition the desired properties and constraints are defined in a descriptive manner using the logical operators conjunction ($\wedge$) and disjunction ($\vee$). The operator = means that after the execution of this action the expression of the right side equals the expression of the left side. The constructs, operators, expressions, and symbols are reused from the Temporal Logic of Actions [Lamp 94].

PROCESS connect_s
IMPORT DT-PDU
BODY
  VARIABLES
    state: {"idle","wait connection","connected"};
  INIT ≙ state = "idle";
  PROCESSES
    C: communicate(pdu: pdu_type);
    t: timer(ti: natural);
    ...
  ACTIONS
    Con-Init(pdu: pdu_type) ≙ pdu.type = "DT" $\land$ pdu.sequ = 1 $\land$ state = "idle"
                  $\land$ state′= "wait connection" $\land$ C.send(pdu) $\land$ t.start(5);
    ...
END

Example 8.4/3: Compositional process *connect_s*

8.4.2 Language elements

A process type definition in cTLA has a fixed structure (see Figure 8.4/1). Each section begins with a defined keyword. Some of the elements are optionally.

PROCESS
IMPORT
CONSTANTS
BODY
  VARIABLES
  INIT
  PROCESSES
  ACTIONS
END

Figure 8.4/1: Segments of a cTLA process type definition

PROCESS
Processes are described in a process type definition which is enclosed by the keywords **PROCESS** and **END**. The process header may contain formal type declarations, which are replaced by concrete ones when instantiating the process, e.g.,

PROCESS communicate(pdu_type: ANY)

  . . .

END

IMPORT

cTLA supports the importing of definitions contained in other process type definitions. These processes have to be listed after **IMPORT,** e.g.,

IMPORT timer, address;

Similarly to LOTOS, cTLA demands the definition of all symbols, constants, data types, and functions used in the specification. Such definitions may be imported from previously defined modules.

CONSTANTS

Constants can be introduced directly in the process type definition in the **CONSTANTS** segment, e.g.,

CONSTANTS
Maxpdu $\triangleq$ 10;
DTpdu $\triangleq$ [type = "DT", conn: int; sequ: int; eom: bool; data: byte];

A constant may be an identifier which is equal to a certain type or it may refer to a data structure. The latter can be used to define the structure of service primitives and protocol data units.

BODY

The proper specification of the process type is contained after this keyword.

VARIABLES

The variables used in the process have to be declared in this section. These variables form the state space of the process. The variables are only accessible inside the **BODY**-part. The syntax of the variable definition corresponds to definitions in programming languages, e.g.,

VARIABLES
source-addr: address;
dest-addr: address;
conn: natural;
sequ: natural;
eom: bool;
data: [natural $\rightarrow$ byte];

Each variable is associated with a data type. cTLA distinguishes system-defined and user-defined data types. The former are data types, such as *int, natural, short, bit, byte,* and *bool,* which can be used by default. Furthermore, enumeration types are allowed. User-defined data types can be imported from previously defined modules.

INIT

The key word **INIT** specifies the initial state of the process by assigning initial values to the variables, e.g.,

INIT ≜ state = "idle" ∧ phase = "CONNECT" ∧ to = false;

A cTLA process always identifies the state defined in **INIT** as the beginning of the execution.

PROCESSES

The section **PROCESSES** appears only in compositional process definitions. It declares the process instances which are used in the composition. A process instance is defined by a name and the respective process type, e.g.,

PROCESSES
C: communicate(pdu_type);
t: timer;

In system action definitions the actions defined in the processes can be accessed by the instance name followed by the related action, e.g.,

C.send(sd);
t.start(5).

ACTIONS

The action definition part describes the actions belonging to the process. An action describes a transition transferring the system from a given state to the next state. The current state is referenced by variables, the next state by primed variables, e.g.,

ACTIONS
Con-Init(pdu: pdu_type) ≜ pdu.type = "DT" ∧ pdu.sequ = 1 ∧ state = "idle"
∧ state'= "wait connection" ∧ C.send(pdu) ∧ t.start(5);

Action definitions can contain actual parameters. The variables, the initial state (**INIT**), and the actions of a process define a state transition system which describes a set of state sequences. A state sequence starting from the initial state models a certain process behavior. An action describes a number of transitions [Herr 00].

8.4.3 Formal semantics

Like the other formal description techniques introduced in this chapter, cTLA possesses a formal semantics. It is directly based on TLA [Lamp 94]. Unlike other FDTs which concentrate more on a structured and readable formal description, cTLA was designed with the objective of explicit verification support. The close relation to TLA enables TLA-based verification.

Each cTLA process instance corresponds to a TLA formula. This correspondence defines the formal semantics of cTLA. Formally, a cTLA process, whether simple or compositional, can be expressed through a canonical TLA formula. The following example shows the canonical formula C for the process *Timer* defined above:

$$C \triangleq \text{INIT} \wedge \square \, [\, \exists \, to, t \in natural: \text{start}(t) \vee \text{reset}() \vee \text{time-out}(to)]_{(to,t)}$$

The formula states that the predicate INIT holds in the first state of every state sequence modeled by C and that the expression which follows the conjunction operator has to hold in all states of all state sequences. The expression $[pp]_{(to,t)}$ defines that either the predicate pp holds or a **stuttering step** takes place in which the annexed variables do not change their state, i.e., $to' = to$ and $t' = t$. Stuttering steps are needed for refinement proofs. The actions may have parameters of the given variable types. Accordingly, a cTLA process specifies that the initial process state fulfills INIT and that any state change must either comply with an action or be a stuttering step.

The TLA formulae which are derived from cTLA formulae possess certain constraints to facilitate coupling with cTLA actions. So a process may only have access to variables defined within the process. Actions have to be uniquely identified to be used as references to process actions in compositional processes. Furthermore, some rules are introduced to guarantee liveness [Herr 00].

8.4.4 Example

In order to demonstrate the cTLA description principle we show here a fragment of the XDT protocol specification, namely the connection set up phase. According to Section 2.3, the set up phase is formed by the processes *connect_s* and *connect_r* which are shown here. We assume here that the simple cTLA process *response* for responding service primitives as well as the service primitive and PDU types (*sp_type*, *pdu_type*) have been defined in other processes. Further we use in this example two standard functions defined in cTLA: *unchanged* to indicate the variables which do not change when an action is executed, and *stutter* to express stuttering steps.

PROCESS connect_s
IMPORT SP, PDU;   ! Import of service primitive and
  BODY   ! PDU definitions
  VARIABLES
    state: {"idle","wait connection","connected"};
    phase: ("CONNECT", "DATA TRANSFER");
    to: bool;
  INIT $\triangleq$ state = "idle" $\wedge$ phase = "CONNECT" $\wedge$ to = false;
  PROCESSES
    C: communicate(pdu_type);
    t: timer;
    R: response(sp_type)   ! Service primitive to user
  ACTIONS
    Con-Init(XDATrequ: sp_type, DT: pdu_type) $\triangleq$
         XDATrequ.sequ = 1 $\wedge$ state = "idle" $\wedge$ state' = "wait connection"
         $\wedge$ C.send(DT) $\wedge$ t.start(5) $\wedge$ unchanged(phase,to);
    Con-Conf(XDATconf: sp_type, ACK: pdu_type) $\triangleq$
         C.receive(ACK) $\wedge$ ACK.sequ = 1 $\wedge$ state = "wait connection" $\wedge$ t.reset
         $\wedge$ R.response(XDATconf) $\wedge$ state' = "connected"
         $\wedge$ phase = "DATA TRANSFER" $\wedge$ unchanged(to);
    Con-Abort(XABORTind: sp_type) $\triangleq$
         t.time-out(true) $\wedge$ state = "wait connection" $\wedge$ state' = "idle"
         $\wedge$ R.response(XABORTind) $\wedge$ unchanged(phase);
    Tick $\triangleq$ t.tick;
END

PROCESS connect_r
IMPORT SP, PDU;   ! Import of service primitive and
  BODY   ! PDU definitions
  VARIABLES
    state: {"idle", "connected"};
    phase: ("CONNECT", "DATA TRANSFER");
  INIT $\triangleq$ state = "idle" $\wedge$ phase = "CONNECT";
  PROCESSES
    C: communicate(pdu_type);
    R: response(sp_type)
  ACTIONS
    Con-Init(DT, ACK: pdu_type, XDATind: sp_type) $\triangleq$
         C.receive(DT) $\wedge$ DT.sequ = 1 $\wedge$ state = "idle" $\wedge$ R.response(XDATind)
         $\wedge$ C.send(ACK) $\wedge$ state'= "connected" $\wedge$ phase = "DATA TRANSFER";
END

The two process definitions above describe the properties that the two entities should fulfill regarding the connection set up. To complete the specification we have to specify the complete system. This is done below with the definition of the process *connect* including the process instances of the XDT entities *XS* and *XR*. Since we only consider the connection set up in this example, *XS* and *XR* are instantiations of the processes *connect_s* and *connect_r*, respectively. The actions defined in *connect* establish the relation between the respective processes defined in *connect_s* and *connect_r*. In two definitions in *XR* only the stutter function is performed. This indicates that there are no state changes in *XR*, only in *XS*. Furthermore, we introduce a process for the global time *sTick*. This can be defined in cTLA as an internal invisible action using the key word **INTERNAL**.

PROCESS connect
IMPORT SP, PDU;
BODY
   PROCESSES
      XS: connect_s;
      XR: connect_r;
   ACTIONS
      sCon-Init(XDATrequ, XDATind: sp_type, DT, ACK: pdu_type) $\triangleq$
         XS.Con-Init(XDATrequ: sp_type, DT: pdu_type)
         $\wedge$ XR.Con-Init(DT, ACK: pdu_type, XDATind: sp_type);
      sCon-Conf(XDATconf: sp_type, ACK: pdu_type)) $\triangleq$
         XS.Con-Conf(XDATconf: sp_type, ACK: pdu_type) $\wedge$ XR.stutter;
      sCon-Abort(XABORTind: sp_type) $\triangleq$
         XS.Con-Abort(XABORTind: sp_type) $\wedge$ XR.stutter;
   INTERNAL
      sTick $\triangleq$ XS.tick $\wedge$ XR.stutter;
   END

8.4.5 Applicability

cTLA is the only descriptive specification technique that was developed especially for the description of communication protocols and distributed systems. The significant advantage of cTLA is its explicit support of verification. As a temporal event-based system, it is possible to rewrite cTLA processes in a canonical form. This form can be used to verify the system behaviors by introducing an appropriate verification mechanism. It is also possible to formulate properties – safety and liveness ones – and to prove whether they hold in the specification. cTLA possesses a relatively small set of language elements. The basic elements are processes. Simple processes can be composed to make more complex ones. Properties of the simple processes are transferred to the composed process by superposition. The correctness of the properties of the composed processes can be proved by means of a theorem prover [Herr 02] or model checker [Krae 09a]. cTLA supports the description of both services and protocols. It allows one to verify that the specified service is really provided by the specified protocol (see Section 11.1). Of course the elaboration of a cTLA specification for a complex protocol is cumbersome because many processes have to be defined and verified. For that reason, a framework for transfer protocols which contains a lot of verified components has been developed [Herr 00, 02].

The use of cTLA in practical protocol design is limited. This is because the user needs experience in cTLA, its semantics TLA, and related verification methods. This is often not a given. It is also difficult for a developer unfamiliar with cTLA to trace the developed modules. Like LOTOS, cTLA does not support those features which protocol engineers like to have in a specification: an explicit representation of major states and interactions. Moreover, cTLA does not provide appropriate means for representing local actions and access to data structures. cTLA specifications are quite abstract. They leave much freedom to the implementer, but they also require experience of how to derive implementations. For that reason, cTLA can be considered more as a supplementary technique which is especially useful for verification purposes. Due to its program-like structure, it can also be used as a base for model transformations, e.g., onto programming languages like JAVA and C++, and verification languages like PROMELA.

8.5 Data format description – Example: ASN.1

The data formats of the service primitives and protocol data units used in services and protocols are described separately from the protocol procedures. As we have seen in the preceding sections the formal description techniques use different methods for the data format definition. SDL uses an abstract data type notation; LOTOS the more sophisticated ACT ONE. Estelle used Pascal data types, which proved, however, too implementation-oriented. Nowadays the **abstract syntax notation ASN.1** is often used for the description of data formats. ASN.1 was originally developed in the context of the ITU-T X.400 message handling system for solving the data conversion problem of applications in heterogeneous environments (see below). It was integrated into the OSI reference model. Later it became a widely accepted standard for describing data formats in protocols. It has even been kept alive in the today's TCP/IP world. SDL and the test notations TTCN-2/-3 (see Section 14.6) adopted ASN.1. For that reason, ASN.1 should not remain unmentioned in an introduction to *Protocol Engineering*.

8.5.1 Basic concepts

ASN.1 (*Abstract Syntax Notation One*) aimed originally at converting machine-specific encodings so that data are consistently interpreted in heterogeneous networks. Later it was used more and more for data type descriptions. The development began in the 1980s. ASN.1 was first defined in the ITU-T X.409 standard, which belonged to the X.400 message handling series. From 1984 onwards it was considered the notation-of-choice for the specification of OSI application layer protocols. Two years later it became an ISO standard, and again two years later a self-contained ITU-T standard. The standard was revised several times in 1989/ 90, 1994, 1997, and 2002.

The ASN.1 standard consists of two parts: the actual *abstract syntax notation*, now defined in ITU-T recommendation X.680ff and ISO/IEC 8824ff, and the *encoding rule*, which define how ASN.1 data values are encoded at bit level for transfer syntaxes. There are various encoding rules. They are defined in the ITU-T X.690ff and ISO/IEC 8825ff standards [ISO 8824], [ISO 8825]. The first encoding rules were the *Basic Encoding Rules* (BER). The division of ASN.1 into two levels is due to the conversion approach originally applied with it.

ASN.1 was designed to solve the problem of varying data representations in computer systems which result from the heterogeneous data representation modes of different machine architectures (e.g., *Big* and *Little Endian* presentation) and from the diversity of programming languages which all possess their own internal coding. In heterogeneous networks this represents a problem because distributed environments need a unique interpretation of data. Communication protocols with binary coded protocol data units overcome this problem by the use of a "common language": the unique bit representation. Thus, both sides can consistently interpret PDU headers and trailers (if used). This does not solve, however, the problem of the application data which are passed as user data to the protocol stack and which would remain untouched unless special measures are taken to guarantee a consistent interpretation. The ASN.1 approach is a widely accepted solution for this. Another solution is the textual coding of protocol data, e.g., using ASCII coding, as applied in many Internet application protocols, e.g., HTTP and SIP.

The ASN.1 approach ensures the consistent and unambiguous interpretation of data in a heterogeneous network environment by defining an **abstract syntax** for a distributed application (or a class of distributed applications). This abstract syntax is described in ASN.1. It defines a generic representation for the data types and values used in the distributed application which is independent of their concrete coding in the individual computers, i.e., of their **local syntax**. In order to exchange data between end systems an appropriate encoding is required to ensure that the coded data are properly recognized by the peer machine. This encoding is described by the **transfer syntax**. It encodes the data as triplets consisting of the type, the length, and the value. The transfer syntax relates to the abstract syntax. It specifies how the data is to be transmitted according to the abstract syntax. Note that several transfer syntaxes may be defined for an abstract syntax. The transformation from the local syntax into the transfer syntax and back is determined by associated **encoding rules**.

Which abstract syntax and which of the transfer syntaxes are applied for an application is negotiated between the partners. Figure 8.5/1 illustrates the principle. The agreed combination is called the **presentation context**. Thereby context negotiation and the transfer process run in the presentation layer, although the abstract syntax actually relates to the application layer.

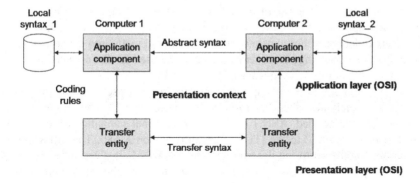

Figure 8.5/1: Presentation context

Figure 8.5/2 depicts the principle using type definitions of different programming languages to more clearly demonstrate the role of the abstract syntax.

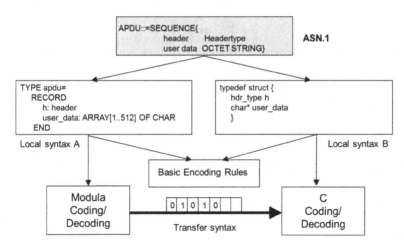

Figure 8.5/2: Use of abstract syntax

ASN.1 does not prescribe the transfer syntax to be applied. Most frequently the *Basic Encoding Rules* (BER) defined first are used. In the meantime further more efficient, but more complicated coding patterns have been proposed, e.g., the *Packed Encoding Rules* (PER), the *Canonical Encoding Rules* (CER), and the *Distinguished Encoding Rules* (DER) [ISO 8825]. Furthermore, a mapping on XML (*Extensible Markup Language*) was defined.

The abstract computer-independent description of data structures let ASN.1 very quickly become a popular description technique for data formats in the communication field. There are ASN.1 descriptions of many protocols, not only for conversion purposes. The use of ASN.1 is supported by compilers which translate ASN.1 descriptions into high-level programming languages (C, C++, Java). The ASN.1 compiler can either translate the specification directly into data types of the respective target language or generate a code to be used for the conversion of the abstract syntax into/from a sequence of bytes (see Figure 8.5/3).

ASN.1 is not a formal description technique in the sense of the definition in Chapter 7. It solely describes data formats. In contrast to ACT ONE, no operations over the data are defined. ASN.1 possesses an informal semantics which is contained in Amendment 2 to the ITU-T Recommendation X.680. The following introduction is confined to the description notation ASN.1. It gives an overview of the most important concepts. We do not consider the encoding rules which do not concern the topic of this book. For this, we refer to the more comprehensive introductions to ASN.1 in [Larm 99] and [Dubu 00], which also describe the various encoding rules in detail.

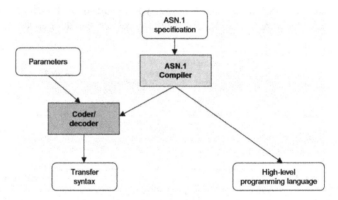

Figure 8.5/3: Application variants of an ASN.1 compiler

8.5.2   Structure of an ASN.1 description

Module

The basic element for structuring an ASN.1 specification is the *module*. A specification can consist of one or several modules. On the other hand, a module can contain several definitions, e.g., to facilitate their coherence. A module definition has the following syntactic structure:

module name DEFINITIONS::= BEGIN
                      EXPORTS *export list*
                      IMPORTS *import list*
                      definitions
                      END

It consists of the module header with the name of the module and the module body. The module name can be used as a reference to the abstract syntax in negotiations. The module body contains the type and the value *definitions* of the data structure or the abstract syntax to be described. There is no fixed order prescribed for arranging the definitions. Repeated blanks or blank lines are interpreted as one blank. Further there is the possibility to export and/or import definitions to/from other modules.

Lexical conventions
Unlike many programming languages, ASN.1 uses obligatory rules for denoting objects (modules, data types, and values):

- Names of data types and modules begin with a capital letter.
- Names of standard data types only consist of capital letters.
- Names of values begin with a small letter.

Apart from that, usual naming conventions are applied. Names can consist of large and small letters, numbers, and hyphens.
Comments are introduced by the symbol "--". A comment is limited by the end of a line.

8.5.3   Data type definitions

Similarly to other languages, ASN.1 distinguishes simple data types, compound data types, and further specific type forms. New data types can be derived from these data types by a type definition.

Type definition
Beside the value definition the *type definition* is one of the fundamental constructs in an ASN.1 description. It introduces a new data type for the basis type indicated to the right of the assign symbol (::=), e.g.,

    Role ::= BOOLEAN.

The basis type can be a simple or composed type, a subtype, a tagged type, a CHOICE type, or an ANY type. The new data type is equivalent to the basis type.

Simple types
The simple data types (*built-in data types*) in ASN.1 are defined by the standard. These are BOOLEAN, INTEGER, BIT STRING, OCTET STRING, REAL, ENUMERATED, and NULL. Most of these types are familiar from other languages and need no special explanation here. The representation of the type ENUMERATED is shown by the following example:

    Error ::= ENUMERATED{*unknown* | *no-connection* | *sequence-error* | *pdu-error*}.

The specific data type NULL is used if only the information is of interest but not its value. This can be used to signal that a certain event occurred, e.g.,

Signal ::= NULL.

Composed types

Further data types can be derived from simple and composed types by means of type constructors. These constructors are SEQUENCE, SEQUENCE OF, SET, SET OF, and CHOICE. The included types must not be defined explicitly beforehand because forward and backward references are permitted.

The **SEQUENCE-constructor** defines a data structure which consists of components of different data types (comparably with the *record-* or *struct-*type of other languages). The sequence of the components is significant. The components are identified by their names which can be used at the same time to illustrate their meaning, e.g.,

```
DT ::= SEQUENCE
    {length      INTEGER,
     code        BIT STRING DEFAULT '1110'B,
     sequ_nr     INTEGER OPTIONAL
     COMPONENTS OF DP-type1
     }.
```

In SEQUENCE types the following supplemental specifications can be used additionally:

- OPTIONAL indicates that the component can be contained optionally. The sender of the packet decides whether it is contained.
- DEFAULT <*value*> denotes a default value which can be included optionally into the data type definition. Defaults can only be used if all components of the SEQUENCE type are assigned to different tags (see below). The keyword DEFAULT must not be supplemented by OPTIONAL.
- COMPONENTS OF inserts at this position all components of the indicated SEQUENCE type.

A **SEQUENCE OF-constructor** describes a sequence of elements of the same type (comparable to the *array-*type of many languages), e.g.,

Data ::= SEQUENCE OF OCTET STRING.

The length of the sequence is variable. The order of the elements is fixed.

The **SET-constructor** defines a set. It corresponds to the SEQUENCE constructor except that the order of the component types is not fixed here any longer (as in the *set-*type of some languages). The options OPTIONAL, DEFAULT, and COMPONENT are applied as discussed above.

Similarly the **SET OF-constructor** describes in correspondence to SEQUEN-CE OF a set with elements of the same type, e.g.,

Digits ::= SET OF ENUMERATED {0,1,2,3,4,5,6,7,8,9},

where the order is again not relevant.

CHOICE describes selection from a set of alternative data types (comparable to the *union*-concept in C). The alternative data types are listed after CHOICE included in curly brackets and separated by commas, e.g.,

XDT-pdu-type ::= CHOICE{
   dt pdu-type1,
   ack pdu-type2,
   abo pdu-type3
   }.

From the indicated alternatives exactly one is true in each case.

Sub-types

As in many languages, sub-range types and/or sub-types can be defined in ASN.1. They are derived from the respective basis type by indication of the sub-range which applies to the subtype, e.g.,

Reason1 ::= Error (*unknown* | *pdu_error*)
Index ::= INTEGER(0..99).

ASN.1 provides different means for defining subtypes on which we do not enlarge further here (see [Dubu 00] for this).

Tagging

Up to this point the data type definitions do not differ in principle in ASN.1 from those of many specification and programming languages. The qualitative difference that distinguishes the ASN.1-notation from others consists in adding a unique identification – the **tag** – to each data type by which all simple data types, constructors, and composed types can be identified unambiguously. The tag represents a coding of the data type which is needed for the exchange of type information. It allows the receiver of a data unit to relate the received data with the specified data type. A tag consists of the tag class and the number of the data type or the constructor within this class, respectively. It is included to square brackets and placed in front of the respective type. ASN.1 differentiates four **tag classes**:

- UNIVERSAL,
- APPLICATION,
- PRIVATE,
- context-specific.

The class UNIVERSAL is assigned to data types that apply to all specifications. These are the standardized types. They are defined in the ASN.1-Standard. For example, BOOLEAN possesses the tag [UNIVERSAL 1] and the constructor SEQUENCE the tag [UNIVERSAL 16].

The tag class APPLICATION defines data types that apply only to a certain standard, e.g., for the transport protocol. A tag of this class must be unique for the respective application, i.e., it must be distinguishable from all data types used in this application.

PRIVATE is used for own definitions or user specific extensions of international standards which are used, for instance, in companies or organizations.

Context-specific tags do not possess a special keyword. They are symbolized only by the tag number. The interpretation of the tags is determined by the context in which they are used. Their scope is the marking of the component types in composed data types SEQUENCE, SET, or CHOICE, e.g.,

```
Abo ::= SEQUENCE{
        code      [0] BIT STRING DEFAULT '1101'B,
        conn      [1] BIT STRING,
        reason    [2] Error
}.
```

Implicit tagging

Tagging causes a certain overhead for coding/decoding as well as for writing and reading the specification which is not always required. Therefore the use of tags has gradually been simplified. While in the original ASN.1 explicit tagging was essential, the introduction of implicit and automatic tagging made the handling of tags substantially more comfortable. Implicit tagging means that the coding of data types is suppressed when IMPLICIT is added to the type (except for CHOICE types). It presumes that the type derives clearly from the context, e.g.,

```
Abo ::= SEQUENCE{
        code      [0] BIT STRING DEFAULT '1101'B,
        conn      [1] IMPLICIT BIT STRING,
        reason    [2] IMPLICIT INTEGER
}.
```

Without IMPLICIT, the tags for BIT STRING and INTEGER would be coded and transferred. After decoding the first component of *Abo* the receiver can deduce the data types of the following values. A coding of these types would unnecessarily extend the bit sequence to be transferred. The indication of IMPLICIT before the types prevents this. The data type coding can also be waived for the entire module definition if the uniqueness of the data types is ensured. In this case the IMPLICIT mode has to be indicated in the module header, e.g.,

xdt_data DEFINITIONS IMPLICIT TAGS ::=

```
BEGIN
 . . .
END
```

Analogously, the explicit tagging mode can be assigned to a module by EX-PLICIT TAGS. Furthermore, it is possible to change from implicit tagging to explicit and vice versa by indicating EXPLICIT (or IMPLICIT) before the respec-respective type.

Automatic Tagging

With implicit tagging ambiguous situations may occur occasionally as the fol-lowing example of a modified *Abo* specification illustrates.

```
xdt_data DEFINITIONS IMPLICIT TAGS::=
BEGIN
 . . .
   Abo::= SEQUENCE{
        code    BIT STRING DEFAULT '1101'B,
        conn    INTEGER OPTIONAL,
        reason  INTEGER,
        info    INTEGER OPTIONAL
        }
     . . .
END.
```

Here the decoder is no longer able to distinguish uniquely which values are as-signed to which fields. In order to avoid such conflicts when using implicit tags the automatic tagging mode was introduced. It completely releases the specifier from the explicit indication of tags. If he/she declares AUTOMATIC TAGS in the module definition the tags are generated automatically, e.g.,

```
xdt_data DEFINITIONS AUTOMATIC TAGS ::=
BEGIN
 . . .
   Abo ::= SEQUENCE{
        code    BIT STRING DEFAULT '1101'B,    -- associates tag [0]
        conn    INTEGER OPTIONAL,              -- associates tag [1]
        reason  INTEGER,                        -- associates tag [2]
        info    INTEGER OPTIONAL               -- associates tag [3]
        }
 . . .
END.
```

Automatic tagging implies implicit tagging except for a few exceptions, e.g., CHOICE types. This means that the specifier can in principle forget the tags. For that reason, automatic tagging is the recommended mode today.

Tagged types

In ASN.1 new data types can also be defined using tags. They are called *tagged types*. These are types that are equivalent to the respective basic type, but they have a different tag, e.g.,

Protocol_Class ::= [1] INTEGER.

The new type *Protocol_Class* now has the context-tag [1] instead of the INTEGER tag [UNIVERSAL 2].

Predefined character string types

In order to open ASN.1 to a wider field of application a series of predefined character sets has been introduced using tagged types. Examples of such character sets are: *NumericString, PrintableString, TeletexString, VideotexString, Visible-String, IA5String* (International Alphabet Number 5 = ASCII), *GraphicString*, and *GeneralString*. They are derived from the simple type OCTET STRING. The set of predefined character sets has been continually expanded. In one of the latest language versions the new fonts *BMPString, Universal String*, and *UTF8String* were introduced which allow, in particular, the use of strings on the basis of the ISO/IEC 10646 standards which support signs and symbols of many languages.

Further types

There are other types defined in ASN.1 which we mention here for the sake of completeness. These are OBJECT IDENTIFIER and the so-called useful types. OBJECT IDENTIFIER denotes the description of abstract information objects which can be used to describe the structure of standards or specifications. In this way universally unique identifiers for objects may be defined. The **useful types** encompass data definitions which can appear in many specifications. Currently there are four types defined: *UTCTime* and *GeneralizedTime* to describe time in seconds or other units, *ObjectDescriptor* for describing information objects in the character set *Graphic String*, and EXTERNAL for the integration of data values of other abstract syntaxes.

8.5.4 Value definitions

Another key element of an ASN.1 description is the representation of values. In order to represent the values of simple data types, **value representations** were defined. They are essentially representations of the familiar values in high-level programming languages like TRUE and FALSE for BOOLEAN, integer numbers for INTEGER, binary strings and hexadecimal sequences for BIT STRING and OCTET STRING as well as character strings for the predefined character sets, such as *IA5String* and others (see above).

In addition, there is the possibility to introduce symbolic names for certain values using **value definitions** similarly to a constant declaration. A value definition contains the symbolic name – the *value reference* – and the data type left of the assignment symbol :: = and right of it the value, e.g.,

class0 INTEGER ::= 0
open BOOLEAN ::= TRUE
dt-code BIT STRING ::= '1000'B

Value definitions can also be applied to composite types, e.g.,

states ::= SEQUENCE OF VisibleString
sender states::= {"*idle*","*await*","*connected*"}.

8.5.5 Extensibility

An important feature in the use of ASN.1 is the possibility to extend specifications in order to take changes and extensions of a specification into account. For this reason, the latest version of ASN.1 introduced means to support the upward and downward compatibility of specifications. The extensibility of definitions can be specified in two ways: by using the local extensibility marking "..." or by globally specifying EXTENSION IMPLIED in the module header. The concrete extensions are always included in double brackets "[[" and "]]". Thus, for instance, different versions of a protocol can be defined, e.g.,

{XDT-Version 1.0}   {XDT-Version 2.0}

Ack ::= SEQUENCE   Ack ::= SEQUENCE
    {*conn* [0] INTEGER,   {*conn* [0] INTEGER,
    sequ [1] INTEGER   *sequ* [1] INTEGER,
    ...   [[*credit* [2] INTEGER]]
    }   ...
                                                                 }

The first version defines the *ACK*-PDU as we have used it so far. It contains the extensibility marker "..." to indicate that extensions are possible. The second definition shows the *ACK*-PDU of a possible second protocol version with flow control support. For this purpose, the data unit incorporates a field for updating credits. Further protocol versions can be defined by including the extensions in double brackets.

The extension mechanism allows the decoder to accept data units which contain unknown components. It recognizes through the extensibility marker that the data unit contains extensions which do not belong to the current protocol version. They are treated as optional components and the data unit can be delivered to the application.

8.5.6 Constraints

In certain ASN.1 definitions it is possible to define restrictions concerning the contents of certain elements. These restrictions are defined in **constraint specifications**. There exist different constraint specifications: *user defined constraints, tabular constraints,* and *component relational constraints.* The last two relate to information objects, which we do not consider here. *User defined constraints* are a special form of comment to describe restrictions which would be too expensive to express by other ASN.1 means, e.g.,

> PDU code ::= BIT STRING (CONSTRAINED BY { -- each string must contain a 1 in
> the first bit --}).

8.5.7 Parameterization

ASN.1 offers the possibility of parameterization of type and value definitions. The formal parameters are listed after the type or value identifier, e.g.,

> PDU-type1{INTEGER: *min*, INTEGER: *max*}::=
> SEQUENCE{
> *length* INTEGER(*min..max*),
> *code* BIT STRING DEFAULT '1110'B,
> *sequ_nr* INTEGER OPTIONAL
> COMPONENTS OF DP-type1
> } .

The actual parameters are indicated in the references to the type and/or value definition, e.g.,

> Small-DT ::= PDU-type1{10,100}
> Large-DT ::= PDU-type1{10,1000} .

8.5.8 Example

We conclude the introduction to ASN.1 as usual with an example specification; in this case with the description of the XDT service primitives and PDUs. In order to demonstrate the use of tags we apply implicit tagging rather than the simpler automatic tagging. The service primitives and PDUs are described using SEQUENCE types, for which PRIVATE tags are introduced. They are collected in CHOICE types. For demonstration purposes, we define the PDU identification code by means of value definitions. The *XABORTind* primitive serves as an example to highlight value assignment to composite types by introducing an error code in contrast to the original XDT specification.

```
xdt-data DEFINITIONS IMPLICIT TAGS::=
BEGIN
  -- XDT sub-services
  XDT-connect ::= CHOICE{
            xdatrequ    XDATrequ-type,
            xdatind     XDATind-type,
            xdatconf    XDATconf-type,
            xabortind   XABORTind-type
            }
  XDT-data-transfer ::= CHOICE{
                xdatrequ   XDATrequ-type,
                xdatind    XDATind-type,
                xdatconf   XDATconf-type,
                xbreakind  XBREAKind-type,
                xabortind  XABORTind-type,
                xdisind    XDISind-type
                }


  -- Auxiliary type definitions

    XDATrequ-type    ::= [PRIVATE 0] DP-type1
    XDATind-type     ::= [PRIVATE 1] DP-type1
    XDATconf-type    ::= [PRIVATE 2] DP-type2
    XBREAKind-type   ::= [PRIVATE 3] DP-type3
    XDISind-type     ::= [PRIVATE 4] DP-type3
    XABORTind-type   ::= [PRIVATE 5] DP-type4
    DP-type1 ::= SEQUENCE{
                conn        [0] INTEGER,
                sequ        [1] INTEGER,
                source-addr [2] BIT STRING OPTIONAL,
                dest-addr   [3] BIT STRING OPTIONAL,
                eom         [4] BOOLEAN,
                data        [5] SEQUENCE OF OCTET STRING
                }
    DP-type2 ::= SEQUENCE{
                conn        [0] INTEGER,
                sequ        [1] INTEGER
                }
    DP-type3 ::= SEQUENCE
                conn        [0] INTEGER,
                sequ        [1] NULL
                }
```

```
DP-type4 ::= SEQUENCE{
                conn        [0] INTEGER
                reason      [1] ENUMERATED{unknown, no-connection,
                                              out-of-order}
        }
```

-- XDT-PDUs
```
XDT-pdu-type ::= CHOICE{
                dt      PDU-type1,
                ack     PDU-type2,
                abo     PDU-type3
        }
PDU-type1 ::= [PRIVATE 10] SEQUENCE{
                length       [0] INTEGER,
                code         [1] BIT STRING DEFAULT dt-code,
                source-addr  [2] BIT STRING OPTIONAL,
                dest-addr    [3] BIT STRING OPTIONAL,
                conn         [4] INTEGER,
                sequ         [5] INTEGER,
                eom          [6] BOOLEAN,
                data         [7] SEQUENCE OF OCTET STRING
        }
PDU-type2 ::= [PRIVATE 11] SEQUENCE{
                code         [0] BIT STRING DEFAULT ack-code,
                conn         [1] BIT STRING,
                sequ         [2] INTEGER
        }
PDU-type3 ::= [PRIVATE 12] SEQUENCE{
                code         [0] BIT STRING DEFAULT abo-code,
                conn         [1] BIT STRING,
                reason       [2] ENUMERATED{unknown,
                                              no-connection, out-of-order}
        }
```

-- XDT value definitions
```
dt-code     BIT STRING::= '1000'B
ack-code    BIT STRING::= '1001'B
abo-code    BIT STRING::= '1010'B
```

END -- *XDT-Data format description*

8.6   Protocol description with UML 2

To say it at the very beginning UML is not a formal description technique as defined in this chapter and like the specification languages presented in the preceding sections. So in principle no words should be spent on UML here. But UML has been applied in recent years for describing protocols and probably will be applied more often for this purpose in future. Therefore, it is necessary to speak about UML in this context. We do not intend to introduce UML here in the manner we did this for the various FDTs beforehand. There are a lot of books and tutorials on UML available on the market which introduce the language. What we are discussing here is the use of UML for describing communication protocols.

The purpose and the origin of UML are different from that of the formal description techniques presented in this chapter. UML is a standardized language developed by the OMG (*Object Management Group*) for the modeling of systems which is used in software engineering to support and facilitate software development. It aims at the development of software blueprints as a basis for the software development process. UML is based on the object oriented language paradigm. It is primarily a graphical language which can be used in different phases of the software life cycle to specify, construct, visualize, and document software objects or artifacts [Booc 05], [Lano 09]. UML provides a vocabulary and the rules to combine words of this vocabulary to create models and to work with them. The models serve the communication among people involved in a project. They can be refined and varied using different viewpoints.

UML is a general-purpose modeling language that can be applied to many application areas, such as business processes, systems engineering, and representation of organizational structures. As a consequence, UML is a very complex language with a large number of diagrams and constructs, which make the learning and use of the language not easy. The development of UML has passed through several stages since its creation in the 1990s. The current version is UML 2, to which we refer here.

When comparing UML with the formal description techniques of this chapter one can find a lot of overlaps concerning their deployment, application, and the description elements used, but there are just as many differences. UML is above all a modeling language whose purpose is to develop models and not to document a concrete design process. The models developed can be mapped onto different platforms and languages, including formal description techniques. FDTs are more focused on their application field, e.g., on communication systems or protocols. They do not aim at developing models for a broader application range. The modeling capabilities of FDTs are limited by the semantic model defined through their formal semantics.

UML offers all the elements needed to describe communication services and protocols. It provides 13 diagram types, which are grouped into structure and behavior diagrams. This broad range of diagrams allows the user to model protocols in a natural way, i.e., in a behavior- or communication-oriented way. In contrast, most FDTs force the users to follow the given semantic constraints of the language when describing a system or protocol like the process-oriented description in LOTOS or the agent-oriented one in SDL. Two of the various UML diagrams can be directly used for protocol description: the state machine diagram and the sequence diagram. The *state machine diagram* can be used to produce FSM or EFSM presentations of protocol entities. It differs in part from the representation we used in Chapter 7, e.g., there is a start state, but in principle similar representations can be produced. Figure 8.6/1 shows the simplified FSM/EFSM specifications of the XDT entities.

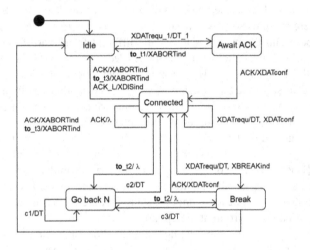

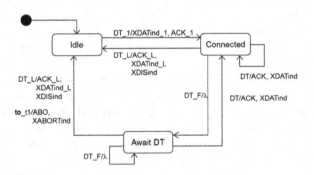

Figure 8.6/1: UML 2 state machine diagrams of the XDT protocol entities

The *sequence diagram* can be used for the communication-oriented representation of the protocol message exchange. In UML 2 *Message Sequence Charts*, as introduced in Section 8.2, has been coopted as sequence diagrams so that this very popular description language can also be used in the context of UML. Figure 8.6/2 depicts a fragment of the XDT protocol as a sequence diagram. But other diagrams, such as use case diagrams, activity diagrams, communication diagrams and others, can also be used in protocol design. It is a large advantage of UML that a broad range of representations can be used for protocol design, protocol description, and documentation which offer different views on the designed protocol and thus support reasoning about the various features of the protocol.

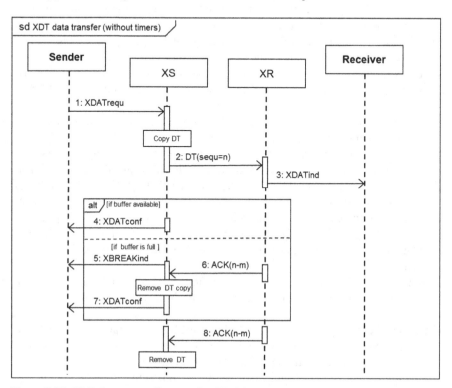

Figure 8.6/2: UML 2 sequence diagram of an XDT fragment

UML is an enabler for model-driven development technologies in which parts of the resultant implementation are automatically generated from the model. In contrast to earlier approaches, a greater focus is put on the architecture of the software system to be developed and less on a complete automated code generation process. This abstraction promotes simpler models with a greater focus on the problem space. The model-driven development process comprises several model levels; of particular importance are the *platform independent model* (PIM) and the *platform specific model* (PSM). FDTs are also used in the various development phases of the protocol development process, but their use is always related to a concrete design. Compared to model-driven development they correspond more to a platform specific model rather than to the platform independent model.

Another significant difference between UML and FDTs is that UML does not possess a formal semantics. This is because UML aims at supporting a wide range of models which can be mapped on various platform specific models. UML and part of its semantics can be explained by UML itself. For this, the *Meta-Object Facility* (*MOF*) was introduced which provides a meta-modeling architecture to define UML. It is designed as a four-layered architecture with a meta-meta-model at the top layer. This model is the language used by MOF to build meta-models, such as the UML meta-model that describes UML itself. These models describe elements of models in the related languages, e.g., models written in UML. The last layer is the data layer which is used to describe real-world objects. This kind of meta-modeling is not the same as the formal semantics discussed in Chapter 7 and 8. So UML cannot directly benefit from the advantages of formal semantics. To overcome the formal semantics problem three approaches are applied [Wet 05]:

- A frequently applied approach is to map a subset of UML diagrams as a work-around to existing formal methods.
- An alternative approach is to merge UML with a formal language, e.g., by defining UML profiles as has been done in the UML profile *SDL Combined with UML* defined by ITU-T in the standard Z.109 [ITU-T 109]. Profiles provide extension mechanisms which allow the specialization of meta-classes from existing meta-models to tailor them for specific application areas. The Z.109 recommendation specifies a UML subset using stereotypes, tagged values, constraints, and notational elements to work in an SDL environment.
- Another possibility is of course the definition of a formal semantics for a defined subset of UML diagrams as done, for instance, in [Kali 10].

On the other hand, UML has attracted huge attention and many more users than the FDTs introduced here. Many people are familiar with the basic structures of UML and use them in practice. Students learn them in their basic courses on software engineering. Thus the number of people is constantly growing who are familiar with UML and are capable of using it. In addition, much research has been carried out on UML and its applicability meanwhile. The great attraction and application of UML can be therefore also seen as a chance to bring formal methods to a broader audience. UML offers the user sufficient means to describe communication protocols and their services. It can therefore be expected that it will be more widely used for describing protocols. The semantics problem will be a matter of further research. A possible approach for applying UML for protocol development is presented in [Kali 10].

Further reading
   Since SDL has been a widely used language for protocol description as well as for the design of telecommunication systems, there are many publications about the language and its application. Further introductions to the language can be found in [Mits 01] and [Dold 03]. The first book considers the language in the context of performance engineering, while the second one focuses on simulation

and validation. It describes in particular the use of the SDL tools *Tau* and *ObjectGeode* for performing simulations of SDL specifications. We further refer to the conference series [FORTE] and [SDL Forum], where various papers on different aspects of the use of SDL have been published. Last but not least, we re-refer to the web site of the SDL Forum Society (http://www.sdl-forum.org/) which contains information about recent publications, conferences, and workshops on SDL. At this web site the reader can also find information about the on-going revision of SDL 2000 towards SDL 2010.

Regarding MSC, there are no book publications. A comprehensive introduction to MSC-2010 can be found in [Haug 01]. Further tutorial material and other information are also contained at the SDL Forum Society web site.

There are various publications which introduce LOTOS. A very comprehensive introduction is given in the tutorial of Bolognesi and Brinksma during the standardization of the language [Bolo 87]. Another comprehensive introduction that also considers various semantic models can be found in the book of Bowman and Gomez [Bowm 06]. A further tutorial can be found at the CADP toolbox web site [CADP].

Comprehensive descriptions of cTLA are contained in [Herr 00] and [Herr 02]. Currently, cTLA is used to define formal semantics for UML diagrams. Examples can be found in [Krae 09b] and [Kali 10].

Beside the standard there are two books that give a detailed introduction to ASN.1. These are the already cited books [Larm 99] and [Dubu 00]. They contain descriptions of the various encoding rules which we did not consider here. ASN.1 encoding with the Basic Encoding Rules is also described in [Shar 08].

Exercises

(1) Explain the description approach applied in SDL, its basic elements and the differences between them. How are SDL specifications structured? Which description principle related to the classifications given in Chapter 7 is enforced by SDL?

(2) SDL supports the separation of automata descriptions into sub-automata. Describe how this can be done.

(3) Explain how state transitions from one state into various states are described in SDL. What kinds of triggering events exist? How can additional transitions be added to the triggering events? How is the next state indicated?

(4) What is the purpose of the *save*-symbol in SDL? When must it be used?

(5) Describe the various kinds of interactions between agents. Give examples of when they should be used.

(6) Modify the SDL specification of Section 8.1 to integrate an explicit connection set up into XDT as described in exercise (11) of Chapter 2. Change both the service and the protocol specification.

(7) Modify the SDL specification of Section 8.1 to integrate the data delivery regulation described in exercise (13) of Chapter 2. Change both the service and the protocol specification.

(8) Modify the SDL specification of Section 8.1 to integrate the explicit connection release into XDT as described in exercise (15) of Chapter 5. Change both the service and the protocol specification.

(9) In exercise (6) of Chapter 5 we replaced the *go back N* procedure by *selective repeat*. Replace accordingly the *go back N* procedure of the SDL specification in Section 8.1 by a *selective repeat* procedure. Sketch the integration of the latter into the SDL specification.

(10) Explain the description approach applied in MSC and its basic elements. What is the advantage of this kind of description?

(11) Describe the explicit connection set up of exercise (11) in Chapter 2 using MSC for the service and protocol specification. Consider the rejection of a connection in the same chart.

(12) Describe the data delivery regulation of exercise (13) in Chapter 2 using MSC for the service and the protocol specification.

(13) Describe the explicit connection release of exercise (15) in Chapter 5 using MSC for the service and the protocol specification.

(14) Describe the replacement of the *go back N* procedure by *selective repeat* of exercise (9) using MSC.

(15) Explain the description approach applied in LOTOS and its basic elements. How is a LOTOS specification structured? What is the difference between *Basic* and *Full* LOTOS? Which description principle related to the classifications given in Chapter 7 is enforced by LOTOS?

(16) Explain the difference between processes which terminate with **stop** and **exit**. What process functionality corresponds to these terminations?

(17) Give for the process

process UV[a,b,c,d]: **exit** :=
U[a,b,c,d] || V[a,b,d]
where
    process U[t,u,v,w]: **exit** :=
        t;u;**exit** [] u;w;**exit** [] v;**exit**
    endproc (* U *)
    process V[t,u,w]: **exit** :=
        t;u;**exit** [] u;w;**exit** [] t;**exit**
    endproc (* V *)
endproc (* UV *).

the alternative representation using only the action prefix and the *choice*-operator. Draw the behavior tree for the resulting behavior expression. Change the process *UV* so that the resulting behavior expression contains nondeterministic behavior.

(18) Rewrite the process

process PQ[a,b,c,d]: **exit** :=
P[a,b,c,d] ||| Q[d]
where

    process P[t,u,v,w]: **exit** :=
    t;u;**exit** [] u;w;**exit** [] v;**exit**
    endproc (* P *)
    process Q[t]: **exit** :=
    t;**exit**
    endproc (* Q *)
endproc (* PQ *)

using only the action prefix and the *choice*-operator. What do the resulting event sequences represent?

(19) What is the purpose of hiding? What can it be used for?

(20) Two processes synchronize at gate *g* with the value *true*. What kind of event offer has to be used? Write the synchronization down. If either *true* or *false* can be exchanged what event offer can be taken and what does the synchronization look like?

(21) Compare the definition of labeled transition systems with that of finite state machines. What do they have in common and what are the differences?

(22) Describe an explicit connection set up service including a possible rejection at the responder side in the monolithic, constraint-oriented, state-oriented, and resource-oriented specification styles.

(23) Modify the LOTOS specification of Section 8.3 to integrate an explicit connection set up into XDT as described in exercise (11) of Chapter 2. Change both the service and the protocol specification.

(24) Modify the LOTOS specification of Section 8.3 to integrate the regulated data delivery into XDT as described in exercise (13) of Chapter 2. Change both the service and the protocol specification.

(25) Similarly to exercise (9) sketch the replacement of the XDT *go back N* by *selective repeat* in the LOTOS specification of Section 8.3.

(26) Modify the LOTOS specification of Section 8.3 to integrate the explicit connection release into XDT as described in exercise (14) of Chapter 2. Change both the service and the protocol specification.

(27) Explain the description approach applied in cTLA. What are the basic language elements of cTLA? What is the difference in the description compared to the other FDTs introduced beforehand?

(28) In Section 8.4 we specified the XDT connection set up in cTLA. Give accordingly the corresponding specification for the explicit connection set up as described in exercise (11) of Chapter 2.

(29) Outline the presentation of time and the modeling of timers in the presented description techniques and discuss their applicability for protocol description.

(30) Describe the description principle applied in ASN.1 including its basic language elements. Explain in particular the role of tagging. What is it needed for?

(31) Transform the following ASN.1 definition

```
PDU-type1 ::= [PRIVATE 10] SEQUENCE{
                 length [0] INTEGER,
                 code   [1] BIT STRING DEFAULT dt-code,
                 source-addr [2] BIT STRING,
                 dest-addr [3] BIT STRING OPTIONAL,
                 conn [4] INTEGER,
                 sequ [5] INTEGER,
                 eom [6] BOOLEAN,
                 data [7] SEQUENCE OF OCTET STRING
             }
```

into a data type definition in any programming language of your preference.

(32) Change the XDT data format definition of Section 8.5.8 to introduce the service primitives and the protocol data units needed for the explicit connection set up as described in exercise (11) of Chapter 2.

Part III: Development of communication protocols

The third part of the book deals with the typical development steps of communication protocols. It first presents the protocol life cycle and discusses the differences to traditional software development. Subsequently, the main stages of the protocol life cycle are introduced and discussed in more detail. These phases are: design, specification, verification, performance evaluation, implementation, and testing.

The chapter *Design* covers the phases design and specification. It gives a brief overview of approaches proposed for a systematic protocol design. Since the design process is closely related to the development of the (formal) protocol specification to document design decisions, we consider afterwards rules and recommendations for the development of formal specifications.

In the chapter *Verification* we first discuss typical errors that may occur when designing a communication protocol. Thereafter we introduce the most important techniques to verify the correctness, consistency, and completeness of protocol designs. The methods we consider in detail are reachability analysis, Petri net-based verification, algebraic verification, and model checking.

The chapter *Performance evaluation* outlines methods for the evaluation of the expected performance behavior of the designed protocol in the considered target execution environment. These evaluations may be used to optimize the protocol design and to look for alternative implementation solutions.

In the chapter *Implementation* we describe the steps and decisions that have to be passed through to implement a protocol. We present the basic approaches used for protocol implementations: the server model and the activity thread model including related interfaces. Furthermore, we consider several special implementation methods. We give an example implementation of the XDT protocol for the server and the activity thread models. Finally we give an overview of automated implementation techniques.

The chapter *Testing* deals with the testing of protocol implementations. We consider the two main forms of protocol testing: the conformance and the interoperability tests. Based on the ISO 9646 conformance testing methodology, we introduce the characteristic architectures, concepts, and procedures for running conformance tests. In a separate section we present various methods for the derivation of test cases which are not part of the standardization. We consider both the derivation of test cases from finite state machines and from labeled transition systems. Next we briefly discuss the use of passive testing methods. Thereafter we argue the need for interoperability tests and present various architectures for their execution. The chapter ends with an overview on test description languages. We present the basic features of the standardized test notations TTCN-2 and TTCN-3 which are used preferably for describing test cases and test scenarios in the protocol area. As in the other chapters, most examples are related to the XDT protocol.

The final chapter *Outlook* concludes the book with a discussion on the extent of the use of formal description techniques in practice, related issues, tool requirements, and conditions for their widespread use.

9   Protocol development process

Communication protocols are implemented for the most part in software. The development stages of a protocol from its design to integration/installation correspond principally to the phases known from software development [Somm 00]. There are, however, a number of differences that give the protocol development process its own specific character. We discuss these differences in this chapter. First we give a short introduction to the main phases of the protocol development.

9.1   Development phases

The phases of the protocol development process are often presented using the waterfall model as depicted in Figure 9.1/1. The results of each phase are associated with the arrows which symbolize the transitions between the phases. We only deal here with the phases between requirements analysis and protocol installation. Phases like protocol operation and maintenance are not considered here, since they do not differ fundamentally from those in normal software development.

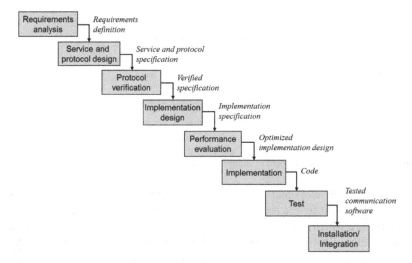

Figure 9.1/1: Waterfall model of the protocol development process

The waterfall model is a fairly rough representation of the protocol development process which highlights in particular the different stages. Dependencies and interactions between the stages are not expressed. In order to be able to describe the specifics of protocol development more accurately we use a more detailed development model here. It is represented in Figure 9.1/2. In contrast to the water-fall model, the phases are indicated by arrows, while the respective results are indicated in rectangles. We introduce the stages next. The characteristic protocol properties which influence the development process are discussed afterwards.

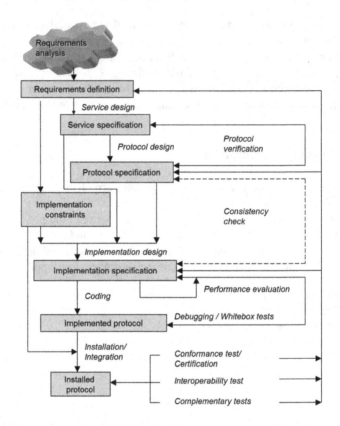

Figure 9.1/2: Phases of the protocol development process

The protocol development begins like any software development with **requirements analysis** to fix the requirements on the protocol to be developed. The requirements are usually written down informally. The subsequent design process consists ideally of two steps: the **design of the service** and the **design of the protocol**. Sometimes only the protocol is designed. The service, if required, must be derived indirectly from it. This is often the case with Internet protocols because the service concept is not part of the TCP/IP architecture (cp. Section 4.3.2). The designed service and protocol are documented in the *service* and the *protocol specification*, respectively. These specifications are the blueprints or reference specifications for the further development steps.

The design phase is followed up by the verification stage in which the functional correctness of the design is proved. In general, the design and the verification processes require several iterations. **Protocol verification** differentiates between the verification of special and general properties. The *verification of the specific properties* examines whether the designed protocol really provides the specified service. The *verification of the general properties* proves the logical consistency of the design. In practice, however, a complete verification of the protocol design is usually not possible so errors in the service and protocol specification are sometimes discovered even years later.

The protocol design does not refer to a specific target system. It has a generic character, since protocols should run under any execution environment or operating system, respectively. Due to the implementation independence of the protocol specification, it does not contain any system-related specifications. In order to implement the protocol on a concrete target system a third design phase – **implementation design** – is needed. It maps the protocol onto the target system taking the constraints of the execution environment into account. This includes also the selection of protocol options and implementation-related refinements of the protocol specification to dissolve abstractions, such as nondeterminisms or internal events. The decisions made are fixed in the *implementation specification* which forms the basis for the **coding** of the protocol.

The implementation process may be accompanied by a **performance evaluation** to assess whether the specified protocol meets the desired performance requirements in the target system. This allows the implementer to optimize the implementation design and to reason about implementation alternatives. Such evaluations are especially of interest for protocols that have to satisfy real-time requirements, such as multimedia protocols. Performance analyses require additional implementation-dependent information about the target system, such as resource availability, time constraints, and the expected workload. These nonfunctional parameters are usually not contained in a formal specification. They must be added in an appropriate way. Based on this extended specification an assessable performance model is generated. The execution of the performance model results in various performance measures. This is done by analytical methods or simulation.

The implementation process may be accompanied by further validation steps. Possible validations could be a consistency check between the protocol specification and the implementation specification or the use of program verification. In practice, however, this is rarely done due to the complexity of the protocols, especially as the implementation specification is often not explicitly worked out. Consistency checks are usually left in practice to the final test phase. Tools for automated code generation ensure consistency through defined transformation rules. Their use though is limited.

The **protocol test** has the task to detect errors in the implementation of the protocol. Different kinds of tests are applied in the protocol development process. Errors made during the implementation and coding phase are detected and fixed by classical white box testing and debugging. The main form of protocol testing is the **conformance test** which proves compliance between the implemented protocol and the specification. The conformance test is a black box test that considers only the exterior behavior of the implementation. The conformance test is mainly deployed to prove compliance with the protocol standards. Compliance can be confirmed in an authorized test laboratory in a **certification** procedure which issues an official certificate as a quality measure. For the integration of protocol implementations in real network environments, another test plays an important role in practice: the **interoperability test**. It tests the interoperability capabilities of various implementations of the same protocol. This is to identify differences in the interpretation of the specification/standard by the implementers as well as the use of different protocol options and parameters. **Additional tests** are the *robustness test*, which examines the robustness of the implementation against incorrect inputs, and the *performance test*, which evaluates the performance of the implementation.

Finally the tested protocol is integrated in the execution environment and configured according to its demands. Only now network addresses and time-out values are set.

9.2   Singularities of protocol development

Protocol development differs from traditional software development by a number of singularities. Some of these are reflected directly in the protocol development process, but mostly they influence the various development stages. Comparing the protocol development process with traditional software life cycle models, the presence of several specification levels is in evidence first. The **service specification** corresponds in its essence to the requirement specification of software development, which specifies the expected exterior behavior of a program or a module. The service specification describes the interactions at the service interface, i.e., the interactions the service users may observe. It makes no statements about how the service is provided by the service provider. This is the task of the **protocol specification**, which defines which interactions at the system interface have to take place to provide the service. Consequently, the protocol specification can be interpreted as an *abstract implementation* of the service specification. This also explains why the development of formal description techniques for protocols has been a challenging task compared to traditional software specification. Protocol specifications describe abstract implementations rather than only summarizing requirements. Unlike conventional software, a protocol is implemented several times on different computer systems with various operating systems. This has two consequences. First, the protocol description must be implementation independent, i.e., it must be sufficiently abstract and does not rely on a specific operating system. Second, implementation independence forces the protocol description to leave certain decisions open and shift them to the implementation to ensure system independence and to support a broad application range. This is often solved by means of protocol options. The mapping of the protocol description in a specific target environment requires therefore a further refinement of the specification concerning the constraints of the target system. For this, a third specification is required: the **implementation specification**.

The different purposes of the service and protocol specifications also explain the need for a specific **protocol verification**. The purpose of the protocol verification is to prove that the designed protocol really provides the specified service, i.e., that the abstract implementation of the service is correct and consistent. The protocol verification (ideally) confirms the correctness of the service and protocol specifications as a precondition for their multiple implementations.

One consequence of the implementation independence of protocol descriptions is the need for international standardization of protocols. **Standards** play an important role in the protocol development process. All protocols used today in open networks are published as standards. Internet protocols are published in *Requests for Comments* (RFCs). The majority of standards are described informally. The elaboration of standards is often the result of long empirical design work of working groups in international standardization bodies, such as the IETF, the ITU-T, and industry consortia. Systematic design methods are rarely used. After elaborating the standard the purpose of the working group is mostly finished. Implementations of the protocol are usually performed independently from the original design. Errors in the standards are only detected by subsequent verifications, often in the academic environment. Hence, there is rarely a consistent development of communication protocols from scratch, i.e., from requirements analysis via design and verification to implementation and installation. The majority of the protocol developers are hardly involved in the protocol design itself but rather in the subsequent phases of its implementation and validation. The standards form the interface between the two stages of protocol development.

The importance of standards in the protocol development process explains the need for additional tests. First, it must be proved whether a protocol implementation is in compliance with the standard. This is tested in the **conformance test**. The outcome can be officially assessed by a **certificate**, which is especially needed as a quality measure for commercial use. The conformance test alone is not sufficient to guarantee the interoperability of various implementations of a protocol. The reason for this is the freedom that the standards leave to the implementers, e.g., the already mentioned protocol options. So it may happen that two conforming implementations do not run together. Therefore, a further test – the **interoperability test** – is required to examine the interoperability of various implementations of the same protocol. Other requirements, such as the robustness of the implementation and its performance, are not covered by the functional conformance test. For this, complementary tests may be applied.

10   Design

The protocol development process, as it was described in the previous chapter, contains several design phases: the service design, the protocol design, and the implementation design. Although the design phases comprise in detail many important and creative design decisions, relatively little attention has been paid to the design issue in the literature. Many publications use the word *design* in their headlines, but they refer more to the specification and the validation phase rather than to the design process itself. Nowadays protocols are still prevailingly developed empirically using more or less heuristic design methods. In contrast to the other phases of the development process, no established methods or techniques exist for protocol design. Therefore, we restrict ourselves in this chapter to a brief overview of interesting approaches related to systematic protocol design. Since the design process is closely related to the development of the (formal) protocol specification to document design decisions, we also discuss some issues concerning specification development in this chapter.

10.1   Systematic protocol design

Communication protocols are mainly developed empirically, mostly in standardization bodies, at universities, or in research institutions. Often they are the result of a long development process in working groups, e.g., in the IETF. Systematic design methods are rarely applied. This is because systematic design methods, on the one hand, are still not mature enough and, on the other hand, the various demands on protocols regarding data formats, services provided, communication relations, and interactions with the environment are hard to cover with existing design methods.

The design issue has attracted large theoretical interest because systematic design methods promise interesting benefits, such as reduced error rates, a faster development speed, and documentation support. Various approaches have been reported using CCS/LOTOS models [Kant 96], FSM/EFSM models [Higa 93], and in particular different types of Petri nets [Yama 07].

Design methods for protocols can be divided into synthetic and analytical approaches [Prob 91], which we consider next.

Synthetic design methods

Synthetic design methods have been intensively investigated since the beginning of *Protocol Engineering* [Zafi 80]. The basic idea is to synthesize the protocol by completing a given partial draft. This can be done either interactively or automatically, by applying a given set of rules or a derivation algorithm, respectively. The main benefit of the synthetic approach is its ability to ensure important correctness properties, such as deadlock and livelock freedom, and termination (see Chapter 11) through the design. This allows one in principle to avoid an explicit verification phase, but most approaches are tied to certain assumptions (e.g., synchronous communication, limited state space) that restrict this benefit (see [Prob 91]).

There are two approaches to deriving a protocol specification from a given partial draft: (1) starting from the service specification or (2) using the peer entity specification. Examples of the first approach are the methods described in [Prob 91], [Higa 93], [Kant 96]. The approach of [Prob 91] uses finite state machines. It analyses the interactions at the service interface and generates the related transitions according to predefined transformation rules. The rules are determined by the structure of the service specification, the communication direction of the service primitives, and their causal dependencies. The method assumes a reliable communication channel. The derived protocol specification meets important properties, such as deadlock and livelock freedom. It contains no unspecified events. An extended version of the approach also supports the specification and treatment of parallel processes at the service access points and the use of an unreliable transmission medium.

An example of the derivation of the protocol specification from the peer entity is given in [Rama 85]. The approach starts from a Petri net specification of the entity. It is converted into an FSM representation and verified for correctness. From this specification the partner FSM is derived using various transformation rules. This can be done automatically or interactively. The derived FSM is mapped into a Petri net again. It was used to re-design the ITU-T X.21 protocol. Later it was extended for unreliable communication.

A different approach is the structured synthesis proposed in [Choi 87]. This technique applies an interactive synthesis based on previously designed smaller protocol units that represent closed interaction patterns, which are derived from typical interaction scenarios, such as connection set up. These units possess exactly defined interfaces via which they are connected with the other units. The resulting design is finally converted into an FSM representation. The method guarantees a deadlock-free synthesis with no unspecified events. The applicability of the method was also demonstrated by re-designing the X.21 protocol. A similar approach – the SDL design patterns – is presented below.

In summary, it has to be mentioned that protocol synthesis is primarily of theoretical interest. The scope of the various approaches is not limited to communication protocols. It is much broader and comprises distributed applications and systems in general, collaborative computations, control systems, and others [Yama 07]. The assumptions made are often simplifying or use contexts which are not typical for real-life communication protocols. So in [Kant 96], the existence of a central controller and more than two entities is assumed. The controller sends synchronization messages to coordinate the different process runs. In substance, synthesis methods provide means to map a given service specification (or a peer entity) into a protocol specification based on a relatively simple message exchange pattern. For this, they can ensure a correct design according to the applied description method or technique, respectively. These methods do not take into account design aspects – and this is their limitation – which cannot (or only with great difficulty) be derived from the service specification, such as data format specifications, error handling procedures, and others. Especially, protocol functions that are related to the underlying layer, such as flow control, fragmentation, connection mappings etc., cannot be derived this way. For this reason, protocol synthesis will have limited importance as a design approach for real protocols in the near future.

Analytical design methods

The analytical design methods correspond to the traditional approach of a step-wise protocol design based on more or less accurate requirement definitions. The first design steps are typically ad hoc; e.g., by defining the exchanged messages or describing the first interactions. For this, MSCs are often used (cp. Section 8.2). These designs are verified, revised, and refined in several iteration steps until the protocol (fragment) is completely specified. In contrast to the synthetic design methods, these approaches do not guarantee an error-free design. Therefore the design has to be verified.

In order to diminish the ad hoc nature of this approach systematic design methodologies are needed. Such a methodology, for example, was developed for LOTOS and tested in several case studies [Viss 92], but it did not achieve practical relevance. Another example is the SDL design pattern approach described in [Gotz 03], [Dors 05].

The **SDL design pattern approach** is based on the design pattern technique applied in software engineering for reuse of design decisions. An SDL design pattern is a reusable, generic template, described in SDL, for a recurring protocol sequence. It is stored in a pattern pool. The integration of SDL design patterns into the design is part of the overall protocol development process. The objective of this process is the development of an SDL specification. The starting point is a set of design requirements which are analyzed and summarized in an analysis model consisting of an architectural part described in terms of a UML object model and collaboration scenarios described in MSC. Based on the analysis model the designer selects appropriate patterns from the pattern pool (see Figure 10.1/1). The selected patterns are adapted to the given embedding context creating pattern instances. The adaptations are restricted by constraints of the SDL context, and by renaming and refinement rules in the pattern definition. Finally the pattern instance is included in the SDL specification. Thereafter, the next set of design requirements is considered. This results in an incremental design process that eventually leads to a complete SDL specification.

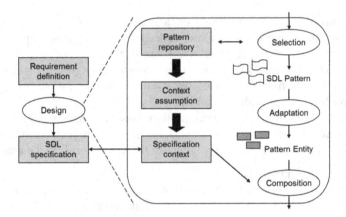

Figure 10.1/1: SDL design pattern in the design process

An SDL design pattern definition consists of several parts. Each pattern begins with an identifying *name*, an *intention*, which informally describes the purpose of this pattern, and a *motivation*, which gives examples of the pattern usage. The introduction part is followed by a *structure* description which graphically shows the involved design components, e.g., service users or protocol entities, and their relations. *Message scenarios* describe the interaction of the pattern with the environment. These can be represented by message sequence charts. The *SDL fragment* describes the syntactical structure of the pattern and the context in which the pattern is applicable. The remainder of the design pattern contains various rules for the adaptation and incorporation of the pattern into the design context. Figure 10.1/2 shows a fragment of an example pattern.

In order to illustrate the design process using SDL design patterns we sketch here the design process following [Gotz 03]. The design process starts from the informal service and protocol description. First a partitioning is carried out to derive the aforementioned requirement subsets. The decomposition is based on heuristics gathered in various case studies. The following list of heuristics is considered for the service specification:

H_1 *To start with, define the system architecture: identify entities and channels, and compose them.*

H_2 *To build up communication functionality, start with a reliable medium.*

H_3 *Decompose the communication functionality, e.g., according to protocol phases or related functional units.*

H_4 *In systems with multicast communication, start with the unicast case and generalize this to the multicast case later.*

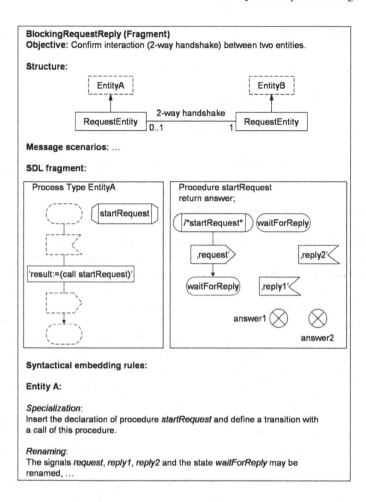

Figure 10.1/2: Example of an SDL design pattern (source [Gotz 99])

For a typical communication service, the following decomposition would be derived applying the heuristics H_1, H_2, and H_3:

Step I: Service architecture

Step II: Connection set up phase

Step III: Data transfer phase

Step IV: Data release phase.

For the protocol specification, protocol-specific heuristics are applied, such as

H_5 *Refine the service design*

H_6 *Add flow control, if applicable*

H_7 *Add multiplexing, if applicable*

H_8 *Gradually relax the reliable communication assumption by taking transmission errors and/or reordering into account, if applicable*

and others. A demonstration of the design process for the *InRes* protocol is given in [Gotz 03].

The SDL design pattern approach supports the reuse of design templates and experience of various applications. It speeds up the development of the specification, and facilitates the documentation of the design as well as its validation, since refinements and adaptations can more easily be traced back. Experiments have shown that the approach remarkably reduces error rates during the design phase [Gotz 03]. The focus of the SDL design pattern approach, however, is more oriented towards an incremental and systematic development of SDL specifications rather than to a creative protocol design process as discussed above. Many creative design decisions, such as system architecture design or message exchange, are described in terms of UML and MSC. Nevertheless, the approach can essentially improve the quality of the service and protocol specifications and help to diminish some of the problems encountered when developing formal specifications, as discussed in the following section. The approach has been successfully applied to the engineering and re-engineering of several communication protocols and systems, such as the Internet *Stream Protocol* ST2+, a subset of the RTP protocol, a controller area network, a light control in a building, and others. The basis for a successful application is the size of the pattern pool which has grown up in various projects, although the number of patterns required for a specification has proved to be not that large.

10.2   Specification development

After discussing different aspects of the design process, we now address the development of formal specifications. Although much has already been said about the specification in the previous chapters, certain aspects of specification development have not yet been mentioned. This we do now.

The specification documents the design decisions. Since the design of a protocol usually requires several iterations, it is recommended to use formal description techniques already during the design phase to verify the various versions of the draft and, where appropriate, to assess their performance. For this reason, there is no sharp line between the design process and the specification development. Nevertheless, the service and protocol specifications represent important steps in the protocol development process because both specifications provide the basis for the further protocol development stages, which have particular demands in terms of accuracy and completeness. Important aspects for the development of both specifications are the selection of the description technique and the way the specification is accomplished.

10.2.1 Selection of the description technique

The selection of the formal description method or technique is a priori not an easy decision because there is no method that meets all requirements. The existence of standard description techniques has laid an emphasis on these languages, but the existence of several languages has partitioned the users in "fan communities". Sometimes, other techniques, e.g., in-house solutions, are preferred in order to use existing tools or for administrative reasons.

As long as the development of new protocols is not directly linked to a certain formal description technique, there will always be a broader range of techniques and methods which may be applied. On the one hand, this may be prejudicial, since, as we have seen in Chapter 8, changing between FDTs is not that easy and their use requires experience. On the other hand, it may be useful because different methods and techniques emphasize varying aspects of the design. For instance, more abstract representations, such as Petri nets or temporal logics, are better suited for analysis and verification purposes than descriptions in SDL, which better support the implementer. The combined use of different formal techniques is, therefore, an advantage for the protocol and system development process as a whole. The problem is the mapping of the various representations (possibly automatically) onto each other preserving the semantics of the specification. This is very difficult to achieve due to the complexity of the formal descriptions.

Now the question is what are the criteria to select the description method or technique, respectively? Generally speaking, one should select that technique which meets best the requirements of the protocol or system to be designed. In practice, the decision is much more complicated because many criteria may influence the selection. The selection criteria can be differentiated into general and specific ones.

General selection criteria
The general selection criteria relate to the context of the application of the formal description technique or method. Important criteria include:

- *Pursued objectives*
  The description techniques are based on different semantic models and consequently have divergent properties which support the various phases of the protocol development process differently. Therefore, the selection depends substantially on the objectives of the respective design.

- *Administrative background*
  Often, a company or organization prescribes the use of certain description techniques. A typical example is the use of SDL in the telecommunication sector.
- *Psychological aspects*
  Users' experience and training have a considerable influence on the selection of formal techniques. It may also influence administrative decisions.
- *Availability of tools*
  The support of the description technique through applicable, mature, and/or commercially available tools can often be a decisive factor in the selection.

Special selection criteria

The special selection criteria relate to the specific characteristics of the description techniques themselves. They reflect the users' assessment of how the demands on formal description techniques are met, as we formulated them at the beginning of Chapter 8. Some important selection criteria are listed in Table 10.2/1. The assessment is of course essentially influenced by subjective factors.

Applicability	*Is the description technique appropriate for the design, i.e., does it meet its specific requirements? Does it allow one to specify service and protocol in a reasonable form? What is the application range of the technique?*
Interpretation	*Does the description technique guarantee a unique, comprehensible, and readable presentation, which avoids different interpretation and thus makes varying implementations of the protocol unlikely?*
Naturalness	*Does the description technique correspond to the needs of the application area and its related requirements? Does it support the intuitive reasoning of the users?*
Homogeneity	*Do the features of the description technique belong to the same model world or do they complement each other?*
Completeness	*Does the description technique allow one to describe all relevant requirements of the design?*
Abstraction	*Does the description technique possess the capability to abstract away irrelevant details?*
Ease to learn	*What is the effort required to learn the description technique?*
Design support	*Can the description technique be applied during the design phase? How does it support the subsequent phases up to implementation and testing?*
Tool support	*What kinds of tools are available?*

Table 10.2/1: Specific criteria for the selection of a description technique

10.2.2   Development of formal descriptions

Creating a service and a protocol specification is usually an ambitious and time-consuming process. It can take several months and requires a lot of experience as well as a good understanding of the protocol by the specifier. The use of formal description techniques during the design phase supports this process beneficially. FDTs allow iteratively developing the specification (see Figure 10.2 /1). In addition, they provide a clear theoretical background for the design process. The different design steps can be formally verified and their consistency with the former design level proved. Prototypes can also be derived to validate the different design decisions (see Chapter 11 for this). Nevertheless, the development of a specification remains expensive and often requires several iterations.

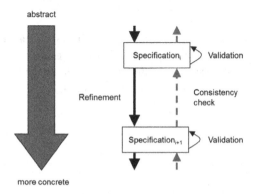

Figure 10.2/1: Step-wise development of a specification as a result of the design process

The ideal case of developing a formal specification as a direct result of the design process occurs seldom in practice. Often formal specifications are worked out based on the informal description of a standard because most protocols are not designed systematically. They are often the result of a long development process in standardization bodies or working groups. The development of the respective formal description is a subsequent activity which is often not accomplished by the designers themselves.

Moreover, there are no fixed rules concerning how to develop a formal description. The basic problem is the finding of an appropriate structure for the specification, which also optimally supports subsequent development steps, in particular the derivation of implementations [Köni 00]. This is not easy to achieve due to the complexity of the descriptions. A possible approach is to structure the specification according to functional aspects, e.g., taking the protocol phases into account, as we did in the introductory chapters. Another way to find appropriate structures is the usage of dedicated specification styles, as proposed for LOTOS (cp. Section 8.3.8). But there is also a subjective impact of the specifier on the specification structure. As with the programming of larger programs, the complexity of the description gives the specifier enough freedom for an individual specification style.

This holds in particular for constructive techniques which represent quasi-implementations of the protocol or system design on a more abstract level (cp. Section 7.3). Thus, the resulting specification is not always optimal and some of the benefits of formal descriptions may get lost. This can only be avoided if authorized formal descriptions are provided by standardization bodies for use as reference specifications. Only thus, the uniqueness and binding character of the specifications as well as an optimal specification structure can be ensured. This is not yet the case. With few exceptions, most formal descriptions are developed in the academic environment. They can hardly be used as binding reference specifications because they are mostly not complete. Furthermore, formal descriptions are often only available after the first protocol implementations have appeared. This reduces their importance.

Further reading

As with Chapters 7 and 9, this chapter extracts facts which are contained in many publications on protocols and their description. Besides the cited papers we again recommend the proceedings of the FORTE conference series [FORTE] including its predecessor PSTV (*Protocol Specification, Testing, and Verification*) for further studies.

11 Verification

The protocol verification phase has the task to prove the logical correctness and operation of the protocol design as it is documented in the service and protocol specification. Its goal is to ensure prior to coding that all the specified design requirements are worked out accurately and of course to detect design errors. The protocol design is, strictly speaking, not finalized and the specification not completed, as long as its correctness has not been proven formally. Since the protocol specification forms the basis for various protocol implementations in different execution environments, great importance is attached to the protocol verification to ensure the functional feasibility of the protocol. This is the reason why protocol verification has been established as an independent stage in the protocol development process (cp. Chapter 9). The protocol verification phase, like protocol specification and protocol testing, is one of the most intensively explored stages of the protocol development process. Many approaches have been proposed and investigated. Some of them have contributed successfully to the detection of design errors in real-life protocols [West 89], [Holz 91], [Lai 98], [Gord 00]. In this chapter we give an overview of the most important methods of protocol verification and their fields of application.

The term protocol verification is not always applied uniformly in the literature. Sometimes the term protocol validation is used synonymously. In this book we apply the differentiation used in software engineering [Somm 00]. *Protocol validation* aims at answering the question: "*Are we building the right product?*" It comprises the process of evaluating the functional and non-functional aspects of the protocol design in relation to the user requirements. Protocol validation is a more general process that comprises various activities of the protocol development process like performance evaluation, prototyping, and various forms of protocol testing (see Figure 11.1/1). We consider them in the subsequent chapters.

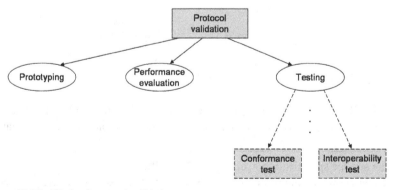

Figure 11.1/1: Kinds of protocol validation

Protocol verification, in contrast, tries to answer the question *"Are we building the product right?"* It formally proves whether the service and the protocol are specified correctly. This is the focus of the current chapter.

11.1   About protocol verification

Protocol verification has the goal to formally prove the correctness, completeness, and consistency of a protocol design documented through its specification. The notion of *correctness* refers to the functional correctness of the design including the provision of the specified service within a finite time. *Completeness* demands the consideration of all possible events and options including related reactions. *Consistency* relates to the absence of internal contradictions in the design.

Exactly speaking, the protocol verification pursues two goals: to prove that the protocol design is consistent and that the specified protocol really provides the specified service[1]. Note that the formal proof that an implemented protocol is in compliance with the protocol specification is not part of the protocol verification. This is checked by the conformance test (see Chapter 14). Protocol testing relates to the protocol implementation rather than to the protocol design. Testing, however, cannot give evidence about the correctness of an implementation because it is often incomplete and does not examine all the possible protocol behaviors. Protocol verification and protocol testing are therefore complementary techniques in the protocol development process.

In accordance with the aforementioned two goals, protocol verification is divided into verification of general properties and verification of special properties (see Figure 11.1/2).

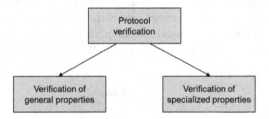

Figure 11.1/2: Kinds of protocol verification

The **verification of general properties** proves properties which must be fulfilled regardless of the specific semantics of the designed protocol. It targets mainly

---

[1] The service specification itself cannot be verified in this sense, as it is the reference against which the protocol is verified. But, it is possible to verify the consistency of the service specification.

the consistency and completeness of the design. The most important properties are summarized in Table 11.1/1. For each property, we give the respective protocol behavior.

No unreachable actions	*The protocol does not contain any actions which will never be executed.*
Deadlock freedom	*The protocol will never reach a state which it cannot leave any more and in which, consequently, no further interactions with the environment are possible.*
Livelock freedom	*The protocol will never enter an unproductive cycle (e.g., the repeated exchange of the same message) which it cannot leave by itself.*
Fault tolerance and resynchronization	*After an error or in an abnormal situation, the protocol will return within finite time to a state from which it can continue with a specified behavior.*
Completeness	*The protocol does not contain unspecified events, i.e., for all possible events a reaction is specified.*
Termination	*The protocol will always reach one of the possible final states; in cyclic protocols the initial state.*

Table 11.1/1: Important general properties to verify

The **verification of special properties** examines properties that are determined by the semantics of the designed protocol. The purpose of this verification is to prove that the designed protocol provides the specified service.

11.2   Verification techniques

Verification techniques for communication protocols can be generally divided into

- model-based,
- deductive, and
- hybrid

methods. *Model-based verification* checks the correctness, completeness, and consistency of the specification using proof techniques which operate directly on the semantic model of the applied formal description technique. Examples of model-based verification are the reachability analysis of finite state machines and the static and dynamic analysis of Petri nets.

Deductive verification is based on the use of axioms and inference rules to prove the correctness of the design. It uses the syntax of the description technique as a formal basis extended by axioms on semantic relationships and inference rules, thus forming a calculus which purely syntactically permits conclusions on the correctness of the specified statements. Syntactic deduction leads to a chain of theorems that are derived from each other and proved. These proofs require experience and are often performed by hand. A theorem prover can support this process. The proof of protocol invariants is part of the deductive verification, such as the order of message sequences or buffer limits. Manual verifications, however, have proven too expensive, lengthy, and error-prone. They are of little importance for practical protocol verification, particularly as not all properties of interest can be verified with reasonable efforts [Holz 91].

Hybrid techniques try to take advantage of both approaches by combining the good tool support of the model-based techniques with the clear deduction rules of syntactic verification. The best known example is model checking.

The choice of the verification method depends crucially on the used description technique or method, respectively. Different techniques are applied to the various specification methods. The standardized formal description techniques have not been designed for the specific needs of verification. They are primarily designed to meet specification requirements. Therefore many formal protocol descriptions cannot be directly used for verification. They must be transferred into a suitable intermediate representation which can be used as input for the verification process.

In the subsequent sections we present the most important verification techniques for communication protocols. We discuss their application fields and the conditions for their use.

11.3   Reachability analysis

The most commonly used verification method for FSM/EFSM based protocol descriptions is **reachability analysis** which aims at the exhaustive exploration of all possible behaviors of the protocol entities by generating all reachable states and transitions described by the finite state machines.

11.3.1   Reachability graph

For this purpose, the reachable states of the "protocol systems" are generated, which comprises the two entities and the communication channel between them. Starting from the initial state, a graph is generated that contains all reachable states as nodes and the associated state transitions as edges. This graph is called a **reachability graph**. The states of the reachability graph represent global system states.

Figures 11.3/1-2 illustrate the principle for the connection set up of the XDT protocol according to Figures 7.4/1 and 7.5/1. The figures only represent the major states of the two entities. Pictures a) and b) in Figure 11.3/1 contain the state-transition graphs of the sender and the receiver entity. Picture c) depicts the protocol system including respective input and output events. The sender and receiver entities *XS* and *XR* are linked by separate channels. It is assumed that these channels have a capacity of two messages in each direction. The reachability graph of the overall system is represented in Figure 11.3/2. For each system state, the current states of the entities and in square brackets the respective channel assignments are indicated. The initial and final states are indicated by stronger lines.

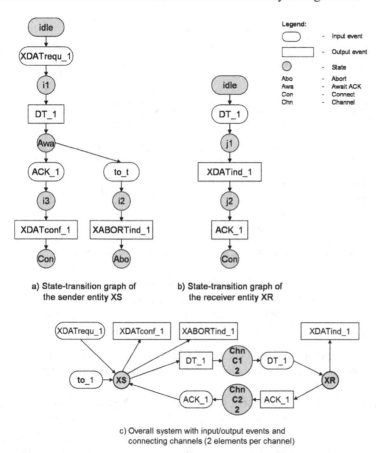

a) State-transition graph of
the sender entity XS

b) State-transition graph of
the receiver entity XR

c) Overall system with input/output events and
connecting channels (2 elements per channel)

Figure 11.3/1: Protocol system for the connection set up of the XDT protocol

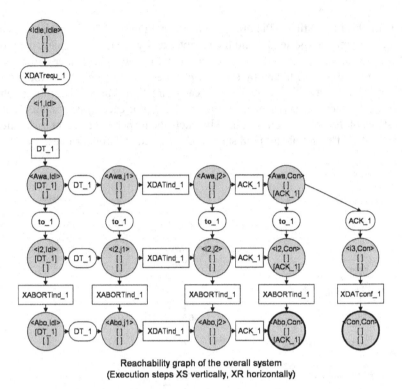

Reachability graph of the overall system
(Execution steps XS vertically, XR horizontally)

Figure 11.3/2: Reachability graph for the connection set up of the XDT protocol

The objective of the reachability analysis is to explore which states of the protocol can be reached and whether the execution paths to get there are correct. With the help of the reachability analysis both general and special properties of the protocol design can be proved. General properties are proved as follows:

- **Deadlock freedom:** The protocol is deadlock-free if there are no states in the reachability graph, except the final states, without a successor state (which therefore cannot be left).
- **Livelock freedom:** The protocol is livelock-free if there are no execution sequences which can be infinitely repeated without achieving visible progress in protocol execution.
- **No unreachable actions:** The protocol does not contain any unreachable actions if all specified actions can be assigned to at least one edge of the reachability graph.
- **Termination:** The protocol terminates correctly if the reachability graph reaches the expected final states.

Specific protocol properties, e.g., the adherence to certain PDU sequences, can be formulated as invariants of states by logical expressions, which are proved when reaching the state. Furthermore, the reachability graph can be inspected with respect to the equivalence of the externally visible behavior [Krum 90]. Thus, it can be shown that the protocol specification really provides the specified service. Reachability analysis consists of two steps: the generation of the reachability graph and its subsequent analysis. The graph is generated iteratively by traversing all possible execution paths of the protocol system. The derivation begins with the initial state by generating the successor state for all executable transitions. Each generated state is stored. In addition, each new state is examined to see whether it has been already reached via another execution path to avoid the state is being analyzed several times. The generation of the reachability graph terminates when no new successor state is found. Consequently, it does not terminate for an infinite state space.

In the 1990s *on-the-fly* techniques were developed which connect the graph generation with the analysis of system properties. The graph generation stops when an error in the specification has been revealed. The benefit is that this avoids the storing of the graph states for further analysis (see below). Figure 11.3/3 contains the algorithm for an *on-the-fly* analysis. The presented principle is that of *full search*, in which all states of the graph are inspected. The algorithm uses two sets: the *working set S* and the *set of generated states W*. The set *S* contains all states that still have not been fully analyzed, i.e., their successor states have not been fully generated. The set *W* contains all states generated up to now. In case of a successful completion of the analysis these are all reachable states of the system.

```
full_search()
   {add(W,q0);                          // q0 - Initial state
    add(S,q0);
    while ¬ empty(S) do
      {q = select(S);
       remove(S,q);
       if (error_state(q))
          {error_report()};              // Abort analysis
       forall successor states p of q     // Generation of successor states
          {if (¬ member(W,p))
             {add(W,p);
              add(S,p);
             }
          }
      }
   }
```

Figure 11.3/3: Principle of full search (after [Holz 91])

Depending on how the states are removed from the working set *S* two types of searches are distinguished (see Figure 11.3/4):

- breadth-first search, and
- depth-first search.

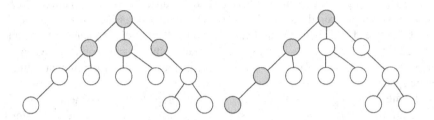

Figure 11.3/4: Breadth-first vs. depth-first search

In **breadth-first search** the working set is organized as a FIFO queue, i.e., the states are entered and removed to/from the set according to the *first-in first-out* principle. This has the advantage that error states with short execution paths are revealed first. However, the working set is larger. **Depth-first search** organizes the working set as a stack. The states are analyzed according to the *last-in first-out* principle (LIFO). The main advantage of depth-first search is that the execution path from start to the error state can be read out directly from the stack, when an error has been detected. It is implicitly given by the storing sequence of the working set. Breath-first search, in contrast, must reconstruct the path from the states already stored in the working set.

11.3.2 State space explosion

State space explosion phenomenon

Reachability analysis has to perform two operations on the stored states [West 89]:

- It must compare global states regarding their equivalence to prevent the multiple analyses of states.
- It must be able to return to the analysis of a former state.

This requires that the states are stored in an appropriate manner. This can lead to a very high demand on memory. While for a pure FSM specification only the major states have to be considered, the analysis of the in practice relevant EFSM-based specifications has to take also the minor states, i.e., the various assignments to variables and input queues, into account. If the specification further consists of several sub-automata the reachability graph can, due to the interleaving of the events, quickly reach a size that no longer allows an exhaustive state exploration because the states cannot be stored any longer. This phenomenon is called **state space explosion**. It represents the central issue of the applicability of reachability analysis, although the number of reachable states that can be analyzed has increased considerably in the past two decades. Even smaller protocols often reach a state space size from 10^5 to 10^9 states as the following assessment of the XDT protocol demonstrates. It takes the major and minor states into account, where for the latter only the possible value ranges are counted. We omit the input queue for the sake of simplicity.

XDT	Sender entity	Receiver entity
Major states	5	3
Minor states	*sequ*: n	*N*: n
	last: 2	
	buffer: k	
	N: n	
	i: k	

The constants n and k indicate the number of data units to be transferred and the size of the buffer to store unconfirmed DT-PDUs. If we assume the values 50 and 5 for n and k, the state space of the XDT protocol comprises $93.75 * 10^6$ states, i.e., approximately 10^8 states.

Exhaustive search remains therefore restricted to smaller protocols (up to 10^9 states). Most protocols have a larger state space. However, not all states and interleaving sequences are of interest for the protocol execution and the error search. Mechanical detection and removal of such states might be more difficult than the continuous analysis of the state area. Therefore, other procedures have been required to cope with the complexity of the state space.

Coping with the state space problem
The state space explosion problem has been studied intensively. A number of approaches have been developed. Some important ones are sketched here. More detailed representations can be found in [Holz 91], [Lai 98], and [Clar 00].

Decomposition and partitioning
Decomposition and partitioning is one the oldest approaches to solve this problem [Chow 85]. It uses the relative autonomy of protocol parts and phases by analyzing these parts separately which results in smaller state spaces for each. But this method hardly covers dependencies between the protocol parts.

Projection
This approach reduces the size of the reachability graph by model simplification without changing the externally visible behavior of the protocol automata

[Lam 84], [Krum 90]. For this purpose, a projection function is created for each function to be verified by grouping states and the associated events in one state. As a consequence, the logical behavior of the whole protocol cannot be analyzed any longer. This requires several projections.

Controlled partial search

Controlled partial search analyses only a subset of the reachable states to hold the number of states to be stored within feasible limits. The principle of the full search of Figure 11.3/3 is modified for this so that not all successor states of the reached state are generated:

> **for some** *successor states p* **of** *q*   // Generation of successor states
> {**if** ($\neg$ *member*(W,p))
>   {*add*(W,p);
>   *add*(S,p)
>   }
> }

The size of the state space which can be analyzed by partial search depends on the applied search method and the available memory. It should be arranged that the main protocol sequences are covered, but this cannot be guaranteed. The coverage of controlled partial search has some commonalities with the test coverage (see Section 14.3.4) because only parts of the state space are examined. As with testing, criteria have to be formulated to evaluate the quality of the search. Here the analysis coverage and the error detection rate are used. The *analysis coverage* is characterized by the ratio of the analyzed states to the number of all possible system states. This measure indicates how well the search covers the possible system states, but it gives no indication whether the relevant protocol sequences are covered. The error detection rate is defined by the ratio of detected errors to the total number of existing errors, though this is difficult to capture.

There are a couple of different techniques to control the partial search. They range from *depth restricted search*, via *scattered search, guided search, probability-based search* to *partial ordering search*. A detailed description of these techniques can be found in [Holz 91].

Random search

In contrast to controlled partial search, *random search* (*random walk*) selects the next state to be analyzed arbitrarily (see Figure 11.3/5). The analyzed states do not to have be stored. Random walk is a method for very large systems, when it is no longer possible to store a reasonable set of states in order to apply other analysis methods. The random search is independent of the size of the system to be analyzed. Like testing (see Chapter 14), it can only detect errors, but it cannot prove the absence of errors because it is not decidable whether all achievable states were analyzed. A good error detection rate has nevertheless been stated for longer analysis times [West 89].

```
random_search()
  {p:= q0;                                    // q0 - Initial state
  repeat until analysis stop
    {if (error_state(p))
      {error_report();
       p:= q0
      }
    else p:=a successor state of p
    }
  }
```

Figure 11.3/5: Principle of random search (after [Holz 91])

Symbolic Algorithms

An essential reduction of the presentation of the state space can be achieved by using a symbolic representation. For this, the reachability graph is represented by mapping successor relations between states of the reachability graph onto *ordered binary decision diagrams* (OBDDs) [Brya 86], [McMi 93], a very popular representation for Boolean functions. They provide a canonical representation for Boolean functions which is often much more compact than other representations and can be manipulated very efficiently. OBDDs are widely used, especially in hardware verification [Eben 05]. Unlike the methods mentioned previously, the state space is not generated explicitly when using OBDDs. It is represented by Boolean functions as described in [McMi 93], [Clar 00].

OBDDs are a variant of the more general binary decision diagrams (BDDs). A BDD is a rooted directed acyclic graph which is derived from a binary decision tree by merging isomorphic sub-trees and by using two types of terminal nodes: 0-terminal and 1-terminal nodes (see Figure 11.3/6). Each non-terminal node is labeled by a variable x_i and has two successor nodes $low(v)$ and $high(v)$. A binary decision diagram B with root v determines a Boolean function $f_v(x_1, \ldots, x_n)$ as follows [Clar 00]:

(1) If v is a terminal node:
   - if $(value(v) = 1$ then $f_v(x_1, \ldots, x_n) = 1$
   - if $(value(v) = 0$ then $f_v(x_1, \ldots, x_n) = 0$
(2) If v is a non-terminal node with $var(v) = x_i$ then f_v is the function
   $f_v(x_1, \ldots, x_n) = (\neg x_i \wedge f_{low(v)}(x_1, \ldots, x_n)) \vee (x_i \wedge f_{high(v)}(x_1, \ldots, x_n))$.

Figure 11.3/6a shows an example of a BDD. The solid lines are used for *high*-edges, whereas dashed lines indicate a *low*-edge. Ordered binary decision diagrams are graphs which apply a strict ordering of the variables on all paths from the root to the terminal nodes. Figure 11.3/6b shows the respective OBBD for our example. Note that the representation has been reduced further by merging the isomorphic sub-trees which appear when applying a strict variable ordering to the BDD in picture a). A further reduction can be achieved when besides the merging of isomorphic sub-trees also all nodes with identical successor nodes are removed (see Figure 11.3/6c). These graphs are called *reduced ordered binary decision diagrams* (ROBDDs).

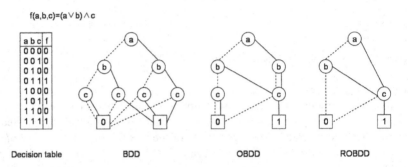

Figure 11.3/6: Binary ordered diagrams

The variable ordering decisively determines the size of an OBDD. Finding an optimal ordering for variables is difficult. Deciding whether a given ordering is optimal is NP-complete [Brya 92]. Heuristics have been developed to find appropriate variable orderings, especially for circuit verification.

The use of OBBDs has led to substantially more compact representations of the state space. Compared to explicit state algorithms, analyses with 10^{20} and with refined techniques even up to 10^{120} states are reported [Clar 00]. Symbolic algorithms though are mainly used for circuit verification rather than in protocol verification.

Partial order reduction

Partial order techniques exploit the independence of concurrently executed actions as they result from applying the interleaving model (cp. Section 1.2.4). They proceed from the assumption that the concurrent actions are executed independently of each other. The order of their execution does not change the final result. The kernel idea of the partial order reduction approach is not to generate the full state space with all interleaving sequences but only a partial space which takes only one interleaving sequence into account. This requires a relation to check whether two actions are independent of each other. Examples of partial order reduction techniques are the *stubborn sets* of Valmari [Valm 92], the *sleep sets* of Godefroid [Gode 96], and the *ample sets* of Peled [Clar 00]. The stubborn sets approach, for example, divides at each state the set of executable transitions into two subsets: the set of "stubborn" transitions – the *stubborn set* — and the set of non-stubborn transitions. The stubborn set contains generally a subset of all con-currently executable transitions that are not affected by the switching of other transitions and they do not themselves affect other transitions. Only one of the possible interleaving sequences of this subset is taken into account when generat-ing the state space. It is not trivial though to determine this subset. Often heuristics are applied [Clar 00].

Supertrace algorithm

Another way to mitigate the state space explosion problem is to improve the storable number of states, given by the ratio of available space and the number of bytes needed to store a state. This was done in the *supertrace algorithm* developed by Holzmann that is described in [Holz 91]. The algorithm reduces the memory needed to store a state to one bit so that a larger reachable space can be analyzed. A new state is stored in the memory using a hash function. This function always returns the same value for the same state thus indicating that the state already has been reached. Hash conflicts are the steering element here. If state space is sparse and the available memory is sufficiently large the method shows good results. It behaves like full search for smaller protocols. When this relation declines, the al-gorithm converts into a randomized partial search for larger protocols. Compared to other controlled partial search algorithms, however, it behaves more optimally.

11.4   Petri net analysis

Petri net analysis is another interesting approach to protocol verification. Its ca-pabilities are briefly outlined in this section. As in Section 7.6, we focus on the verification of place/transition nets. Examples of the use of other net types are contained among others in [Bill 99].

11.4.1   Preparation of the Petri net for analysis

In order to perform a Petri net analysis it is required that the specification either exists as a Petri net or can be derived automatically from the protocol specification (cp. Section 7.6). If the specification consists of several networks the partial nets have to be merged at the fusion places. Figure 11.4/1 shows the Petri net for the connection set up phase of the XDT protocol that has been formed from the sub-nets of the protocol parts *connect_s* and *connect_r* (cp. Figure 7.6/4). The fusion places are grey. In addition, the behavior of the environment must be modeled to ensure that the net has a bounded state space. The interactions at the service inter-face are modeled through the behavior of the service users. The network in Figure 11.4/1 contains further some fusion places which are only connected by an edge. These places refer to timers and to the beginning of the DATA_ TRANSFER phase which are not modeled here. The DATA_TRANSFER place represents the final place reached, when the connection is established successfully. Some of the places and transitions are numbered. We use these numbers as references in later figures. The indices *s*, *r*, and *e* used here stand for sender, receiver, and environment.

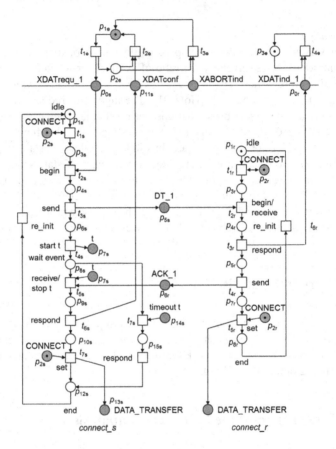

Figure 11.4/1: Petri net of the XDT connection set up

A simplified form to present a Petri net is an incidence matrix, which is used in various analyses. It is based on a fixed indexing of places and transitions (see Figure 11.4/2). This representation represents only in part the structure of the net. So it does not contain, for instance, the marking. The **incidence matrix** $C: S \times T \rightarrow$ $\{-1,0,+1\}$ of an ordinary Petri nets is defined by:

P \ T	t_{1s}	t_{2s}	t_{3s}	t_{4s}	...
	0	-1	0	0	
p_{1s}	-1	0	0	0	
p_{2s}	0	0	0	0	
p_{3s}	+1	-1	0	0	
p_{4s}	0	+1	-1	0	
p_{5s}	0	0	+1	0	
p_{6s}	0	0	+1	-1	
p_{7s}	0	0	0	+1	
p_{8s}	0	0	0	+1	
:			...		

Figure 11.4/2: Fragment of the incidence matrix for the XDT connection set up

$$c_{ij} := \begin{cases} -1, & if \quad p \in \bullet t \ and \ p \notin t \bullet. \\ +1, & if \quad p \notin \bullet t \ and \ p \in t \bullet. \\ 0 & otherwise \end{cases}$$

A matrix element c_{ij} describes how many token are removed from or added to a place $p_i \in P$, when the transition $t_j \in T$ fires once. In ordinary Petri nets c_{ij} accepts only the values -1, +1, or 0. The values -1 and +1 indicate the decrease or increase in the number of tokens, respectively. The value of 0 may indicate that the token number is not changed because the place was not involved in the firing of the transition. A zero value may also be caused by a so-called *side condition* (see Figure 11.4/3). This is a link between a place and a transition by two opposite-directed edges (in nets often represented by a double-arrow (see Figure 11.4/1)). Side conditions are not visible in the incidence matrix because the number of tokens in p_i remains unchanged.

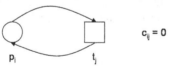

Figure 11.4/3: Side condition

Figure 11.4/2 shows a fragment of the incidence matrix for the net presented in Figure 11.4/1. The fragment comprises the places and transitions marked in Figure 11.4/1 with p_{0s}, p_{1s}, ... and t_{1s}, t_{2s}, ... Note that a side condition exists regarding place p_{2s}, when transition t_{1s} fires.

11.4.2 Behavioral properties of Petri nets

To verify communication protocols with the help of Petri nets it is necessary to map the protocol properties onto properties of the Petri net to assess them by means of the net analysis. The most important properties of place/transition nets are boundedness, liveness, and reversibility. These properties are orthogonal and cannot be derived from each other. So a reversible net, for example, may be bounded or not bounded and live or not live.

Boundedness

A Petri net $N = (P, T, F, m_0)$ is called *bounded* if the marking set $R_N(m_0)$ (cp. Section 7.6), i.e., the set of all reachable markings from the initial marking m_0, is finite. Otherwise, the network is *unbounded*. A Petri net is bounded exactly, if there is a number $n_p \in Nat$ for each place $p \in P$, so that for all $m \in R_N(m_0)$ we have $m(p) \leq n_p$, i.e., the number of tokens on place p does not exceed a certain value n_p for each marking. A Petri net with $n_p = 1$ for all places is called *safe* or *1-bounded*. Boundedness is a safety property (cp. Section 7.8) which excludes undesirable system properties, such as the requirement of unlimited resources or channel capacities. At the same time it is an important prerequisite for the analysis of the nets. Unbounded Petri nets are more difficult to analyze.

Liveness

A Petri net $N = (P, T, F, m_0)$ is said to be live if for all transitions $t \in T$ and each marking $m \in R_N(m_0)$ there exists a successor-marking $m' \in R_N(m)$ of m in which t is enabled. In a live net each transition is able in principle to fire again. Liveness expresses the ability of the modeled system that its elements can be executed again and again. The verification of liveness may be costly and impractical for large systems. For that reason, different levels of liveness have been introduced [Mura 89].

Important net properties are related to liveness:

- *Reachability*
  A marking and/or a state m' is reachable if there exists a sequence of transitions that transfers the net from the initial marking m_0 to the marking m', i.e., $m' \in R_N(m_0)$.
- *Deadlock freedom*
  A Petri net $N = (P, T, F, m_0)$ is *deadlock-free* if it never reaches a marking or a state $m \in R_N(m_0)$, respectively, in which no transitions are enabled and consequently no more transitions can fire. A live net is also deadlock-free. One distinguishes between partial and total deadlocks. In a partial deadlock there is a state $m \in R_N(m_0)$ and a subset $T' \in T$ of transitions, so that for all states $m' \in R_N(m)$ reachable from m there is no transition from T' which is enabled in m'. These transitions are not live. A partial deadlock blocks only a subsystem, while other parts of the system can be executed. A *total deadlock*, in contrast,

blocks the entire system, i.e., it reached a state in which no transition can fire any longer.

• *Dead transitions*
A Petri net $N = (P, T, F, m_0)$ may contain transitions that will never fire. Dead transitions indicate unreachable actions in the modeled system. Transitions that are already dead in the initial marking m_0 are called m_0-dead, but transitions may also later become dead after reaching another marking m. A Petri net that contains dead transitions is not live.

• *Livelock freedom*
A Petri net $N = (P, T, F, m_0)$ is livelock-free if the net never reaches a marking $m \in R_N(m_0)$ from which it can repeat endlessly the same transition sequence (unproductive cycles). Livelocks can arise, for example, through conflicts (cp. Section 7.6).

Reversibility
A Petri net $N = (P, T, F, m_0)$ is said to be reversible if m_0 is reachable from m for any marking $m \in R_N(m_0)$ so that the net is always able to return to the initial state independently of the current marking. Note that it is not always necessary to return to the initial state but rather to other selected states. These states are called home states [Mura 89]. Reversibility implies system features, such as fault tolerance and self-synchronization, that indicate whether the system can return after an error or from an abnormal state to a state with a specified reaction.

11.4.3   Analysis methods

The analysis methods of Petri nets may be divided into three classes [Hein 98]:

• Net-based animations,
• static analyses, and
• dynamic analyses.

Net-based animations
Net-based animation checks the functional behavior of the modeled system by simulating the token flow. There are various tools. Net-based animation is a special form of prototyping and not, strictly speaking, a verification method according to the discussion in the introductory section of this chapter. It may give a deeper insight into the operation of the modeled system, but it is not a substitute for systematic net analyses.

Static analyses
Static analyses inspect the net without creating the state space. They derive behavioral net properties from the structure of the net. The methods of static analysis are simpler than those of the dynamic analysis. They often require less memory, since they do not generate the reachable states of the net. Static analyses serve primarily for the analysis of general properties. The main methods are:

- net reduction,
- structural analysis, and
- net invariants.

Net reduction

The complexity of the nets is one of the major weaknesses of Petri nets. Net reduction attempts to reduce the net size by substituting subnet structures by smaller ones preserving the net properties. Reduction rules have been defined for this. Simple examples are the fusion of series of places and/or transitions or the elimination of self-loop places and/or transitions [Mura 89]. A set of reduction rules is said to be *complete*, if they transform each net into a minimal one that possesses the same properties with respect to boundedness and liveness. However, relatively few reduction rules can be defined for ordinary Petri nets, such as place/transition nets, so net reduction is of little importance for these nets.

Structural analyses

Structural analysis examines local structures of the net. These are the nodes and their immediate environment (pre- and post-transitions or -places). For example, in a net in which the number of input and output places is equal for all transitions it can be concluded that the number of tokens remains constant, i.e., the net is bounded. Vice versa, it can be concluded from the existence of transitions that do not possess input places that the network is unbounded, as these transitions can always fire. Such analyses allow statements on boundedness and liveness even for complex nets without generating the set of reachable states.

Net invariants

The incidence matrix defines equations whose solution allows one to derive statements about the dynamic net behaviour and the modelled system, respectively. The goal is to derive net invariants related to places and transitions, for short **P- and T-invariants**. To determine such invariants the following equations are derived from the incidence matrix

$$C \cdot \underline{t} = 0 \text{ and } \underline{p} \cdot C = 0$$

where $\underline{t} = (t_1, t_2, ..., t_m)$ and $\underline{p} = (p_1, p_2, ..., p_n)$ represent vectors of transitions and places. The equation system for determining a place invariant is, for example,

$$c_{11} \cdot p_1 + c_{21} \cdot p_2 + ... + c_{n1} \cdot p_n = 0$$
$$c_{12} \cdot p_1 + c_{22} \cdot p_2 + ... + c_{n2} \cdot p_n = 0$$

$$\cdots$$

$$c_{1m} \cdot p_1 + c_{2m} \cdot p_2 + ... + c_{nm} \cdot p_n = 0.$$

Each vector $I_P = (p_1, p_2, ..., p_n)$ that fulfills this equation system is a P-invariant. A P-invariant refers to a set of places whose weighted sum of tokens is constant, i.e.,

$$m \cdot I_P = m_0 \cdot I_P$$

for all reachable markings $m \in R_N(m_0)$ in N. If $m \cdot I_P = 1$ then exactly one place can possess a token. This is called a 1-P-invariant. The places in the protocol part *connect_r* in Figure 11.4/1 without the fusion place CONNECT, for example, fulfill this condition. From the finite number of tokens of a P-invariant I_P it follows that the associated places are bounded. If in a net all places belong to a P-invariant I_P the net is bounded. Thus, P-invariants are a criterion to decide boundedness. Sometimes the equation system $\underline{p} \cdot C \leq 0$ is used. The solutions are called sub-invariants. A network is structurally bounded iff it can be completely covered with sub-invariants. P-invariants can be used for the verification of properties which imply a finite number of tokens. If the number of tokens is finite for a certain set of places then the fulfillment of these system properties can be deduced.

Similarly, each vector I_T that fulfills the equation system $C \cdot \underline{t} = 0$ is a T-invariant. A T-invariant I_T denotes a set of transitions whose firing reproduces a marking m. If one of the values $t_1, t_2, \ldots, t_m$ is greater than 1 then the associated transition must fire multiply to reproduce the marking. T-invariants describe possible cycles in the reachability graph (see below). Not all derived T-invariants are executable. This is because of side conditions (see Figure 11.4/3) and the fact that the initial marking is not taken into account in the computation. With the help of T-invariants, for example, statements about liveness can be formulated. All transitions which belong to an executable T-invariant are not dead regarding the initial marking m_0. A necessary condition for the liveness of a bounded net is that all its transitions may be covered with T-invariants.

Dynamic analyses

Dynamic analysis methods have to be applied if the required net properties cannot be derived by the less expensive static analysis methods. The classical approach here is also state space exploration by generating the reachability graph of the modeled system. The **reachability graph** of a Petri net $N = (P, T, F, m_0)$ is the graph

$$RG_N = [R_N(m_0), K_N] \text{ with } K_N = \{[m,t,m'] \mid m, m' \in R_N(m_0) \wedge t \in T \wedge m \xrightarrow{t} m'\}$$

which contains as nodes all markings m reachable in N and as transitions the actions which transfer the system to a new state or marking. The procedure for generating the reachability graph corresponds to that described in Section 11.3.1.

Figure 11.4/4 shows the beginning of the reachability graph for the Petri net of Figure 11.4/1. In this example we use marking vectors to represent the states of the state space. They indicate the places with tokens for the reached marking m:

$$\underline{m} = (m(p_1), m(p_2), \ldots m(p_n)).$$

m_0	1s	2s	1e	3e	1r	2r			
m_1	3s	2s	*	*	*	*			
m_2	1s	*	0s	*	*	*	2e		
m_3	1s	*	1e	*	3r	*			
m_4	3s	*	0s	*	1r	*	2e		
m_5	3s	*	1e	*	3r	*			
m_6	3s	*	0s	*	1r	*	2e		
m_7	1s	*	0s	*	3r	*	2e		
m_8	3s	*	1e	*	3r	*			
m_9	1s	*	0s	*	3r	*	2e		
m_{10}	3s	*	0s	*	3r	*	2e		
m_{11}	4s	*		*	3r	*	*		
m_{12}	6s	*	5s	*	3r	*	*		
m_{13}	8s	*	5s	*	3r	*	*	7s	
m_{14}	6s	*		*	4r	*	*		
m_{15}	8s	*		*	4r	*	*	7s	
m_{16}	6s	*		*	5r	*	*	7s	0r
m_{17}	8s	*		*	5r		*	7s	0r
m_{18}	15s	*		*	5r	*	*	7s	0r
m_{19}	8s	*	6r	*	7r	*	*	7s	0r
m_{20}	8s	*		3e	5r	*	*	7s	
m_{21}	9s	*		*	7r	*	*		0r
m_{22}	8s	*	6r	3e	7r	*	*	7s	
m_{23}	10s	*	11s	*	7r	*	*		0r
m_{24}	9s	*		3e	7r	*	*		
m_{25}	12s	2s	13s	*	7r	*	*		0r

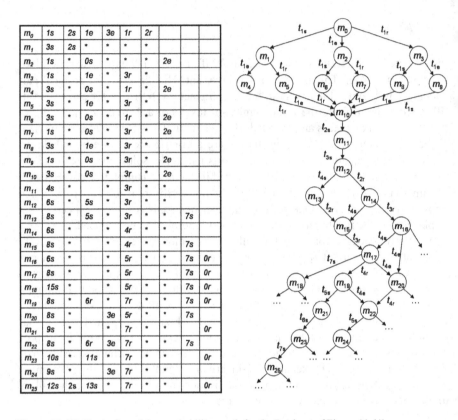

Figure 11.4/4: Beginning of the reachability graph for the Petri net of Figure 11.4/1

To simplify the presentation in safe or 1-bounded Petri nets often only those places are indicated that are marked in a state. This is also done in Figure 11.4/4. The table on the left-hand side contains the places with tokens in that marking. The places are indicated by the index of the place as used in Figure 11.4/1. Places that are not affected by the firing of a transition are indicated with "*".

The reachability graph is only finite for a bounded net. If the reachability graph cannot be derived then the **coverability graph** is computed. The computation is more complex. It is based on equivalence classes over infinite sets of states. The coverability graph can decide the boundedness of the net, but not other properties like reversibility, or liveness.

As with reachability analysis for state machines, the state space explosion phenomenon is the restrictive factor for dynamic analysis in Petri nets. In order to limit the state space to be analyzed similar methods are applied as described in Section 11.3.2 for reachability analysis, e.g., binary decision diagrams and partial order reduction techniques, such as the stubborn set and the sleep set methods.

Petri net analyses can be used to prove both general and special properties of the specification, in particular by analyzing the reachability graph [Hein 08]. The **general properties** can be verified as follows:

- **Boundedness:** The Petri net is bounded if the generation procedure for the reachability graph terminates. If the graph cannot be generated it cannot necessarily be concluded that the net is unbounded. A reason for this may be the lack of memory for storing the generated states. Instead the coverability graph may be calculated, but this is much more expensive. It, however, allows one to verify the boundedness of the net.
- **Dead transitions:** Transitions that will never fire are recognized by the fact that there are no edges in the graph which are labeled with these transitions, i.e., there is no state transition performed by these transitions.
- **Total deadlock:** A marking which cannot be left is represented in the reachability graph by a node without outgoing edges. Such a node is also called a leaf.
- **Liveness:** In order to determine whether a net is live the reachability graph is partitioned into strongly connected components. Such a component relates to a set of states in which each state is reachable from each state. A strongly connected component is called terminal if no other strongly connected component is reachable in the partitioned graph. The latter need not be generated explicitly. It only reflects the procedure. The net is live, if all transitions are in terminal strongly connected components.
- **Partial deadlock:** A partial deadlock occurs when one or more of the terminal strongly connected components of the reachability graphs do not contain all transitions. When the system progresses in these areas it will happen that parts of the system do not progress because one or more transitions do not become enabled any more, while other parts of the system keep progressing.
- **Livelock:** The possibility that the system contains unproductive cycles is reflected in the reachability graph by the fact that not all transitions are included in all cyclic execution paths of the graph. If this is the case there would be the possibility that a cyclic execution path can be omitted.
- **Reversibility:** A Petri net is reversible if the reachability graph is strongly connected, i.e., it is possible to return from each state to the initial state.

For the verification of **special properties,** different approaches can be chosen:

- **Model checking of special behavior properties:** In Petri net analysis model checking is also applied to prove whether desired system properties hold. The properties are formulated in temporal logics and proved by generating the reachability graph. We enlarge on model checking in Section 11.7.
- **Verification of the protocol specification against the service specification:** The question whether the specified protocol provides the offered service can be decided by means of Petri nets. For this purpose, both specifications, the

service and the protocol specification, are required in a Petri net representation. In the service specification the edges are labeled exclusively with service primitives. The reachability graph is generated for both nets. In both graphs all internal state transitions, i.e., state transitions that are not visible at the service interface, are labeled as the empty transition ε. Subsequently, both graphs are minimized and compared. The protocol specification is consistent with the service specification if there is an isomorphic relationship between the minimized reachability graphs of the service and protocol specifications. In [Gord 00], this approach was applied to colored Petri nets to check the compliance between the service and the protocol specification of the mobile communication protocol WAP Class 2 Wireless Transaction Protocol. Several inconsistencies were revealed.

In summary, Petri nets can be considered a useful approach for the verification of the protocol design. A major strength of Petri nets is their ability to analyze many properties which are relevant for distributed systems and protocols. Also the possibility of static analyses is advantageous. However, the size of the net increases quickly for ordinary Petri nets, even for small protocols like XDT. This requires resources and computing time. The use of net reduction methods or other net types can reduce the problem. Examples of successful use of colored Petri nets are described in [Bill 04] and [Bill 08]. Another problem with Petri net-based protocol verification is that the errors indicated by the analysis relate to errors in the Petri net, but they do not refer directly to the origin of the error in the source specification. This requires additional analyses. The crucial point, however, remains the elaboration or the derivation of the Petri net protocol specifications, as already argued in Chapter 7. This requires a good theoretical knowledge and experience. Therefore, the application of Petri nets in practical *Protocol Engineering* is limited.

11.5   Algebraic verification

After considering the verification of FSM- and Petri net-based specifications in the previous sections we now focus on aspects of the verification of algebraic specifications on the basis of labeled transition systems (LTS) (cp. Sections 7.7 and 8.3.6). In order to verify LTS specifications, similar techniques as for finite state machines, such as reachability analysis and model checking, can be used. Reachability analysis is subsumed by model checking, which will be discussed in Section 11.7. The special requirements of model checking in the context of algebraic specifications are described in detail in [Bowm 06]. We do not enlarge on this in this section. We focus on another important aspect on the verification of algebraic specifications: the checking of correctness relations.

11.5.1   Correctness relations

Formal verifications based on correctness relations pursue the objective to compare different specifications to prove whether they are equal or refinements of each other under the associated semantics [Bowm 06]. For this, various correctness relations have been defined to characterize the equivalence with or the relation to other specifications. These relations can be roughly grouped into equivalence relations, refinement relations, and implementation relations.

Equivalence relations express an equivalent behaviour between two specifications and/or behaviour expressions. The relation is reflexive, symmetric, and transitive. To assess the equivalence of two specifications observation criteria are applied. Two systems are said to behave equivalently if they are indistinguishable by the applied observation criteria, where only the external behaviour is taken into account (cp. Section 7.7). Concerning the observation criteria an internal or an external view can be applied. The *internal view* defines a relationship between two specifications with regard to their states and transitions. The *external view* introduces an external observer to decide this question. Examples of these two views are observation equivalence and testing equivalence (see below).

Refinement relations are used to assess specifications during the development process. They describe relations between specifications in a step-wise refinement process, e.g., by defining a preorder (see Section 14.3.2). In contrast to equivalence relations, refinement relations are only reflexive and transitive.

Implementation relations represent a less strong form of refinement. Instead of demanding that any subsequent stage should be somehow externally equivalent they permit integration of steps needed towards an implementation specification [Ledu 92]. So an implementation must be, for instance, more deterministic than the specification. In contrast to refinement specifications, implementation specifications are asymmetric relations, i.e., they are only reflexive. The service and protocol specifications are an example of such an asymmetric relation. An implementation relation demands that observations of the implementation can be related to the specification. Hence, an implementation relation defines the conditions for the conformance between a specification and an implementation of it.

In the remainder of this section we focus on equivalence relations. Implementation relations are considered in the testing chapter (see Section 14.3.2).

11.5.2   Bisimulation

Unlike numerical equivalence, where the equivalence of expressions can be determined by the value, the equivalence of two LTS or behaviour expressions cannot be derived from the syntactical structure alone. Consider, for example, the two expressions in Figure 11.5/1. They are syntactically different, although their observable behaviour is the same because each of the three alternative paths in the right-hand expression executes *a;b*.

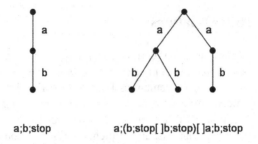

a;b;stop   a;(b;stop[ ]b;stop)[ ]a;b;stop

Figure 11.5/1: Two syntactically different behaviour expression (after [Bowm 06])

The basic method applied to prove the equivalence of two LTS expressions is bisimulation. The basic idea behind **bisimulation** is that two systems are considered equivalent if they behave in the same way in the sense that one system simulates the other and vice-versa, i.e., they cannot be distinguished by their externally visible behavior, although they may be syntactically different. Two types of bisimulation exist: strong and weak bisimulation.

Strong bisimulation

Strong bisimulation is a binary relation $R \subseteq S \times S$ on the set of all states of a labeled transition system. Two states P and Q are strongly bisimilar, denoted $P \sim Q$, if $(P,Q) \in R$ implies for all $a \in Act$:

(1) if P -a→ P' then $\exists Q'$: Q -a→ Q' $\wedge$ $(P',Q') \in R$ and
(2) if Q -a→ Q' then $\exists P'$: P -a→ P' $\wedge$ $(P',Q') \in R$,

where the notation s -a→ s' denotes a transition of the Labeled Transition System from state s into state s' when executing action $a \in Act$. Strong bisimulation implies that two bisimilar states are able to simulate all actions of the other state including internal actions and that they are transferred into a bisimilar state again. Bisimilar specifications possess a structural equivalence so that each state of one specification must have a bisimilar counterpart in the other specification. Figure 11.5/2 demonstrates this for two bisimilar behavior expressions of the initial behavior of the XDT receiver entity (cp. Figure 7.7/3b)). The respective LOTOS expressions are given beneath. The dotted lines connect the bisimilar states.

Strong bisimulation considers all actions including the internal action i. Consequently, the two behavior expressions

XDATind; i; XABORTind and *XDATind; XABORTind*

are not strongly bisimilar, although they cannot be distinguished from outside. This strong equivalence notation often turns out to be too restrictive. Weak bisimulation repeals this restriction.

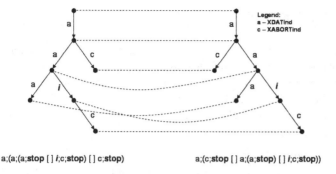

a;(a;(a;stop [ ] *i*;c;stop) [ ] c;stop)   a;(c;stop [ ] a;(a;stop) [ ] *i*;c;stop))

Figure 11.5/2: Strong bisimulation

Weak bisimulation

Weak bisimulation does not take internal actions into account. This means that any transition $a \in Act$ in B_1 may be followed by one or several internal actions which are skipped in B_2 and vice versa, but again both are transferred into weakly bisimilar states. A transition $a \in Act$ from a state s into a state s' that can be followed by one or more internal actions i is denoted by $s -\hat{a} \rightarrow s'$ in the following. Two states P and Q are weakly bisimilar, denoted $P \approx Q$, if $(P,Q) \in R$ implies for all $a \in Act$:

(1) if $P -\hat{a} \rightarrow P'$ then $\exists Q': Q -\hat{a} \rightarrow Q' \wedge (P',Q') \in R$ and
(2) if $Q -\hat{a} \rightarrow Q'$ then $\exists P': P -\hat{a} \rightarrow P' \wedge (P',Q') \in R$.

Figure 11.5/3 shows a weak bisimulation for the example above.

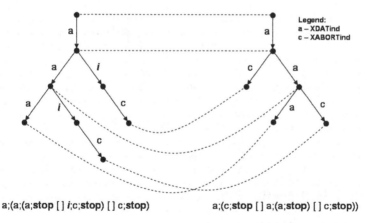

a;(a;(a;stop [ ] *i*;c;stop) [ ] c;stop)   a;(c;stop [ ] a;(a;stop) [ ] c;stop))

Figure 11.5/3: Weak bisimulation

11.5.3   Equivalence relations

Equivalence relations define conditions under which the behavior of two labeled transition systems is considered to be equivalent. The most common equivalence relations are the bisimulation equivalence ($\sim$), observational equivalence ($\approx$), testing equivalence ($\approx_{TE}$), and trace equivalence ($\approx_{TR}$). Bisimulation equivalence is the strongest among these relations, trace equivalence the weakest of them:

$$\sim \,\subset\, \approx \,\subset\, \approx_{TE} \,\subset\, \approx_{TR}.$$

Bisimulation equivalence

Two labeled transition systems are bisimilar and/or strongly equivalent, if there is a strong bisimulation between them which includes the initial states of both systems. Figure 11.5/4 gives some examples. The first two behavior trees meet the condition, not the one below. Here the initial state and the states reached after executing the first *a* are no longer bisimilar. In the initial state there is nondeterminism regarding *a* and in the successor state either *a* and *i* or only *c* are expected and not *a* and *c* as in the other two trees.

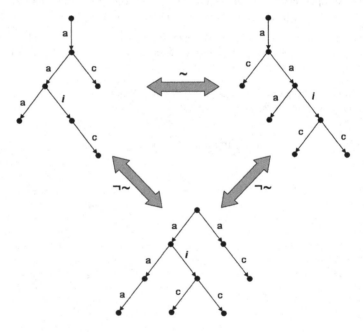

Figure 11.5/4: Bisimulation equivalence

Observational equivalence

Observational equivalence and/or weak equivalence holds if there is a weak bisimulation relation between the considered systems which includes the initial states. Intuitively this means that the externally observable behavior of both sys-

tems is the same. Figure 11.5/5 gives examples for both cases. Algorithms to efficiently determine bisimulation and observational equivalence are described in
[Fern 91].

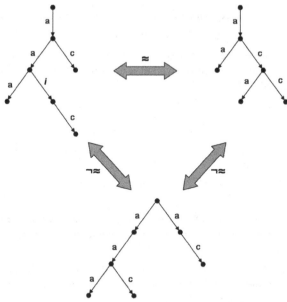

Figure 11.5/5: Observational equivalence

Testing equivalence

In contrast to bisimulative and observational equivalence which apply the internal view, testing equivalence is based on the *external view*. It goes back to De
Nicola and Hennessy [DeNi 84] and describes the relationship between two expressions through a set of observations $obs(o) \in OBS$ collected in experiments by
an external observer o.

Testing equivalence characterizes two labeled transition systems as equivalent
if they cannot be distinguished by a test [Bowm 06]. Tests are experiments that
evaluate the behavior expressions using an external object, the **observer** o (see
Figure 11.5/6). The observer is also described as a labeled transition system. It
communicates synchronously with the observed system S, i.e., S can execute an
observable action if and only if the observer synchronizes with this action: $o\|S$.

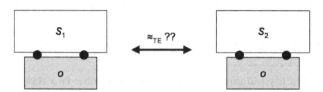

Figure 11.5/6: Observer

A $test(T,S)$ of a labeled transition system S consists of a set of test cases $T = (t_1, t_2, \ldots t_m)$ which examine the system behavior in individual experiments. Test cases are traces.

A **trace** $\sigma \in L^*$ is a sequence of observable actions which transfers a Labeled Transition Systems from state s into a state s', $s \xrightarrow{\sigma} s'$, where L^* denotes the set of all possible finite action sequences over the set of labels L. The set of all traces which transfers a labeled transition system S from the initial state s_0 into any possible state, is described by

$$traces\,(S) = \{\sigma \in L^* |\; s_0 \xrightarrow{\sigma}\}^2.$$

The execution of a test case $t\|S$ can induce the following observations

$$obs(t,S) = <\{\sigma \in L^* |\; t\|S \xrightarrow{\sigma}\}, \{\sigma \in L^* |\; t\|S \Rightarrow t'\|S' \wedge \forall\, a \in L\!: t'\|S' \neg \xrightarrow{a}\}>.$$

The observer can either observe the expected event sequence or it ends after executing a trace σ in a state in which no further events can be observed, i.e., it has reached a deadlock.

Two labeled transition systems S_1 and S_2 are testing equivalent $\approx_{TE}$ if they cannot be distinguished by executing all test cases $t \in T$, i.e., they show the same observable behavior including deadlocks:

$$S_1 \approx_{TE} S_2 \Leftrightarrow\; test(T,S_1) = test(T,S_2)\quad \text{or}$$
$$S_1 \approx_{TE} S_2 \Leftrightarrow\; \forall\, t \in T\!: obs(t,S_1) = obs(t,S_2).$$

Figure 11.5/7 shows an example with three LOTOS processes. The processes terminate except for the action sequence $a;a;c$ which induces a deadlock. The processes X and Y are testing equivalent, but not observational equivalent. Process Z is not testing equivalent to X and Y. The reason is the deterministic behavior of Z. It always accepts the test case $a;c$, while X and Y do not always do so because after accepting a they transfer into a state in which they may accept only action a or c, but not both.

Trace equivalence

Trace equivalence is the weakest of the equivalence relations considered here. Intuitively, it means that both systems accept the same sequences of actions. Between two labeled transition systems trace equivalence holds if all possible sequences of actions $\sigma \in L^*$ that each of the systems accepts are the same (see Figure 11.5/8):

$$S_1 \approx_{TR} S_2 \Leftrightarrow traces(S_1) = traces(S_2)$$

---

[2] The notation used to represent the transition between two states in a labeled transition system is $s \xrightarrow{\sigma} =_{def} \exists\, s'\!: s \xrightarrow{\sigma} s'$.

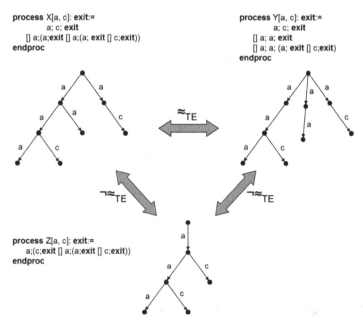

process X[a, c]: **exit**:=
   a; c; **exit**
   [] a;(a;**exit** [] a;(a; **exit** [] c;**exit**))
endproc

process Y[a, c]: **exit**:=
   a; c; **exit**
   [] a; a; **exit**
   [] a; a; (a; **exit** [] c;**exit**)
endproc

process Z[a, c]: **exit**:=
   a;(c;**exit** [] a;(a;**exit** [] c;**exit**))
endproc

Figure 11.5/7: Testing equivalence

Trace equivalence does not take internal actions, nondeterminisms, and deadlocks into account. For example, action a represents an acceptable trace for both trace equivalent behavior expressions in Figure 11.5/8, although it induces a deadlock in the first expression. Trace equivalence also holds between the processes in Figure 11.5/7.

Finally it has to be mentioned that equivalence between behavior expressions can also be defined based on refusals. This semantics is called *refusal semantics*. Trace-refusal semantics, for instance, can distinguish behavior which is considered equal by trace equivalence. For more details see [Bowm 06].

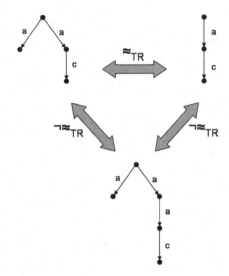

Figure 11.5/8: Trace equivalence

11.5.4   Congruence relations

Equivalence relations do not possess the substitution property, i.e., if two behavior expressions have been proved equivalent they cannot be replaced by each other. This is because they may behave differently when they are part of another context. In order to substitute expressions stronger relations are required. Such relations are termed **congruence relations** [ISO 8807], [Bowm 06]. They are especially useful for the incremental development of specifications. Congruence is related to the notion of context. A **context** $C[\ ]$ is a behavior with a formal process parameter $[\ ]$ which can be replaced by a behavior expression, i.e., $C[B]$. Congruence is an equivalence relation that states that two behavior expressions B and B' can be substituted for any context C.

There are different kinds of congruence relations as well, e.g., bisimulation congruence, testing congruence, and pre-congruence. Strong and weak bisimulation are congruence relations for the *Basic* LOTOS operators. The proof is contained in [Bowm 06]. Strong bisimulation congruence ($\sim_c$) is substitutive for all operators, weak bisimulation congruence ($\approx_c$) only for a subset of the operators. Some examples of weak bisimulation congruence are given below:

$B_1\ [\ ]\ B_2\ \approx_c B_2\ [\ ]B_1$
$B_1\ [\ ]\ (B_2\ [\ ]B_3)\ \approx_c (B_1\ [\ ]B_2)\ [\ ]B_3$
$a;\ i;\ B_1\ \approx_c a;\ B_1$
$B_1|[\ ]|\ B_2\ =\ B_1|||B_2$

A comprehensive list of rules is contained in [ISO 8807].

11.5.5   Tool support

A number of tools have been developed to decide equivalence relations as described above (see [FORTE]). The most established and mature one is CADP (*Construction and Analysis of Distributed Processes*) [CADP], a tool suite for the design of communication protocols and distributed systems. It has been developed by the VASY team at Inria Rhône-Alpes. The main focus of CADP is the verification of LOTOS specifications, but it also supports other input notations, such as finite state machines and communicating automata. CADP provides two compilers, CAESAR and CAESAR.ADT, to translate LOTOS specifications including data format descriptions into C code to be used for simulation, verification, and test case generation. It provides various tools for the assessment of bisimulation equivalence and model checking. In addition, it supports reachability analysis, algorithms for deadlock and livelock detection, on-the-fly verification, and symbolic verification using binary decision diagrams.

11.6   Deductive verification

Deductive verification can be applied to prove statements on properties in descriptive specifications (cp. Section 7.8) that the designed protocol should meet. As we learnt earlier these statements are usually formulated in a temporal logic. A deductive system for a temporal logic consists of axioms and inference rules. A statement or formula p is said to be provable if there exists a finite sequence of statements leading to statement p so that each statement is an instance of an axiom and/or follows from previous statements by applying one of the inference rules [Emer 90]. Examples of axioms of the linear time logic used in Section 7.8 are:

$\Box p \Rightarrow p$	(*reflexivity*)
$\Box(p \Rightarrow q) \Rightarrow (\Box p \Rightarrow \Box q)$	(*consequence closure*)
$\Box p \Rightarrow \Box\Box p$	(*transitivity*)
$\Box(\Box p \Rightarrow \Box q) \lor \Box(\Box q \Rightarrow \Box p)$	(*linearity*)
$\Box(\Box(p \Rightarrow \Box p) \Rightarrow p) \Rightarrow (\Diamond\Box p \Rightarrow p)$	(*discreteness*)

The inference rules consist of general rules, such as

(1) *if* p *is provable then also* $\Box p$ *is provable*   (*rule of generalization*),
(2) *if p and p* $\Rightarrow$ *q are provable then also q is provable*   (*rule of modus ponens*),

and specific rules which refer to the used specification language, e.g., cTLA. The axioms and inference rules extend the specification language to a calculus. With the help of such a calculus a purely syntactic proof is possible by applying the axioms and inference rules and transforming formulas into new ones. A temporal formula which was derived in this way is called a **theorem**. Thus, the syntactic deduction leads to a chain of theorems that are derived from each other. An important prerequisite is the choice of a suitable deductive system which ensures that the derived theorems are valid. A deductive system is sound if every provable formula is valid. It is complete if every valid formula is provable.

Deductive verification performed by hand is time consuming and requires special knowledge and experience. The process can be supported by tools that enforce the correct use of axioms and interference rules. These tools are called **theorem provers**. A fully automated proof is usually not possible, as the deduction systems for many specification languages are inherently incomplete and their efficiency is not acceptable. Therefore, interactive theorem provers are preferred.

The use of deductive verification in practical protocol development is rare. This is explained, besides the high efforts required to perform the proof, by the limited availability of protocol specifications in a temporal logic or hybrid technique, such as cTLA (cp. Section 8.4). Approaches like the framework concept [Herr 00] can facilitate the verification process using specification module libraries with associated proven theorems. But they presume the development of corresponding frameworks for certain protocol classes. This is hard to do in practice. Temporal logics, however, are widely applied as a complementary technique for the proving of correctness claims as with model checking, which we consider in the following section.

11.7   Model checking

The methods presented in the preceding sections each pursue the goal to verify the entire system design. The analyses often encounter the boundaries of practicality, since they are too expensive and too lengthy. A complementary approach to verify a formal description or model, which often leads more quickly to the desired results, is model checking. This has become a popular and preferred method for verifying communication protocols, distributed systems and circuit designs.

Model checking is an automated proof technique that systematically checks whether a system design satisfies claimed properties [Clar 00], [Holz 04]. It can be applied to designs specified with finite state machines, Petri nets, or labeled transition systems. The properties to be checked are formulated in temporal logics. Two types of temporal logics are applied. Linear temporal logics are mainly used for software verification and, of course, for protocol verification. Computational tree logics are preferred for the verification of circuit designs. The checking process generates the reachability graph and proves the validity of the formulated property. LTL-based model checkers preferably apply *on-the-fly* verification (cp. Section 11.3.1), while CTL-based checkers often use compressed state space representations using binary decision diagrams (cp. Section 11.3.2). The latter are also called *symbolic model checkers*. The result of model checking is *yes* or *no*. The model checking algorithm will either terminate with *true* to indicate that the property holds or with *false* if the property is not satisfied. In the latter case a counterexample may be presented that shows why the formula does not hold.

Unlike the methods considered previously, the model checking algorithm needs a finite state space to terminate with a definite answer. The state space exploration is limited by the available memory to store the state space. The state space explosion problem is therefore the central issue of model checking. To reduce the state space the same methods are applied as we have got to know in connection with reachability analysis (cp. Section 11.3.2).

11.7.1 Model checking with LTL

In this section we describe the principle of LTL-based model checking as it is applied for protocol verification.

Kripke structures and Büchi automata

In model checking the systems to be modeled are mapped onto Kripke structures [Clar 00]. A Kripke structure is a state transition graph which consists of a set of states, a set of transitions between them, and a labeling function that assigns properties to each state which are true in this state.

A **Kripke structure** is defined as a four-tuple $<S,s_0,R,L>$ with

S – finite, non-empty set of *states*,

$s_0 \in S$ – *initial state*,

$R \subseteq S \times S$ – a *transition relation*, and

$L: S \to 2^{AP}$ – a *function* that labels each state with a set of atomic propositions (AP) that are true in that state.

A path in a Kripke structure represents a computation run. The labels at each state allow it to pursue changes along the execution timeline.

In model checking (or in reachability analysis) the state exploration algorithm has to determine that a computation run reaches a valid final state [Holz 04]. Many distributed systems, such as reactive systems and communication protocols, show an infinite behavior. Such infinite computation runs are called ω-runs. Automata which accept finite and infinite runs are correspondingly named ω-automata.

An ω-automaton is defined as a quintuple $<S,s_0,L,T,F>$ with

S – finite, non-empty set of *states*,

$s_0 \in S$ – *initial state*,

L – finite set of *labels*,

T – set of *transitions* $T \subseteq S \times L \times S$, and

F – set of *final states* $F \subseteq S$.

An infinite run shows a correct behavior if the automaton passes infinitely often certain final states. In communication protocols the initial state is often such a final state, as, for instance, in both XDT entities. Figure 11.7/1 shows the finite state machine of the XDT receiver entity. The final state is marked with a double line.

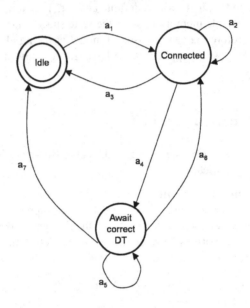

Figure 11.7/1: Finite state machine of the XDT receiver entity with final state

Infinite runs can be described by means of Büchi acceptance named after the Swiss mathematician J.R. Büchi who defined them in 1960 for the acceptance of infinite words. Let σ be an infinite ω-run and σ^ω the set of final states that appear infinitely often in T, then the acceptance of σ is defined by **Büchi acceptance**:

An accepting ω-run of a finite state machine $<S,s_0,L,T,F>$ is any infinite run σ with $\exists s_f\colon\; s_f \in F \wedge\; s_f \in \sigma^\omega$.

An automaton with the Büchi acceptance condition is called a **Büchi automaton,** where the final states are called *accepting* states here. Kripke structures can easily be transformed into Büchi automata. A Kripke structure corresponds to an ω-automaton where all states are accepting ones. The labels form the accepted alphabet.

Mapping temporal logic to automata

Vardi and Wolper showed in [Vard 94] that any LTL formula can be translated into a Büchi automaton. Figure 11.7/2 shows the respective automata for two formulae. These formulae correspond to rules (3) and (4) of our XDT service specification in Section 7.8.

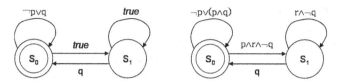

Figure 11.7/2: Automata for rules $\Box(p \Rightarrow \Diamond q)$ and $\Box(p \Rightarrow r \,\mathcal{U}\, q)$

This mapping permits one to mechanically convert the properties to be proved, described as LTL formulae, into Büchi automata.

Principle of model checking

The model checking process begins with the modeling of the considered system in the chosen formal method. As we see below an intermediate representation is often required as input. Next the property to be proved has to be formulated. Both the system model and the property are converted into Büchi automata. In the next step the synchronous product of the automata is formed (see Figure 11.7/3). The resulting automaton is again a Büchi automaton. Next reachability analysis is performed for the product automaton. If all states are reachable then it contains those behaviors that satisfy the LTL formula and, thus the property to be proved. Instead of exploring all correct behaviors it has been found that it is more efficient to search for behaviors that do not fulfill the LTL formula. For this, the LTL formula is negated before being transformed into a Büchi automaton. If a behavior is found that satisfies this formula the analysis will be stopped and the found state will be indicated as a counterexample to the correctness claim to be proved.

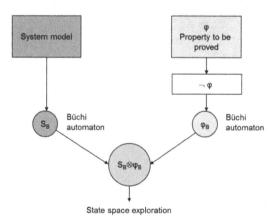

Figure 11.7/3: Model checking procedure

11.7.2 SPIN model checker

Various model checkers have been developed. The most well-known ones are SMV and SPIN. SMV (*Symbolic Model Verifier*) [McMi 93], [Clar 00] and its successor NuSMV [NuSMV] are CTL-based model checkers for finite state machines, while **SPIN** is an LTL-based model checker. The latter has become the most popular model checker for distributed systems and communication protocols. The SPIN model checker was developed at Bell Labs by Gerard Holzmann in the 1980s and 1990s. The tool has attracted a large user community. A yearly workshop has been established to report recent developments and applications. SPIN stands for *Simple Promela Interpreter*. **PROMELA** (*PROcess Meta Language*) is the input language for this verification tool. It aims at modeling process synchronization and coordination in concurrent software systems. Although it contains many features of modern programming languages as well as many notational conventions of the C programming language, it is not a computational language. PROMELA is a language for building verification models. We do not introduce the language here. Instead we refer to the introduction to PROMELA and all theoretical and practical aspects of SPIN given by Holzmann himself in the SPIN primer [Holz 04]. Figure 11.7/4 gives as an example a fragment of the PROMELA specification of the XDT protocol part together with some SPIN outputs to demonstrate the principle. A complete PROMELA specification of the XDT protocol may be found at the book web site. PROMELA is similar to our model language, although they have different origins. This is because both languages apply the process- and communication-oriented description principle (cp. Section 7.1).

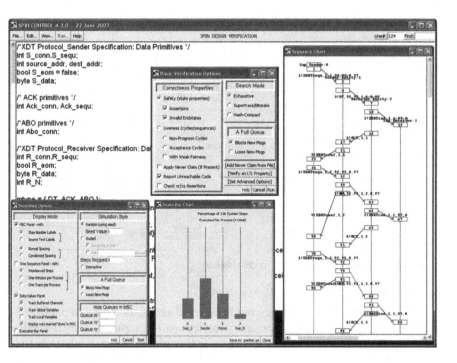

Figure 11.7/4: Fragment of the PROMELA XDT specification together with SPIN outputs

The workflow of the SPIN model checker is depicted in Figure 11.7/5. It starts with a verification model of the designed protocol or distributed system specified in PROMELA. The model as well as the properties to be proved may optionally be input by the graphical front-end XSPIN which provides different functions, such as graphical displays of message flows and time sequence diagrams. A line editor can be used instead. The PROMELA parser proves the syntactical correctness of the specified model. Next the verifier can first prove in an interactive simulation whether the verification model fulfills basic properties. The simulation is random by default. If the verifier wants to prove a certain property the correctness claim has to be formulated as an LTL formula. The PROMELA specification together with the property is input to a verifier generator which generates an *on-the-fly* verifier. The reduction algorithm applied in state space exploration can be selected as a compiling option. The verifier executes itself. If a counterexample to the correctness claim is found a special file is generated which can be used as feedback for the SPIN simulator which then operates in the guided mode to pursue the system behaviour until the deviation from the expected behaviour is found. For a detailed introduction to the use of the SPIN model checker, we refer to the already mentioned SPIN primer [Holz 04].

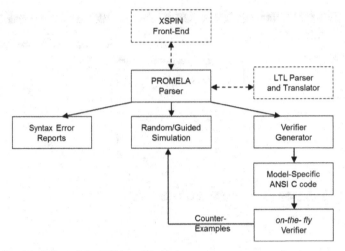

Figure 11.7/5: Workflow of the SPIN model checker

Further reading

There are only a few books devoted to protocol verification because most verification books provide a more general overview on this topic. A comprehensive introduction to protocol verification is given in the first Holzmann book [Holz 91]. Many important aspects of protocol verification are also considered in the SPIN primer [Holz 04] as well, which, however, has a broader focus. Verification techniques for communication protocols, especially reachability analysis and Petri net-based methods, are also described in the book of Lai and Jirachiefpattana [Lai 98]. The book is in part related to Estelle.

Overviews on Petri net analysis techniques are given among others in the tutorials of Murata [Mura 89] and Heiner, Gilbert, and Donaldson [Hein 08]. Although the latter is devoted to biochemical networks it describes the basic Petri net principles which are also relevant for protocol description and analysis.

More details about algebraic verification techniques in the context of LOTOS and LTS covering both equivalence relations and model checking are given in the comprehensible introduction to concurrency theory by Bowman and Gomez [Bowm 06].

An excellent introduction to the fundamentals of model checking can be found in the book of Clarke, Grumberg, and Peled [Clar 00], which is recommended for an introduction to this topic. The same applies to the SPIN primer [Holz 04] which besides an introduction to PROMELA and SPIN contains a well written overview on the relevant fundamentals of model checking. A more theoretical introduction to this topic is given in [Baie 08].

Exercises

(1) What is the objective of protocol verification? What is the difference from protocol testing?

(2) Discuss the terms validation and verification. What are the differences between them?

(3) Protocol verification distinguishes between the verification of general and special properties. Explain these properties.

(4) Give examples of typical protocol properties to be verified.

(5) Characterize the verification techniques applied in protocol verification.

(6) What are the most important methods for protocol verification?

(7) What is the objective of reachability analysis? Sketch how the reachability graph is generated. Explain how important properties, such as deadlock and livelock freedom, no unreachable actions and termination, can be proved with the help of the reachability graph.

(8) What is the reason for the state space explosion issue? What measures are taken to mitigate the problem?

(9) Interleaving may increase the state space explosion problem considerably. What kinds of methods are applied to handle this issue in reachability analysis?

(10) Generate the reachability graph for the explicit XDT connection set up of exercise (11) in Chapter 2. Take the protocol system of Section 11.3.1 as a basis.

(11) Introduce the XDT protocol changes of exercises (10) and (11) of Chapter 7 (explicit connection set up, regulated data delivery) into the Petri net of Figure 11.4/1. Regarding exercise (10) consider only the successful set up, not the refusal.

(12) Give the incidence matrix for the Petri net of Figure 7.6/1.

(13) Explain the Petri net properties boundedness, liveness, and reversibility. Decide whether the Petri net of Figure 7.6/1 fulfills these properties.

(14) Explain the net properties reachability, deadlock freedom, dead transitions, and livelock freedom.

(15) Evaluate the Petri net given below of the explicit connection set up (without timers) regarding the properties mentioned in exercise (14). Assume that the fusion places *XDATconf* and DATA_TRANSFER are correct terminations.

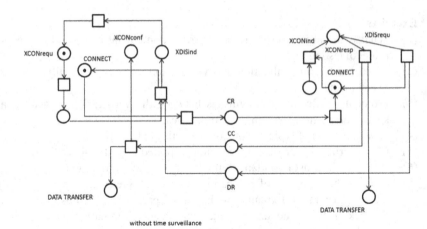

without time surveillance

Correct the net if it contains any errors.

(16) Describe the most important verification methods applied to Petri nets.

(17) Give the beginning of the reachability graph for the correct network of exercise (15) using marking vectors like in Figure 11.4/4.

(18) Sketch how important net properties can be proved on the basis of the reachability graph.

(19) What verification methods are applied to algebraic specifications?

(20) Explain the differences between equivalence, refinement, and implementation relations.

(21) What is the purpose of bisimulation? What is the difference between strong and weak bisimulation?

(22) Which of the behavior expressions
a; i; b; **stop** [] b;(i; c; **stop** [] b; a; **stop**) and
b;(c; **stop** [] b ;(c; **stop** [] a; **stop**)) [] a; b; **stop**
is weakly bisimilar to the expression a; b; **stop** [] b;(b; a; **stop** [] c; **stop**) ?
Explain your decision.

(23) Are the behavior expressions
a; i; b; **stop** [] a ;(i; b; **stop** [] b ;(c; i; **stop** [] a; **stop**)) and
a;(i; b; **stop** [] b;(c; i; **stop** [] a; **stop**))
strongly bisimilar? Explain your answer.

(24) Describe the differences between bisimulation, observational, testing, and trace equivalence. What is the relation between them?

(25) If the expressions in exercise (24) are not strongly bisimilar what equivalence relation do they meet?

(26) Given the behavior expression c;b;(c; **stop** [] i; a; **stop**)) [] a; b; **stop**. Construct behavior expressions that are bisimulation, observational, testing, and trace equivalent to it.

(27) Explain the verification principle applied in model checking. Define the terms Kripke structure and Büchi automaton. Describe the model checking procedure.

(28) Translate the property $\Box(S.XDATrequ \Rightarrow \Diamond (S.XDATconf \ W \ state \equiv break))$ into a Büchi automaton.

(29) Formulate LTL conditions for the regulated data delivery of exercise (11) of Chapter 7 which might be proved with model checking. Translate them into a Büchi automaton.

12 Performance evaluation

We are now approaching the implementation phase. The implementation begins with an implementation design that will be considered in detail in Chapter 13. During implementation design it may be useful to assess the expected performance behaviour of the designed protocol in the target execution environment. Implementers often require quantitative measures like throughput or response time to optimize their implementation and to reason about implementation alternatives.

Software development and performance analysis are often considered two rather independent areas having their own models, methods, and tools. Considering performance evaluation as an "afterthought" induces various disadvantages because changes have to be introduced into the implementation to meet the performance requirements that do not correspond to the original specification. For this reason, the performance evaluation community argues for integration of performance evaluation in the development process [Mits 01]. This has also been investigated for the protocol development process. The approaches applied are considered in this chapter.

12.1 Objectives

Service and protocol specifications, as we have considered them until now, describe the functional behavior of services and protocols. In order to allow evaluation of the performance of a protocol design, **non-functional properties** related to time and resources have to be added to the specification (see Figure 12.1/1). These properties include characteristics of the hardware devices, the achievable degree of parallelism, concurrency due to non-sharable resources, scheduling strategies, processing speeds, the available bandwidth, buffer sizes, timer settings, the specification structure, the description of the expected load behavior (load model), traffic characteristics etc.

Based on the specified quantitative performance measures – and this is the benefit of the integrated approach – an executable performance model can be derived. The model is completed by a load or traffic model which specifies, for instance, the packet arrival rate (i.e., packets/sec). The execution of the performance model results in various performance measures depending on given input parameters which describe the available resources and the workload. The simple M/M/1 model well known from queuing theory is an example of such a performance model. In practice, however, much more complicated models are applied.

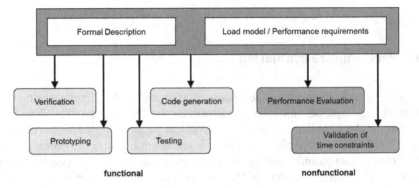

Figure 12.1/1: Functional and non-functional aspects of a formal description (source [Mits 99])

The objective of the performance analysis is to assess the performance behavior of the designed protocol related to the specified parameters (throughput, response times, end-to-end delay, packet loss rates, etc.), in order

- to find performance bottlenecks in the protocol and the used runtime environment (see Chapter 13),
- to validate time constraints, and
- to compare implementation alternatives.

Furthermore, statements on the likelihood of time-outs, the duration of event sequences, and the resource utilization can be derived [Herm 98], [Hint 01]. The obtained analysis results allow the protocol engineer to evaluate whether the designed protocol principally fulfills the expected performance requirements and to tune system parameters, such as timer values, window and buffer sizes, and others. Further, they give the protocol engineer a better understanding of the consequences of protocol changes.

Unfortunately, performance evaluation cannot be carried out in an implementation-independent way. Without an orientation on a certain execution environment, performance predictions have little meaning [Heck 91]. Therefore, there are restrictions on how performance evaluation can be applied during the early design phase. On the other hand, changes in the protocol design should be made as early as possible to minimize their costs. In order to make early performance evaluations possible, specification-oriented methodologies, e.g., for SDL [Mits 99], [Mits 01] and LOTOS [Woli 93], [Herm 98], were developed which support the specification of non-functional properties and provide tools for model-based performance analyses. The model is defined by the semantic model of the respective FDT and a machine model based on the implementation specification (see Section 13.1.1).

Performance evaluation has generated much interest within *Protocol Engineering*. The first work on this topic was already published in the 1980s. The interest in this sub-discipline, sometimes also called *performance engineering*, is especially large in areas with high performance requirements, such as high performance communication and mobile communication. Nevertheless, performance analysis is still a relative specialized discipline due to the difficulty of finding appropriate performance models [Mits 01].

12.2   Specification of non-functional aspects

Current formal description techniques do not support the quantitative specification of non-functional properties. They must be added, e.g., by comments or other means. Sometimes modified MSCs are used. The ideal case would be an integrated specification of functional and non-functional aspects, as shown in Figure 12.2/1 to automatically generate a performance model.

The information that has to be added to the formal specification comprises among others [Woli 93], [Herm 98], [Mits 99]:

- the integration of time,
- the quantization of nondeterminisms, and
- the specification of resource requirements.

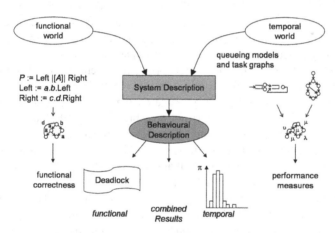

Figure 12.2/1: Integrated description and analysis of functional and non-functional aspects (source [Herm 98])

Integration of time

Formal description techniques usually allow only a limited representation of temporal aspects, mainly for monitoring timers in protocol procedures whose primary purpose is to avoid deadlocks. Performance analysis requires the intervals in which events may occur to be expressed. This changes, however, the semantics of the formal description techniques. Thus, safety and liveness properties can get lost due to time restrictions.

According to [Woli 93], there are three ways to introduce time into formal description techniques:

- *Delaying individual preconditions*
  A delay is enforced between the fulfillment of a precondition and the time it becomes effective. Such delays have to be formulated separately for each precondition.
- *Delaying events*
  A delay is enforced between the fulfillment of all preconditions and the occurrence of the event.
- *Introducing an execution duration of events*
  Instead of assigning a duration time of zero, as usually assumed, a certain amount of time is introduced for handling events.

Standardized formal description techniques do not define time in this form. Various proposals to integrate time in formal description techniques have been discussed. We present here some examples for the languages SDL and LOTOS.

In SDL, the treatment of time is most advanced compared to other standardized formal description techniques, but it primarily serves the time surveillance of the communication (cp. Section 8.1.2.3). The time is incremented by a clock outside the system. No unit is defined. The expiration of a timer (time-out) does not directly lead to a reaction, since the event is enqueued into the input queue of the agent and only processed when all the events ahead are removed from the queue. Furthermore, there are no uniform rules for the time behavior of channels. They can delay the signal transmission or not, but it is not defined how long a delay lasts. Therefore no statements can be made on the execution duration of certain statement sequences. Moreover, it is not possible to define the quantitative load model required for performance evaluation. Several proposals have been made to extend the SDL semantics through time, such as *Timed SDL* by Bause and Buchholz [Baus 93], *SPECS* by Bütow, Kritzinger et al. [Büto 96], and timed extensions by Bozga et al. [Bozg 01]. The first approach introduces for a relatively small subset of SDL probabilities for the switching of transitions and exponential time durations for their execution. Resources and work load, however, cannot be specified. The second approach introduces a time semantics to SDL, which ensures among other things that the exchange of signals over channels and the processing of actions lasts a specified time. The third paper proposes the use of annotations to express non-functional aspects in the specification. Two kinds of annotations are introduced: *assumptions* to express a priori knowledge or hypothesizes on the execution environment and *assertions* which express expected behavior. The proposed annotations are urgencies, durations, and periodicity of actions to control the time progress. Furthermore, a flexible channel concept is proposed that foresees message losses, reordering, propagation delay etc.

LOTOS in its original form does not contain features to represent time or to support performance evaluation. Timers and their functionality can only be modeled at separate processes as we did in Section 8.3.8. Time was only introduced in

E-LOTOS (*Enhancement to LOTOS*) [ISO 15437], an attempt to extend the language to meet new requirements of distributed systems. To represent time E-LOTOS introduces a time domain which is defined as a set of values of the sort *time*. The time domain can be discrete or continuous. There are two notations to describe time statements: the *duration of an offer* (cp. Section 8.3.4), which limits the period in which an offer can take effect, and the *delay prefix* for delaying the execution of actions. A detailed introduction is given in [Leon 97]. Another approach to the representation of time in LOTOS is the *Timed Interacting Systems* (TIS) described in [Woli 93] (see below).

Quantization of nondeterminisms
In addition to the integration of time, statements on nondeterminisms (cp. Section 1.2.4) have to be taken into account for performance evaluations. This is done by specifying probabilities for the execution of state transitions or the switching of transitions. However, the simple indication of probabilities can be difficult because it is not always known how many and which events are involved in the nondeterministic selection. To solve the problem the assignment of weights to events was proposed from which the probability of the triggering of a transition can be derived [Woli 93]. The quantization of nondeterminisms can be further refined using priorities. SDL and LOTOS support the presentation of nondeterminisms, but not their quantization. In both languages nondeterminism can be explicitly expressed by specifying different reactions to the same event or implicitly through spontaneous transitions (*none*) in SDL (cp. Section 8.1.2.5), and the internal action *i* (cp. Section 8.3.2) in LOTOS. An approach to integrating stochastic modeling and analysis into LOTOS is presented in [Herm 98].

Quantization of resource requirements
Delays in the execution of processes are caused by lack of resources which may have different effects in load situations. Therefore, performance analysis needs statements about the used system resources, such as processors, memory, input/output channels, or bandwidth. As discussed above, such statements are not possible without a focus on a dedicated target system. In practice, a machine model is usually specified to estimate the performance behavior of the system in response to a given load. Examples are given below. Since standardized formal description techniques do not support the specification of these data, additional notations are used.

12.3   Performance modeling techniques

After setting up the formal description extended by quantitative performance measures including a workload description, an executable performance model has to be derived, i.e., the extended specification must be transformed into a quantitatively assessable representation that is executable or solvable. The following solution techniques are usually applied [Mits 99]:

- *Stochastic modeling using queuing networks*
  Here a class of so-called product-form queuing networks can be solved exactly by analytical techniques. Further approximation methods are applied for models including non-exponential distributions, priorities, and blocking.
- *Markov chain techniques*
  Markovian models are mapped to a set of linear equations that can be solved by numerical methods, e.g., Gaussian elimination or iteration techniques. Here also the problem of state-space explosion occurs. Nowadays already models with many million states can be solved.
- *Discrete event simulation*
  Simulation is applied when analytical and numerical techniques cannot be applied. The problems with simulation are to find an appropriate simulation model, which does not contain too many details, to prove its correctness, and to interpret the large amounts of statistical data.

Hybrid techniques which try to combine the benefits of different approaches are applied as well.

12.4   Tools

In the last two decades a number of tools for performance evaluation have been developed, mostly for SDL. We present three approaches as examples here. An overview of the whole range of approaches is given in [Mits 01].

SPECS

The SPECS tool (*SDL Performance Evaluation of Concurrent Systems*) applies the above-mentioned supplement of the SDL semantics with time by Bütow, Kritzinger et al. (see [Büto 96]). It aims at the evaluation of concurrent systems which are specified in SDL-92. Accordingly a system is modeled by blocks which are executed on processors with varying speeds. The tasks belonging to each block are described as processes. They are executed concurrently if they belong to different blocks, otherwise their execution is quasi-parallel. Different weights can be assigned to the processes. By changing the weights and the assignment of the blocks to the processors the engineer can adjust the relative process speeds and thus evaluate different system behaviors.

SPECS consists of a compiler, a graphical user interface, a simulation environment, and a trace analysis tool (see Figure 12.4/1). The compiler translates a subset of SDL/GR into an internal code. The graphical user interface gives interactive user guidance and presents the progression and results of the simulation. It allows the user to specify the quantitative characteristics of the target environment, e.g.,

- Selection of the processes and blocks considered during the simulation,
- Setting channel attributes (reliability, distribution of the delay time (determined, exponential, even)),

- Determining the capacity of the input queues of the processes,
- Setting the process weights and the block execution or processor speeds, respectively.

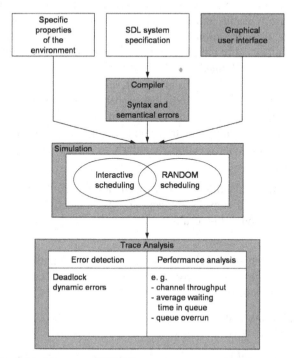

Figure 12.4/1: Functional structure of SPECS

The resulting model is executed on a virtual machine. The scheduling of processes can be incidentally or interactively controlled. In addition, a step-wise execution is possible. The observed execution sequences are evaluated in the trace analysis tool for various performance measures, such as throughput per channel, state throughput, medium, and maximum length of the process queues. In [Wet 05] the tool *proSPEX* is presented which transfers the methodology to UML 2.

TIS

Timed Interacting Systems (TIS) [Woli 93] is a LOTOS extension for performance evaluation. It is not defined as a superset of LOTOS, but many LOTOS language elements can be translated directly into TIS. The latter contains three elements to describe performance requirements:

- *Time*
  Global time is represented by a single object – the *ticker*. The progression of time is described by discrete time units – the *ticks*. A process can define several local clocks which progress with each tick generated by the global ticker.

The time is explicitly assigned to time-related actions as a parameter to determine delays of preconditions and the execution duration of interactions.

- *Resources*
  In a TIS specification global, passive resources – *facilities* – can be defined. Facilities are reusable and non-shareable resources. Their availability is a prerequisite for interactions. There are several different types of facilities, which again consist of equal elements. For each facility type, a serving strategy, e.g., FIFO, is defined. ·

- *Quantification and restrictions of nondeterminisms*
  Two operators are introduced: the probability-related *choice*-operator to specify the probabilities for the selection of the various alternatives, and the *parallel racing*-operator to restrict nondeterminisms by allowing the parallel execution of time-related actions (similarly to our *par event*-operator in Section 1.2.4).

The performance evaluation of a TIS specification is performed by simulation. It supports an animated step-wise execution, the simulative execution, and the graphical representation of the results.

QUEST
The QUEST approach [Hint 01] is based on the usage of time-consuming machines that model congestions of processes due to limited resources. The concept consists of two components:

the language QSDL and
the QUEST tool.

QSDL (*Queuing SDL*) extends SDL by constructs for the specification of resources and work load. To remain compatible with the SDL standard these constructs are added in the form of annotations, i.e., specific comments, to the specification. The resources are modeled by means of the machines which are assigned to the processes. Figure 12.4/2 shows this for an example specification. A machine provides a set of time-consuming services (see Figure 12.4/3). It is modeled by a waiting room, a number of servers, and a scheduling strategy. The machine services are invoked by SDL signals.

By adding workload models and defining respective mappings of the workload to the machines an assessable performance model is generated. The modeling of the workload is supported by various random distribution functions. Traffic patterns can also be described by load generators which can be implemented as QSDL processes. An important option is the use of multiple-state sources, such as Markov modeled Poisson processes (known as MMPP) or Markov modeled Bernoulli processes (known as MMBP), which allow a flexible description of different traffic patterns ranging from file transfer to audio/video transmissions.

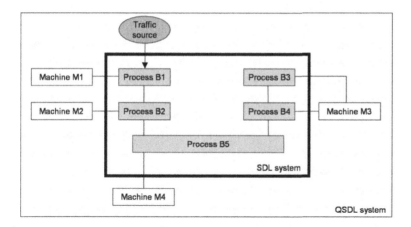

Figure 12.4/2: Assignment of machines to processes in QSDL

The QUEST tool transfers a QSDL description automatically into an executable simulation program. The performance evaluation is supported by different evaluation components and graphical display options. The latter allow among other things an online visualization of the system behavior for analyzing certain behavior moments, such as the impact of bursts or packet losses on the performance. Apart from the transient "short-term behavior" also stationary performance measures can be calculated. An application of QUEST to the performance modeling of TCP is presented in [Hint 01].

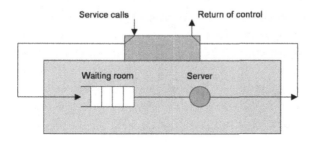

Figure 12.4/3: Modeling of a machine in QSDL

Further reading

Similar to some previous chapters, this chapter extracts facts on dedicated approaches on performance evaluation in the protocol field. Besides the cited papers we recommend the proceedings of the FORTE conference series [FORTE] including its predecessor PSTV (*Protocol Specification, Testing, and Verification*) for further studies. The interested reader can find a comprehensive application to SDL and MSC in the book of Mitschele-Thiel [Mits 01].

13   Implementation

After verifying the protocol design and possibly evaluating its expected performance the protocol can be implemented in a concrete execution environment. Although at first glance it may not seem so, the implementation is one of the most expensive stages of the protocol development process. It requires a multitude of decisions which have a considerable influence on the efficiency and correctness of the final protocol realization. The implementation stage receives anyhow less attention in *Protocol Engineering* research compared to the other phases of the protocol development process which is expressed in the small number of publications on this subject. One of the reasons is that implementation experiences are rarely generalized and published because of their strong system relation and the subjective character of implementations. In addition, the implementation phase provides few starting points for formalizations. Implementation in the context of formal description techniques means primarily **prototyping**, i.e., the execution of specifications on a computer. It primarily serves the validation of the protocol procedures during design. FDT compilers usually support this possibility. The efficiency of the generated code plays a minor role in this form of implementation.

In this chapter we give an overview of the key implementation techniques for communications protocols and explain the resultant problems. In contrast to the previous chapters, the focus is less on formal aspects but on the description of protocol implementation techniques that are not bound to formal descriptions. Only towards the end of the chapter we present approaches to automatically derive implementations from formal descriptions.

13.1   From protocol specification to implementation

The core problem of a protocol implementation is the mapping of the specified protocol functionality into the given target system. Experience of protocol implementations in practice has shown that the quality and efficiency of a protocol is far more determined by the implementation than by the design [Clar 89]. There are two main reasons for this. (1) Protocol specifications are implementation independent and rarely contain implementation requirements. This gives the implementers much freedom for an individual design of the protocol implementation. The quality and efficiency of the coded protocol therefore depend much on the individual skills and experience of the implementer. (2) Protocol implementations are heavily determined by the execution environment of the target system, notably by the operating system in which they are embedded. An overwhelming majority of the actions needed for the protocol execution are processed in the execution environment. Since the anticipation of implementation decisions is explicitly avoided in protocol specifications, there is a wide range of possible compliant implementations of a protocol, even in the same execution environment. This range may be used differently depending on the given system constraints. Therefore there is no universal recipe for an advantageous implementation of any protocol. Each implementation requires individual design decisions. There exist, however, a number of approaches and techniques developed over the years that can be used depending on the given implementation context. As an introduction we consider, therefore, the various steps of an implementation a little closer. They are depicted in Figure 13.1/1.

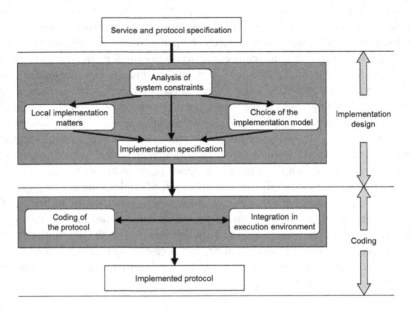

Figure 13.1/1: Implementation steps

13.1.1   Implementation design

The objective of the implementation design is to optimally map the protocol design, documented in the service and protocol specifications, onto the execution environment of the target system. This additional design phase is needed for two reasons. First, the logical model defined by the (implementation independent) protocol specification, e.g., the layer model, is not necessarily preserved in the implementation. The logical model provides primarily a basis for a comprehensive structuring of the protocol procedures. Its structures often turn out to be inefficient for implementations. Therefore completely different structures may be chosen. Second, protocol specifications often contain options and guidelines which can be decided only at implementation level.

Analysis of system constraints

A protocol implementation is always targeted to a concrete execution environment. Consequently, the implementation has to take its features and constraints into account. These are the operating system used, possible implementation languages, and existing libraries. Sometimes it may also be important whether there is a specialized execution environment supporting protocol implementations (see below).

Local implementation matters

Protocol specifications often leave certain decisions to the implementer for reasons of implementation independence. Such decisions are referred to as *local implementation matters*. They relate typically to the design of the interfaces to the execution environment, to protocol options, and to implementation choices. Moreover, nondeterminisms in the protocol specification must be dissolved, since protocol implementations are as a rule deterministic. Nondeterminisms give room for different implementation choices (cp. Section 1.2.4). The implementer has to refine the specification and make concrete decisions for the possible options. These decisions require a high degree of experience, a good knowledge of the protocol, and a sure instinct as these decisions can affect the conformance and the interoperability capability of the protocol implementation [Svob 89].

Choice of the implementation model

An important decision during implementation design is the choice of the implementation model which determines how the implementation is mapped onto the process structure of the execution environment. This mapping does not necessarily mean a one-to-one mapping, since protocol specifications often only describe the behavior of an entity regarding one connection, whereas the implementation has to support a dynamically changing number of connections. Two basic implementation models have been established: the server and the activity thread models that we introduce in the next section. The evaluation of implementation choices can be supported by performance analyses as described in Section 12.

Implementation specification

The implementation design may be documented through an *implementation specification*. It forms the basis for the subsequent coding process. In contrast to the protocol specification, the implementation specification is basically related to the target system. The character of the implementation specification though is not as precisely determined as that of the protocol specification because it is mostly an internal working document of the implementation process. When using informal protocol descriptions usually only the key implementation decisions are fixed, while in the case of formal descriptions the implementation specification usually refines the protocol specification with implementation-specific decisions. Only automated protocol implementations require an explicit implementation specification as a starting point for the code generation (see Section 13.6).

13.1.2   Coding

The subsequent implementation of the protocol in the narrow sense consists of two complementary steps: the coding of the protocol and its integration in the execution environment.

Protocol coding

The program code can mostly be derived relatively straightforwardly from the specification. A lot of additional functions, however, are required that cannot be derived directly from the specification, such as functions for the timer and the buffer management. Such functions must be provided by the execution environment.

Execution environment

The implementation of communication protocols strongly depends, as already mentioned above, on the execution environment. A protocol cannot be implemented independently of the execution environment. It forms the implementation environment of the protocol. The execution environment possesses a high share in the execution of the protocol. This share is often much higher than that of the proper protocol [Svob 89], [Clar 89], [Hutc 91], [Held 95]. Therefore, protocols with high efficiency demands, such as TCP/IP, are preferably implemented in the operating system kernel to execute the high share of actions belonging to the execution environment as efficiently as possible.

There are three variants for the inclusion of a protocol in an execution environment:

- integration into the operating system,
- integration into the application, and
- use of a protocol-specific execution environment.

Usually transport-oriented protocols are embedded in the operating system, while application-oriented ones are implemented as applications or as part of them. The implementation environment is formed here by the operating system and, if needed, by a few additional functions. In this approach the protocol implementation is bound to the operating system. If the protocol implementation is not sufficiently supported by the operating system complementary functions must be provided. In this case it is recommended to use a protocol-specific execution environment (see Figure 13.1/2) which covers the given operating system and provides a uniform interface to the protocols. This simplifies the integration of protocol software and facilitates its portability. In addition, the implementation environment can be better tailored to the specific needs of the protocol implementation. Examples of such implementation environments are presented in [Hutc 91], [Lang 99b], and [Popo 06]. Separate implementation environments are of special importance for the automatic derivation of protocol implementations. They are mostly applied here (see Section 13.6).

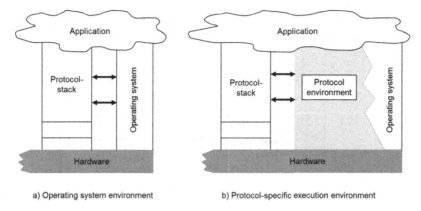

a) Operating system environment   b) Protocol-specific execution environment

Figure 13.1/2: Execution environments for protocol implementations

13.2   Implementation models

The mapping of the protocol entities onto the process structure of the execution environment is one of the key elements of the protocol implementation. A variety of mappings is conceivable, for example, one process or thread per entity, several processes or threads per entity, or several entities per process. The mapping depends on the requirements of the implementation and the features of the given execution environment. Mainly two process implementation models are applied for protocol implementations [Svob 89]:

- server model, and
- activity thread model

as well as further refinements.

13.2.1 Server model

The *server model* implements relatively straightforwardly the extended finite state machine principle. It represents the most popular protocol implementation method. The name originates from the implementation principle (see Figure 13.2/1) that maps the protocol entity onto a cyclic sequential process which serves an associated input queue. The process acts like a server that in every cycle reads an event from the queue, analyzes it, and branches depending on the reached state to the associated transition. After executing the transition and possibly writing an output event into the input queue of the next server process it returns to the central waiting point or loop, respectively, to read the next input event or to wait for the occurrence of a new event if the input queue is empty. Internal events can be handled in two ways: either using a shared variable, which is queried cyclically, or writing the event like the external events into the input queue.

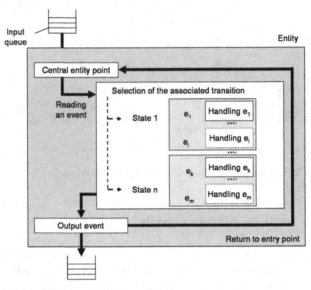

Figure 13.2/1: Principle of the server model

The server model can also be applied for the implementation of several protocol layers. This can be done using a single process or several (see Figure 13.2/2).

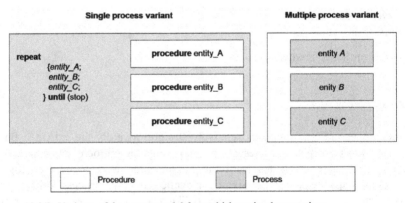

Figure 13.2/2: Variants of the server model for multi-layer implementations

If a single process is used all entities are implemented as procedures within this process. Each procedure follows the described implementation principle of the server model. The execution order is defined by the implementation environment. In general, the procedures are called successively in round-robin manner. In the multi-process solution each entity is mapped on an operating process. The processing order of the entities is determined by the scheduling strategy of the execution environment. If round-robin is applied there is no difference to the processing sequence of the single process solution

13.2.2 Activity thread model

The activity thread model goes back to Clark [Clar 85]. It implements a protocol entity through a set of procedures. Each procedure processes an event. It corresponds to a transition in a protocol automaton. The call of a procedure represents an exchange of an event between two protocol entities within a protocol stack (see Figure 13.2/3). An incoming event triggers the call of the corresponding procedure. If the transition possesses an output event the associated procedure of the next protocol entity is called. Thus incoming events can trigger a sequence of procedure calls – the **activity thread** – across several layers. This implementation principle is beneficial above all when implementing several layers because the events are not stored, but executed immediately.

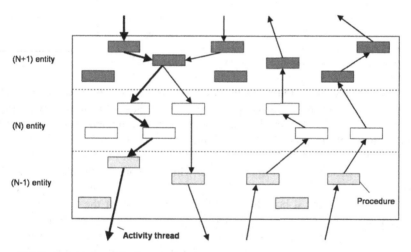

Figure 13.2/3: Activity thread implementation

Activity threads can be executed in parallel in both directions, i.e., top-down and bottom-up. This concurrency requires special synchronization means for access to shared variables.

There are a number of other problems which have to be solved when applying the activity thread principle, e.g., the handling of spontaneous transitions and internal events. There are two options: either calling a special procedure within the entity or using shared variables to spread the information. Another problem is the interface with the execution environment. Here a hybrid solution with the server model approach has proved convenient that stores the external events in an entry input queue which is read out cyclically. This brings, however, another problem with it. The associated procedures are not called directly from the environment. They have to be activated within the waiting loop. Thus, activity threads can run serially within the same process.

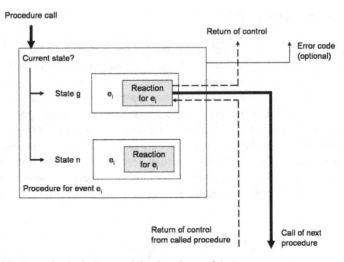

Figure 13.2/4: Execution paths in an activity thread procedure

The possible execution paths in an activity thread procedure are illustrated in Figure 13.2/4. When the procedure is called, first it has to be checked whether the event is accepted in the current state. This requires a unique presentation of the states to which all procedures must have access (see also Section 13.5). If the event is not expected in this state the procedure cannot be executed. In this case, an optional error code is returned together with the control to the calling procedure to inform about this (see Section 13.4.2). If the event is expected the procedure can be executed and it branches to the associated code of the transition. In case there is an output event the associated procedure for the next entity is called. An activity thread terminates when a transition has no output event or the event is not expected in the current state. In this case, the control is returned to the calling procedure and eventually to the initial point of the activity thread. Note that several states may be considered in a procedure for a given event. This is due to the fact that the same event may be expected in different states. Therefore the current state of the entity has to be determined at the beginning of the procedure.

Comparison of the models

Comparing the two models the server model approach represents the simpler and more straightforward implementation of a protocol entity. Its performance though is significantly lower than that of the activity thread implementation because the events have to be stored between layers and process changes are more frequent during execution. With the activity thread model, very efficient implementations can be achieved, since the events are processed immediately after their occurrence without any process change. The activity thread model, however, requires a very careful design. Problems to be solved include the handling of concurrent threads, the resolution of possible cyclic procedure call sequences, and the treatment of internal events.

13.3   Interface design

The design of the interface between the layers and with the execution environment is an important task of the implementation design. It maps the logical service interfaces onto the interaction mechanisms of the given execution environment. Furthermore, additional mechanisms may be introduced as, for instance, an atomic execution of the events or a flow control to regulate the data exchange at the layer interface. Sometimes special data interface units are introduced for the data exchange which may contain several service data units or in the case of a long payload only a subset of the data to be transferred.

The interface design depends on the implementation model applied. Two principal realizations are distinguished:

* the buffering interface and
* the procedure interface.

Buffering interfaces are used in server model implementations; procedure interfaces in activity thread ones. Note that the rendezvous principle as applied in some formal description techniques, such as LOTOS (cp. Section 8.3), to express the semantic concept of synchronous interaction is rarely used in real-life protocol implementations because it lowers the efficiency.

13.3.1 Buffering interface

Buffering interfaces transfer service data units or other events asynchronously via queues or process channels (see Figure 13.3/1). Depending on the mapping of the logical model onto the process structure, buffering interfaces can be realized across processes or internally in one process. In the first case, service access points can be implemented, for instance, using two opposed queues. In the second case various solutions are possible as operating system operations are rarely needed.

The drawback of the buffering handover is the efficiency loss due to data storing and queue management. Regarding the latter, the use of a common queue for all events of the protocol stack in which the event is stored together with the identifier of the destination entity has proved more favorable [Lang 99b].

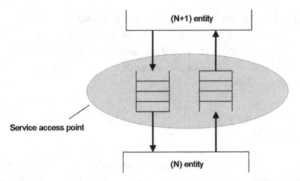

Figure 13.3/1: Buffering interface

13.3.2 Procedure interface

A procedure interface transfers an event with the procedure call. The event is processed immediately (see Figure 13.3/2). There must be a procedure for any possible event. The calling procedure is blocked until the control is returned from the called procedure.

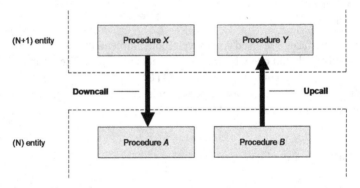

Figure 13.3/2: Procedure interface

The procedure calls are called as downcalls or upcalls, respectively, depending on their direction. A **downcall** refers to a call of a procedure of the (N)-entity by an (N+1)-entity to handover an event to the service provider. An **upcall** corresponds to a call in the opposite direction to indicate reactions of the service provider. An upcall may also be used by the (N)-entity for a query to the (N+1)-entity to optimize its own behavior.

The procedure interface implementation must ensure that no blockings occur between the events created in the activity thread due to existing dependencies. This is because the calling procedure has to wait until the event is processed. It may also happen that an event cannot be processed completely in one procedure.

Thus, logically related actions may be distributed on various procedures which in part may merge. This can lead to calls at the same level or even in the opposite direction, so that cyclical call sequences may occur. Such situations should be avoided wherever possible because they may cause blocking due to internal dependencies.

For this reason, a merged variant of both interfaces is sometimes used in which the procedure calls are only applied in one direction (see Figure 13.3/3). Accordingly, a downcall and an upcall interface are distinguished. The downcall interface is mostly applied for application-oriented protocols, the upcall interface in lower layer implementations.

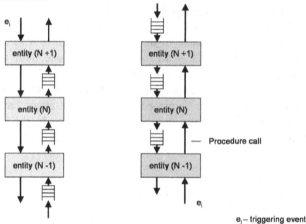

Figure 13.3/3: Downcall and upcall interface

13.4   Example

Before we enlarge on specific implementation issues, we want to demonstrate the principle of both implementation models by means of an example implementation of the XDT protocol in the programming language C. We consider only the implementation of the sender entity. Starting point for our example implementations is the EFSM representation of the XDT sender entity in Figure 7.5/1. We consider first the server model implementation.

13.4.1   Server model implementation

The server model implementation of the XDT sender entity can be derived straightforwardly from the EFSM representation in Figure 7.5/1. The structure is simple. It follows the principle represented in Figure 13.2/1. The entity is mapped onto a *while*-loop. After reading-out an event from the input queue the transition to be executed is determined based on the current state. There is a little deviation compared to the EFSM representation in Figure 7.5/1. We do not implement an explicit state for *go back N* because this would lead to a less manageable implementation. The reason is that this state will only be reached after this internal event has entered the input queue and been read-out again. Instead, *go back N* is directly integrated into two transitions in the state CONNECT. Note further that the presented implementation is not complete. It contains only the XDT layer, but not the implementation of the environment. In addition, it also does not take into account robustness requirements, such as responses to false input events etc. The procedures of the buffer and timer management are also not represented.

The implementation possesses an input queue that is read-out with *get_queue*. It serves two output queues: one queue for the XDT user (*put_user_queue*) and one for the Y-layer (*put_Y_queue*). The XDT service primitives are represented in a simplified way through the name of the primitive together with the associated parameters. Since the XDT-PDUs are mapped one-to-one onto the Y-service primitives, we refrain from using Y-primitives and enqueue the PDUs directly in the Y-queue. There is another presentation problem regarding the abovementioned *get_queue* operation. All events dequeued from the input queue have a different type. In order to preserve clarity we describe all input events by the type *event* and assume that the auxiliary variable *E* to which the events are assigned accepts the specific type.

```
/* TYPE DEFINITIONS AND FUNCTIONS */
typedef enum {true,false} boolean;
typedef enum {IDLE,AWAIT_ACK,CONNECTED,XBREAK} states;
typedef enum {XDATrequ,DT,ACK,ABO,timeout_t1,timeout_t2} event;
typedef struct {int sequ;boolean eom;data_array data} DT_type;
typedef struct {int sequ,source-addr,dest-addr; boolean eom; data_array data}
                                                        XDATrequ_type1;
typedef struct {int conn,sequ; boolean eom; data_array data} XDATrequ_type;
typedef struct {int conn,sequ } XDATconf_type, ACK_type;
typedef struct {int conn} XABORT_type, XBREAK_type;
typedef [ ]char data_array;
                        /* Functions for building PDUs and service primitives */
DT_type build_DT1(XDATrequ_type1);
DT_type build_DT(XDATrequ_type);
XDATconf_type build_XDATconf(int,int)
XABORT_type build_XABORTind(int);
XBREAK_type build_XBREAKind(int);
XDIS_type build_XDISind(int);
DT_type get_buffer(int);                 /* Functions for buffer management */
int put_buffer(DT_type);
void free_buffer(int);
void put_user_queue(event);             /* Functions for queue management */
```

```
void put_Y_queue(DT_type);
event get_queue();
void start(int,int);                        /* Functions for timer management */
void reset(int);


/* DECLARATION OF THE VARIABLES OF THE SENDER ENTITY */
int N, last, sequ;
int conn ;                                  /* Connection reference      */
int t1, t2;                                 /* Timer                     */
event E;                                    /* Auxiliary variable        */
states state;                               /* Current state             */
boolean not_stop = true;


/* TRANSITIONS */
while(not_stop)                             /* Central waiting loop      */
  {E = get_queue();                         /* Reading-out of an event   */
     switch(state)                          /* Current state  ?          */
        {case(IDLE):                        /* State IDLE                */
           {if (E == XDATrequ)
                {state = AWAIT_ACK;         /* IDLE ← XDATrequ          */
                 sequ = 1;
                 N = 0;
                 start(t2,50);              /* Timer connection set up   */
                 put_Y_queue(build_DT1(E)); /* Transfer to Y-layer       */
                }
          break;
          }
        case(AWAIT_ACK):                    /* State AWAIT_ACK           */
           {if (E == timeout_t2)            /* AWAIT_ACK ← Time-out*/
                {state = IDLE;              /* No connection set up      */
                 put_user_queue(build_XABORTind(conn));
                }
            if (E == ACK)                   /* AWAIT_ACK ← ACK          */
                {if (E.sequ == 1)
                    {conn = E.conn;         /* ACK.conn                  */
                     N= 1;
                     state = CONNECTED;
                     put_user_queue(build_XDATconf(conn,1));
                     reset(t2);             /* Reset timer t2            */
                     start(t1,500);         /* Start activity timer t1   */
                     start(t2,50);
                    }
                }
```

```
    break;
    }
case(CONNECTED):                                /* State CONNECTED          */
    {if (E == XDATrequ)                         /* CONNECTED ← XDATrequ */
      {sequ++;
        put_Y_queue(build_DT(E))                /* Transfer to Y layer      */
        if (XDATrequ.eom)                                      /* last PDU ?     */
          last:=sequ;
        if (put_buffer(DT) == 0)                           /* Buffer full ?   */
          {state = XBREAK;                                 /* Break          */
            put_user_queue(build_XBREAKind(conn));  /* XBREAKind       */
          }
      }
    if (E == ACK)                               /* CONNECTED ← ACK    */
      {reset(t1);
        reset(t2);
        if (E.sequ > N)                         /* ACK with correct number  */
          {N = E.sequ;
            free_buffer(N);
            if (N == last)                               /* last ACK ?       */
              {put_user_queue(build_XDISind(conn)); /* Connection release */
                state = IDLE;
              }
          }
        start(t1,500);
        start(t2,50);
      }
    if (E == timeout_t2)                        /* CONNECTED ← timeout_t2 */
      {int i;
        for (i=1; (i ≤ sequ - N); i++)                     /* go back N       */
          put_Y_queue(get_buffer(N+i));
      }
    if (E == ABO)                               /* CONNECTED ← ABO      */
      {state = IDLE;                            /* Protocol abortion by receiver */
        put_user_queue(build_XABORTind(conn));
      };
    if (E == timeout_t1)                        /* CONNECTED ← timeout_t1 */
      {state = IDLE;                            /* Inactive receiver        */
        put_user_queue(build_XABORTind(conn));
      };
    break;
    }
```

```
case(XBREAK):                             /* State XBREAK    */
  {if (E == timeout_t2)                   /* XBREAK ← timeout_t2    */
    {int i;
     for (i=1; (i ≤ sequ - N); i++)       /* go back N       */
        put_Y_queue(get_buffer(N+i));
    }
   if (E == ACK)                          /* XBREAK ← ACK       */
     {reset(t1);
      reset(t2);
      if (ACK.sequ > N)                   /*ACK with correct number */
        {N = ACK.sequ;
         free_buffer(N);
         put_user_queue(build_XDATconf(conn,sequ));
         state = CONNECTED;               /* Break finished    */
        }
      start(t1,500);
      start(t2,50);
     }
   if (E == ABO)                          /* XBREAK ← ABO         */
     {state = IDLE;                       /* Protocol abortion by receiver*/
      put_user_queue(build_XABORTind(conn));
     }
   if (E == timeout_t1)                   /* CONNECTED ← timeout_t1 */
     {state = IDLE;                       /* Inactive receiver   */
      put_user_queue(build_XABORTind(conn));
     }
   break;
  }
 }
}
```

13.4.2. Activity thread implementation

We now consider the activity thread implementation of the XDT sender entity. It consists of a set of procedures. These procedures can also be relatively readily derived from the state transition graph in Figure 7.5/1 by searching the transitions that belong to the external events of the (N+1)- or the (N-1)-layer. The transitions in turn may contain output events which trigger a procedure call in the higher or lower layer, respectively. Problems occur, as discussed above, if mutual dependencies between the procedures have to be taken into account.

As for the server model implementation, we consider again only the XDT layer. For that reason, our example implementation contains only procedures which can be called by another entity or internally. These are the procedures for the events *XDATrequ, timeout_t1, timeout_t2, ACK* und *ABO*. The implementation does not contain the procedures for events like *XDATconf, XBREAKind, XABORTind, XDISind*, or *DT*, which belong to the implementation of the XDT service user and the Y-layer which are not considered here. In the declaration these procedures are marked as *external*. Analogously to the server model implementation, we use procedure calls for the Y-primitives that refer to the name of the transported PDU, e.g., *call_DT, call_ACK*, and *call_ABO*.

In contrast to the server model implementation, we introduce return codes in this implementation. A return code informs the calling entity whether the procedure was executed completely or not. The return code "1" indicates a successful execution of the procedure in our example, the return code "0" that it failed. In the procedure *call_ACK* we use additionally the code "2" to indicate that the passed *ACK* is wrong. We demonstrate the use of the return code when calling procedures of the Y-layer. The respective error handling is carried out by the procedure *failure* which is not further specified here.

Another problem of this implementation represents the access to the global variables of the entity by concurrent threads. We solve this problem in our implementation by including all variables in the structure ECB (*entity control block*). The access to the ECB is exclusive and protected by semaphores. For clarity reasons, the latter are not represented in the following.

```
/* TYPE DEFINITIONS */
typedef enum {true,false} boolean;
typedef enum {IDLE,AWAIT_ACK,CONNECTED,XBREAK} states;
typedef [ ]char data_array;
typedef struct{int sequ;boolean eom;data_array data} DT_type;
typedef struct {int conn,sequ,source-addr,dest-addr; boolean eom;
                                data_array data} XDATrequ_type;
typedef struct {int N, last, sequ; states state; boolean no_buffer} ICB_type;


/* PROTOTYPE DEFINITIONS FOR ALL PROCEDURES */
int call_XDATrequ(XDATrequ_type);        /* Procedures of the XDT sender entity */
int call_timeout_t1()
int call_timeout_t2()
int call_ACK(int,int);
int call_ABO(int);
extern void call_XDISind(int);           /* Procedures of the XDT user  */
extern void call_XDATconf(int,int);
extern void call_XABORTind(int);
extern void call_XBREAKind(int);
extern int call_DT(DT_type);             /* Procedures of the Y-entity  */
ICB_type *ECB;                           /* Entity Control Block        */
int conn;                                /* Number of the connection    */
int t1,t2;                               /* Timer declarations          */
DT_type build_DT1(XDATrequ_type);        /* Function DT_1 coding        */
```

```
DT_type build_DT(XDATrequ_type);           /* Function DT coding        */
DT_type get_buffer(int);                    /* Buffer functions          */
int put_buffer(DT_type);
void free_buffer(int);
void start(int,int);                        /* Timer functions           */
void reset(int);
external void failure();                    /* Error handling function   */


/* PROCEDURES OF THE XDT SENDER ENTITY */
int call_XDATrequ(XDATrequ_type XDATrequ)   /* Procedure for XDATrequ    */
    {int rc;
     DT_type DT;
     switch(ECB → state)
       {case(IDLE):                          /* IDLE ← XDATrequ           */
          {ECB → state = AWAIT_ACK;          /* Connection set up         */
           ECB → sequ = 1;
           ECB → N = 0;
           start(t2,50);
           rc = call_DT(build_DT1(XDATrequ));
           if (rc == 0) failure();           /* Evaluation return code    */
           return(1);
          break;
          }
        case(CONNECTED):                     /* CONNECTED ← XDATrequ */
          {ECB → sequ++;
           put_buffer(DT);
           rc = call_DT(build_DT(XDATrequ));
           if (rc == 0 ) failure();          /* Evaluation return code    */
           call_XDATconf(conn,ECB → sequ);   /* Confirmation sending      */
           if (XDATrequ.eom)                 /* last PDU ?                */
           ECB → last = ECB → sequ;
           if (no_buffer)                    /* Buffer full ?             */
             {ECB → state = XBREAK;
              call_XBREAKind(conn);          /* Break                     */
             }
           return(1);
          break;
          }
        default: return(0);                  /* Procedure not executable  */
       }
    }
```

```
void call_go_back_N()                          /* Procedure for go back N    */
  {int i,rc;
  for (i=1; (i ≤ ECB → sequ – ECB → N); i++)
  rc = call_DT(get_buffer(ICB → N+i));
  if (rc == 0) failure();                       /* Evaluation return code     */
  }

int call_ACK(int c,sequ)                        /* Procedure for ACK-PDU      */
  {switch(ECB → state)
      {case(AWAIT_ACK):                         /* AWAIT_ACK ← ACK           */
         {if (sequ == 1)                         /* correct ACK                */
            {ECB → state = CONNECTED;
            conn = c;
            call_XDATconf(conn,1);
            reset(t2);
            start(t1,500);
            start(t2,50);
            return(1);
            }
         else return(2);                         /* wrong ACK                  */
        break;
        }
      case(CONNECTED):                          /* CONNECTED ← ACK           */
         {if (sequ > ECB → N)                     /* correct ACK                */
            {reset(t1);
            reset(t2);
            ECB → N = sequ;
            free_buffer(sequ);
            if (sequ == last)                     /* last ACK ?                 */
               {call_XDISind(conn);               /* Connection release         */
               ECB → state = IDLE;
               }
            start(t1,500);
            start(t2,50);
            return(1);
            }
         else return(2);                         /* wrong ACK                  */
        break;
        }
```

```
        case(XBREAK):              /* XBREAK ← ACK           */
            {if (sequ > ECB → N)   /* correct ACK            */
              {reset(t1);
               reset(t2);
               ECB → N = sequ;
               free_buffer(ECB → N);
               call_XDATconf(conn, ECB → sequ);   /* Break finished    */
               start(t1,500);
               start(t2,50);
               return(1);
               }
             else return(2);       /* wrong ACK              */
            break;
            }
        default: return(0);        /* Procedure not executable   */
        }
    }

int call_ABO(int conn)            /* Procedure for ABO-PDU       */
    {switch(ECB → state)
        {case(CONNECTED):         /* CONNECTED  ← ABO        */
         case(XBREAK):            /* XBREAK  ← ABO           */
            {ECB → state = IDLE;
             call_XABORTind(conn);   /* Abort by receiver       */
             return(1);
            break;
            }
        default: return(0);        /* Procedure not executable   */
        }
    }

int call_timeout_t1()             /* Time-out activity timer     */
    {switch(ECB → state)
        {case(CONNECTED):         /* CONNECTED ← timeout_t1*/
         case(XBREAK):            /* XBREAK ← timeout_t1     */
            {ECB → state = IDLE;
             call_XABORTind(conn);
             return(1);
            break;
            }
        default: return(0);
```

```
            }
         }

      int call_timeout_t2()                    /* Time-out ACK timer          */
         {switch(ECB → state)
            {case(AWAIT_ACK):                  /* AWAIT_ACK ← Time-out */
               {ECB → state = IDLE;
                call_XABORTind(conn);          /* no connection set up        */
                return(1);
                break;
               }
             case(CONNECTED):                  /* CONNECTED ← timeout_t2 */
             case(XBREAK):                      /* XBREAK ← timeout_t2      */
               {call_go_back_N;                 /* go back N                  */
                return(1);
                break;
               }
             default: return(0);                /* Procedure not executable    */
            }
         }
```

13.5   Specific implementation issues

Independently of the chosen implementation model, a number of problems have to be solved for each implementation. Some of these problems are discussed in this section.

13.5.1   Entities

Additional functions

The implementation of a protocol entity requires some additional functions that do not always depend on the chosen implementation model. Some of these functions are:

Activation of the entity

If the input queue is empty the entity has to wait. Active waiting should be avoided for efficiency reasons. When using a buffering interface cyclic queries of the input queue can be used to leave the waiting state. This can be implemented by an interprocess communication mechanism that supports multiple alternatives. In the procedure interface activation is triggered by the call of the respective procedure.

Reading-out and analyzing events
Each event read-out from the input queue must be analyzed regarding type, correctness, and content. It has to be removed from the input queue to avoid multiple activations of the event.

Access to the transition
The incoming event and the current state of the entity determine the transition to be executed. The access to the code of the transition takes place centrally in server model implementations and is decentralized in activity thread implementations (cp. Section 13.4). In both cases there are two ways to access the transition code: the programmed and the table-driven access. The *programmed access* determines the transition using nested *if*-and/or *case*-statements (see Figure 13.5/1a). The resulting code is relatively extensive in this case. For larger nesting depths (> 4), this kind of access has proved less efficient than the *table-driven* one [Held 95]. The latter is based on the use of a two-dimensional matrix (see Figure 13.5/1b) that contains the transitions, e.g., represented by a reference to the transition code or by control parameters for a general transition procedure. The indices for the transition access are the major states, possibly also important minor states (see below), and the input events.

Atomic execution of transitions
The semantics of some formal description techniques demand an atomic execution of transitions. In this case, the actions of the transition must be protected by a synchronization mechanism that ensures that all outputs and all changes of variables only become visible after executing the transition.

Representation of states
In both implementation models it is required that the state of the entity is uniquely represented. One distinguishes between major and minor states. *Major states* are the states that are explicitly indicated in the specification. They are usually implemented by a simple variable that indicates the current state. *Minor states* represent the current values of the entity variables $V_1 \dots V_n$. The number of possible minor states is determined by the value ranges of these variables. Hence, the set of all possible states of an entity is:

$$\{\text{major states}\} \times \text{value range } V_1 \times \dots \text{value range } V_n.$$

Connection management
The implementation of connection-oriented protocols requires special measures for the management of the connections in the entities. For this, the entities use connection tables which contain information about the managed connections (cp. Section 2.1), e.g., the local and the destination address, connection end points (if used), the current state of the connection, and others. The table entries are the local connection references. For each incoming event, the entity has to determine which connection the event belongs to.

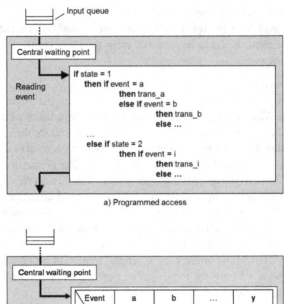

Figure 13.5/1: Access to the transitions

The connection management itself can be implemented in two ways: either by direct integration into the entity code or by setting up a process or thread for each connection. The first variant is more expensive to implement, since separate data areas must be kept for the entity variables of each connection. Both variants require a mechanism for reacting to requests for new connections.

Note that formal description techniques handle connection management differently. Frequently, only the behavior of the protocol is described, which corresponds to one single connection. In such cases, connection management has to be added to handle various connections. If the connection management cannot be described by the means of the formal description technique it must be provided through the implementation, e.g., by the runtime environment.

Coding and decoding of PDUs

The coding and decoding of PDUs including their analysis take up a not insignificant part of protocol implementations measured in either lines of code or execution time. Before sending a PDU, the protocol control information and the user data have to be written into the specified PDU fields, i.e., they have to be shifted to the specified bit positions. Since protocol data units are mostly independent of each other, usually separate coding/decoding procedures are used for each PDU type. The data are transferred to the procedure as parameters. Sometimes larger data units have to be segmented (cp. Section 5.6). In this case, the coding procedures have to include a segment offset into the PDU headers.

The decoding of the protocol data units in the receiver entity consists of two steps. First it must be checked whether the received PDU is the expected one (otherwise, it is usually discarded), and whether it was transferred correctly. Then the contents can be extracted and analyzed. When segmented data units are received, the complete service data unit must be re-established based on the segment offset in the PDU headers.

Mapping between SDUs and PDUs

The mapping of service data units onto protocol data units is often not explicitly described in protocol specifications. The segmentation, blocking, and chaining of data units is quite often considered a local implementation matter. For segmentation, for instance, this decision depends on whether the underlying protocol or connection requires a maximum value for the length of the protocol data units to be transferred.

13.5.2   Interfaces

When buffering interfaces are used, two further aspects have to be taken into account: the application of flow control mechanisms at the service interface and the atomic execution of events.

Interface flow control

In addition to the compensation of processing speed differences between peer entities, flow control mechanisms (cp. Section 5.8) can also be deployed for the regulation of the interaction between adjacent entities at the service interface[1]. Frequently used mechanisms are:

- *Finite input queues*
  Effective regulation can be achieved by the use of finite queues for each (N)-connection. If the queue between the (N)- and (N-1)-layer is full, no further events can be read-out from the input queue of the (N)-entity. A back-pressure occurs which may continue upwards to the application. The same applies analogously to the other direction.

---

[1] The break state (*XBREAKind*) of the XDT protocol is an example of such a flow control mechanism at the service interface. It is though part of the protocol and thus does not represent an implementation feature.

- *Flow control through buffer allocation*
  The principle of finite input queues can also be implemented with the help of buffer allocations by providing only a limited number of buffers for the data exchange between adjacent layers in each direction. The receiving entity delays the return of an empty buffer until it has in turn processed the received data and forwarded them.
- *Additional service primitives*
  Additionally, implementation-specific service primitives may also be introduced through which similar mechanisms can be implemented as are used between the peer entities, e.g., the granting of loans.

Atomic execution of events

Buffering and procedure interfaces resolve the atomicity of interactions at the service interfaces. This may result in event sequences which deviate from the specified ones. In order to ensure the atomicity of interactions, if demanded in a specification, again implementation-specific primitives can be used. For example, a *DISCONNECT request* primitive does not automatically trigger the removal of PDUs of this connection in the opposite queue. This can be achieved by a 2-way handshake through an additional service primitive, e.g., *DISCONNECT completed*, which confirms the removal of these protocol data units [Svob 89].

13.5.3   Buffer allocation and management

The exchange of service data units at the service interface requires the use of appropriate exchange mechanisms. An obvious and simple solution would be the exchange of data through buffers. This requires a buffer pool in each layer. A buffer is allocated for encoding a protocol data unit which is then transferred as service data unit to the next layer. Here the contents can be copied into a new buffer to add the protocol control information (PCI) of the associated protocol. Blocking, chaining, and segmentation can also be easily realized this way. This approach has proved, however, not to be efficient. Since the data units to be transferred may be pretty large, copying may cost a lot of time, especially as it is repeated at each interface. Today it is expected that protocol implementations should avoid the copying of data units within a protocol stack, wherever possible [Clar 89], [Svob 89]. Instead shared data areas are used which all entities can access. Now only the references to the respective data areas have to be exchanged. The use of references, however, makes the mapping between service and protocol data units more complicated. In order to ensure efficient transfer of data units across multiple layers mainly two techniques are applied:

- *Offset method*
  The offset method reserves a sufficiently large buffer in which the user data (payload) and the protocol control information (header) of all layers are stored (see Figure 13.5/2). The encoding of a protocol data unit can now very simply be done by writing the header information in this buffer and setting a reference

to it. At receiving side, the entity stores the received PDU again in a buffer from which all header information and user data can be read-out in each protocol. The references can be deleted accordingly. When segmentation, chaining or blocking is needed, however, some copy operations are unavoidable.

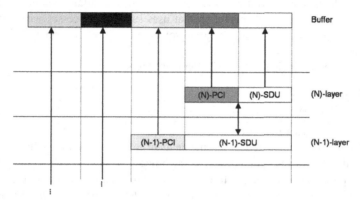

Figure 13.5/2: Offset method

- *Gather/Scatter method*
  The gather/scatter method stores the data that form a PDU in separate buffers (see Figure 13.5/3). Instead transfer descriptors are exchanged between layers that refer to the stored data (PCIs, user data) and thus "gather" the scattered data. This method supports in particular segmentation and blocking. At least one copying though can hardly be avoided within the protocol stack to compile the data for sending and to separate when receiving, if demanded.

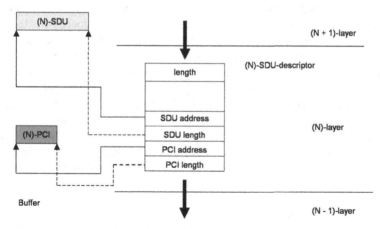

Figure 13.5/3: Gather/Scatter method

13.5.4   Timer implementation

Although timers usually possess a relatively simple control functionality (*start*, *reset* and *time-out*), their implementation is not as easy as it looks. An entity, for example, which runs several connections, may need in certain situations a large number of timers. An implementation that uses separate processes with separate channels for interprocess communication for the timers may overload the operating system.

There are two principal ways to implement timers:

- by an independent process or
- within a process.

Implementation as a process

The timer is implemented as an independent process. The timer functions are exchanged between the protocol and timer process as events. This allows use of the timer process by different entities, which helps in particular server model implementations. It requires, however, additional interprocess communication. The timer process accepts start and reset orders from the entities. Start messages contain the address of the calling entity for feedback, the time-out interval, and an order ID selected by the protocol entity. The reset order contains the feedback address and order ID to identify the timer to stop. The timer process periodically monitors the received orders taking the current time into account, and generates a time-out signal for the client entity when time elapses. The time-out message contains the order ID, so that the entity can identify the respective timer.

Implementation within a process

If the overhead for interprocess communication is to be avoided the timer can also be implemented within the entity. The interface can be presented by procedures for starting, resetting, and querying the timer. The query procedure is the most problematic one because it may conflict with entity activation and the reading-out of events from the input queue (cp. Section 13.5.1). Required blocking in this context should not prevent entity activation by other incoming events, while conversely waiting for new events should not delay the handling of a time-out. In activity thread implementations there is the additional problem that the entity may only be activated by an external procedure call. Therefore, the procedures should contain timer queries and respective time-out reactions. A specific solution has to be foreseen for situations when no external events occur, but time-outs are pending. This may be solved by an additional procedure "Test for time-outs" that is activated periodically by the runtime environment.

13.5.5 Special protocol-related implementation techniques

Several special implementation techniques have been developed, especially in the context of high performance communication which has triggered not only the development of new protocols but also tried to increase the efficiency of their implementations. Examples of such implementation techniques are integrated layer processing and parallel protocol implementations. **Integrated layer processing (ILP)** is an efficient implementation technique for protocol stacks especially to support multimedia applications [Abbo 93], [Ahlg 96]. It aims at reducing the number of memory accesses by executing data manipulation operations of different layers simultaneously, when these data are in the main memory. Typical examples of such data manipulation operations are cyclic redundancy checks (CRC), data compression/decompression, and data encryption/decryption. The data manipulation operations which are processed form the so-called ILP-loop. ILP implementations can achieve significant efficiency improvements, but are more sophisticated in the design because the ILP loop does not interrupt the protocol's normal execution. In case of a protocol error a conventional implementation must be provided additionally.

The goal of **parallel protocol implementation techniques** was to exploit the parallelism inherent in communication protocols by mapping parallel executable units onto different processors and thus increasing the data throughput. The types of parallelism taken into account were the parallelism of layers, connections, data flow directions, PDUs, and protocol functions. Especially the last two forms appeared promising. Often though, the performance gain is balanced by the organizational overhead. In addition, the derivation of suitable parallel units appears non-trivial. Both approaches – integration layer processing and parallel execution – are rarely applied any more. This is due to progress in computer processor technology which sufficiently supports multimedia applications nowadays. For that reason, we do not go in details here and refer the interested reader to the referenced literature. Both techniques were also investigated regarding their applicability for FDT-based implementations [Lang 99b], [Gotz 96b]. It has been shown that they are applicable in this context and may lead to performance improvements.

Besides the development of efficient implementation techniques which map the specification more or less directly onto optimal implementation structures, there have been various activities that deal with the **optimization of the runtime environment**. Even if these approaches seem "far away" from the viewpoint of formal protocol descriptions they represent an essential element in the development of efficient communication software. An example is the x-Kernel [Hutc 91], which tried to reduce the non-negligible share of the operating system in protocol execution by providing special functions for optimizing data and control flow as well as minimizing copy operations. Such optimized execution environments may particularly be used in execution environments with a limited number of applications.

13.6   Automated protocol implementation

As already argued in former chapters, the development of a complete complex formal protocol description is a long process. The derivation of a running implementation from it may take as long as the development of the specification. This means the protocol is "described" quasi two times, once in the FDT and again in the programming language used for coding. This can almost double the time required. This double effort has motivated investigations to automatically generate implementations from a given formal specification. This would allow various implementations to be generated based on a given specification. This intention has failed up to now due to the insufficient efficiency of the generated code which usually does not meet the demands of real-life communication. We come back to this issue at the end of this section. For this reason, automated code generation from formal descriptions serves primarily for prototyping, i.e., for executing the specifications to validate them or to trace certain protocol sequences. All FDT compilers nowadays support this feature and provide outputs for the generation of executable code. The efficiency of the generated code plays a minor role for prototyping.

The ideas and techniques of automated protocol implementation coincide with the approaches of model-driven software development. Here too, the objective is to generate code from the model developed. Approaches to automated protocol implementation though go back to the 1980s.

Benefits of automated protocol implementation

The automated derivation of protocol implementations from formal descriptions offers a number of advantages. The most important one is undoubtedly the significant (time) gain in the implementation process, but other benefits are also quite remarkable. Automated implementations may reduce the likelihood of implementation errors because the compiler generates the code according to a defined transformation procedure which has to be designed and proved during compiler development. For the same reason, generated code usually has a better compliance with the specification than manually written code. Automated code generation also avoids subjective implementation styles. Last but not least, it allows a faster adjustment to protocol changes which have to be carried out only at specification level.

Constraints of automated protocol implementation

Automated protocol implementation is substantially different from traditional manual implementation. It is subject to a number of restrictive conditions which have to be taken into account when generating the code. We discuss these differences on the basis of Figure 13.6/1 in the following.

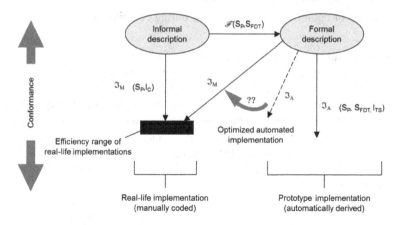

Figure 13.6/1: Constraints of automated protocol implementation

A manual implementation $\mathfrak{I}_M$ maps a given (often informal) specification of the protocol onto the execution environment of the target system. The semantics of the (informal) protocol specification S_P and the implementation context I_C (execution environment, implementation language of the target system) form the constraints of this mapping. The implementation is designed individually and impacted by the subjective style of the implementer. He/she has the possibility to optimally adapt the implementation to the given environment, while respecting conformity with the specification. If the implementer starts from a formal description $\mathcal{F}(S_P)$, this serves as a basis for the unique interpretation of the protocol specification. The semantics of the formal description technique, however, needs not necessarily be preserved in the implementation as long as the protocol procedures are correctly implemented. For example, a TCP implementation derived from a LOTOS specification does not preserve synchronous communication.

This situation changes when automated implementation techniques are applied. They start from a formal protocol description $\mathcal{F}(S_P)$. In contrast to a manual implementation, an automated implementation $\mathfrak{I}_A$ has to take the formal semantics S_{FDT} of the applied FDT and its implementation environment I_{TS} into account. The implementation generation is performed automatically. A correct implementation can only be guaranteed if the FDT semantics is preserved. The simplest form of transformation is the direct implementation of the formal FDT semantics S_{FDT}, as most FDT compilers do. The transformation is easy to perform and its correctness can be readily validated. The main goal of such implementations is prototyping. The efficiency of the generated code is usually not sufficient for real-life protocol implementations[2] [Held 95], [Gotz 96b]. In order to deploy this code in real-life protocol implementations further optimizations are required. This can be done in

---

[2] Here we understand real-life protocol implementations to mean implementations that meet the performance requirements of real networks.

two ways: by manual adjustments of the generated code, as often done in practice, or by means of optimizing transformations during compilation, which we consider below.

Principle of automated code generation

The principle of code generation is basically the same in all approaches to automated protocol implementations [Held 95], [Lang 99b] (see Figure 13.6/2). The starting point of the code generation process is the **implementation specification** (cp. Section 13.1.1) which contains the implementation-related information and refinements needed for code generation on the target system. Even for prototyping, additional information about the runtime environment is required. If this information is missing the generated code will contain gaps which require manual post-processing.

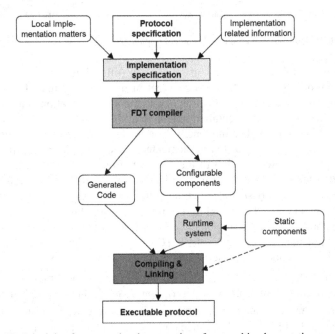

Figure 13.6/2: Principle of automated code generation of protocol implementations

The FDT compiler generates executable code from the implementation specification. Here the FDT compiler applies a specific **implementation model** which describes the structure of the automatically generated implementation, its components, and the manner of their interaction. The implementation model defines the transformation rules for the FDT compiler to map the formal description onto executable code including the service interface and the integration into the execution environment.

Unlike a manual implementation, where the implementation model is selected during implementation design, the implementation model for the automatic implementation has to be designed during the compiler development. At that time, neither the potential applications nor the implementation contexts are known.

The generated code must be embedded into the target system. For automated protocol implementations, the use of a separate, manually coded implementation environment which is placed between the operating system and the protocol stack code has turned out to be appropriate (cp. Figure 13.1/2). This is an FDT-related execution environment that provides all functions that cannot be derived automatically, in particular functions of the FDT semantics. Such an implementation environment facilitates the generation of implementations for different implementation contexts. The separate execution environment virtually forms the "**runtime system**" of the FDT compiler, which though is more strongly connected to the operating system than with conventional compilers. The separate runtime environment contains primarily routines for integrating the code into the operating system and special routines, e.g., for interface interactions, timer management, buffer management, and event scheduling. The routines may be parameterized by the compiler to better adapt them to the presetting of the implementation model. The runtime system can exist either as source code, which is then translated together with the generated code by the compiler of the target language into executable code, or as object code which is linked together with the generated code.

Experience with such implementations has indicated that approximately 40-70 per cent of the code can be generated automatically [Held 95], [Lang 99a]. This strongly depends on the type of the protocol implemented. It is, however, worthwhile to note that the manually coded routines of the runtime system are reused for other implementations.

Optimized code generation

The core problem of automated protocol implementation consists of the fact that the chosen implementation model defines a fixed transformation scheme. The structure of the implementation and the separation of functions are strongly influenced by the semantics of the respective formal description technique. The rigid implementation model limits the effectiveness of the implementation, since very little room is left for local implementation matters and individual optimizations. These can only be carried out subsequently.

Existing FDT compilers, e.g., [CADP], [Cind], aim primarily at prototyping. They straightforwardly map the FDT semantics and contain some optimizations to reduce the overhead incurred by the FDT semantics. Complex elements, such as efficient PDU coding/decoding or cross-layer implementations are usually not supported. The generated code can rarely be deployed in protocol implementations that can be deployed in real networks. To do so an optimized code generation is required. Several approaches have been published which have tried to increase the efficiency of the generated code, e.g., by optimizing the access to the transition code or by parallel execution [Held 95], [Gotz 96b], but the efficiency increase was limited. Two other approaches have proved more promising: (1) the integration of advanced manual implementation techniques and (2) the support of a flexible adaptation to the given implementation context. The first approach was pursued in [Henk 97]. It describes an approach to mapping EFSM-based specifications, e.g., in SDL, onto an activity thread implementation which achieves significantly higher code efficiency. The approach also avoids the copying of data units. The problem of such transformations is that they may violate the FDT semantics. For example, data units may get lost or the order the events occur may change compared to the specification. In [Henk 97], this is prevented through specific runtime mechanisms. An approach which resolves these semantic conflicts already at compile time is presented in [Köni 00]. It is based on a re-ordering of *output*-statements in the transitions. The principle was applied in the experimental SDL compiler COCOS (*Configurable Compiler for SDL*) [Lang 99a] that flexibly adapts to a given implementation context using a variable implementation model. The compiler supports different implementation techniques: the server model, the activity thread model, and integrated layer processing (ILP). It also includes techniques to avoid the copying of data units. Figure 13.6/3 shows the principle of implementation with COCOS.

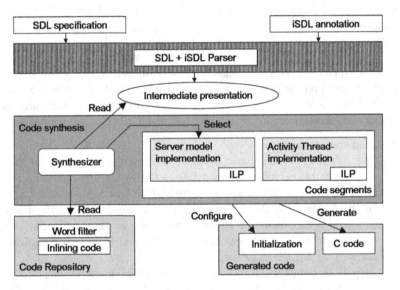

Figure 13.6/3: Principle of code generation with COCOS

The compiler has two inputs: the SDL specification and the iSDL annotation. The latter is an implementation-oriented annotation which selects the implementation model and provides information about the target hardware, e.g., the number of processors or the memory organization. It is embedded as comments in the SDL specification. Both specifications are translated into an intermediate representation which forms the starting point for various analyses including performance predictions for various implementation options. A synthesizer generates the implementation from the intermediate format according to the selected implementation model. The intermediate representation also contains the runtime system. Note that ILP implementations are not generated alone, but always in context with another implementation to which the system switches when protocol errors occur (cp. Section 13.5.5). The code repository contains segments to support the code generation, e.g., word filters for the adjustment of data formats between different data manipulation operations in ILP implementations or efficient (manually coded) code segments to be included in the generated code.

Applications of the COCOS compiler to different specifications have shown significant performance gains compared to existing commercial FDT compilers. For example, the derivation of an activity thread implementation from an SDL specification of the TCP/IP stack outperformed an implementation generated with the *Cadvanced* compiler of the former SDT tool suite of Telelogic Tau by 120 per cent [Lang 99b].

Despite such results, the automated generation of protocol implementations based on today's formal description techniques will be always a trade-off between the implementation duration, the required efficiency, and the degree of automation of the implementation. This is mainly due to the semantic constraints of the specification languages and the relative rigidity of the transformation process. Possible approaches for solving these problems, besides a flexible adaptation to the implementation environment and the use of modern implementation principles, are modifications of the specification languages and the development of implementation-oriented specification styles. For this reason, implementations with high performance demands are hardly the primary application field for automated protocol implementations. These are rather application protocols or novel protocols to quickly generate a running implementation on the basis of a formal protocol description that can be further optimized, if needed.

Further reading

As already argued in the chapter there are not that many publications which deal with the specific problems of protocol implementations. Besides the cited work a description of protocol implementation principles including an FSM library for protocol implementations can be found in the book of Popovic [Popo 06]. A comprehensive introduction to protocol implementation principles is also given in the already mentioned book of Mitschele-Thiel [Mits 01]. The book describes in particular the implementation of SDL systems.

Exercises

(1) Describe the basic steps of protocol implementation design and coding. Discuss in particular the role of local implementation matters and the integration into the execution environment.

(2) What is the purpose of prototyping? What is it used for?

(3) Explain the principle of the server and the activity thread model. What are the issues the implementer faces when using these models? Discuss the return of control and error information in activity threads.

(4) Explain the use of buffering and procedure interfaces in the context of these models.

(5) Sketch an implementation of the XDT receiver entity with an explicit connection set up as described in exercise (11) in Chapter 2.

(6) Sketch the same implementation using the activity thread model.

(7) Integrate the regulated data delivery mechanism of exercise (13) in Chapter 2 into the server model implementation of exercise (5).

(8) What approaches exist to implement the access to the transition code?

(9) How can states be represented in implementations?

(10) How can the connection management be implemented?

(11) What methods exist to optimally handle the exchange of SDUs within a protocol stack?

(12) How can timers be implemented in protocols?

14 Testing

The protocol test has the task to check whether the implemented protocol works correctly and is in compliance with the specification. In contrast to verification, which tries to prove the correctness, accuracy, and consistency of the protocol design, i.e., of its specification, testing focuses on implementations. Protocol verification and testing are therefore complementary methods. While verification is based on formal proofs, protocol testing validates physically existent, executable implementation by experiments. A test always relates to a dedicated implementation. It cannot make statements on other implementations derived from the same specification. The well-known statements on software testing also apply to protocol testing, such as that the goal of testing is to detect errors in the implementation or a test can only confirm the presence of errors but not their absence. Consequently, the protocol test cannot guarantee the correctness of an implemented protocol; it can only increase trust in the functionality and reliability of the implemented protocol.

In this chapter we introduce the basic methods and techniques applied in protocol testing. After a brief overview of the various types of protocol testing, we focus on the conformance and the interoperability test which represent the primary forms of protocol testing. We first introduce the fundamentals of the ISO test methodology. After that, we deal with the derivation of test cases that are not covered by standardization. Finally, we give an outlook on test description languages, in particular the TTCN test notations. As in other chapters, we use the XDT protocol as an example for the representation of test cases.

14.1 Types of protocol tests

Protocol testing represents a variant of the testing of parallel and distributed systems. Compared to the testing of sequential programs, there are a number of differences [Baum 94], such as the non-reproducibility of events, the combinatory overlay of processes, the lack of a global system view with defined conditions, limited observability and control of the implementation, and the use of distributed test systems. The intrinsic distinctiveness of protocol testing compared to software testing, however, is the use of several specification levels, as discussed in the previous chapters (cp. Chapter 9), the role of standardization, and multiple implementations of communication protocols. The task of protocol testing is therefore not only to demonstrate that the implementation meets a given functional specification – the *service specification* – but also to show that the associated abstract implementation – the *protocol specification* – is interoperable with other implementations of the protocol. The proof of interoperability of protocol implementations is complicated by protocol options and local implementation matters, and last but not least also by the incompleteness and ambiguity of informal protocol descriptions.

Protocol testing is the most important validation method for communication protocols in practice. This has several reasons. The use of verification methods is limited in practice because of the complexity of protocol specifications. Moreover, it only relates to the design and not to the implementation of the protocol. The mapping of a (verified) protocol specification onto a concrete implementation includes a variety of steps and decisions that may be sources of errors as we have seen in the preceding chapter. This process is difficult to formally verify, since implementation details are often not disclosed. Hence, the correct functioning of a protocol implementation can only be validated by testing.

Protocol testing comprises different types of tests. They can be roughly divided into:

- debugging,
- conformance test,
- interoperability test, and
- complementary tests.

Debugging

As always in programming, there is a need to find bugs or other defects in the code when implementing the protocol. This task is usually performed by the implementer. The methods and principles applied here correspond to those of traditional software testing, such as the testing of single protocol parts as well as integration tests to examine their interactions. These tests are primarily **white box tests** that are based on knowledge of the source code and its structure (module structure, data structures, and control flow). The test cases can be derived directly from the source code. Other typical test methods like code inspection, walkthroughs, or code supplements (queries, intermediate expressions) can also be applied to get information about the internal processes. These are general test methods which are not only typical of protocol testing.

Conformance test

The first characteristic protocol test is the conformance test that checks whether an implementation is in compliance with the specification. The conformance of an implementation with the respective specification is a necessary precondition for the interoperability of protocol implementations. The significance of the conformance test derives from the existence of protocol standards. It validates compliance with the respective standard. Hence, it is an important means for the enforcement of protocol standards. The conformance test is a much sharper test than debugging. It consists of a set of fixed rules, and is typically not performed by the implementer. The conformance test is a **black box test** that checks the externally visible functional behavior of the protocol implementation. The test cases are derived from the specification; neither the program code nor other information about the structure of the implementation are used for this. One speaks therefore also of **specification-based testing**. The input events contained in the test cases stimulate the implementation. Its reactions, i.e., its outputs, are recorded and then compared with the expected specified behavior for compliance. The localization of the origins of possible errors is not among to the tasks of this test. They must be found by subsequent tests, e.g., white box tests.

Interoperability test

The conformance test alone is not sufficient to guarantee the interoperability of different implementations of a protocol, i.e., to ensure a correct interaction between the implementations as specified. The choice of different protocol options as well as local implementation decisions may cause implementations that comply with the same standard to not be interoperable. The proof of this capability is the task of the interoperability test which has gained increasing importance in recent years. Figure 14.1/1 depicts the relationship between the conformance and interoperability tests.

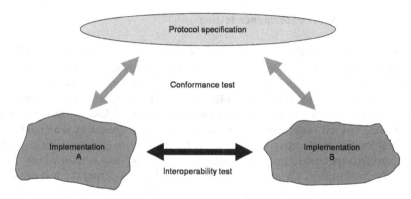

Figure 14.1/1: Conformance versus interoperability test

Complementary tests

The above tests do not cover all properties that a protocol implementation should fulfill. Therefore, additional tests are needed. Typical complementary tests are:

- *performance tests* which evaluate the adherence to performance targets, such as response time or throughput, by measurements, and
- *robustness tests* which examine whether the implementation is stable in the case of incorrect inputs.

These tests apply similar methods to those used in software testing. Therefore, we concentrate in the following on the conformance and interoperability tests.

14.2 Conformance test

The aim of conformance testing is to demonstrate that a given implementation of a protocol is in compliance with the underlying protocol specification. In practice, the conformance test is above all a test for adherence to protocol standards. It gives the user and/or the purchaser of the communication software confidence that the purchased product fulfills the respective standard and is potentially able to interoperate with other implementations of that protocol. Compliance with the standard may be confirmed by a certificate. The theoretical challenge of the conformance test lies in the fact that it is a black box test. The test runs do not take any information about the inner structure of the implementation into account. All test cases are derived from the related protocol specification. Conformance tests of communication protocols are nowadays based on established procedures. Before we speak about these procedures we give a short overview on the principle of conformance testing.

14.2.1   Principle of conformance testing

The task of a conformance test is to prove whether an implemented protocol $I_j \in$ $\Im$ (with $\Im$ – set of all possible implementations of S) behaves exactly like the protocol specification S which it was derived from, or in other words: whether I_j meets the conformance relation I_j **conforms_to** S. The conformance test refers to the functional behavior of the protocol implementation as defined by the specification S, i.e., to their observable interactions with the environment. The conformance test compares the observable external behavior of the implementation with the (expected) specified behavior. To prove this a test system is used which models the environment of the specification S and replaces it during the test run (see Figure 14.2/1). Here it is assumed that the interface between the specification and the environment is implemented correctly for the test (*correct interface assumption*) [Petr 96].

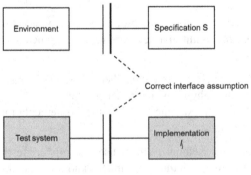

I_j *conforms to* S ??

Figure 14.2/1: Principle of the conformance test

The question now is, when does an implementation I_j conform to the specification S, i.e., when is the relation I_j **conforms_to** S satisfied? Generally speaking, this is true, when the observable behavior of the implementation I_j, i.e., its outputs on the stimuli (inputs) of the test system, is in accordance with the behavior defined in the specification S. Strictly speaking, this depends, however, on the applied implementation relation (cp. Section 11.5.1). For example, when trace preorder is used (see Section 14.3.2), an implementation I_j already conforms to S if the event sequences that I_j accepts are contained in the event sequences of S:

$$I_j \text{ } \textbf{conforms\_to} \text{ } S \Leftrightarrow \text{traces}(I_j) \subseteq \text{traces}(S).$$

Usually several compliant implementations $\Im_S \in \Im$ may be derived from a given specification S (see Figure 14.2/2). This is a consequence of the implementation independence of protocol specifications, which only specify the expected external behavior of the protocol entities but make no statements on their implementation. Any implementation of this specification which is in accordance with the respective conformance relation is compliant.

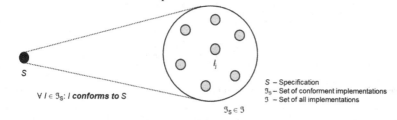

$\forall I \in \Im_S: I$ *conforms to* S

S – Specification
$\Im_S$ – Set of conforment implementations
$\Im$ – Set of all implementations

$\Im_S \in \Im$

Figure 14.2/2: Conforming implementations of S

To run a conformance test appropriate test data have to be provided to stimulate the implementation I_j. The test data needed for testing a certain feature of the protocol, e.g., the connection set up, form a **test case**. A test case represents an experiment that is executed on the implementation I_j to check whether it meets a certain property defined in the specification. This property determines the **test purpose**. The set of all test cases needed to confirm the conformance of an implementation is called the **test suite** (see Figure 14.2/3).

During test execution the implementation is tested against the test suite. The observed reactions (outputs) of the implementation on the input stimuli form the **test outcome**. The latter is compared with the specified behavior to derive a **conformance statement** which is finally expressed in the form of a **test verdict**. Usually, three test verdicts are used: *pass* – if the test is passed successfully, *fail* – if the test is failed, and *inconclusive* – if the test outcome is not unique. The last verdict can be assigned, for instance, when the reason for a (negative) test outcome cannot be uniquely assigned to the implementation because it may also be caused by the test environment (e.g., an error in the underlying communication medium). The conformance relation **conforms_to** introduced above is satisfied if the outcome of the test suite TS is *pass*:

I_j **conforms_to** $S \Leftrightarrow I_j$ passes TS.

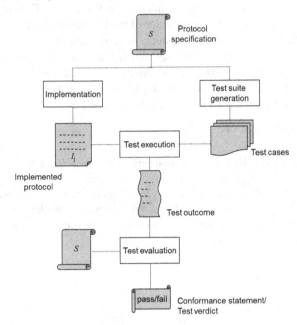

Figure 14.2/3: Steps of the conformance test process

In order to execute the test a **test system** is required which mounts the implementation – usually referred to as the **implementation under test (IUT)**. Test systems are usually implemented as distributed systems. The basic architecture of such a test system is depicted in Figure 14.2/4. The test system interacts with the IUT through special **points of control and observation (PCOs)** to input the stimuli into the IUT and to observe the respective reactions. The interaction is performed by means of service primitives and PDUs. It may also happen that an IUT does not react to a stimulus with an output. This is called an empty output or *quiescence*. A test system usually consists of a lower and an upper tester. The **lower tester** controls the interaction with the IUT. It represents the peer entity of the IUT and is connected through the (N-1)-interface to it. The **upper tester** observes and controls the IUT at the (N)-service interface. It represents the service user. Depending on the positioning and the functionality of the lower and the upper tester different test methods are distinguished, which we introduce later.

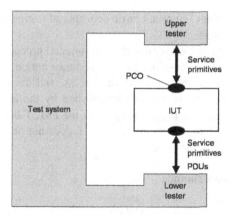

Figure 14.2/4: Basic architecture of a test system

14.2.2   ISO test methodologies CTMF and FMCT

The development of appropriate methods for conformance testing represented a great challenge for *Protocol Engineering* in the 1980s and 1990s and led to a broad range of research activities. This is also reflected in a special conference series on the testing of communication protocols – the *TestCom conference* (see [TestCom]). The methods and procedures for executing conformance tests for OSI protocols were summarized by the ISO in the **OSI conformance testing methodology and framework (CTMF)** [ISO 9646]. The standard is very comprehensive. It contains seven chapters which cover a broad spectre of testing procedures and framework specifications ranging from general concepts, over abstract test suite specifications, test realizations, and test laboratories to the test notation TTCN that we consider at the end of this chapter. Although OSI concepts are no longer the focus of interest, this methodology still represents the basis of conformance testing. It has sustainably influenced research on protocol testing and given rise to many important methods and techniques. For that reason, we introduce here a couple of fundamental notions of this methodology.

CTMF describes a general framework for conducting conformance tests. It defines the notion of conformance and the steps needed to assess the conformance of an implementation, and provides guidelines for the practical execution of conformance tests in test laboratories. How test cases are provided is not prescribed by the methodology. This remains the responsibility of the testing laboratories.

As we have seen in the previous section, conformance testing comprises both practical and theoretical aspects. Therefore CTMF was supplemented in the mid-1990s by **Formal Methods in Conformance Testing (FMCT)** [ISO 13245] which describes the use of formal methods in conformance testing. The FMCT standard is not as comprehensive as CTMF. It focuses on those aspects of the test methodology for which the use of formal resources is relevant. The FMCT standard more precisely defines important basic concepts of testing methodology, such as the conformance notion.

In the following sections we outline the fundamental procedures of conformance testing. In particular, we consider the conformance notion, the abstract testing methodology, the conformance assessment process, and the test execution. The reference to the respective standards is established by the abbreviations CTMF and FMCT, respectively. We begin always with the FMCT definitions. For those aspects of the testing methodology which FMCT does not dealing with, only the CTMF representation is considered.

14.2.3   Notion of conformance

The definition of when an implementation can be considered as compliant with the specification is decisive for the conformance test. FMCT and CTMF provide slightly different definitions for this.

14.2.3.1 Conformance according to FMCT

In defining the concept of conformance both standards distinguish between static and dynamic conformance. **Static conformance** refers to the instantiation of the specification and the IUT regarding the possible protocol options. It confirms that the options selected by the implementation are allowed.

Dynamic conformance checks whether the behavior of the IUT observable by the test system corresponds to the expected specified behavior according to the applied conformance relation. For this, the implementation relation **imp** is used[1] (cp. Section 11.5.1):

$$\textbf{imp} \subseteq MODS \times SPECS.$$

Here $SPECS$ denotes the set of instantiated specifications and $MODS$ the set of models that model the behavior of the implementations. The introduction of $MODS$ requires some additional explanations. $MODS$ is used to establish a formal relationship between the formal specification and the implementation which cannot be done directly. Therefore, a relationship is established by constructing a formal model $m_{IUT} \in MODS$ of the implementation under test $IUT \in IMPS$, with $IMPS$ – set of all implementations, which is compared with the specification. One can imagine this, for example, by means of a finite state machine that is constructed from the test outcome and then checked for compliance with the specification S. FMCT only assumes that such a formal model exists; it need not be set up ex-

---

[1] The FMCT standard is based on algebraic test theory and uses the corresponding terms. The notion of implementation relation can be equated with the term conformance relation used in the previous section.

plicitly. This assumption is also referred to as a **test assumption** [Brin 97]. It is used to handle implementations as a formal object to define conformance relations formally.

An IUT is dynamically conforming with an instantiated specification S regarding the chosen implementation relation **imp**, iff

$$m_{IUT} \textbf{ imp } S.$$

In this case, m_{IUT} is a compliant model of S with respect to **imp** (see Figure 14.2/5).

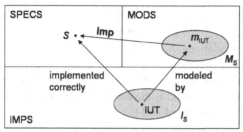

Figure 14.2/5: Relation between *IMPS*, *MODS*, and *SPECS* [ISO 13245]

Since usually several implementations $I_S \in IMPS$ may be compliant to S, there are also several formal models m for which m **imp** S holds. The set M_S then refers to all models which are compliant to S:

$$M_S = \{m \in MODS \mid m \textbf{ imp } S\}.$$

The weaker an implementation relation **imp**, the larger is the set of implementations I_S that conform to S and the easier is the proof of compliance.

Dynamic conformance is defined by means of **dynamic conformance requirements** that determine which observable behavior of an implementation IUT is allowed. A specification represents in total all dynamic conformance requirements. The latter are formulated in a requirement language, e.g., in a formal description technique. Dynamic conformance is described by the satisfaction relation **sat**:

$$\textbf{sat} \subseteq MODS \times REQS,$$

where *REQS* denotes the set of all conformance requirements which can be formulated in the given requirement language. An instantiated specification $S \in SPECS$ is characterized by a set of conformance requirements $R_S \subseteq REQS$. The totality of the instantiated specifications *SPECS* is given by the power set of all conformance requirements: $SPECS = \wp(REQS)$.

An implementation I_S is dynamically compliant to a specification $R_S \subseteq REQS$ if the formal model m_{IUT} meets all conformance requirements in R_S:

$$\forall r \in R_S \colon m_{\text{IUT}} \text{ sat } r,$$

where $r \in R_S$ denotes a single conformance requirement. For the set M_S of all models compliant to S, we have correspondingly

$$M_S = \{m \in MODS \mid \forall r \in R_S \colon m \text{ sat } r\}.$$

14.2.3.2 Conformance according to CTMF

The conformance notion of the previously defined CTMF standard is broader than that in FMCT. Conformance in the CTMF context means the compliance of a protocol implementation or of a real system with one or more ISO protocol standards or ITU recommendations. Note that this compliance relates only to the protocol specification, but not to the service specification! It is assumed that a conforming protocol implementation provides the specified service correctly. This assumption is ultimately only valid if the correctness of the service provision by the protocol can be formally verified and the interoperability with other implementations is given.

Like FMCT, CTMF distinguishes between static and dynamic conformance requirements. The **static conformance requirements** define the necessary preconditions for the conformance of an implementation. They define the technical preconditions for a test run, e.g., which of the specified functions and capabilities may be combined in an implementation. In particular, they specify the subset of capabilities required for interoperability between implementations. This includes global requirements, such as the support of protocol classes, as well as detailed specifications regarding the value ranges of parameters and time-out intervals. Moreover, specific decisions regarding the implementation of certain protocols as well as dependencies between the protocol layers may be given.

The **dynamic conformance requirements** define the expected or allowed protocol behavior. They include all those requirements that concern the dynamic protocol flow, such as state transitions, expected service primitives and PDUs, protocol termination, error measures, etc. The dynamic conformance requirements can to a large extent be derived from the protocol specification. Their validation forms the main part of the testing process. The conformance requirements are formulated as commandments and prohibitions. They are differentiated into:

- *mandatory requirements* which must always be observed,
- *conditional requirements* which have to be met only under certain circumstances, and
- *options* which take the specifics of the implementation into account.

14.2.4   Test architecture

The **test architecture** describes how the IUT is embedded in the test system. It defines the **test interface** used to access the IUT. Depending on the positioning of the lower and the upper tester and of the test objectives pursued, various test architectures are distinguished.

14.2.4.1 Test architecture in FMCT

The test architecture in FMCT is characterized by the components depicted in Figure 14.2/6. These include:

* the test system,
* the implementation under test (IUT),
* the test context,
* the points of control and observation (PCOs), and
* the implementation access points (IAPs).

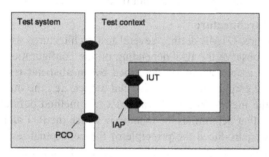

Figure 14.2/6: Test architecture according to FMTC

The *test system* is the active object in the testing process. It executes the test cases, records the reactions of the IUT, analyzes it, and derives the test verdicts. The IUT is embedded in an environment, the *test context*. It is assumed that the test system has no direct access to the IUT. Its behavior can only be controlled and observed indirectly through the test context, namely through the points of control and observation, the *PCOs*, and the implementation access points, the *IAPs*. PCOs and IAPs may coincide. In this case, the test system can directly control and observe the IUT.

The influence of the test context on the testing process must be taken into account in the modeling. The test context is defined as a function $c: MODS \to MODS$. The model of the implementation in the corresponding test context c is then denoted by $m_{\text{IUT},c}$. The inclusion of the test context requires a clarification of the test assumption of Section 14.2.3.1 to the extend that conformance is no longer determined by the construction of the model m_{IUT}, but of the model $m_{\text{IUT},c}$. Accordingly, the implementation relation **imp** must be supplemented by the context-dependent implementation relation **imp$_c$**:

$$m_{\text{IUT}} \text{ imp}_c \, S \Leftrightarrow m_{\text{IUT,c}} \text{ imp } c(S).$$

The implementation relation **imp$_c$** is weaker than **imp**:

$$m_{\text{IUT}} \text{ imp } S \Rightarrow m_{\text{IUT}} \text{ imp}_c \, c(S),$$

since all conforming implementations of S are compliant in any other test context, while not all implementations that meet **imp$_c$** may prove as compliant in another test context.

14.2.4.2 Test architecture in CTMF

In contrast to FMCT, CTMF describes how tests can be set up in practice. It defines several variants on how the test components can be arranged. To generalize their description CTMF introduces the notion of conceptual test architecture.

Conceptual test architecture

As argued before, CTMF defines several test architectures which vary in how they control and observe the IUT depending on the configuration of the options. The different test architectures are described by an **abstract test methodology**. The term *abstract* emphasizes the conceptual aspect, i.e., the implementation independence of the methodology. The abstract test method defines a **conceptual test architecture** that determines the manner in which the IUT and the test system interact. We have introduced the principle of the conceptual test architecture already in the introduction of Section 14.2.1 (cp. also Figure 14.2/4). Based on the conceptual test architecture, different abstract test methods (ATMs) are defined. As a consequence, the term **test method** is rather preferred in practice than *test architecture*.

CTMF, like FMCT, regards the IUT together with the test context in which it is embedded. The test context and the IUT form the **system under test (SUT)**. Two types of SUTs are distinguished: *end systems* and *relay systems*. The terms IUT and PCO are used as in FMCT, while the term *implementation access point* (IAP) is not used. An IUT may contain one or more protocols. Accordingly, one speaks of *single protocol IUTs* and *multi-protocol IUTs*. For the test of relay systems, it is demanded that the IUT shall include at least the protocol layer which performs the mapping between the different networks.

The abstract test methods differ in the number and positions of the PCOs for the interaction between the test system and the SUT, and thus in the degree to which they can control and observe the IUT. The positioning of the PCOs also determines the type of the test events (ASPs[2] or PDUs) that may occur at these points. Figure 14.2/7 shows the possible positions of the PCOs in test architectures.

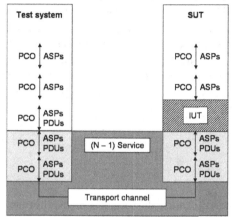

Figure 14.2/7: Possible positions of PCOs

Lower and upper tester

As already mentioned in Section 14.2.1, the conceptual test architecture differentiates between a lower and an upper tester. The **lower tester** (LT) represents the "peer entity" of the IUT (see Figure 14.2/8). It communicates with the IUT through the (N-1)-service interface. As a rule, the access is indirect, since the lower tester is usually located on another computer than the IUT and communicates with it or the SUT via the (N-1)-service. It is assumed that the (N-1)-service provider is tested and works correctly, reliably, and stably. The **upper tester** (UT) accesses the (N)-service interface of the IUT. This access may be direct or indirect. To run a test the two testers have to cooperate. This cooperation is usually realized by means of **test coordination procedures** (TCPs). In some test methods a test management protocol is used.

The lower tester controls the test execution. It usually initiates the test runs. In contrast to the upper tester, it is contained in all test architectures. The abstract test methods differ, therefore, primarily through the presence and the position of the upper tester as well as the way the two testers are coordinated.

Notations

Before explaining the various abstract test methods, we introduce two notations used in [ISO 9646] to facilitate the following descriptions.

ISO 9646 refers to the highest and the lowest layer of the IUT by N_t ($t = top$) and N_b ($b = bottom$). If there is only one layer in the IUT then $N_t = N_b$. This nota-

---

[2] ASP – *Abstract Service Primitive*. The attribute *abstract* is added to the service primitives in the abstract testing methodology to emphasize their implementation independence.

tion can also be applied to the description of the layers in the SUT and the lower tester. In all abstract methods the stimuli sent via the lower tester's PCO are specified using (N_b-1)-ASPs and/or (N_b)- to (N_t)-PDUs.

The second notation concerns the denotation of the abstract test methods for end systems. Four categories of abstract test methods are distinguished: local (L), distributed (D), coordinated (C), and remote (R), respectively, which are labeled by the first letter. The abstract test methods are further differentiated depending one the number of protocols contained in IUT. Accordingly, the labels S (*single-layer*) and SE (*single-layer embedded*) are used. Based on this, the following name scheme is derived:

$$\begin{Bmatrix} L \\ D \\ C \\ R \end{Bmatrix} \begin{bmatrix} S \\ SE \end{bmatrix}$$

Under this scheme, LS denotes the local test method for the test of a single layer and LSE the local test of an embedded layer.

Abstract test methods for end systems

In the following we present the basic abstract test methods for end systems. These are the local, distributed, coordinated, and the remote test method. We explain the principle of the embedded test only for the local test method. Regarding the other test methods, we refer to the ISO 9646 standard and [Baum 94].

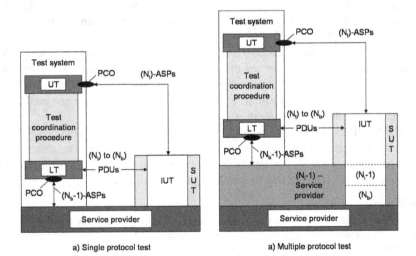

Figure 14.2/8: Local test method

Local test method

The local test method is characterized by the fact that both the lower and the upper tester are located on the same computer (see Figure 14.2/8). Since the test coordination procedure is executed locally, the synchronization between the two testers is simplified significantly. Synchronization problems occurring with the other methods, such as delays and loss of data, do not exist here. The local test method uses two PCOs. One is assigned to each tester. For the (N)-service interface of the IUT, a standardized hardware interface is required for access during the test run.

The embedded test uses basically the same architecture. The objective here is to test the protocol (N_i) that is embedded in a protocol stack without direct access to it. The protocol can be only accessed through the test context, in this case the adjacent protocol layers. In order to stimulate and observe the protocol the test system can only access the IUT by means of the (N_t)-ASPs at the upper PCO and the (N_b-1)-ASPs at the lower PCO. The (N_b-1)-ASPs carry the PDUs of the layers (N_b) to (N_t).

Distributed test method

In contrast to the local test method, the distributed test method integrates the upper tester into the SUT (see Figure 14.2/9). The positions of the PCOs remain the same. In order to access the IUT through the upper service interface only a user interface or a standardized programming interface is required. For the test coordination, only requirements are defined without giving the procedures themselves.

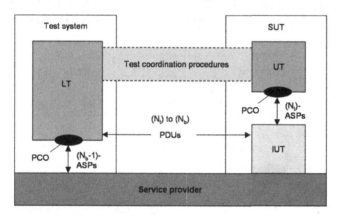

Figure 14.2/9: Distributed test method

Coordinated test method

Unlike the previous methods, the coordinated test method uses only one PCO that is positioned at the bottom of the lower tester (see Figure 14.2/10). It does not require direct access to the service interface of the IUT. Further a test management protocol (TMP) is used instead of a test coordination procedure. In practice a standard protocol is usually applied. Thus, the upper tester represents an entity of the applied test management protocol.

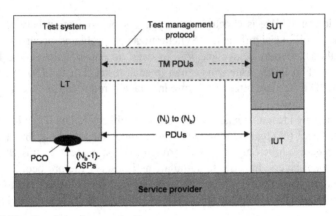

Figure 14.2/10: Coordinated test method

Remote test method

The remote test method has basically the same structure as the coordinated method (see Figure 14.2/11), but it puts weaker demands on the design of the upper test interface. It uses a test coordination procedure, but the demands on it are formulated relatively weakly. Certain minimum requirements may be formulated in the abstract test suite (see below), but there is no obligation for their implementation. There is no explicit upper tester. Its function must be taken over by the SUT.

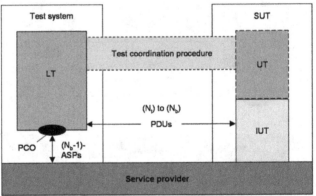

Figure 14.2/11: Remote test method

Multi-party test methods

These test methods were later supplemented by multi-party test methods which consider not only one communication relation, i.e., one connection, but several communication relations in parallel. Multi-party test methods represent a variant of a distributed test architecture in which the tests are executed and evaluated in parallel. Multi-party test methods are particularly appropriate for the testing of application-oriented protocols.

The principle of the multi-party test methods is depicted in Figure 14.2/12. To control and observe the IUT several lower and upper testers are deployed that operate in parallel. The testers are coordinated by the **lower tester control function** and **upper tester control function**. Lower and upper testers are synchronized by test coordination procedures. Moreover, there are also architectures with only one upper tester or without an upper tester.

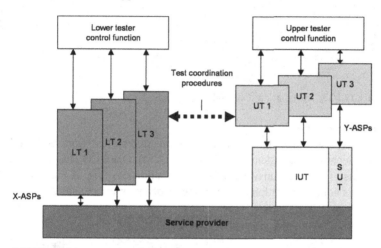

Figure 14.2/12: Multi-party test method

Abstract test methods for relay systems

CTMF defines further test methods for the testing of intermediate systems (routers, gateways)[3]: the loop-back method and the transverse method, abbreviated YL and YT, respectively.

Loop-back method

The loop-back test method tests an intermediate system that connects two networks in layer N_t from one of the two networks (see Figure 14.2/13). The test system is connected to that network through two PCOs which are located remotely from the (N_t) intermediate system.

The testing of connection-oriented protocols requires that the two outbound connections are connected at the remote end to a loop, but it is left open whether this is done in the intermediate system or in the other network. When connectionless transmissions are tested, it is required that the second network sends the PDUs back to the other PCO. The advantage of the loop-back test method is the use of only one test system that controls the entire test execution from one network. But this is also its drawback because the behavior of the intermediate system can only be observed from one network.

---

[3] We use hereafter the term *intermediate system* which is preferably used for relay systems nowadays.

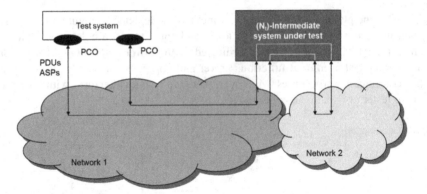

Figure 14.2/13: Loop-back test method

Transverse test method

The transverse test method tests the intermediate system from both networks using two separate test systems (see Figure 14.2/14). One PCO is assigned to each test systems. Thus the transverse test method allows testing of the intermediate system in its normal operation by observing its behavior at both sides.

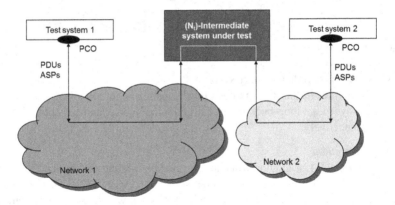

Figure 14.2/14: Transverse test method

14.2.5   Test suite

CTMF and FMCT define the role and the structure of test suites generically. The standards do not make statements on how to derive test suites. This is the responsibility of the test laboratories. We enlarge upon this in Section 14.3.

14.2.5.1 Test suite in FMCT

FMCT describes the derivation of a test suite TS for a context-dependent implementation relation $\mathbf{imp_c}$ from a formal specification S by the function $\mathbf{gen_c}^{imp}$:

$\textbf{gen}^c_{imp}$: $SPECS \rightarrow \wp\,(TESTS)$.

Hereby $SPECS$ denotes the set of instantiated specifications and $\wp\,(TESTS)$ the set of test suites in a given test notation $TESTS$. The derivation of a test suite is bound to the used implementation relation and the given test context. Another implementation relation or a modified test context generates another test suite. All models of implementations conforming to S must be contained in the set of compliant models M_{TS} of the test suite TS to decide whether an IUT is compliant to S:

$\forall m \in MODS$: $m\ \textbf{imp}_c\ S \Rightarrow m \in M_{TS}$, with $TS = \textbf{gen}^c_{imp}(S)$.

Test suites are differentiated into three classes with respect to their ability to recognize compliant or non-compliant implementations:

- *exhaustive*: A test suite TS is called exhaustive if the set of models M_{TS} that are compliant to the test suite TS represents a subset of the set of compliant models M_S, i.e., $M_{TS} \subseteq M_S$. All implementations that pass the test are compliant with S. A non-compliant implementation cannot pass the test. However, there may also be conforming implementations which do not pass the test.
- *sound*: A test suite TS is sound if the set of conforming models M_S is a subset of the set M_{TS}, i.e., $M_S \subseteq MT_{TS}$, i.e., all compliant implementations pass the test. There may, however, also be non-compliant implementations that pass the test suite and thus remain undetected.
- *complete*: A test suite TS is complete if it is sound and exhaustive, i.e., $M_S = M_{TS}$. A complete test suite can exactly distinguish between compliant and non-compliant implementations.

Ideally, a test suite should be complete. But this is rarely feasible, since the derivation of exhaustive test suites is very expensive. For this reason, the only practicable demand is that a test suite should be sound.

14.2.5.2 Test suite in CTMF

Test suites are defined as abstract test suites in CTMF. An **abstract test suite (ATS)** is a complete set of test cases needed to test the dynamic conformance requirements of a protocol. The add-on *abstract* indicates again that it is not an executable test suite, yet. An abstract test suite consists of a set of test cases (see Figure 14.2/15). They form the main elements of a test suite.

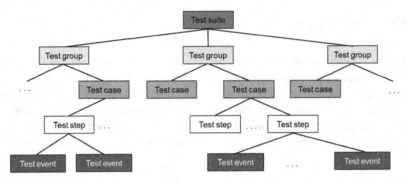

Figure 14.2/15: Structure of a test suite

A **test case** comprises the test activities for a specific test objective – the **test purpose**. Possible test purposes may be, for instance, to test whether a connection can be established successfully, whether connection requests may be rejected, or whether the transfer order of PDUs is observed during data transmission. The test purposes are derived from the dynamic conformance requirements. The execution of a test leads to a **test verdict** (*pass, fail, inconclusive*) (see Section 14.2.7.2). Test cases must be independent of each other so that they can be executed alone to avoid that the test execution does not have to be cancelled after detecting an error. Thus, further test cases can be executed to investigate other functions of the IUT.

A test case can consist of several test steps (see Figure 14.2/15) which in turn may consist of several test events. **Test steps** can be arbitrarily nested. They can also be stored in test step libraries. A **test event** describes an atomic interaction between the IUT and the test system, e.g., the exchange of an abstract service primitive. The test cases in turn can be united to form **test groups**. They can be nested arbitrarily. A test purpose can be also assigned to them. The ISO 9646 standard provides in Part 2 guidelines for the design of a test suite.

A test case consists basically of three components:

- the **test preamble** that transfers the IUT from the start state to the state where the test body begins,
- the **test body** that contains the actual test steps according to the chosen test purpose, and
- the **test postamble** that leads the IUT back to the start state or another stable testing state.

The start state of a test case can be either the idle testing state or a stable testing state. The *idle testing state* is a testing state in which no connections are set up with the protocols under test and the state of the IUT is independent of previously executed test cases (no preamble is required for this state). *Stable testing states* are states to which the IUT returns without further activities of the lower tester (e.g., beginning of the data transfer phase). If the test body ends in a stable testing state no postamble is required.

14.2.6   Test realization

The test realization is only considered in CTMF. Part 4 of the ISO 9646 standard describes the implementation of the abstract test methodology and the necessary **means of testing** needed for the derivation, selection, parameterization, execution, and recording of test cases. We consider here only the implementation of the abstract test methods. The latter concerns first of all the implementation of the lower and the upper tester as well as the coordination between them.

Lower tester
To implement the lower tester usually two methods are applied: the encoder/decoder method and reference implementation.

Encoder/decoder method
The encoder/decoder method simply implements the encoding/decoding of the PDUs and service primitives that form the test case. The protocol to be tested is not implemented in the lower tester. This is the advantage of the method because it avoids the effort for the implementation of the protocol in the lower tester. The test cases can be flexibly adapted to the test course. On the other hand, each test case has to be coded individually. For this, the context of the test must be taken into account in the preamble and the postamble. In the case of very many test cases, this may be as costly as the implementation of the protocol itself [Baum 94].

Reference implementation
When using a reference implementation, the lower tester contains a (tested) implementation of the protocol. The implementation is complemented by additional components, such as error generators, a configuration module, and a test driver to realize various protocol behaviors. The advantage of this approach is that the entire protocol is executed by the lower tester, but this requires a larger implementation effort. Therefore, in practice the encoder/decoder version is preferred.

Upper tester
There are several possibilities to implement the upper tester. It can be realized as a self-contained component or directly integrated into the SUT as in the remote test method. It is also possible that the test engineer can directly access the IUT via the user interface.

Test coordination procedure
As with the upper tester, the test coordination procedures can be implemented in different ways. Usually, they are realized by a scenario interpreter, implemented in the upper tester, which reads service primitives from a predefined file. Another possibility is the use of a test management protocol. If the test engineer can direct-

ly access the user interface he/she can take over the coordination function depending on the test progress.

There are basically two possible approaches for the feedback between the upper and lower testers: the use of the protocol under test itself (*inband*) or the establishment of a separate connection between the two testers (*out of band*). In the inband variant, the test data are transferred as payload through the protocol under test. The basic disadvantage of this approach is that the untested protocol is used for the coordination which may cause undesirable interactions between the IUT and the test system. For connectionless protocols, it is further not possible to guarantee reliable transfer of the test data. In the *out of band* variant a separate connection is established for the exchange of the test data which bypasses the IUT (see Figure 14.2/16). This solution is applied in the *ferry clip* method outlined next.

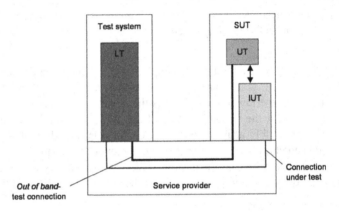

Figure 14.2/16: Out-of-band feedback between upper and lower tester

Ferry clip method

The ferry clip method is a frequently used technique for implementing the feedback between the test system and the SUT. It is not part of CTMF. The ferry clip method facilitates in particular the synchronization between the lower and the upper testers in distributed test settings, where additional problems may occur due to transmission delays and communication errors during coordination.

The ferry approach can be traced back to Zeng and Rayner [Zeng 86] and was originally designed for the testing of intermediate systems to return the test data by means of a "ferry" from the IUT to the test system. This principle was later applied to reduce the complexity of the test software in the SUT, especially in the upper tester, by relocating some of its functions in the test system. Figure 14.2/17 shows the ferry clip principle. The lower and upper testers are located in the test system as in the local test method so that the synchronization can be done locally. The connection between the test system and the SUT is established by the ferry clip through an independent communication channel. There exist a *passive* and an *active ferry clip*. The former is integrated into the SUT and takes over the passive part of the ferry clip protocol: the interaction with the IUT and the transfer of the test outcome back to the test system. The passive ferry clip is driven by its active counterpart, which coordinates the entire test run in the test system together with the two testers.

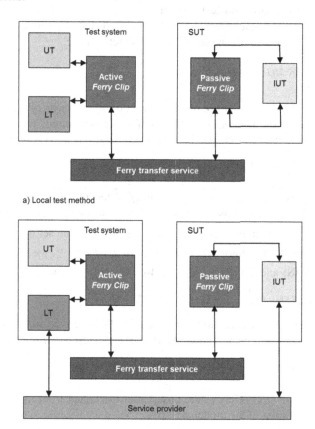

a) Local test method

b) Distributed test method

Figure 14.2/17: Ferry clip method

The large benefit of the ferry clip approach is the decoupling of the SUT and the test system. The control of the test execution including the synchronization between the upper and lower tester are shifted to the test system. All abstract test methods introduced above can be realized using the ferry clip approach. Figure 14.2/17 shows the local method which can be implemented if there is a direct access to the lower interface of the IUT (see Figure 14.2/ 17a)), otherwise the distributed solution has to be applied (see Figure 14.2/17b).

14.2.7   Test execution

14.2.7.1 Test execution in FMCT

Test execution function and test verdicts

The execution of a test suite $TS \subseteq TESTS$ on an IUT in a given test context c is described in FMCT through the test execution function **exec**:

$$\mathbf{exec}: TESTS \times MODS \rightarrow OBS.$$

The execution of a test with **exec** results in a set of observations $obs \in OBS$ regarding the model of the IUT $m_{IUT,c} \in MODS$. These observations, which are stored in a log file, form the *test outcome* from which the *test verdict* **verd** is derived:

$$\mathbf{verd}: OBS \rightarrow \{\mathit{pass,fail}\}$$

FMCT distinguishes the test verdicts *pass* and *fail* depending on whether the model of the implementation satisfies the model of the test suite ($m_{IUT,c} \in M_{TS}$) or not ($m_{IUT,c} \notin M_{TS}$). A test suite TS correspondingly subdivides the set of models of the implementation $MODS$ into two disjoint subsets $M_p(TS) = \{m_{IUT,c} \in MODS \mid m_{IUT},c$ **passes** $TS\}$ and $M_f(TS) = \{m_{IUT,c} \in MODS \mid \neg\ (m_{IUT},c$ **passes** $TS)\}$:

$$MODS = M_p(TS) \cup M_f(TS) \text{ and } M_p(TS) \cap M_f(TS) = \varnothing.$$

The test verdict for the execution of a test suite TS is derived from the observations of all test cases of the test suite. An IUT passes a test case $t \in TS$ if

$$\text{IUT } \mathbf{passes}\ t \Leftrightarrow \mathit{verd}_t(\sigma) = \mathbf{\mathit{pass}}$$

holds, where $\sigma \in OBS$ refers to the observations obtained from the execution of the test case t relating of the model $m_{IUT,c}$:

$$\mathbf{exec}(t,m_{IUT,c}) = \sigma.$$

An IUT passes a test suite $TS \subseteq TESTS$ if and only if the IUT passes all test cases $t \in TS$, i.e.,

$$\mathit{IUT}\ \mathbf{passes}\ TS \Leftrightarrow \forall t \in TS\text{: }\mathit{IUT}\ \mathbf{passes}\ t.$$

Test purpose

The subset of models of the implementation $m_{IUT,c} \in MODS$ that fulfills the relationship $\mathit{IUT}\ \mathbf{passes}\ t \Leftrightarrow \mathbf{verd}_t(\mathbf{exec}(t,m_{IUT,c})) = \mathbf{\mathit{pass}}$ meets the *test purpose* P_t of t:

$$P_t = \{m \in MODS \mid \mathbf{verd}_t(\mathbf{exec}(t,m)) = \mathbf{\mathit{pass}}\}.$$

The goal of the execution of a test case t is therefore to prove whether $m_{\text{IUT,c}}$ is contained in P_t, i.e.,

IUT **passes** $t \Leftrightarrow m_{\text{IUT,c}} \in P_t$.

If an IUT passes the test suite *TS* then this means that the model of the IUT $m_{\text{IUT,c}}$ is contained in all test purposes $P_{t,i}$, i.e.,

IUT **passes** $TS \Leftrightarrow m_{\text{IUT,c}} \in P_{TS}$ with $P_{TS} = \cup P_{t,i}$, $i=1,...,n$.

The set of formal test purposes P_{TS} of *TS* is a superset of the set of compliant models M_S, i.e., $P_{TS} \supseteq M_S$. If all conforming models $m_{\text{IUT,c}}$ pass a test suite *TS* generated for a set of test purposes P_{TS}, i.e., $P_{TS} = M_S$, then this test suite is sound (cp. Section 14.2.5.1).

14.2.7.2 Test execution in CTMF

Although test execution looks quite simple in FMCT, it is much more complicated and extensive in practice. In CTMF, the test execution is defined by the conformance assessment process. It comprises all activities that must be adhered to in order to prove the conformance of an implementation against the respective standard. The conformance assessment process consists of three phases: test preparation, test execution, and test evaluation including test report.

Test preparation

The test preparation includes several steps, such as selection of the test method, the provision of the needed test cases, and the preparation of the IUT as well as of the deployed test tools. Furthermore, a *system conformance statement* has to be filled out which contains administrative information and statements about the protocols to be tested. One of the main activities of test preparation is to fill out the conformance declarations PICS and PIXIT. They contain information from the implementer about the implemented protocol and the system under test.

The **protocol implementation conformance statement (PICS)** documents in questionnaire form, the *PICS form*, statements of the implementer on the protocol implementation, such as the protocol classes and options used, the value ranges of the parameters, e.g., the PDU sizes, or the time-out values set. The PICS document is needed for the static conformance assessment, the provision of the test suite (e.g., for adapting it to the selected protocol options), and as a reference document for the evaluation of the test outcome. The structure of the PICS form is specified in Part 2 of the ISO 9646 standard.

The **protocol implementation extra information for testing (PIXIT)** contains information on the SUT, e.g., the SAP addresses, information about the realization of the upper tester in the SUT, information about the protocol stack, and administrative information, such as the SUT version, the associated PICS form, and more. The PIXIT declaration must be filled out by the test client and the test laboratory for each abstract test suite against which the IUT is being tested.

PICS and PIXIT are also required to transform an abstract test suite into an **executable test suite (ETS)**. CTMF offers different ways to do this depending on how the test cases are selected and parameterized (see Figure 14.2/18). The transformation is supported by a set of rules in order to ensure consistency between the abstract and executable test suites. Thus, it is required among other things that each executable test case corresponds to an abstract test case. The test purpose and the possible test verdicts of an abstract test case have to be maintained in the executable form. Furthermore, no inspections of the PDU parameters should be performed during the test run which go beyond those defined in the abstract test suite.

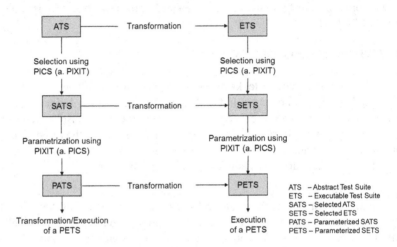

Figure 14.2/18: Derivation of executable test suites

Test execution

The test execution represents the conformance assessment process in the narrower sense. The steps of this process are predefined (see Figure 14.2/19). They determine how the static and dynamic conformance requirements including PICS and PIXIT are incorporated in the test process.

The test consists of a static and a dynamic conformance assessment. In the **static conformance assessment** the PICS is evaluated regarding the relevant static conformance requirements (cp. Section 14.2.3.2). The subsequent **dynamic conformance assessment** comprises the actual test execution. The test suite is parameterized based on PICS and PIXIT. The conformance assessment process cannot be fully performed for each protocol implementation due to cost reasons. Therefore CTMF distinguishes four types of tests which gradually make statements on the conformance and thus reduce the test efforts:

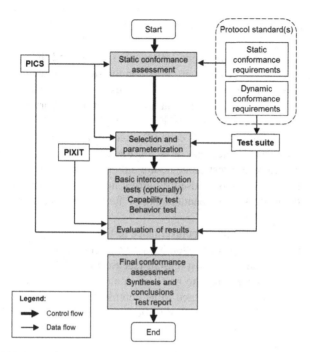

Figure 14.2/19: Conformance assessment process (according to [ISO 9646])

- **Basic interconnection test** that proves whether the IUT supports the basic requirements of the specification. It is a preliminary test to find out whether the implementation actually possesses the necessary capabilities to justify the continuation of the test.
- **Capability test** that determines whether the IUT includes the capabilities specified in the PICS. It is a further preliminary test to limit the test efforts.
- **Behavior test** that examines the compliance with the dynamic conformance requirements and represents the actual conformance test.
- **Conformance resolution test** that makes yes/no statements on specific compliance requirements. The resolution tests serves for a selective test of implementation capabilities (e.g., reset mechanisms). It is optional and can be used to resolve controversial issues.

The execution of the parameterized executable test suite (PETS) (cp. Figure 14.2/18) and the recording of the test outcome in a log file are called the **test campaign**. The latter comprises the basic interconnection test (optional), the capability test, and the behavior test.

Test evaluation

Upon completion of the test campaign, the test is evaluated based on the test log file and a **test report** has to be written. The test log file contains all interactions that were observed at the PCOs during the test campaign – the **observed test**

outcomes. In addition, information regarding the abstract test cases used is also contained.

The test evaluation compares the test events (inputs) and the related test outcomes with the expected behavior as defined in the specification. This comparison eventually results in a test verdict. The test cases and the expected outcomes are described by means of special test notations. The most important one is TTCN which we will introduce at the end of this section. The test evaluation can be partially automated. A test outcome is called *foreseen* or *expected* if it corresponds to the specified test case. Otherwise, it is *unforeseen* or *unexpected*, respectively. Reasons for an unforeseen test outcome are either errors in the test case or abandonment. The former may be caused by errors in the specification or the implementation of the test case. An abandonment of the test case is triggered by the test system.

It has to be pointed out that a conformance test can make no final statement on the conformance of an implementation because only a limited number of test cases can usually be executed due to cost reasons (see Section 14.3.4). Moreover, the influences of the test context have to be taken into account. Therefore, a tested implementation can only be considered to be compliant as long as the contrary has not been proved. The aim of the test must be to minimize the probability of counter examples.

Test verdict

CTMF, like FMCT, distinguishes the test verdicts **pass** and **fail**, but since it is a more practical standard it also takes into account that there may be other reasons why a test may fail, e.g., influences of the test environment as mentioned above. For this reason, CTMF defines *inconclusive* as a third test verdict. The verdict **inconclusive** (*not convincing*) is assigned if it cannot be decided uniquely from the test outcome whether the test was successful or not. For example, such a situation may occur when a connection set up test failed. This may be caused by an error in the IUT or by the (N-1) service provider. In such a case, additional tests or a repetition of the test run are needed.

Test report

The results of the conformance tests are summarized in a **test report**. Two test reports are distinguished. The **system conformance test report** documents the conformance status of the system under test (SUT). It summarizes the conformance assessments of the single protocols contained in the system. The **protocol conformance test report** contains the outcomes of all executed test cases including references to the related records of the test results. It also includes links to further documents relevant to the assessment process. It is produced for each protocol of the tested system.

Repeatability, comparability, and verifiability of test results

In order to achieve high confidence in the results of conformance tests repeated tests should produce the same outcome. This, however, is not always feasible because of the concurrency of the test processes as well as the limited invariance of the implementations with respect to time and environment [Baum 94]. The developers of abstract test cases and the test laboratories should therefore do everything possible to minimize the likelihood that repetitions of the same test cases result in different test outcomes.

The comparability and verifiability of the test results are other important requirements on the conformance assessment process. This requires a series of measures which cover the entire testing process. The comparison of test results requires special care in the design and specification of the test cases, the test tools, and all other related procedures of the process. Further, it should be ensured that the test outcomes may be rechecked to prove that all conformance assessment procedures were executed correctly. Therefore, test laboratories are obliged to record all test outcomes to allow verification.

14.2.8 Certification and test laboratories

The confirmation of conformance is evidence about the quality of an implementation. As in other areas of software development, this may be confirmed by formally **awarding a certificate** to it. This process is called **certification**. The certification process is an important measure for the enforcement of protocol standards just as in the case of with other software products, such as compilers. Certification is ultimately justified commercially. It gives the customer of the communication software the confidence that the purchased product possesses the properties defined in the standard. On the other hand, it should help to avoid expensive tests at the customer side.

The issuing of a certificate is an administrative act that is bound to the fulfillment of a series of formal rules. Therefore, the certification is entrusted to designated test laboratories and other official certification bodies. For conformance testing, a test laboratory should be accredited. The accreditation is based on a longer review of the test laboratory to determine whether the test laboratory meets the requirements on the execution of conformance tests as defined in [ISO 9646]. This includes among other things, evaluations of whether the test laboratory is capable of running the tests, whether the appropriate tools are available, and whether the staff has the necessary expertise. The requirements on test laboratories and test customers are formulated in Part 5 of CTMF. Three types of test labs are distinguished:

- *First Party Testing Laboratories*: These are the test laboratories that belong to the organizations or enterprises which implement the protocol or provide an implementation.

- *Second Party Testing Laboratories*: These are test labs of the customers or users of the protocol implementation which themselves want to assess the conformance of the product acquired.
- *Third Party Testing Laboratories*: These are test laboratories that are independent of the developers and users and which test the protocol on their behalf.

Part 5 of the ISO 9646 standard defines the requirements that test laboratories and test customers must fulfill in this context to ensure that the test results obtained in different test laboratories for the same or similar implementations are comparable. It contains requirements on the testability of implementations regarding the abstract test methods, general requirements on test laboratories and test customers for each conformance test, the exchange of technical and administrative information, the coordination between test laboratory and test customers regarding test configuration and test environment, and the structure and content of the test reports. This is primarily of organizational concern. Moreover, various activities have been launched to harmonize test results at a national and international level.

For conformance testing, tests carried out by an independent third party laboratory test are undoubtedly the desired goal (also called *third party guarantee*). This goal was originally pursued with the development of the OSI conformance testing methodology. The approach, however, proved often to be too costly. Therefore, other forms of the mutual recognition of test results have been introduced, such as registration and developer statements. **Registration** means the test results are recorded in a publicly accessible register managed by an organization (*second party guarantee*). An example was the U.S. NIST GOSIP register at the times when the OSI technology was still pursued in the United States. Inclusion in the register is based on predefined criteria. Registration can be used as a complement to a certification in this field. It is informative rather than carrying the liability of a certificate. The registration is not limited to implementations. It can also comprise test suites, test tools, and test services. In a **developer statement** the developer publishes its own test results (*first party guarantee*). Such a declaration does not usually have the objectivity of a certificate, but it is significantly cheaper. In Europe manufacturers may self-certify against the relevant harmonized standards and make an EU *Declaration of Conformity*. The European Telecommunications Standards Institute (ETSI) (http://www.etsi.org/) elaborates standards which can be used for this.

To sum up, the original idea of certifying the compliance of implementations to protocol standards has not proved feasible. Nowadays it is applied in a restricted, economically justifiable manner.

14.3 Derivation of test cases

The provision of test cases is one of the core problems of conformance testing. The derivation of test cases, however, is not defined by CTMF or FMCT. It remains the responsibility of the testing laboratories. Test cases are predominantly derived manually. For a number of protocols, test cases have been standardized. In addition, automatic derivation methods are also used. High theoretical claims have been made for the derivation of test cases from formal descriptions. There are different approaches, but few feasible solutions have been developed. This mainly stems from the fact that the theory of test case derivation only provides applicable methods for the semantic models of

- finite state machines (FSM) and
- labeled transition systems (LTS).

There are no straightforward solutions for more complex semantic models, such as the extended finite state machines (EFSM) and the structured labeled transition systems (SLTS), which are the basis of standardized FDTs. Here intermediate steps are required (see Section 14.3.3).

In this section we give an overview of the most important approaches to derive test cases from finite state machines and labeled transition systems. Furthermore, we outline approaches to derive test cases from specifications in standardized formal description techniques. We conclude with the derivation of test cases for our example protocol XDT.

14.3.1 Derivation of test cases on the basis of finite state machines

FSM-based methods are the most widely used procedures for deriving test cases for testing protocol implementations.

14.3.1.1 Principle of testing

The test of a communication protocol that is described by means of a finite state machine proves whether the IUT correctly executes the specified transitions and reaches the expected states. The outputs of the IUT are recorded. Testing a transition $(s_i, s_j, p_k/o_l)$

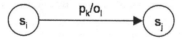

consists of three steps:

(1) Bring the IUT by the shortest path from the initial state to the start state s_i;
(2) Stimulate the IUT with the input p_k and observe the output o_l;
(3) Check whether the expected state s_j is really reached.

These steps can be set in correspondence with the test phases preamble, test body, postamble of CTMF (cp. Section 14.2.5.2) as follows. The *preamble* corresponds to step (1). It transfers the IUT by external stimuli to the desired start state. The *test body* comprises the steps (2) and (3). These include the execution of the transition under test and verify that the expected state has been reached. It may be followed by a *postamble* that transfers the IUT back to the initial state. For this, a *reset capability r* is often used which describes this reset. Here it is assumed that the IUT generates a *null output* when the reset function is applied.

The ability to transfer an IUT from the initial state into any desired state is called **controllability**, correspondingly the ability to recognize the reached state is **observability**. Controllability and observability of an implementation determine their **testability** which represents an indicator of whether a protocol is easy or difficult to test. For example, additional points of observation which in contrast to the PCOs only record the occurring events increase the testability of an implementation. Test methods that lead to shorter test suites also increase testability. A protocol design which purposefully supports the testing phase is called **design for testability** [Vuon 94], [Köni 97], which, however, did not obtain much importance in protocol design.

Fault model

The FSM-based test theory does not use the terms implementation relation and model of the implementation, as introduced in Section 14.2.3.1. The conformance relation is defined here through the so-called *fault model* [Petr 96]. It takes into account that a variety of errors can be contained in the various implementations derived from a specification S. A fault model defines a set of possible fault types that can occur in the implementations. When a test suite is derived, it relates to the defined fault model. The test suite will detect any error in the implementations which belongs to the considered fault types [Math 08].

A **fault model** $F(S)$ for a specification S defines the set of conforming implementations concerning a given type of errors or a certain error class. It divides the set of implementations $\mathfrak{J}$ derivable from S into the set of compliant implementations I_p in relation to $F(S)$ and the set of non-compliant implementations I_f concerning this relation (see Figure 14.3/1). The set of non-compliant implementations I_f is referred to as the **fault domain** of the specification S in relation to $F(S)$. Non-compliant implementations can also be obtained by changes (mutations) in the specification S, e.g., by inserting false outputs, or by changing or omitting transitions. An implementation that is derived from such a thus changed specification is called a **mutant**.

The ability of a test suite TS to reveal errors of a certain error model $F(S)$ is referred to as **fault coverage**. It is a measure to estimate the detection power of a test suite. A test suite $TS_{F(S)}$ has **full fault coverage** in relation to $F(S)$ if it detects all mutants defined by $F(S)$, i.e.,

$$\forall i \in I_f \Leftrightarrow \exists t \in TS_{F(S)}: \neg (i \text{ passes } t).$$

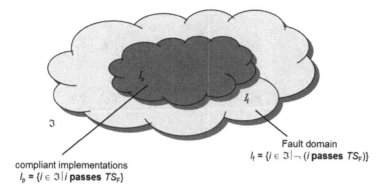

Figure 14.3/1: Fault domain of a specification S in relation to the fault model $F(S)$

Fault models for finite state machines are mainly based on the following four error classes:

- *Output faults*: A transition produces an output error if the transition in relation to the start state and the triggering input event results in a different output than specified.

- *Transfer faults*: A transition causes a transfer fault if the transition in relation to the start state and the triggering input event ends in another state than specified.

- *Extra state faults*: The number of states in the implementation is larger than specified. In this case the implementation also contains transfer faults to these states.

- *Missing state faults*: The number of states in the implementation is lower than specified. The reason is often an incomplete and nondeterministic specification [Petr 96].

The derivation methods presented below have different fault detection powers regarding these error classes. A test suite derived with the transition tour method can only detect output errors, while test suites generated with the W-method may reveal errors from all four classes.

14.3.1.2 Derivation methods

There are various methods for the derivation of test cases from finite state machines. We introduce here the four main approaches: the transition tour method, the DS-method, the W-method, and the UIO sequence-method. These four methods differ primarily in how they check after executing the transition $(s_i, s_j, p_k/o_l)$ that the expected state has been reached. To illustrate the methods we use the example automaton presented in Figure 14.3/2.

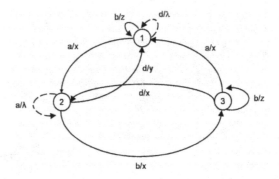

Figure 14.3/2: Example automaton

Assumptions

In order to run a test based on finite state machines the automaton should fulfill certain properties which have proved useful for testing. The finite state machine should be

- *minimal*, i.e., there are no two equivalent states,
- *strongly connected*, i.e., each state is reachable from every other state,
- *deterministic*, i.e., each input in a given state triggers exactly one transition, and
- *completely specified*, i.e., there exist a transition for each allowed input of the automaton in each state.

Furthermore, it is assumed that

- the IUT possesses a known maximum number of states m that may be greater than the specified number of states n,
- all inputs and outputs are known,
- the IUT reacts to each input within a known finite time, and that
- the IUT possesses a reset function r, if needed.

The example automaton in Figure 14.3/2 meets these requirements. It is *minimal*, since there are no two states with the same input/output behavior, and *strongly connected*, since each state is reachable from every state. For example, this condition would not be satisfied if the transition b/x in state 2 did not exist. The automaton is *deterministic* because there is exactly one transition assigned to each input in every state. This would not be fulfilled if there existed, for example, for input a in state 1 a further transition a/y. Finally the machine is *completely specified* because there is one transition for each allowed input of the FSM in each state. The latter condition needs some explicative comments. Protocol automata are often not fully specified, since certain events do not occur in some states. This is what we did in the description of the XDT protocol in Section 7.4. To convert this presentation into a completely specified automaton transitions must be added in every state for previously unspecified inputs. For these, we use self-loop transitions that end in the same state and have no output. The empty output is represented by λ^4. In Figure 14.3/2 dotted lines are used to mark these transitions.

Derivation methods have been also investigated for FSMs that do not fulfill these conditions or only in part, e.g., nondeterministic automata. These methods are restricted by other, mostly less general constraints. The interested reader can find various approaches in the proceedings of the conference series *FORTE* and *TestCom* [FORTE], [TestCom].

Transition tour method

A transition tour is an input sequence that transfers the automaton from the initial state back to the initial state passing each transition at least once. Example 14.3/1 contains a transition tour for the incompletely specified finite state machine as shown in Figure 14.3/2 (i.e., the dotted transitions are not included).

State	1	1	2	1	2	3	2	3	3	1
Input	b	a	d	a	b	d	b	b	a	

Example 14.3/1: Transition tour for the example automaton of Figure 14.3/2

The transition tour method is the simplest of the derivation methods considered here. It may also be applied to incompletely specified automata. The transition tour method generates shorter test suites than the other methods. The length of a transition tour[5] can be estimated by $O(pn)$ with p the number of inputs and n the number of states. The fault detection power is lower compared to the other methods. A transition tour can only detect output errors. It is not capable of recognizing transfer errors, as it does not check the reached state. Figure 14.3/3 shows this in an example. Picture a) contains a slightly modified variant of the example automaton of Figure 14.3/2 in which the transition b/z in state 3 has been replaced by the transition b/x. The transition tour remains unchanged, but the output behavior is now different. It is no longer capable of detecting the wrong implementation of the transition d/x in state 3 in picture b).

The derivation of a transition tour is based on the well-known Chinese rural postman problem from graph theory. It is about finding the shortest path in a strongly connected graph whereby every edge is passed at least once. The tour is also called accordingly the *Chinese Postman Tour*.

---

[4] This means that the IUT does not produce any output for a defined finite time.
[5] The length of a test suite is a measure of the test effort; the shorter a test suite the lower the cost for executing the tests. The maximum length of a test suite is often used to compare the various derivation methods. It is estimated using the O-notation by the number of states and possible inputs.

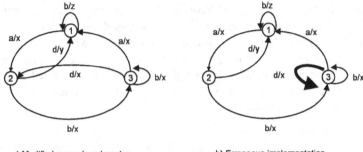

a) Modified example automaton   b) Erroneous implementation

Figure 14.3/3: Example of the limited detection capability of a transition tour

A test suite derived this way may contain redundant inputs because some transitions have to be executed several times to eventually cover all transitions. These redundant inputs may be minimized.

DS-method

The DS-method was developed by Gonenc [Gone 70]. It uses a so-called distinguishing sequence to verify that the expected state really has been reached. A **distinguishing sequence** (DS) is an input sequence that generates for each state of the automaton a different output sequence which uniquely distinguishes the state from other states. The DS-method is also applicable to an incompletely specified automaton if a distinguishing sequence can be found. The shortest distinguishing sequence for our incompletely specified example automaton is *bab* (see Example 14.3/2).

State	Distinguishing sequence	Output
1	bab	zxx
2	bab	xxz
3	bab	zxz

Example 14.3/2: Distinguishing sequence for the example automaton of Figure 14.3/2

The distinguishing sequence stimulates the IUT after the transition to be tested has been executed. Accordingly, a test case consists of the preamble, the input for the transition to be tested, the distinguishing sequence, and the reset function *r* as postamble. The latter is often put at the beginning. The test case for the test of the transition *b/x* in state 2 of our example automation is then:

rabbab.

In order to derive a test suite the state cover or the transition cover has to be determined. The **state cover** *SC* is defined as the set of all input sequences including the empty sequence ε that transfer the automaton from the initial state to the state where the transition under test starts. The **transition cover** *TC* includes additionally the transition to be tested. Figure 14.3/4 shows the transition cover for our example automaton.

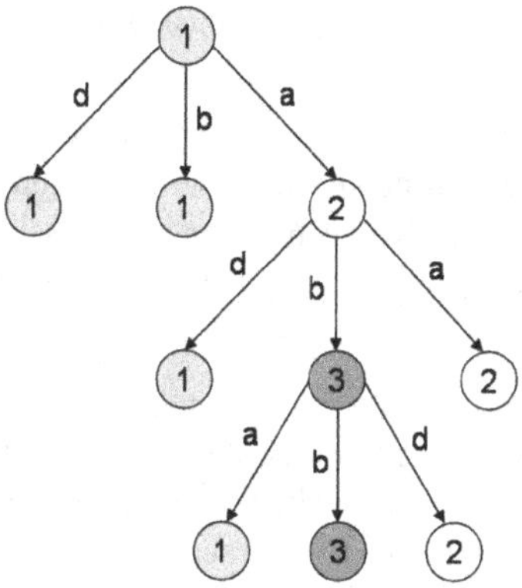

Figure 14.3/4: Transition cover for the example automaton

The transition cover is preferred for test suite generation. It can be derived as follows.

Given: FSM = $<S,I,O,T,s_0>$ with *n* nodes
Output: TC

begin
state:=s_0
TC:= {ε}
i:=1
while $i \leq n$ do{
for all nodes at level *i-1* in *TC* **do**{
select a node *n* at level *i-1*
if (node is not contained at any level between 1 and *i*-1)
for all transitions of *n* **do**{
add $t \in T$ **to** *TC*
}
else *n* is leaf node
i:=i+1
}
}
end

The test suite TS_{DS} for a given finite state machine is formed by concatenation of the transition cover TC with the distinguishing sequence DS and the reset function r:

$$TS_{DS} = \{r\} \times \{TC\} \times \{DS\}.$$

Accordingly the test suite for our example automaton is

rbbab rabab radbab rabbab rabbbab rabdbab rababab

The maximum length of a test suite for the DS-method is $O(pn^2)$. The DS-method has higher error detection power than the transition tour method beside output errors because it may also reveal transfer and missing state faults. The issue though is that for most real protocols no distinguishing sequence can be determined.

W-method
If a distinguishing sequence cannot be determined one or several partially distinguishing sequences can be used to check the reached state. These sequences are called **characterizing sequences**. They trace back to Vasilewski [Vasi 73] and form the core of the W-method [Chow 78]. A characterizing sequence distinguishes a state s_i not from all other states of the FSM, but only from a subset of states. If the state is supposed to be uniquely distinguished from all other states then several characteristic sequences have to be used. The set of these characterizing sequences is called the **characterization set** W. The latter can be derived from so-called P_1 tables, with I – set of inputs [Gill 62]. The method for constructing the W-set is described in [Math 08]. The W-method can also be applied to incompletely specified automata if the set W can be identified.

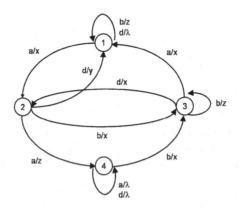

Figure 14.3/5: Extended example automaton

To illustrate the difference to the DS-method we extend our example state machine (see Figure 14.3/5). The input sequence *bab* is no longer a distinguishing sequence for the new automaton, since it produces the same output for the states 2 and 4:

State	Distinguishing sequence	Output
1	bab	zxx
2	bab	xxz
3	bab	zxz
4	bab	xxz

A clear distinction between the states can be achieved by means of the characterization set $W = \{ba, d\}$ which generates the following outputs:

State	ba	d
1	zx	λ
2	xx	y
3	zx	x
4	xx	λ

λ - empty output

Similarly to the DS-method, the test suite TS_W for a finite state machine is again formed by the concatenation of the transition cover TC with the characteristic set W and the reset capability r:

$$TS_W = \{r\} \times TC \times W.$$

The transition cover for the extended example automaton is

$$TC = \{\varepsilon, a, b, d, aa, ab, ad, aaa, aab, aad, aba, abb, abd\}$$

and the resulting test suite TS_W

rba rd raba rad rbba rbd rdba rdd raaba raad rabba rabd radba radd raaaba raaad raabba raabd raadba raadd rababa rabad rabbba rabbd rabdba rabdd.

We can optimize the test suite by removing all test cases that are contained as a partial sequence in other test cases:

rba rbba rbd rdba rdd raaba rabba radd raaaba raaad raabba raabd raadba   raadd rababa rabad rabbba rabbd rabdba rabdd.

The W-method can also be used for the testing of implementations that implemented a greater number of states m than the specified number of states n, where m must be known. In this case, W has to be replaced by the distinguishing set Z [Chow 78] which is defined by:

$$Z = (\{\varepsilon\} \cup X \cup X^2 \cup \dots \cup X^{m-n}) \times W = X[m\text{-}n] \times W$$

with X – set of inputs
n – number of specified states
m – number of implemented states.

For $m=n$, Z is equal to W.

The W-method has the highest error detection power of the methods presented here. It can reveal errors from all four error classes. However, the W-method generates much longer test suites than the other methods introduced here, since for each characterizing sequence, the automaton must be retransferred from the initial state into the state to be checked. The maximum length of the test suite is estimated for $m \neq n$ with $O(mn^2 p^{m-n+1})$ and for $m = n$ with $O(pn^3)$ [Vasi 73].

Wp-method

An extension of the W-method, which under certain conditions permits one to generate shorter test suites, is the partial W-method Wp described in [Fuji 91]. The Wp–method is similar to the W-method. It divides the test generation procedure into two phases and applies in the second phase a state identification set W_i instead of the characterization set W. The state identification set is a sequence of inputs that uniquely distinguishes the state from the other states. The union set of all state identification sets is the characterization set W (for the derivation of the state identification sets see [Math 08]). The Wp-method is applicable to all implementations which meet the initially given assumptions, also to implementations with $m > n$ states. It has the same fault detection capability as the W-method.

UIO sequence method

The UIO sequence method uses unique input/output sequences (*UIO sequences*) to check the reached state. A UIO sequence is a minimal sequence of input/output pairs that uniquely distinguishes a state from all other states, i.e., it defines an input/output behavior for the state that is different from the remaining states. If an input sequence is the same for several states then the output sequences must be different for these states. If the input sequence for all states is the same the outputs of all states have to be different. This corresponds to the distinguishing sequence, which represents a special case of UIO sequences.

A procedure to derive minimal UIO sequences is described in [Math 08]. The method is also applicable to incompletely specified finite state machines. The UIO sequences for our extended example automata of Figure 14.3.5 are the following:

State	UIO sequence	Output
1	bad	zxy
2	d	y
3	d	x
4	d	λ

The test suite for the extended example automaton is then:

rbad rbbad rad radbad rabd rabdd rabbd rababad raad raabd;

with the optimized variant

rbad rbbad radbad rabdd rabbd rababad raad raabd.

The UIO sequence method in its original form has a significant defect. It assumes that the UIO sequences derived from the specification also apply to the implementation. This cannot always be guaranteed. Faulty implementations of some transitions can cause some states of the IUT to possess the same UIO sequences, although they should be different according to the specification.

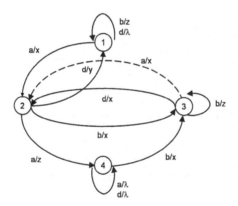

Figure 14.3/6: Erroneous implementation of the extended example automaton

Figure 14.3/6 shows this case for our extended example automaton. With the wrong implementation of the transition (s_3, s_1), the UIO sequence is the same for states 1 and 3. This issue is solved through the UIOv method [Vuon 90] which additionally checks that each state of the IUT is characterized through the specified UIO sequence. This requires for every state a test sequence of maximally $q(n + 2n^2)$ test events. Maximally $(n-1)$ steps are needed for each UIO sequence to bring the FSM into the state to be verified, maximally $2n^2$ steps for the input of the UIO sequence and one for the reset function; q denotes the number of different input sequences[6].

The UIO sequences and thus the derived test suites are much shorter than the distinguishing and the characterizing sequences. Experiments have shown that UIO sequences usually need no more than six stimuli [Ural 92]. The maximum length of a test suite is $O(pn^2)$. However, the UIO sequence method has a lower error detection power. It detects all output errors and most errors from the other error classes. The detection capability of the UIOv method is even higher.

Comparison of the methods

Finally we compare the presented test derivation methods regarding fault detection capability and test suite length as a measure of the cost of the test execution. A comparison of the fault detection capability for the four error classes shows that only the W-method is able always to detect all types of errors (see Table 14.3/1). In return, it requires essentially longer test suites (see Figure 14.3/7).

Errors / Method	Output faults	Transition faults	Extra state faults	Missing state faults
Transition tour	×	-	-	-
DS-method	×	×	-	×
W-method	×	×	×	×
UIO sequence	×	(×)	(×)	(×)

× - always detected
(×) - almost always detected

Table 14.3/1: Fault detection capability of the presented methods

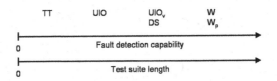

Figure 14.3/7: Fault detection capability versus test suite length of the presented methods

Example

As in the other chapters, we finish with the XDT example and derive test cases for the XDT receiver entity using the transition tour, the DS, and the UIO sequence methods. For this purpose, we adapted the FSM representation of the XDT receiver entity of Figure 7.4/1 by abbreviating multiple outputs by a single symbol (see Figure 14.3/8). In addition, the automaton was converted into a fully specified

---

[6] Since equal input sequences have to generate different output sequences, other output sequences cannot be observed after proving that the UIO sequence belongs to the q specified UIO sequences.

state machine by adding in all states the transitions for those input events that were not contained in this state so far. They are again represented by dotted lines. As in Figure 7.4/1, the *DT*-PDUs were differently labeled according to their different semantic meaning. If we refrain from doing this we have only two input events and have a non-deterministic automaton which we do not consider here.

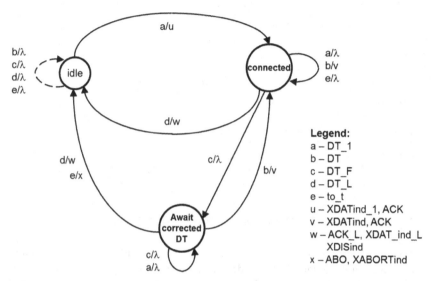

Figure 14.3/8: Completely specified FSM of the XDT receiver entity

Transition tour

The transition tour for the incompletely specified FSM of the XDT receiver entity is:

a d a b c b c c d a c e

or when using the regular event names

DT_1 DT_L DT_1 DT DT_F DT DT_F DT_F DT_L DT_1 DT_F to_t.

Regarding the timeout event *to_t,* we assume as in SDL that it is enqueued as an external event in the input queue.

Distinguishing sequence

There is a distinguishing sequence for the XDT receiver entity: *ae*, but it generates many empty outputs λ and is, therefore, not very practical.

UIO sequences

UIO sequences allow slightly better distinction, but only for the completely specified automaton so that a longer test suite is required. The UIO sequences are:

- State *idle:* a/u
- State *connected*: a/λ e/λ
- State *await*: e/x[7].

By using the reset function *r* we arrive at the following test suite:

r a a e   r a a a e   r a b a e   r a e a e   r a d a   r a c e   r a c b a e   r a c a e
r a c c e   r a c d a   r a c e a

which can be optimized to

r a a e   r a b a e   r a e a e   r a d a   r a c b a e   r a c a e   r a c c e   r a c d a
r a c e a,

or with its original identifiers

r DT_1 DT_1 to_t   r DT_1 DT DT_1 to_t   r DT_1 to_t DT_1 to_t
r DT_1 DT_L DT_1   r DT_1 DT_F DT DT_1 to_t   r DT_1 DT_F DT_1 to_t
r DT_1 DT_F DT_F to_t   r DT_1 DT_F DT_L DT_1   r DT_1 DT_F to_t DT_1.

14.3.2   Derivation of test cases on the basis of labeled transition systems

Test cases that come from LTS specifications represent sequences of actions which lead from the start state to a dedicated state according to the specified test purpose. The basis for the derivation of test cases is the behavior tree of the specification or behavior expression, respectively (cp. Section 7.7). It describes the reachable states (see Figure 14.3/9). The behavior tree can be derived according to the *transition derivation system* defined in [ISO 8807] or by a simulation in which all possible state sequences are executed. The latter is supported, for instance, by the CADP tool [CADP]. The test cases that are derived depend on the applied implementation relation (cp. Section 11.5.1).

In contrast to FSM-based testing, an LTS test case does not check whether the IUT actually reached the specified state. It merely checks the execution of the specified sequence of actions. A transition into an incorrect state can only be detected if the subsequent behavior causes an error. For this reason, sufficiently long tests have to be performed so that the wrong behavior can ultimately be detected. From a theoretical point of view, this is fulfilled, since test suites derived from an LTS specification are endless, in contrast to those from finite state machines. A

---

[7] One may argue that the empty outputs are not very convenient for test execution, but the XDT automaton has not been designed for a test example but rather as an example protocol for demonstrating protocol principles.

labeled transition system is based on an infinite state space [Miln 89]. In practice, however, the length of the test cases must be limited.

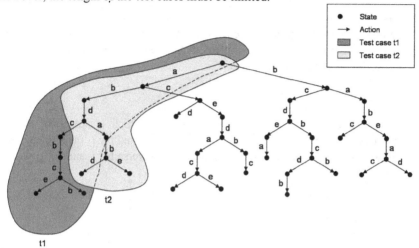

Figure 14.3/9: Behavior tree with test cases

Testing relations

Unlike Chapter 11 where we discussed the equivalence of expressions based on equivalence relations, we now focus on implementation relations that describe the relation between the specification and the implementation. As stated in Section 11.5.1, implementation relations are asymmetric relations which require that the implementation is equivalent in its external behavior. This is tested using external **observers** (see Figure 14.3/10) as already introduced in Section 11.5.3.

Figure 14.3/10: External observers

An implementation I is compliant to a specification S if all observations $obs(o, I) \in OBS$ from I obtained by the observer o may be related to the observations of o regarding S in the same environment:

$$I \textbf{ conforms\_to } S =_{\text{def}} \forall obs \in OBS: obs(o,I) \subseteq obs(o,S).$$

This relation is called the **testing relation**. Different testing relations may be defined by varying the experiments and thus the observations made. Examples of such testing relations are *trace preorder, testing preorder, failure preorder,* **conf**-*relation, input/output testing relation,* **ioco**-*relation,* and many others. We give some examples here. Overviews on the various testing relations can be found in [Tret 96 a,b], [Brin 97], and [Bowm 06].

Trace preorder

The trace preorder relation weakens the trace equivalence of Section 11.5.3. It only demands that all traces of the implementation must be contained in the traces of the specification, but not vice versa:

$$I \leq_{tr} S \Leftrightarrow traces(I) \subseteq traces(S),$$

i.e., an implementation may only show behaviour which is specified. Figure 14.3/11 contains some examples. So the relation is fulfilled for I_1 (as implementation) regarding I_2 and I_3 (as specification), but not vice versa for I_2 and I_3.

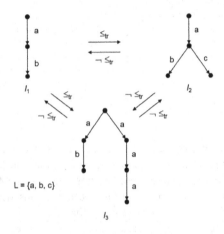

Figure 14.3/11: Trace preorder

Testing preorder

Analogously to trace preorder, the testing preorder relation weakens the testing equivalence introduced in Section 11.5.3. Testing preorder between an implementation I and a specification S exists if the traces recorded by observer o for I are also observed for S and each deadlock in I is also included in S, but not necessarily vice versa:

$$I \leq_{te} S \Leftrightarrow \forall obs \in OBS: obs(o,I) \subseteq obs(o,S).$$

Testing preorder allows the implementation to be more deterministic than the specification, but it cannot do more than S allows, i.e., the implementation may not contain actions that are not specified. Figure 14.3/12 illustrates this relationship. I_2 (as implementation) is not in testing preorder with I_1 (as specification), since the action c observed in I_2 is not specified in I_1. But I_1 is in testing preorder to I_2 and I_3 because the actions $a;b$ are also observed for both specifications.

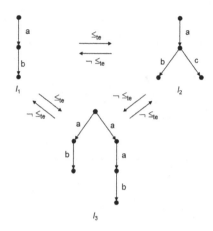

Figure 14.3/12: Testing preorder

conf-relation

Another weaker implementation relation is the **conf**-relation which is related to testing preorder. It restricts all observations only to those traces that are contained in S. This corresponds to conformance testing, i.e., **conf** requires that an implementation does what it should do [Tret 96b]. The **conf**-relation regards an implementation *I* as compliant to a specification *S* if the implementation can execute the traces of the specification and shows the same refusal behavior[8], i.e., *I* cannot refuse more than *S* or in other words: *I* cannot deadlock in an environment where *S* does not.

For this, the observations of the implementation have to be compared with the traces of the specification. Since this cannot be done directly, a new process *T*(*S*) is introduced that behaves inversely to *S* and acts as observer. The traces of *T*(*S*) and *S* are equal, i.e.,

$$traces(T(S)) = traces(S).$$

This process is called a **canonical tester**. The canonical tester of *T*(*S*) is again the specification *S*: *T*(*T*(*S*)) = *S* (see Figure 14.3/13).

The canonical tester evaluates the conformance between *I* and *S* through a test run *T*(*S*) ∥ *I* in which it examines whether *I* synchronizes with the traces specified in *S*. The relation **conf** is fulfilled, i.e., *I* passes *T*(*S*), iff

$$I \textbf{ conf } S \Leftrightarrow \forall obs \in OBS: obs(o,I) \cap traces(S) \subseteq obs(o,S).$$

---

[8] As already mentioned in Section 11.5.3, equivalence between behavior expressions can also be defined considering refused behavior. *Refusal semantics* may distinguish behavior that is considered equal by certain equivalence relations (see [Bowm 06] for more details).

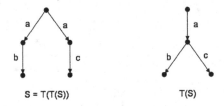

Figure 14.3/13: Canonical tester

The **conf**-relation is a more liberal version of the testing preorder. It allows that an implementation may contain actions that are not prescribed in the specification (see Figure 14.3/14).

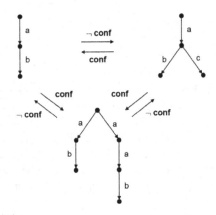

Figure 14.3/14: conf-relation

A canonical tester can be generated for each specification. The concept of the canonical tester is in particular of interest as a theoretical model. It has not achieved practical relevance, since it relies on the assumption of synchronous communication between the IUT and its environment. This assumption is not realistic for many applications. Furthermore, sufficiently practicable procedures for the derivation of test cases have not been found. Since the canonical tester reflects the whole specified behavior, it is generally expensive to determine it. This is often only done for *Basic* LOTOS. The consideration of data has proved to be very difficult [Brin 97].

ioco-relation

A more practical testing relation is the **ioco**-relation developed by Tretmans [Tret 96a,b]. Unlike normal labeled transition systems, the **ioco** approach distinguishes between inputs and outputs. It uses a special form of LTSs: the *Input/Output Transition Systems* (IOTS). An IOTS divides the set of labels in an LTS into the disjoint sets L_I and L_O for inputs and outputs:

$$IOTS(L_I, L_O) \subseteq LTS(L_I \cup L_O) \quad \text{with } L_I \cap L_O = \{\varnothing\} \text{ and } L_I \cup L_O = L.$$

It is further required that all inputs are always enabled:

forall states s, **forall** $?a \in L_I$: $s \overset{?a}{\Rightarrow}$

Figure 14.3/15 gives an example of an IOTS. The inputs are labeled by a question mark, the outputs correspondingly by an exclamation mark. States in which the IOTS generates no output on an input are referred to as *quiescence*, denoted by δ. In Figure 14.3/15 this is the case in the right execution path after the first input $?a$. Traces that contain *quiescence* are called *suspension traces* (*Strace*):

$$Straces(s) = \{\sigma \in (L_I \cup L_O \cup \delta)^* \mid s \overset{\sigma}{\Rightarrow}\}$$

In the behaviour tree quiescence is represented by a transition which returns to the same state.

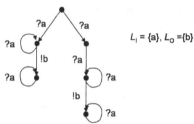

Figure 14.3/15: Example of an input/output transition system

The **ioco**-relation assumes that the specification is given in the form of a labeled transition system, i.e., $SPECS = LTS(L_I \cup L_O)$, while the implementation is modeled by an input/output transition system, i.e., $MODS = IOTS(L_I, L_O)$:

ioco $\subseteq IOTS \times LTS$.

An implementation I meets the implementation relation **ioco** with respect to a specification S iff

I **ioco** $S \Leftrightarrow \forall \sigma \in Straces(S)$: $out(I$ **after** $\sigma) \subseteq out(S$ **after** $\sigma)$

with

I **after** $\sigma = \{p' \mid p \overset{\sigma}{\Rightarrow} p'\}$,

$out(P) = \{!x \in L_O \mid s \overset{!x}{\rightarrow}, s \in P\} \cup \{\delta \mid s \overset{\delta}{\rightarrow} s, s \in P\}$

$s \overset{\delta}{\rightarrow} s \Leftrightarrow s \overset{L_O}{\nrightarrow} s \Leftrightarrow \forall !x \in L_O : s \overset{!x}{\nrightarrow}$.

Figure 14.3/16 shows as examples the various outputs of the IOTS behavior expression.

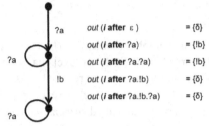

out (*i* after ε)	= {δ}
out (*i* after ?a)	= {!b}
out (*i* after ?a.?a)	= {!b}
out (*i* after ?a.!b)	= {δ}
out (*i* after ?a.!b.?a)	= {δ}

Figure 14.3/16: Outputs after various inputs

The **ioco**-relation implies that the specification can be more comprehensive than the implementation. Accordingly, everything that happens in the implementation must be defined in the specification, but not necessarily vice versa. Figure 14.3/17 shows some examples.

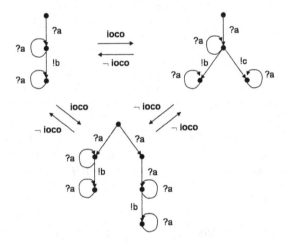

Figure 14.3/17: **ioco**-relation

Derivation of test cases

A test case for the considered relations can be taken as a finite and deterministic labeled transition system, whose final states are the test verdicts *pass* and *fail* [Tret 96b]. Figure 14.3/18b gives an example for the **ioco**-relation. The set of labels $L = L_I \cup L_O \cup \{\theta\}$ is determined by the input and output sets, and the timer θ. The latter is used to control quiescence. The expiration of θ indicates that the implementation did not make any output during the period δ. In every state of the test case except the final states indicated by ***pass*** or ***fail***, the following interactions are possible: an input, various outputs, or quiescence. Figure 14.3/18 gives an example including the test execution. The test case in b) is derived from the specification

given in a)[9] as shown below. Picture c) contains an implementation to which the
test case is applied. The test execution is represented in d). Here *iut'* and *iut"* refer
to the states that the IUT reaches after executing the respective test cases.

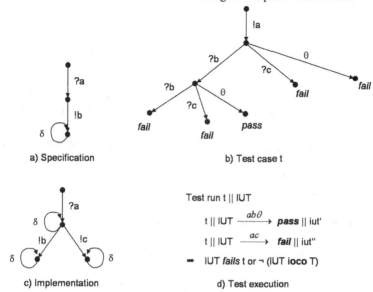

a) Specification

b) Test case t

c) Implementation

d) Test execution

Figure 14.3/18: Test case and test execution for the **ioco**-relation

An **ioco** test case is derived recursively. It starts with the definition of the test purpose. The latter is defined by a trace which determines the input behavior to be
analyzed. First, the final state is determined, which has to be reached after a successful execution of this trace. The verdict **pass** is assigned to this state (*Step* 1).
After this, the first input of the trace, $?a \in L_I$ in our **ioco** example, is assigned to
the initial state (or another chosen starting state) s (*Step* 2):

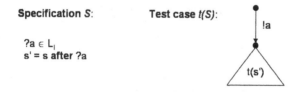

Specification S:

$?a \in L_I$
$s' = s$ **after** $?a$

Test case t(S):

In the next step the reached state $s' = s$ **after** $?a$ is examined for all possible outputs $!x \in L_O \cup \{\delta\}$ (*Step* 3).

---

[9] Note that a test case describes the inverse behavior of the specification. Accordingly, output events of the IUT are presented as input events in the test case
and vice versa.

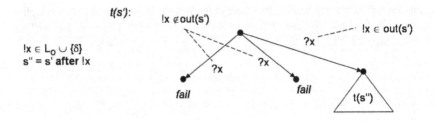

All outputs $!x$ leading to the target state **pass** are considered as allowed outputs ($!x \in out(s')$). The other outputs $!x \notin out(s')$ lead to the state **fail**. The timer θ is handled analogously. If the specification indicates quiescence for a state then $\{\delta\}$ is a valid output, otherwise **fail** follows θ. Steps (2) and (3) are repeated for the remaining sub-trees until the states are reached that were marked with **pass** in step (1). Figure 14.3/19 shows the derivation of the test case from Figure 14.3/18b) for the test purpose $!a\ ?b\ \theta$.

14.3.3   Derivation of test cases from formal descriptions

The derivation methods presented in the previous sections cannot be directly applied to formal descriptions in the standardized FDTs, since the latter are based on extended finite state machines or structured labeled transition systems which have more complex semantic models. Taking the minor states into account, which are related to the variables, the number of states grows explosively so that test case derivation with these methods is less feasible. Therefore, formal descriptions have to be preprocessed for the derivation of test cases and test suites. There are basically two approaches: the direct and the indirect methods (see Figure 14.3/20).

Direct method
The direct approach tries to derive test cases straight from the formal description. This is as a rule only possible for simple specifications and by making simplifying assumptions, e.g., by limiting the number of minor states, so that the methods described in the previous sections are applicable.

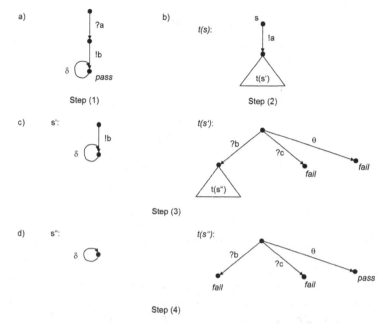

Figure 14.3/19: Derivation of the test case of Figure 14.3/18 b) for the test purpose !*a* ?*b* θ (after [Tret 00])

Indirect methods

Indirect method transform the formal description into an intermediate model, e.g., in an FSM representation, which can then be used for test case derivation with the known procedures. Such an intermediate representation can also be used for different formal description techniques. An example of such an intermediate model was the normal form representation, developed by Sarikaya, Von Bochmann and Cerny for Estelle [Sari 87]. The normal form transfers the Estelle specification into a single automaton in which among others all procedure and function calls, loops, and conditional statements are dissolved. Such a transformation is not possible without loss of information compared to the original formal description. This reduces the fault detection capability of the derived test cases. Their fault detection capability therefore depends strongly on the chosen intermediate model.

The indirect methods are divided into approaches with explicit and implicit test purposes.

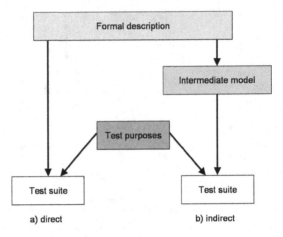

Figure 14.3/20: Derivation of test suites from formal descriptions

Methods with explicit test purposes

These methods start from given test purposes and derive the respective test cases. Instead of test purposes, a fault model can also be used in order to describe the errors to be detected by the test case. The precondition is an accurate formalization of the test purposes which have to be described formally in the case of automated derivation, e.g., by means of MSCs. The methods ensure that the generated test cases are consistent with the specification and the test purposes by a simulative execution of the specification, but they do not guarantee full test coverage. Methods with explicit test purposes represent a pragmatic and flexible way of deriving test cases from formal descriptions. They require accuracy in the formulation of the test purposes. Most tools for the derivation of test cases from formal descriptions use indirect methods. An example is the SAMSTAG method [Grab 97] developed for SDL.

Methods with implicit test purposes

Derivation methods with implicit test purposes pursue the goal to derive a complete test suite from a given formal description. The test purposes are implicitly determined by the derivation procedure. For this, the specification is preprocessed in such a way, e.g., by assumptions about the value ranges of the variables, that it can be transferred into a manageable intermediate FSM or LTS representation from which a test suite can be generated. Derivation methods with implicit test purposes allow the derivation of a complete test suite and ensure complete test coverage with respect to the implicit test purposes. However, due to the restrictions made the consistency between specification and test cases is not fully guaranteed. An example of a derivation method with implicit test purposes is the canonical tester presented in the previous section. So far, however, there are few relevant practical procedures. An approach to an applicable solution for the derivation of test suites from formal descriptions in Estelle and SDL is presented in [Henn 02].

In the literature a variety of approaches and methods for the (automatic) derivation of test cases from formal descriptions in different formal description techniques have been published. The interested reader can find examples among others in the proceedings of the conferences *TestCom* [TestCom] and *FORTE* [FORTE] as well as in the annex to the FMCT standards [ISO 13245]. The proposed methods are usually restricted to subsets of the standardized specification languages or simplified intermediate models. The automatic derivation of test cases will therefore continue to remain a research subject.

14.3.4   Selection of test cases

The execution of the complete test suite is often not possible because of its length, which puts practical and economical restrictions on its execution. For that reason, the number of test runs must be limited to an appropriate subset of test cases in practical test execution. Two criteria apply with priority for the selection of test cases:

- the test coverage and
- the costs of the test execution.

These are conflicting criteria because the reduction of the number of test cases lowers the cost of test execution, but it also reduces the test coverage. Conversely, the expenses increase if the test is more extensive. The selection of an appropriate subset of test cases is therefore an optimization problem with the goal to maximize the test coverage at the lowest possible cost level.

There are basically two ways to select test cases. The selection can be part of the derivation process using test methods with explicit test purposes to generate only selected test cases. The other possibility is selection after deriving the complete test suite.

Test coverage

The test coverage is a normalized measure for a test suite that indicates whether the test suite covers the relevant properties of an implementation and detects related errors. The test coverage for a test suite TS described in the notation $TESTS$ can be interpreted as a mapping on the range 0 to 1:

$$\text{cov: } \wp(TESTS) \rightarrow [0,1]$$

The test coverage represents a measure for the quality of a test suite. It can be used for the comparison of test suites. A test suite TS has higher test coverage than a test suite TS' if it reveals more faulty implementations than the other one, i.e.,

$$F(S) \setminus M_{TS} \subseteq F(S) \setminus M_{TS'} \Rightarrow cov(TS') \leq cov(TS)$$

where $F(S) = MODS \setminus M_S$ is the fault domain of S, M_S the set of conforming implementations, and M_{TS} the set of all implementation which pass TS.

There are in principle two approaches for determining the test coverage

- the specification coverage and
- the fault detection capability.

The *specification coverage* is a measure of the "coverage of the structure" of the specification [Groz 96]. The structure of the specification is determined by the formal description technique applied and the underlying semantic model. When applying finite state machines, for example, possible typical coverages are the execution of all paths (*path coverage*), the execution of all transitions (*transition coverage*), and the passing of all states (*state coverage*). In particular the state and transition coverage possess practical relevance, since the number of execution paths in a finite state machine is infinite in general.

The *fault detection capability* is a measure of the ability of a test suite or a test, case to detect incorrect implementations. There are different interpretations of the fault detection capability in the literature, e.g., as the average probability that a test suite detects any non-compliant implementation or as a metric that indicates how closely a test suite approximates the (infinite) set of tests that fully covers a given specification. FMCT considers the fault detection capability as a normalized measure which indicates whether a test suite achieves full fault coverage with respect to a given fault model $F(S)$ [ISO 13245]. The problem with all these definitions is that they relate more or less to the entirety of possible implementations which is difficult to determine in practice. Therefore, specification coverage is preferred as a measure.

Cost

Cost represents a measure of the efforts needed to run a test. It comprises the expenses for the derivation of the test suite, for its execution, and for the evaluation of the test outputs. The cost of a test suite is in general proportional to its length. A long test suite requires more time and resources for its execution. The cost of the test execution can rarely be defined or measured precisely. It is based on estimates, which are mainly based on the experience of previous test runs. Analogously to the test coverage, we describe the cost of executing a test suite $TS \in TESTS$ by a mapping on the set of real numbers $\mathfrak{R}$:

cost: $\wp\,(TESTS) \to \mathfrak{R}$.

Cost can be used as a measure for the comparison of test suites regarding the effort required for their execution:

$TS' \subseteq TS \Rightarrow cost(TS') \leq cost(TS)$.

The cost of a test suite summarizes the costs of the test cases:

$K_{TS} = \sum_{t \in TS} K_t$

The cost of a test case consists of a fixed part and the cost of its execution.

$$K_t = K_{fix}{}^t + K_{ex}{}^t$$

The fixed costs comprise the efforts for the derivation and implementation of the test case as well as the evaluation of the test outcome. The execution cost consists of the costs of the execution of the preamble, the proper test, and the postamble. The costs of these three test sections in turn summarize the costs of the execution of individual test steps. The estimation of the test costs can be done top-down or bottom-up depending on the whether the entire test or the individual test events are used as starting point. In general, the estimation of the test costs is complicated because different factors, such as the temporal duration of the tests, the staff running the tests, and the technical efforts have to be taken into account. In most cases, different weightings of the test steps are required.

14.4 Interoperability test

The conformance test alone cannot guarantee the interoperability of different protocol implementations. This is easy to see. One of the reasons is the incompleteness of conformance tests due to cost reasons as just discussed. But even if we assume the ideal case of a complete conformance test, interoperability cannot be guaranteed. There are several reasons for this, such as ambiguities of protocol standards, decisions left to the implementers by protocol options and local implementation matters (cp. Section 13.1.1), configuration differences, or faults. This may result in implementations that are not or only partially interoperable with each other (see Figure 14.4 /1).

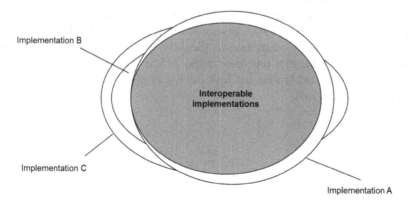

Figure 14.4/1: The interoperability problem

Conformance testing is therefore only a step towards providing interoperable protocol implementations – a necessary precondition – that confirms compliance with the specification or the standard, respectively. To demonstrate interoperability further tests are required.

The interoperability test is a test that is applied in many areas to prove the collaboration capability of systems, devices, or implementations. The task of the interoperability test in the protocol field is to validate the interaction capability of different protocol implementations. The interoperability test provides the buyer or the user of the communication software the certainty that it is able to cooperate with other systems which support the same services. Here, interoperability and interoperability testing should not be equated. Like any other test the interoperability test cannot guarantee absolutely the interoperability of various protocol implementations due to testing limitations.

There are several situations in which interoperability tests can be applied during the development and installation of communication software:

- when developing the implementation to prove that the implementation can in principle collaborate with other implementations,
- when buying the software to validate that the promised interoperability capabilities are provided,
- when installing the software to validate its interoperability with the environment in detail,
- in use to decide specific interoperability problems, and
- when integrating updated versions of the implementation.

The interoperability issue in communications protocols was originally caused by the use of options in protocol specifications. Incompatible option settings, which are nevertheless in compliance with the standard, may yield the situation that conforming implementations are not able to interoperate (see Figure 14.4/2). In the OSI world one tried to overcome this issue by defining protocol profiles (cp. Section 4.1) which, however, have proved too complicated to handle in practice. But there are many others reasons [Seol 04] that may cause interoperability problems, such as different time-out ranges, differences in parameter settings or PDU data formats, and last but not least influences of the execution environment not detected beforehand.

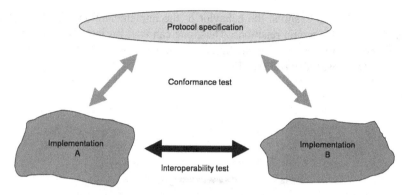

Figure 14.4/2: Conformance test vs. interoperability test

Test architecture

Compared to the conformance test, the interoperability test is a more macroscopic test [Seol 04] which focuses on the interactions of the implementation with other systems, while the conformance test examines the behavior of the implementation. In addition, interoperability tests often relate to the test of two protocol stacks in a real environment rather than to the test of two single implementations. Testing is applied to finished implementations or products in real execution environments with realistic applications. In this way, it implicitly also tests the correct functioning of the protocol entities which is the subject of the conformance test. For this reason, no specific test architectures are defined, unlike for conformance testing. In an interoperability test the implementations test each other quasi mutually. Hence, interoperability tests can also be carried out by people who are not necessarily test specialists. In general, three methods are applied for running protocol interoperability tests:

- *Interoperability tests without monitor*
  Two implementations are tested against each other via a suitable network interface (see Figure 14.4/3a). The test cases are derived from the application scenarios and, if used, from the service specification. The end systems are stimulated by the users via the service interface. The test evaluation is based on the observed reactions at the user/service interfaces and on other emerging effects, such as deadlocks. This type of interoperability test is called a **passive interoperability test**. It is relatively easy to realize. Its drawback is that it only indicates interaction errors, but usually not their causes.
- *Interoperability tests with a passive monitor*
  In this variant the data exchange between the two implementations to be tested is recorded and analyzed by a passive monitor (see Figure 14.4/3b). This provides additional opportunities to detect interoperability errors.
- *Interoperability tests with an active monitor*
  The passive monitoring function is now replaced by an active monitor that is used to influence the data exchange between the IUTs, e.g., by changing or in-

jecting PDUs to examine the behavior of the implementations in more detail and to provoke certain reactions. Thus, one can test, for instance, what protocol options are supported by the implementations. This method is called an **active interoperability test** (see Figure 14.4/3c).

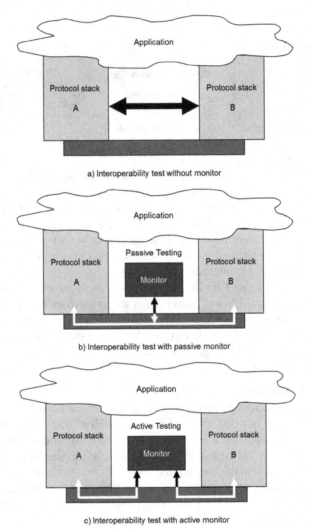

a) Interoperability test without monitor

b) Interoperability test with passive monitor

c) Interoperability test with active monitor

Figure 14.4/3: Methods of interoperability testing

A more generalized test architecture for the interoperability test which applies the concepts of the lower and upper tester (LT, UT) and of the points of control and observation (PCOs) known from conformance testing (cp. Section 14.2.1) is depicted in Figure 14.4/4. Depending on which aspects of interoperability are investigated different architectures, including the three above, may be derived. The choice of test architecture is strongly affected by the access points that the implementations allow to be placed. A detailed discussion of the different variants is contained in [Viho 01]. From the practical point of view, the differentiation into lower and upper tester is not so relevant because an interoperability test in contrast to a conformance test is more strongly controlled by the upper tester rather than the lower tester.

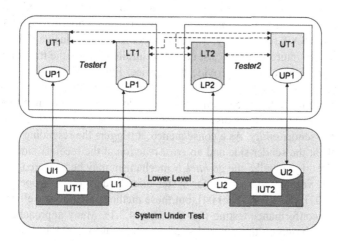

Figure 14.4/4: Generalized test architecture for the interoperability test according to [Viho 01]

One of the main differences between conformance and interoperability testing is the reference specification deployed. Conformance testing is based on the (standardized) specification from which the conformance requirements are derived. The interoperability test, however, is more strongly driven by the usage requirements. These requirements should be summed up in the service specification, as discussed several times in previous chapters, but in practice the service specification is often not worked out explicitly. The interoperability test is, therefore, more frequently based on informal user requirements rather than on predetermined standards.

The difference between conformance and interoperability testing is also reflected in the length of the test suites. Interoperability test suites are significantly shorter than those for conformance testing. An interoperability test requires on average between 100 and 200 test runs compared to approximately 1500 test runs for a conformance test [Heaf 93]. Due to shorter test suites and simpler test architectures, interoperability testing is significantly cheaper than conformance testing. The termination criterion for an interoperability test is primarily the satisfaction of the interoperability statement, while in a conformance test it is above all the cost factor.

Test cases

Interoperability test cases have a different character to conformance test cases. For example, let us consider the test cases for a passive interoperability test of the connection set up in the XDT protocol. The test case for the successful connection set up is *XDATrequ, XDATind, XDATconf*; the test case for the unsuccessful set up attempt: *XDATrequ, XABORTind* or *XDATrequ, XDATind, XABORTind*. The input stimulus is *XDATrequ* in both cases. In contrast to the conformance test, now only the test outputs at the service interface are observed. The test is passed if the primitives *XDATrequ* and *XDATconf* can be observed at the sender SAP and *XDATind* at the receiver SAP, respectively. The test outcome is inconclusive if *XABORTind* is observed. An interoperability test case also implicitly tests the transitions in the protocol entities executed to provide the service. Figure 14.4/5 gives two examples. Picture a) shows the passed transitions for the connection set up (the dotted lines refer to transitions executed if the set up failed). Picture b) refers to an active test in which an *ACK*-PDU is discarded or changed in such a way that it will be rejected by the sender entity. As a consequence, it triggers the resending of the related *DT*-PDU at the sender side and an error reaction at the receiver side due to the repeated PDU. Eventually, the *go back N* mechanism may be triggered.

There are various approaches for systematically deriving interoperability test cases [Bess 02], [Hao 04], [Seol 04], but these methods are not as well established as those for conformance testing (cp. Section 14.3.1). Many approaches, such as [Seol 04], are based on the generation of the reachability graph of the SUT comprising both entities to derive the paths which cover the interactions between the entities.

Running interoperability tests is basically an economical requirement to overcome incompatibility problems between implementations provided by different providers. Unlike conformance testing, there is no general framework or methodology how to perform interoperability tests. The test procedures applied as well as the test cases used are mainly driven by practical requirements rather than based on a theoretical framework. On the other hand, interoperability tests are much shorter than conformance tests and consequently much less expensive. Since interoperability test cases implicitly test the correct implementation of transitions needed for the particular service, one tries to combine both tests to reduce the testing costs. The derivation of test cases that check both the correct interaction of the implementations and compliance with the specification represents the real challenge here.

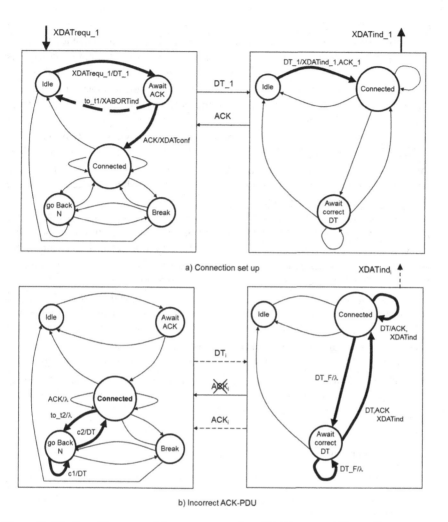

a) Connection set up

b) Incorrect ACK-PDU

Figure 14.4/5: Transitions covered for two test cases in an XDT interoperability test[10]

14.5 Active vs. passive testing

The testing methods we have considered up to now represent active conformance or interoperability tests. In an **active test** a dedicated test system stimulates
the implementation under test and observes the related reactions. As already mentioned, it is scarcely possible to execute a complete test suite in practice. In addi-

---

[10] In this representation the input/output events of those transmissions not covered by the interoperability test case are omitted. For the complete automata, see Chapter 7.

tion, we have seen that all theoretical approaches for deriving test cases are based on certain assumptions, such as a known number of states and knowledge of the input/output set. Moreover, errors can easily occur in an implementation, such as false variable assignments or range overruns, which may be not detected by the derived test cases. Consequently, tests in practice are hardly capable of detecting all errors in an implementation. There remains always an uncertainty about the correctness of the implementation. To cope with this uncertainty passive testing has been proposed as an alternative approach [Lee 97]. In a **passive test** the IUT is monitored in normal operation by recording its input/output behaviors, i.e., their interactions (service primitives, PDUs) with the environment, without interfering with it by external stimuli. The observed interactions are then checked against the specification to detect deviations.

Passive protocol testing consists of two phases. The first phase – called *passive homing* – tries to identify the current state of the IUT, whereas in the second *fault detection* phase one attempts to reveal errors based on detected discrepancies between the passively traced events and the related specification. Thus, the rationale behind passive testing corresponds to a *proof by contradiction*.

The principle of the passive homing phase for an extended finite state machine (cp. Section 7.5) can be described by the algorithm given in [Lee 97] which is represented in slightly simplified form below. Here $\vec{x} = \{x_1, x_2, ..., x_n\}$ denotes the current variable value vector and $e(\vec{y})$ an observed event with its current parameter values $\vec{y} = \{y_1, y_2, ..., y_m\}$. In passive testing no assumption is made about the state of the IUT when the test begins. It need not necessarily be the initial state, i.e., the entity may be in any of the states $S_c = \{s_0, s_1, ... s_{n-1}\}$, and, in addition, the values of the variables are assumed to be unknown.

Given: IUT and observed events	
Output: Error indication	
begin	
$\quad S_c = \{s_0, s_1, ... s_{n-1}\}$	/* Initialize current state set */
$\quad \vec{x} = \{x_1, x_2, ..., x_n\}\ x_i := unknown, i = 1...p$	/* Unknown variable values */
	/* initially */
$\quad$ **for each** $e(\vec{y})$ **do**{	/* Next observed event */
$\qquad S_c' := \varnothing$	/* Possible next state set */
$\qquad$ **for each** transition $t \wedge t.\text{start\_state} \in S_c$ **do**{	
$\qquad$ **if** $(t.\text{event} = e \wedge t.\text{condition}(\vec{x}, \vec{y}))$	/* Is transition fireable ? */
$\qquad\quad \{\ S_c' := S_c' \cup \{t.\text{end\_state}\}$	
$\qquad\qquad$ update $(\vec{x})$	/* Assign new values to */
$\qquad\quad \}$	/* variables */
$\qquad \}$	
$\quad$ **if** $(S_c' = \varnothing)$ **return** fault	
$\quad S_c := S_c'$	
$\quad \}$	
end	

The current state is determined by elimination. Initially, all states are candidates. For each observed event, an executable transition t is searched for. A transition t is executable if the event is expected in the current state and if a possibly defined additional condition over the variables $\vec{x}$ and the parameters $\vec{y}$ becomes true (for details see [Lee 97]). If the transition is fireable the end state is added to the next possible state set S_c. After investigating all possible states S_c is replaced by S_c', i.e., the states which do not wait for this event are eliminated. S_c' contains either the next possible state or is empty. In the latter case no transition has been found for the observed event, i.e., an error must have been occurred. Otherwise the process continues with the next observed event. The algorithm does not describe the relations between the variables and parameters used to formulate additional conditions. It is therefore not capable of revealing the respective errors. An extension of the algorithm to do this is also given in [Lee 97].

Once the current state has been determined the execution paths can be observed. If a deviation is detected the monitored system behaviour (observed input/ output sequence, state sets) can be used to find the source of the error. The causes of a faulty behaviour may also be resolved in an active test, e.g., by using instant replay techniques to force certain execution paths.

Passive testing has attracted large theoretical interest [Tabo 99], [Wu 01], [Netr 03], but its practical importance is limited. This is because protocol errors often cause network and application crashes or other severe faults. Therefore protocols must be tested actively before they can be put into operation. Passive testing is a supplement which may be applied to find further errors, e.g., the origins of some interoperability issues, but it can never be used as a replacement for active tests. The benefit of passive testing is that it can detect errors which are hard to detect in active testing due to its incompleteness, such as extra states, variable range violations, integration errors and so on by monitoring the system under test over a long period in operation. Other claimed benefits, such as no test system [Lee 02], are questionable, since protocols cannot be tested only passively as argued. In addition, passive tests need observation points which cannot automatically be included in implementations.

14.6 TTCN-2

In order to run tests the test cases have to be described adequately. For this, the use of formalized description means is appropriate. Several test description languages have been proposed [TestCom], [Forte] and also some of the specification languages presented in Chapter 8 have been tried. In practice, however, the test notation TTCN which was developed in the context of the OSI conformance testing methodology [ISO 9646] (cp. Section 14.2.2) prevailed because it was in accordance with the requirements on practical test execution at that time.

TTCN (*Tree and Tabular Combined Notation*) is defined in Part 3 of the ISO 9646 standard CTMF. The first version of TTCN was developed in 1992 for description of the test suites for OSI protocols. The characteristic elements of TTCN were behavior trees and tables. In the mid-1990s the notation was expanded for the description of test cases for multi-party tests. This version was published under the name Concurrent TTCN and/or TTCN-2 in the ITU-T recommendation [ITU-T 292], [ETSI 99]. Several years ago the European Technology Standards Institute (ETSI) developed a new version of TTCN, called TTCN-3, which is no longer limited to OSI-based test systems. It also takes other types of tests into consideration. TTCN-3 is not an extension and correction of the earlier versions, but a completely new language. The TTCN core language [ITU-T 161] represents a programming language with test-specific extensions for describing test data, test cases, test configurations, and for handling events. Many of the characteristic TTCN-2 language elements, such as behavior trees and tables are no longer contained in TTCN-3. Because of this breach in the language concept the meaning of the acronym TTCN was reinterpreted. In the TTCN-3 context it means *Testing and Test Control Notation*. TTCN-3 is supported by many organizations and tool providers, but often in such situations the former version continues to be used, especially in industry where many test suites are described in TTCN-2, so that actually two standards exist. For that reason, we give a short introduction to the basic concepts of both versions here.

TTCN-2 is characterized as an informal notation to describe abstract test cases independently from the test methods applied and the protocols being tested. It contains an operational semantics that defines how to interpret the test cases. TTCN-2 provides a notation which reflects the abstract testing methodology defined in the OSI conformance testing methodology [ISO 9646]. As in SDL, the notation divides into two forms: TTCN/GR (*graphical TTCN*) and TTCN/MP (*machine processable TTCN*). TTCN/GR represents the human-readable tabular-oriented form to describe test cases, while TTCN/MP is a canonical representation for computer systems. Among others it is used when transferring TTCN test cases between different computer systems. The two forms are semantically equivalent. We consider here only the TTCN/GR notation and confine ourselves to the basic concepts. These are behavior trees and tables.

14.6.1   Behavior trees

A *behavior tree* describes the events that may occur in a test case. It applies in principle the same concepts as we became acquainted with in Section 7.7 when introducing process calculi. Figure 14.6/1 shows the behavior tree of a test case for the XDT sender entity which tests the connection set up and the beginning of the data transmission at the PCO above the IUT. The relation *father node* → *son node* defines here the temporal sequence in which the test events occur. Sibling nodes denote possible alternative test events.

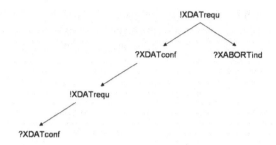

Figure 14.6/1: Behavior tree for a test case of the XDT sender entity

The test case is syntactically represented as follows:

```
U!XDATrequ
  U?XDATconf
    U!XDATrequ
      U?XDATconf
  U?XABORTind
```

The indention determines the temporal sequence of the events. Alternatives, i.e., branches of the tree, are arranged one below the other beginning in the same column. The events are distinguished into events that stimulate the IUT and events observed as reactions of the IUT. Stimuli are labeled with an exclamation mark, reactions correspondingly with a question mark. Before this, the PCO in which the event occurs may be indicated, e.g., L = *Lower Tester*, U = *Upper Tester*. In our test case the following sequences of events may occur:

(!XDATrequ, ?XDATconf, !XDATrequ, ?XDATconf) and
(!XDATrequ, ?XABORTind).

It is also possible to describe the expected behavior at the PCOs of the lower and the upper tester as a behavior tree as is done for the above test run in the following:

```
U!XDATrequ
  L?DT
    L!ACK
      U?XDATconf
        U!XDATrequ
          L?DT
            U?XDATconf
              L!ACK
  U?XABORTind
```

Behavior trees can be decomposed into **sub-trees** which can be described separately (see Figure 14.6/2). This avoids the behavior trees becoming too complex so that they cannot be displayed. The sub-trees are stored in test step libraries.

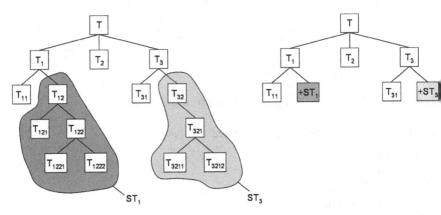

Figure 14.6/2: Separation of sub-trees

14.6.2   Snapshot semantics

The interpretation of behavior trees is defined by the so-called **snapshot semantics**, the operational semantics of TTCN [ITU-T 292], [Baum 94]. We demonstrate the principle of snapshot semantics for the first behavior tree given above which refers only to the upper tester.

The principle of snapshot semantics is to prove whether a received event is the expected one and whether it matches the current event line. For this, the test system passes cyclically through the test case and makes snapshots of the various levels of the behavior tree, always starting with the leftmost alternative. In Figure 14.6/3 the various alternative levels of our example tree are marked by grey rectangles.

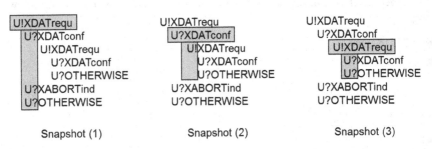

Figure 14.6/3: "Successful" snapshots for our example tree

In each snapshot the tester compares the awaited events with the first event in the input queue of the related PCOs. If this event matches, the related alternative is selected. If the input queue is empty the snapshot is repeated when a new event occurs. Then the tester moves to the next level of indentation and repeats the procedure with the next event. It cannot return to the previous level of indentation (except by using the GOTO construct). To prevent endless waiting in an indentation level an exit can be introduced using ?OTHERWISE, which represents an arbitrary test event that does not coincide with one of the expected alternative test events.

Test Step Dynamic Behavior					
Test Step Name: ABC					
Group: B1					
Objective: Demonstration of TTCN features					
Default:					
Comments: Not related to the above example					
Nr	Label	Behaviour Description	Con-straints Ref	Verdict	Comments
1	F1	+Preamble			DT trans-
2		(I:=0, STOP:=FALSE)			mission
3		REPEAT DATRANS(I,STOP)			(without
		UNTIL [I=K OR STOP]			break)
4		[STOP]			Test
5		+Postamble			abortion
6		GOTO F1			DT trans-
7		[I=K] DATABREAK			mission
8		. . .			(with break)
9		DATRANS(STOP:BOOLEAN,			Local
		J: INTEGER)			sub-tree
10		START T			
11		U!XDATrequ			
12		U?XDATconf (J:=J+1)	XDR		
13		U? OTHERWISE (STOP:=TRUE)		PASS	
14		?TIMEOUT T (STOP:=TRUE)		FAIL	
15				FAIL	
16		DATABREAK			Local
17		. . .			sub-tree

Figure 14.6/4: Example of a TTCN-2 table representation

14.6.3   Tables

Tables are the second basic element of TTCN-2. There is a variety of tables that have to be used in the different parts of the description. We do not introduce them here. Figure 14.6/4 depicts one example table to illustrate the description principle. It shows the description of a test case which, however, is not related to the example given above. The test case description can be connected with constraints concerning the abstract service primitives and PDUs which have to be described in other tables. ASN.1 may be used for this.

14.6.4   Test verdicts

As shown in Figure 14.6/4 test verdicts are indicated for the different outcomes of the test case. This can also be done by using an implicitly defined read-only variable R. The current value of R changes according to the rules given in Figure 14.6/5. Note that there are some additional rules for deriving the final verdict which we do not consider here.

Current value of R	Entry in column *Verdict*		
	(PASS)	(INCONC)	(FAIL)
none	*pass*	*inconc*	*fail*
pass	*pass*	*inconc*	*fail*
inconc	*inconc*	*inconc*	*fail*
fail	*fail*	*fail*	*fail*

Figure 14.6/5: Determination of the test verdict

14.6.5   Distributed test configurations

TTCN-2 supports the description of distributed test configurations. These are test configurations that consist of several test components which run concurrently. They are needed for multi-party test methods (cp. Section 14.2.4.2). The description of distributed test configurations is optional in TTCN-2. For this, special tables and mechanisms are defined.

A distributed test configuration consists of a main test component and one or several parallel test components (see Figure 14.6/6). The main test component MTC takes over the control function of the lower tester. It is responsible for the creation and monitoring of the parallel test components, the management of the PCOs, and the coordination between the testers as well as the derivation of the final test verdict. The parallel test components PTCs are deployed as lower and upper testers.

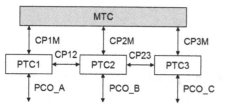

Legend:
MTC - Main Test Component
PTC - Parallel Test Component
CP - Coordination Point
PCO - Point of the Control and Observation

Figure 14.6/6: Example of a distributed test configuration

14.7 TTCN-3

At the end of the last century the TTCN concept was revised fundamentally. The outcome was the language TTCN-3 [ETSI 03] that diverges considerably from its predecessor. This is also expressed in a changed interpretation of the acronym TTCN: **Testing and Test Control Notation**. The reason for this revision was an increasingly wide use of TTCN which exceeded the original scope of the notation. TTCN-2 was primarily designed for the description of test cases for the conformance testing of communication protocols as determined by the OSI test methodology. It turned out to be too restrictive when deployed it for other forms of testing (network integration tests, end-to-end tests, interoperability tests, performance tests) as well as for other application areas (Internet, middleware, mobile communication). But there were also new demands from users of the language, e.g., regarding the table notation, the adoption of ASN.1, the introduction of synchronous communication, and the support of dynamic test configurations. The use of the language, especially the table notation, was a problem for many users.

TTCN-3 represents a much more flexible approach which supports new test requirements. This was achieved through a fundamental change of the notation; in particular the basic concepts behavior tree and table notation have been largely abandoned. TTCN-3 has more the character of a modern programming language, such as C, C + +, or Java, rather than a specific test notation. This promotes its usage and supports tool developments. The new features introduced with TTCN-3 include dynamic test configurations, synchronous and asynchronous communication paradigms, mechanisms for the selection and execution of test cases, harmonization with ASN.1, the module concept, extensibility with the help of attributes, various presentation formats, as well as a defined syntax and operational semantics. Meanwhile, TTCN-3 has become a pretty complex language concept, the definition of which comprises 8 parts [Schi 08]. Nowadays, TTCN-3 is supported by various tool providers.

14.7.1   Basic concepts

Presentation formats

TTCN-3 distinguishes several presentation formats (see Figure 14.7/1). It consists of a textual core language and additional presentation formats, such as the tabular and the graphical formats.

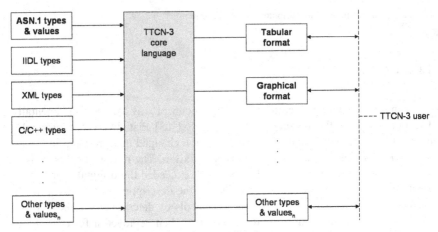

Figure 14.7/1: TTCN-3 core language and presentation formats

The basic notation is the **TTCN-3 core language**. It has three functions [Schi 08]. First, it is a textual language for the description and execution of tests which can be used by test developers, test engineers, and tool developers. Second, it defines an exchange format for test cases between different TTCN test tools and third, it is the semantic basis for the various TTCN-3 representation formats. Data types and values described in ASN.1 (cp. Section 8.5), the Interface Description Languages (IDL), the Extensible Markup Language (XML), and other formats can be imported into the core language for describing data formats. The first presentation format is the table format. It resembles the TTCN-2/GR representation and is mainly supposed to support the migration from TTCN-2 to TTCN-3. The second representation format is the graphical format which uses an MSC-like notation. In this introduction we concentrate on the core language.

The conversion of a TTCN-3 specification from the core language into another presentation format is controlled by attributes allocated to the elements of the core language (see Figure 14.7/2). Three types of attributes are distinguished:

- **encode** for specifying the encoding rules. ASN.1 is defined by default, but also proprietary or application specific rules can be used.
- **display** for setting the representation format, e.g., the table format, the graphical format, or another proprietary format.
- **extension** for the introduction of user-defined attributes.

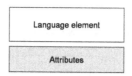

Figure 14.7/2: Attributes

Modules

The basic building block of a TTCN-3 description is the module. A test suite can consist of one or several modules. A **module** is a self-contained unit which can be translated separately. A module consists of a definition and a control section (see Figure 14.7/3). Both parts are optional, but a module may possess several definition parts. The **definition part** contains the definitions of the data types, test data, test system configurations, and test cases used in the module. The **control part** describes the test execution. This can be either the execution of a single test or a sequence of test cases. There are means to control the test case execution depending on the test course. If a test suite consists of several modules the module definitions can be reused in other modules using an *import*-statement. Modules can be parameterized. The parameters are runtime constants which cannot be changed during module execution.

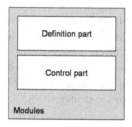

Figure 14.7/3: Structure of a TTCN-3 module

Main components of the description in TTCN-3

A description in TTCN-3 can be roughly divided into four main parts (see Figure 14.7/4): data type definitions, test data, test configurations, and test behavior. These components though do not reflect directly in the syntactic structure of the description.

Data type definitions

Data type definitions form an essential part of a description in TTCN-3 to specify the data formats of the service primitives, PDUs, and other messages to be exchanged. TTCN-3 is a strictly type-oriented language that defines its own data types. Besides all ASN.1 data types and values can be imported and used (cp. Section 8.5). The integration of other type and value systems is foreseen.

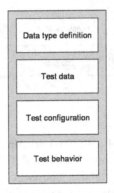

Figure 14.7/4: Main components of description in TTCN-3

TTCN-3 distinguishes like other languages between basic data types, structured types, and special types. The basic data types and the structured types are based on commonly used concepts of modern programming languages. Moreover, there are a number of specific data types, e.g., for the description of test architectures, such as **port** and **component**, or for test cases (**verdicttype**).

Test data
The test stimuli are derived from the data type definitions using **data templates** which create specific value or parameter settings. There are templates for messages and procedure calls. Furthermore, TTCN-3 provides matching mechanisms by which the correctness of responses of the SUT can be checked. Examples of such matching rules are defined values, range limitations, wildcards, the omission of values, and length specifications for strings.

Test configuration
The test configuration describes the test architecture used in a test run. It comprises the description of the test components and their interaction points (ports) as well as their generation, linking, and execution. TTCN-3 supports dynamic test configurations. A test configuration consists of several concurrent test components which execute a specific test behavior, i.e., a test case (see Figure 14.7/5).

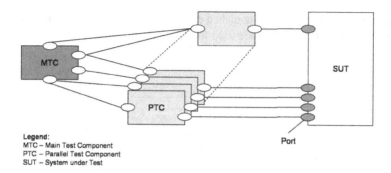

Legend:
MTC – Main Test Component
PTC – Parallel Test Component
SUT – System under Test

Port

Figure 14.7/5: Test configuration

Three types of test components are distinguished:

- the **main test component** (MTC) that is contained in each test configuration,
- the **parallel test components** (PTCs), whose number is not restricted, and
- the **abstract test system interface** as the interface to the SUT.

The parallel test components, which execute partial test runs, are connected with the main test component. Connections between them can be also established. The main test component is generated by the test system before executing a test case. It can dynamically generate and stop parallel test components during test execution. Each test component derives a test verdict and forwards it to the main test component.

The communication between the test components including the test system interface runs via ports (see Figure 14.7/5+6). **Ports** are modeled as infinite FIFO queues. Connections between test components as well as with the test interface begin and end at ports. TTCN-3 supports 1:1 and 1:N communication relations. There are no restrictions concerning the number of connections. However, there are restrictions with respect to the ports between which connections are allowed. The interface to the SUT is modeled by the **abstract test system interface**. The real test interface is not described in TTCN-3. The test execution can start when the test configuration is initialized, i.e., the test components are created and the ports are connected and mapped onto the real test interface of the SUT. During test execution, TTCN-3 distinguishes between connected and mapped ports [Schi 08]. *Connected ports* are for communication with other test components, *mapped ports* for communication with the IUT. Connections and mappings can be set up and deleted dynamically.

TTCN-3 distinguishes between message- and procedure-based communication. **Message-based communication** implements asynchronous data exchange as it is applied in communications protocols. **Procedure-based communication** supports the synchronous communication paradigm. It is primarily used for testing of distributed systems and middleware which use remote procedure calls. Message- and procedure-based ports are distinguished according to the communication paradigm used. Different data templates are used for the generation of test data as well.

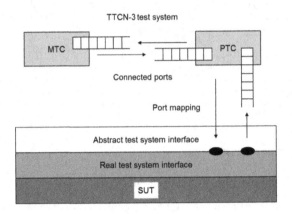

Figure 14.7/6: Conceptual test configuration

Test behavior

The test behavior describes the execution of tests. It defines both the test cases and describes their selection and execution. In TTCN-3 **test cases** are considered as a special form of a function. They are declared like a function in the definition part of a module. A test case description consists of three parts: the interface part, the system part and the behavior part (see Figure 14.7/7).

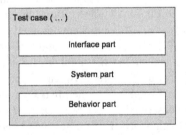

Figure 14.7/7: Test case description

The *interface part* specifies the main test component MTC which executes the test case and determines the ports for communication with the other test components. The *system part* references the test system interface component which defines the ports of the test system. The *behavioral part* describes the test steps of the test case.

TTCN-3 provides a broad range of instructions for the description of the test behavior. These comprise among others control statements, communication statements, timer statements, and behavior statements. One of the most important statements is the **alt**-statement to describe alternative test procedures. The selection of alternatives depends on the test course, i.e., the test outcomes. There is the possibility to define **defaults** to describe behavior that will be executed if none of the alternatives is executable. Defaults can be explicitly enabled and disabled.

A test case is started by the **execute**-statement in the control part of the module. TTCN-3 offers several possibilities to control the test execution. So the test cases can be repeated or other test cases can be activated depending on the test course.

The test execution always results in a test verdict. TTCN-3 distinguishes five test verdicts, which are the values of the data type **verdicttype**. Apart from the test verdicts *pass, fail, inconc*, and *none* known from TTCN-2 (cp. Section 14.6.1), TTCN-3 uses the test verdict *error* when an error occurs in the test system. Each test component assigns a local test verdict which is forwarded to the main test component. The latter collects the local test verdicts and derives a global test verdict for the execution of the test case.

14.7.2 Language elements

In the following we give an overview of the main elements of the TTCN-3 core language. Since the range of language concepts offered by TTCN-3 is very extensive, they cannot be considered comprehensively here. For this, we refer to the standard [ETSI 03] and introductory articles [Schi 08]. We restrict ourselves to an overview of the most fundamental language concepts, whereby we follow the structure of the previous section. The reader will probably be familiar with the principle of a number of language concepts from other languages. They are therefore only mentioned briefly. This applies above all to the data type description which is similar to others concepts presented in this book.

14.7.2.1 Modules

Modules are the building blocks of a TTCN-3 description. They can describe complete test suites or only parts of them. A module consists optionally of a definition and a control part (see Figure 14.7/8), e.g.,

```
module XDT test suite
    {modulpar{integer TS_variant:=1; boolean verdict};
    import XDT data formats from XDT basics;
    control
        {execute(XDT_XS_v12);}
    } // XDT
```

Modules can be parameterized for use in different test contexts. The parameters are listed after **modulpar**. It is also possible to assign default values to the parameters which remain valid as long as no other values are assigned to these parameters during test execution.

Module		
Module definition		
	Imports	Importing definitions from other modules defined in TTCN-3 or other languages
	Data type	User-defined data types (messages, PDUs, information elements, ...)
	Test data	Test data transmitted / received during test execution (templates, values)
	Test configuration	Definition of the test components and communication parts
	Test behavior	Specification of the dynamic test behavior
Module Control		Defining the sequence, loops, conditions, etc. for the execution of test cases

Figure 14.7/8: TTCN-3 module structure (source [Schi 08])

Definition part

The definition part contains all definitions that are globally valid in the module. The range of definitions is quite broad. It ranges from data definitions over the description of communication interfaces to test cases. The possible definitions are summarized in Figure 14.7/9. A characteristic of TTCN-3 is that variables and timers are not introduced in the definition part. They are considered as dynamic language elements that are declared in the control part. For this reason, TTCN-3 does not use global variables. However, variables defined in a testing component can be used by all test cases, functions, etc. which are executed on this component. These variables have the capability to retain their values after the test execution.

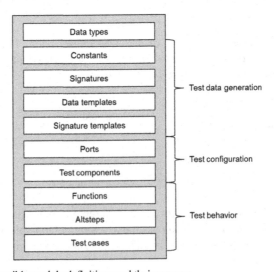

Figure 14.7/9: Possible module definitions and their purpose

TTCN-3 allows the reuse of definitions in other modules as well as the import of definitions from other specifications. Such definitions are included in the definition part with the help of the **import**-statement: **import from** *module name*. When all definitions of a module are imported, this has to be indicated by **all** after the module name. There exist a lot of special rules for the import of definitions. The export of definitions need not be identified explicitly. All definitions of the definition part can be exported by default.

In order to improve the readability and the structure of the description definitions can be grouped, e.g.,

> **group** XDT data formats
> {**const integer** conn := 1;
>
>   . . .
>
>   **type record** XDATrequ_type{ ... };
> } // A grouping of the XDT service primitives and PDUs

Groupings may be nested, i.e., they can contain other groups. The group names in a module need not be unique, but different names must be used at the same hierarchical level. Groupings can also be imported.

Control part

The module control part begins with the key word **control**. It describes the execution of test cases. The control part may contain local declarations, e.g., for constants, variables, and timers, which are needed for controlling the test execution. **Constant definitions** (they can also be contained in the module definition (see above)) have the familiar syntactical structure except the assignment symbol that TTCN-3 uses because the values can be assigned both within and outside of a module, e.g.,

> **const integer** sequ:=50;
>   **boolean** ok:=true;
> **external const integer** max;

Constants which are defined outside of the module have to be labeled with the key word **external**. The TTCN-3-standard does not specify how this assignment is performed.

Variables are declared with the familiar **var**-declaration. They can be initialized, e.g.,

> **var integer** i, j;
>   **boolean** eom:=false;

Timers are declared in a similar way, e.g.,

> **timer** t1, t2;
> **timer** t3:=5E-3;

Optionally, a default runtime (in seconds) can be defined for a timer. The assigned value must be a non-negative number of type **float**. Timers can also be passed as a parameter in functions.

The task of the control part is to determine the execution order of test cases. The execution of a test case is triggered by **execute**, as mentioned above. The test case must first be defined in the definition part of the module (see below). The definition determines the test steps and describes the required test configuration. The statements needed are introduced below. A simple sequence of test cases can be generated by several **execute**-statements. The execution order of the test cases may depend on the test course. To control the execution order including possible repetitions, familiar programming statements can be used, such as the **if-else**-statement, the **for**-statement, the **while**-statement, and the **do-while**-statement. Regarding assignments and expressions, the normal rules apply. The test execution may be stopped by means of the **stop**-statement.

14.7.2.2 Data type definitions

Data type definitions in TTCN-3 are largely based on familiar concepts. In addition, the data type concept has been harmonized with ASN.1. TTCN-3 distinguishes simple base types (e.g., **integer, char, boolean**), basic string types (e.g., **bitstring, hexstring, octetstring, charstring**), and structured types derived from them (e.g., **record, set, enumerated, union**). Compared to ASN.1, there are some syntactic changes, such as the use of **record** instead of SEQUENCE. In addition, a number of specific data types were introduced, such as **objid, verdicttype, address, port, component**, and **default** for the description of the test configuration and the test course. The type **anytype** can be used to refer to all known types of a TTCN-3-module. Examples of data type definitions are given below in the context of message declaration.

14.7.2.3 Test data

Test data are created in two steps. First, their structure is determined by describing the data formats. After that instances of these data formats are generated with concrete value assignments. The data formats are described in data type or signatures definitions depending on whether message- or procedure-based communication is used. For the generation of the test data, templates are deployed.

Message declarations

Messages are declared by means of data type definitions, usually a **record**-type, e.g.,

```
type record XDATrequ
        {integer    conn          optional,
         charstring source_addr   optional,
         charstring dest_addr      optional,
```

```
    boolean    eom,
    char[1..n]  data
  }.
```

Optional components are marked with **optional** as in ASN.1.

Procedure signatures

Procedure signatures, for short signatures, define the procedure interface for procedure-based communication. A signature consists of the procedure name, the parameter list (optional), and the specification of the interaction (blocking, non-blocking), e.g.,

signature request_1(**in integer** a, **out float** b, **inout boolean** c);
signature set(**in integer** x) **noblock**;

In addition to the data type, each parameter is marked by **in**, **out** or **inout** to indicate whether it is an input or an output parameter, or both.

Signatures with the attribute **noblock** refer to a non-blocking call, i.e., the caller does not expect a return value. In the parameter list these signatures may have only **in**-parameters. All other signatures are blocking ones, i.e., synchronous communication is applied in which the caller is usually waiting for a return value, e.g.,

signature request_2(**in integer** a, **inout integer** c) **return boolean**;

The return of a value after completion of the procedure is explicitly indicated by **return** and the type of the return value. In addition, values can also be returned to the caller by means of **out**- and **inout**-parameters. Additionally, **exceptions** can be specified regarding the return value for blocking and non-blocking procedures which may be raised by the called remote component (SUT, test component), e.g.,

signature request_3(**in integer** a, **inout integer** c) **return boolean**;
        exeption (integer);

The conversion of the exceptional values in TTCN-3 data types is system or tool dependent. It is not defined by the TTCN-3 standard.

Data templates

The test data for the individual test cases are derived from the message or signature definitions using data templates. These templates create concrete value assignments to the message components and the parameters of the procedure calls. The following example shows the generation of a message template for the XDT *XDATrequ* primitive.

```
type record XDATrequ_type                template XDATrequ_type XDATrequ_N:=
   {integer conn optional,                 {conn := 10,
    charstring source_addr optional,        source_addr := omit,
    charstring dest_addr optional,          dest_addr := omit,
    boolean eom,                            eom := false,
    char[1..n]data                          data := *
   } // Message definition                 } // Message template
```

With this data template, a *XDATrequ* primitive is generated that is passed to the XDT service provider after successfully setting up a connection. Therefore, the optional address fields are omitted. But it is not the last primitive of a transfer sequence, as *eom* is set to *false*. The wildcard symbol "*" indicates that a sequence of any values may be contained.

TTCN-3 defines various matching mechanisms that make it possible to determine whether the reactions of the SUT (messages or return values of procedures) correspond to the expected values. The data template for a *DT* PDU, for example, that would be sent out by the tester in response to an *XDATrequ* primitive would be

```
type record DT_type                      template DT_type  DT_N
   {integer(0..255) length,                {length := 0 to 255,
    bitstring code,                         code := '1000'B,
    charstring source-addr optional,        source-addr := omit,
    charstring dest-addr optional,          dest-addr := omit,
    integer conn  optional,                 conn := 0 to 10,
    integer sequ,                           sequ := ?,
    boolean eom,                            eom := false,
    char[1..n] data                         data:= *
   } // Message definition                 } // Message template
```

There is a broad range of possibilities for matching the definitions. Some of them are contained in the above example. So *lower* **to** *upper* describes a range of integer values which the expected values may have. The symbol **omit** indicates the omission of a value, "?" any value (wildcard), and "*", as already mentioned above, a sequence of values in an array. In addition, expressions can be given which result in a concrete value.

The definition of signature templates follows a similar scheme. TTCN-3 also defines the parameterization and the modification of templates.

14.7.2.4 Test configurations

The components of the test configuration are described as data types. There are two data type definitions: the *port type definition* and the *component type defini-*

tion. Based on this, the test configuration is created and dynamically adjusted with special configuration operations.

Ports

The port type definition specifies the communication directions of ports. The communication direction is set for each message or signature type, and individual values as well. The directions may be **in** for inbound, **out** for outbound, and **inout** for both directions, e.g.,

type port MP1 **message**
{**in** DT_type;
  out ACK_type, ABO_type;
  inout boolean;
}
	type port PP1 **procedure**
	{**in** proc1;
	  out proc2;
	}

The concept of a message is more generally understood here. It includes both messages that are generated by data templates as well as the current values of expressions. If the port type definition **all** is used, e.g.,

inout all;

then all data types and signatures which are defined in the module can be exchanged via this port.

The communication paradigm of the port is determined by the key word **message** or **procedure**, but also ports can be defined that allow for both forms of communication. They are specified by **mixed**.

Test components

The test component type definition specifies which ports belong to a test component, e.g.,

type component XDT_tester_type
  {**port** MP1 PCO1, PCO2;
   port PP1 PCO3;
   var integer N;
   timer t1;
  }.

The port names used are local to the component, i.e., they can also be used in another component declaration. The port names of a component must be unique.

A component type definition can further contain constant, variable, and timer declarations. These declarations are visible to all functions that execute these components (see *Test cases* below). Variables and timers are bound to the component instance, i.e., a new set of variables and timers will be created with each new instance of the component.

The abstract test system interface (cp. Figure 14.6/12) is also defined as a component because it is conceptually equivalent.

Configuration operations

Configuration operations are used to instantiate the used test configuration and to control and adjust it during the test run. These operations may only be applied in test cases, in functions, and in **altstep**-statements (see below). They are not used in the control part of a module. The configuration operations comprise operations to generate test components, to connect test components, and to control and monitor their execution. The most important operations and the principle of their application are described in the following.

All test components must be explicitly created. An exception is the main test component MTC which is automatically created when a test case is executed. All other components, i.e., the parallel test components, are instantiated by **create**, e.g.,

> **var** XDT_tester_type XDT_tester;
>
> .   .   .
>
> XDT_tester := XDT_tester_type.**create**;

The **create**-operation returns a reference to the generated test component, which is stored in a variable. Along with the test component, all ports will be generated. Their queues are empty. Test components can be created at any point in a behavior definition. The visibility of component references share the same scope rules variables.

After creating the test component it must be connected to the ports of other components or to the test system interface. This can be done with the operations **connect** and **map**. The first one connects the **in**- and **out**-part of the listed ports, e.g.,

> **connect**(XDT_tester: PCO1, **mtc**: PCO1);

The operation **mtc** identifies the main test component. The operation **map** describes the mapping on the test system interface. It merely performs a name mapping through which the communication between the test component and the test system interface is referenced, e.g.,

> **map**(XDT_tester: PCO2, **system**: PCOA);

The operation **system** here analogously identifies the test system interface. For connecting the ports, TTCN-3 defines a set of rules to ensure the consistency of the connections. They are partially checked at compile time, otherwise at runtime. The connections can be released by **disconnect** and **unmap**.

After creating a test component and connecting it with other test components it can be activated using the operation **start**, e.g.,

XDT_tester.**start**(XDT_behavior1);

The **start**-operation binds the associated test behavior to the test component. This behavior is previously defined in a function (see below).

A test component can stop another test component or even itself using the **stop**-operation, e.g.,

  if (verdict = error)
    XDT_tester.**stop**;

There are two possibilities for a test component to stop itself: **stop** and **self.stop**. The operation **self** has a similar function to **mtc** and **system**; it provides a reference to the test component itself. When a test component stops, all resources are released. If the main test component is to stop all parallel test components, this can be abbreviated by

  all component.stop;

Analogously, a test component can stop the main test component. This implies that all ongoing parallel test components will also be stopped, i.e., the test will be terminated.

Furthermore, it can be queried through **running** whether a test component is still active, e.g.,

  if (XDT_tester.**running**)   or   **while(all component.running)**
  {. . .}   {. . .}.

The result value is *true* or *false*. Here again, there is the option to query using **all** whether all components are active. It may be further queried whether one or all component(s) have already finished their work using the **done**-operation, e.g.,

  XDT_tester.**done**   or   **all component.done**.

The **done**-operation is not allowed to be used in logical expressions, only in **alt**-statements (see below). Furthermore, the **running**- and the **done**-operation may only be applied to parallel test components.

Communication operations

TTCN-3 provides various operations for the communication between test components. According to the applied communication paradigm, message- or procedure-based communication can be used. We consider here only message-based communication. Messages can be sent and received by means of the **send**- and the **receive**-operation. The associated port has to be specified for each operation. The data to be sent are either indicated directly as a parameter or specified by a reference to a data template, e.g.,

> PCO1.**send**(5);
> PCO2.**send**(XDATrequ_x) **to** SUT;

Optionally, the communication partner may still be specified through **to**. But this is only required for 1:N communication relations if a particular partner is being selected. Similar rules apply to the **receive**-operation. Now variables or matching templates have to be used instead of parameters for accepting data. Again the sender can optionally be specified after **from**, e.g.,

> PCOx.**receive**(a);
> PCOy.**receive**(XDATrequ_x_M) **from** SUT;
> **any port.receive**;

The **receive**-operation removes the first message from the input queue of the port if it meets the specified matching criteria; otherwise the message remains in the queue. If the **receive**-operation is contained in an **alt**-statement (see below) the next alternative will be processed in this case. A **receive** with no argument removes the message from the queue if any matching criterion is met. The statement **any port.receive** describes the reception of a message at any port.

If the first message is to be read and removed from the input queue the **trigger**-operation has to used, e.g.,

> PCOy.**trigger**(XDATrequ_x_M);

It behaves like a **receive**-operation if the matching conditions are met, otherwise the message is discarded.

Before **send**- and **receive**-operations can be executed, the port has to be started. For this, the **start**-operation is provided, e.g.,

> PCO1.**start**;

The **start**-operation clears the input queue and begins listening to the message exchange. By default, all ports are started implicitly when a test component is created. When the input queue is to be cleared during the active phase of a port, the **clear**-operation is used, e.g.,

> PCO1.**clear**.

A port is closed with **stop**, e.g.,

> PCO1.**stop**;

Thereafter no further operations can be executed on the port. Operations that were initiated before the **stop** are still terminated.

14.7.2.5 Test cases

In TTCN-3 test cases are defined as a specific form of a function (see below). Their execution is started in the module control part by **execute** (see Section 14.7.2.1 above). The return value of a test case is a value of type **verdicttype** that indicates the test verdict. A test case consists of an interface part, a system part (optionally), and the test behavior, e.g.,

```
testcase XDT_V1()
runs on XDT_tester_type          // Interface part
system SUT_type                  // System part
   {
     . . .                       // Test behavior
   }.
```

In the *interface part* the component type of the main test component (MTC) is given after **runs on**. Thus, the ports become visible within the main test component. The *system part* refers to the test system interface with the associated ports. This part can be omitted if only the main test component is instantiated in the test execution. In this case, the MTC type defines the ports of the test system interfaces.

When starting a test case with **execute** the main test component is created implicitly, i.e., without using **create-** and/or the **start**-operations. The ports of the main test component and test system interfaces are instantiated, and the specified test behavior is executed on the main test component.

Test behavior

TTCN-3 offers a wide range of statements for describing the test behavior. We have already introduced some of them. The basic statements were presented during the explanation of the control part of the module (see Section 14.7.2.1), the configuration and communication operations accordingly with the test configurations (see Section 14.7.2.4). Another important group comprises the statements which describe the behavior of the test components regarding the inputs and outputs at the ports.

alt-statement

The most important statement of this group is the **alt**-statement for describing alternative test behaviors, e.g.,

```
alt
  {[] PCO1.receive(XDATconf_1)         // Alternative 1
     {setverdict(pass);
      PCO1.stop;
     }
   [] t.timeout;                       // Alternative 2
     {setverdict(inconc);}
```

```
    [else]                                    // else-branch
      {error reaction_a;
       setverdict(fail);
       stop;
      }
    }.
```

The **alt**-statement follows the same principle as the *wait event*-statement of our model language which we introduced in Section 1.2. The only difference is that the latter does not define an **else**-branch.

The **alt**-statement can be multiply nested. For the selection of an alternative, a snapshot-like semantics as in TTCN-2 is applied (cp. Section 14.6.2). As a last alternative an **else**-branch can be specified, which is executed if none of the triggering events for the other alternatives occurred. It is possible to trigger a new snapshot in the **else**-branch by means of the **repeat**-statement:

```
    [else] {repeat}
```

which can lead to the selection of another alternative. The **repeat**-statement can also be used in other alternatives to trigger a reassessment of the **alt**-statement.

As is familiar from the other formal description techniques the triggering event may also be connected with an additional condition, which here precedes the event in square brackets, e.g.,

```
    [n>9] PCO1.receive(XDATconf_T1).
```

interleave-statement

A special variant of the **alt**-statement, which corresponds to the *par event*-statement of Section 1.2.4, is the **interleave**-statement which applies an interleaving semantics, e.g.,

```
    interleave
      {[] PCO1.receive(XDATrequ_T1)            // Behavior 1
        { ... }
       [] PCO2.receive(ACK_T2)                 // Behavior 2
        { ... }
      }
```

In contrast to the **alt**-statement, the **interleave**-statement reacts to all specified events in parallel, whereby their occurrence is random so that all interleaving sequences are possible (cp. Section 1.2.4). Thus, we can test, for instance, the concurrent arrival of *XDATrequ* primitives and *ACK*-PDUs in an XDT sender entity.

The **interleave**-statement is a shorthand representation. Interleaving semantics can also be expressed by means of the **alt**-statement. The use of the **interleave**-statement is limited to certain statements, such as **done, timeout, receive, trigger,** check etc. Control flow statements, such as **do-while, for, goto, stop, activate, deactivate** etc. are not allowed. In addition, no function calls (see below), no **else**-branch, and no additional conditions can be used.

Timer operations

For timer handling, TTCN-3 provides five operations. The operations **start** and **stop**, and the **timeout** event are known to us in principle from the first part of the book. In the **start** operation the time interval may be specified, e.g.,

t.**start**(20E-3);

otherwise the default interval declared in the timer declaration is taken. The other timer operations are **read** and **running**, e.g.,

x := t.**read**;

. . .

if (t.**running**)
{ *reaction* }

With **read** the elapsed time can be queried, with **running** accordingly whether the timer is active.

Assignment of a test verdict

Each test case results in a test verdict. It is derived from the local test verdicts of the test components (see Figure 14.7/10).

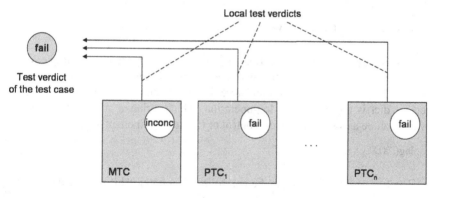

Figure 14.7/10: Derivation of the test verdict

To assign the local test verdicts the statements **setverdict** and **getverdict** can be used. The former sets the test verdict as was shown in previous examples, e.g.,

setverdict(inconc).

The initial value of the local test verdict is *none*. With the operation **getverdict** the current value of the test verdict can be read out for an evaluation, e.g.,

> verdict:=**getverdict.**

The final test case verdict is derived according to the overwriting rules contained in Table 14.7/1. For example, if the current value of the test verdict is *inconc* and another test component returns *pass* then the value of the test verdict remains unchanged, i.e., *inconc*.

Current value of the test verdict	New value to be assigned to the test verdict			
	pass	**inconc**	**fail**	**none**
none	*pass*	*inconc*	*fail*	*none*
pass	*pass*	*inconc*	*fail*	*pass*
inconc	*inconc*	*inconc*	*fail*	*inconc*
fail	*fail*	*fail*	*fail*	*fail*

Table 14.7/1: Overwriting rules for the verdict

The test verdict is returned after executing the test case. It must be stored in a variable in the control part of the module, otherwise it gets lost. This is done most easily by an assignment of the test verdict to a variable after invoking **execute**, e.g.,

> verdict:=**execute**(XDT_XS_v12);

A comparison with the **execute**-statement in the introductory example above (cp. Section 14.7.2.1) shows that **execute** can be invoked both as a procedure and as a function. The former does not store the test verdict. A possibility to store the test verdict is the use of the **log**-operation, which writes a string into a log file which can be assigned to the test control or to a test component, e.g.,

> **log**(„XDT_XS_v12 pass");[11]

The test case execution may be controlled by a timer. This may be done by introducing a time-out in the **execute**-statement, e.g.,

> verdict:=**execute**(XDT_XS_v12, 10E-3);

---

[11] How the logging function is supported by the system is left open in the standard.

In this case, the execution of the test case is terminated by the time-out, i.e., 10 ms in our example. If the test case is not finished at the time-out the test case verdict is set to *error*. The timer used is a system timer that needs neither to be declared nor started.

Functions

TTCN-3 provides the opportunity to structure the description of the test behavior by functions to encapsulate frequently recurring test procedures in separate, recallable units. The syntactic and semantic structure of functions in TTCN-3 corresponds to conventional concepts. Functions may have one or no return value. The latter corresponds to a procedure, but this is not distinguished syntactically by a different keyword. The function can be called in an expression or explicitly in a call statement, e.g.,

```
function break(in DP DP_type) return boolean
    { . . .
      return x;
    };

if break(SP)
    setverdict(fail);
```

The parameterization of the functions applies the same rules as for signatures (cp. Section 14.7.2.3). As usual, a function consists of a declaration part and a statement part. In the *declaration part* constants, variables, and timers can be locally introduced. Constants, variables, timers, and ports that are defined in a component declaration may be used too. In this case, the component type must be specified in the function header after **runs on**, e.g.,

```
function break(in DP DP_type) return boolean runs on XDT_tester_type{...};
```

In the *statement part* all operations for the description of test behaviors introduced above can be used.

Functions may also be declared as being defined externally. In this case, only the interface of the function has to be specified. The declaration is preceded by the keyword **external**. Moreover, TTCN-3 provides a lot of pre-defined functions. These include functions for data type conversion, functions for determining the length or size of data structures, string functions, selection functions, and functions to prove the presence of certain options.

Defaults

Defaults may be used to specify the test behavior to be executed when the explicitly defined behavior cannot be executed because the test course and thus the occurring events do not allow this. Defaults are described with the help of the **altstep**-statement, for short *altstep*, which are scope units similar to functions. *altstep* defines a set of alternatives, so-called *top alternatives*. The description of the top alternatives has syntactically the same structure as the description of the alternatives in the **alt**-statement. Unlike the **alt**-statement, *altstep* defines its own scope in which local constants, variables, and timers may be declared. Access to variables and timers declared in a component declaration is also allowed. For this, the component has to be specified after **runs on**, e.g.,

```
altstep Default_1() runs on XDT_tester_type
  {var integer n:=0;
   [] PCO1.receive(DT_x);
     {n:=n+1;
      if (n>10)
         setverdict(pass);
     }
   [] PCO2.receive(ABO_x);
     {setverdict(inconc);
      stop;
     }
   [] t.timeout                         // t is declared in XDT_tester_type
     {setverdict(fail);
      stop;
     }
  }
```

The alternatives are described by the familiar statements. Functions can be called as well. *Altsteps* can also be parameterized and declared as default.

The invocation of an *altstep* is always connected to an **alt**-statement. There are two options: by an explicit call within an **alt**-statement or implicitly by a default mechanism. The explicit call is indicated like a function call by the name of the *altstep* as an alternative in the **alt**-statement, e.g.,

```
alt
  {[] PCO1.receive { ... }
   [] t1.timeout { ... }
   [] Default_1()                       // explicit call of an altstep
  };
```

When an implicit call is applied, the *altstep* must be activated as a default by means of an **activate**-statement before the point of invocation is reached. For this, default references are used which are stored in predefined variables of the type **default**, e.g.,

```
var default d1 := null;                 // null is an initialization

   . . .

d1 := activate(Default_1());
```

The **activate**-operation inserts the activated default in the default list (see below). It can now be executed. A default can be removed from the default list by **deactivate**, e.g.,

  deactivate(Default_1());

The scope of the operation **deactivate** is local to the test component, i.e., **deactivate** cannot deactivate any defaults of other test components.

Default mechanism

Each test component stores the defaults, i.e., the activated *altsteps*, in a default list which can be updated using the operations **activate** and **deactivate** introduced above. The default mechanism is activated at the end of each **alt**-statement if none of the specified alternatives can be executed according to the current snapshot. It selects the first *altstep* in the default list and waits for the result of the execution. If one of the top alternatives can be selected and executed then the execution is successful. In this case, the execution can be continued accordingly to the specification of the test behavior. Otherwise, the next *altstep* is selected. This process is repeated until either a successful execution is found or no more activated *altsteps* are found. An unsuccessful termination triggers a new snapshot with the related evaluation procedure. If no executable alternative is found this procedure will be repeated until the test component is stopped either by another test component, e.g., the main test component, or a dynamic error occurs that blocks the test component.

14.7.3   Test execution

Besides the TTCN-3 core language and the various presentation formats, the TTCN-3 standard also specifies in parts 5 and 6 the architecture of the test system for executing TTCN-3 test suites [ETSI 07a,b]. The architecture is depicted in Figure 14.7/11.

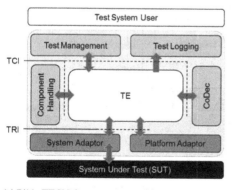

Legend:
TE – TTCN-3 Executable
TCI – TTCN-3 Control Interface
TRI – TTCN-3 Runtime Interface

Figure 14.7/11: TTCN-3 test system architecture

The TTCN-3 test system architecture consist of a set of interacting units that control the test execution, take over the communication with the SUT, and provide external functions including timers. The test system processes the **TTCN-3 executable** (TE) which comprises the executable TTCN-3 code received after compiling a TTCN-3 module and the TTCN-3 runtime system. The TTCN-3 executable interacts with other units, such as the test management, the component handling, and the codec via the **TTCN-3 control interface (TCI)**.

The **test management** (TM) handles the test execution. It provides operations to execute tests and to set module parameters. The **test logging** (TL) is part of the test management. It records the test events. The **component handling** (CH) is responsible for communication between test components. Its application programming interface provides operations to create and delete test components, to establish connections between them, and to manage test verdicts. The **codec** (CD) encodes TTCN-3 values into bitstrings to send them to the SUT and decodes the received values back to TTCN-3 values.

The TTCN-3 executable communicates with the SUT via the **TTCN-3 runtime interface (TRI)**. This defines the interfaces with the system adaptor and the platform adaptor, respectively. The **system adaptor** (SA) provides the operation to communicate with the SUT. The **platform adaptor** (PA) provides timers and external functions. The latter have to be declared in the TTCN-3 modules. Timers have to be implemented outside the TTCN-3 test system.

TTCN-3 tests can also be performed as distributed tests using several test devices (see Figure 14.7/12). The test executable is initiated at each device by the test management. The communication between the parallel test components is again coordinated by the component handler. A special test executable is required to initiate the start test case and to derive the final test verdict.

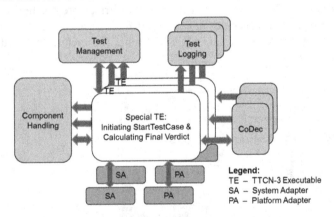

Figure 14.7/12: Distributed TTCN-3 test system

14.7.4 Example

As a final example, we give the TTCN-3 representation of the test case that we used in the introduction to TTCN-2 in Section 14.6. The purpose of the test case is to verify that the IUT of the XDT sender entity *XS* successfully sets up a connection and transfers the first data unit.

We describe the test case by a module. The *definition part* contains the XDT data formats, the data templates, the test component, and the test case. The execution of the test case is represented in the *control part*. Since the XDT data format definitions are familiar from other sections of the book we do not list them here again. Instead we "import" these definitions from the module *XDT_basics*. The definitions are pooled in a group. The data template definitions are also not listed here. The principle has been demonstrated for some XDT data formats above (cp. Section 14.7.2.3). The test architecture used is a local tester. Accordingly, we define a lower and an upper port or PCO, respectively. Note that the communication directions of the ports are seen from the testers' perspective. For this reason, the communication direction **out** is assigned to the primitive *XDATrequ*, for example. Since we have only one test component, the test case description does not contain a system part because the test execution is started by the main test component. The main test component is created implicitly through **execute**.

The test case description reflects relatively straightforwardly the test course that leads to a positive test outcome (*pass*). The negative test outcomes are described by two defaults. *Default_1* is executed when other messages than the specified ones arrive at one of the ports or if the test execution is not completed within 2 seconds. The latter is monitored by the timer *ts*. *Default_2* describes the abandonment of the connection set up triggered by a time-out in the *XS*-IUT. Since this may be caused either by the implementation or by the test system, the test verdict *inconc* is assigned.

```
module XDT_test_1
          // Test of a successful XDT connection set up with one data transmission
  {import group XDT data formats from XDT basics;  // Import definitions

  // Definition part
                                                    // Data templates
    template XDATrequ_type XDATrequ_1:= {...};      // XDATrequ_1
    template XDATrequ_type XDATrequ_N:= {...};      // other XDATrequ
    template XDATconf_type XDATconf_1:= {...};      // XDATconf_1
    template XDATconf_type XDATrequ_N:= {...};      // other XDATconf
    template XABORTind_type XABORTind:= {...};      // XABORTind
    template DT_type DT_1:= {...};                  // DT_1
    template DT_type DT_N:= {...};                  // other DT
    template ACK_type ACK_1:= {...};               // ACK_1
    template ACK_type ACK_N:= {...};               // other ACK
```

```
type port XS_U_type message              // Definition upper port (PCO)
  {out XDATrequ_type ;
   in XDATconf_type, XABORTind_type ;
}
type port XS_L_type message              // Definition lower port (PCO)
  {in DT_type;
   out ACK_type;
}
type component XDT_tester_type
  {port XS_U_type U;                     // Upper port (service interface)
   port XS_L_type L;                     // Lower port (Protocol interface)
   timer ts:= 2.0;                       // Timer for test supervision
}
altstep Default() runs on XDT_tester_type          // Default definition 1
  {[] any port.receive {setverdict(fail); stop}
   [] any timer.timeout {setverdict(fail); stop}
}
altstep AbortDefault() runs on XDT_tester_type     // Default definition 2
  {[] U.receive(XABORTind);              // Set up aborted
     {setverdict(inconc);
      stop;
      }
}

testcase successful_set up() runs on XDT_tester_type
  {activate(Default());                  // Activation Default_1
   U.send(XDATrequ_1);
   ts.start;
   L.receive(DT_1) ;
   activate(AbortDefault());             // Activation Default_2
   L.send(ACK_1);
   U.receive(XDATconf_1);                // Successful set up
   U.send(XDATrequ_N);
   L.receive(DT_N);
   U.receive(XDATconf_N);
   L.send(ACK_N);
   setverdict(pass);
   ts.stop;
   }
// control part
   control
     {verdict:=execute(successful_set up (), 10);}   // Test case execution
} // XDT_Test_1                                       // max. duration 10 s
```

```
// external XDT declarations

module XDT_basics
   {group XDT_data_formats
      {type record XDATrequ_type {...};
       type record XDATconf_type {...};
       type record XABORTind_type {...};
       type record DT_type {...};
       type record ACK_type {...};
      }
   }
```

When considering the example one may wonder why the test case description does not contain an **alt**-statement, although two *altsteps* are activated. For this, we finally refer to a further specific definition in TTCN-3. A single **receive**-statement corresponds to an **alt**-statement with only one alternative. Thus, the statement *L.receive (DT_1)* implicitly opens an **alt**-statement which then also enables the default execution.

Further reading

There have been many papers published about testing communication protocols, most of them in the conference series *TestCom* [TestCom] and *Forte* [FORTE]. The reader is referred to the proceedings for further reading, for references to the original papers about the methods introduced in this chapter, and for information about recent research results. Unfortunately, there are not so many books about this topic.

Introductions to the protocol conformance test methodology can be found in [Sari 93] and [Baum 94]. For detailed information, the reader should look in the standard texts of CTMF [ISO 9646] and FMCT [ISO 13245]. There are few book publications on interoperability testing because it is mainly driven by practical requirements. Here we recommend again the proceedings of the *TestCom* series for recent results and the papers cited in Section 14.4.

More details about the various methods for the derivation of test cases can be found in the original papers referred to in Section 14.3. A comprehensive overview on the FSM-based derivation methods with the algorithms for deriving the various sets is given in the book of Mathur [Math 08]. Further background to the algebraic test derivation methods is given in [Tret 96a,b], [Brin 97], and in the book of Bowman and Gomez [Bowm 06]. A comparison of FSM- and algebraic-based test methods is contained in [Petr 94].

The test description languages TTCN-2 and TTCN-3 are described in several publications. A compact introduction to TTCN-2 is contained in [Baum 94]. An analogous introduction to TTCN-3 is given in the book of Willcock et al. [Will 05]. Further reading on TTCN-3 (tutorials and references to papers) besides the cited papers can be found on the ETSI's official home page on TTCN-3: http://www.ttcn-3.org/.

Exercises

(1) What is a test? What is the difference between testing and verification? What statements can a test make?

(2) Explain the difference between the test types white box and black box testing.

(3) What is the task of conformance testing? Explain the principle of the conformance test and the steps needed to perform it.

(4) Explain the notions test case, test purpose, and test suite. Why is the conformance test a specification-based test?

(5) What is the difference between the test verdicts *pass*, *fail*, and *inconclusive*? How is the test verdict of a test suite derived? Is a protocol implementation error-free if it passed a test suite with verdict *pass*?

(6) How is a protocol test architecture built up in principle? Explain the most basic components and their interaction.

(7) What is the difference between local and distributed test methods?

(8) Describe the main steps of the conformance assessment process in CTMF. Explain the difference between static and dynamic conformance requirements. What is the role of PICS and PIXIT in this process?

(9) How is conformance defined in FMCT?

(10) What is the purpose of certification in the context of conformance testing? Comment on the different forms of guarantees (first, second, third party). What measures of certification are preferred today?

(11) Explain the principle of how a transition is tested in FSM-based testing. How do these steps correspond to the test phases *preamble, test body, postamble* of CTMF? How is the postamble usually presented?

(12) What is a fault model? What are the most important fault models for FSM-based testing? When does a test suite have full fault coverage?

(13) What is a mutant? What can it be used for?

(14) What assumptions should a finite state machine meet to be used as a basis for test case derivation?

(15) What is a transition tour? What is its limitation for testing?

(16) What are the differences between the test derivation methods *Distinguishing Sequence, W-Method*, and *UIO Sequence Method*? When are they used appropriately? How is a test suite principally defined for these methods?

(17) Create the FSM description of the XDT receiver entity for the explicit connection set up as described in exercise 11 of Section 2. Replace the input and output events by a unique letter. Characterize the automaton with respect to the conditions for a test case derivation mentioned in exercise (14)?

(18) Derive a transition tour for the automaton of exercise (17). Construct an erroneous implementation of the automaton that cannot be detected by this test suite.

(19) For the following automaton

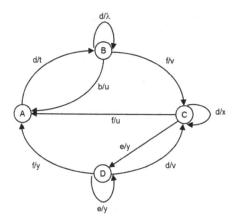

a distinguishing sequence can be determined. Give the test suite for this automaton.

(20) If one output event is changed in the automaton of exercise (19) the distinguishing sequence cannot be applied any more. Determine the characterization set *W* of the changed automaton and derive the test suite.

(21) Derive a test suite for the automaton of exercise (17). What derivation method is appropriate?

(22) Explain the terms implementation relation and testing relation in the context of algebraic specifications. Give examples of testing relations.

(23) Discuss the testing relations *trace preorder* and *testing preorder* in comparison to the equivalence relations *trace equivalence* and *testing equivalence*.

(24) Given the behavior expression $a;(a[]b;c;(e[]f))$ as specification. Determine whether the following observations $a;a$, $a,b;c;d$, $a;b;c$, $a;b;c;f$, $a;a;b$ of an implementation of the above expression are in trace and/or testing preorder with the specification.

(25) Explain the difference of the **conf**-relation compared to testing preorder. What is the role of the canonical tester in this context? Which of the expressions in exercise (24) meet the **conf**-relation?

(26) What distinguishes the *ioco*-relation from the testing relations mentioned before?

(27) Why is the complete test suite often not executed? What criteria are applied for the selection of test cases?

(28) What is test coverage? What types of test coverage are distinguished?

(29) What is the purpose of interoperability testing? Why may conforming implementations fail to be interoperable?

(30) How does the interoperability test differ from the conformance test? What test methods are applied for the interoperability test? Characterize an interoperability test case.

(31) Derive an interoperability test case for the XDT explicit connection set up as described in exercise 11 of Section 2. Indicate the transitions that should be passed in both entities when the test case is executed.

(32) We assume an active interoperability test of the XDT protocol in which all *ACK*s are removed starting from ACK_i. This finally leads to an abandonment of the connection. Indicate all transitions that should be passed in both entities after beginning the removal.

15 Outlook

The goal of this book was to give an introduction to the field of *Protocol Engineering*. Starting from the basic principles of communication protocols we presented various methods and techniques used for the description, implementation, and validation of communication protocols. Throughout the book we tried to find a balance between the theoretical and the practical aspects of protocol development, pointing out at the same time the possibilities and the limitations of the various approaches developed. *Protocol Engineering* was one of the hottest topics in the upswing of computer network technology. Meanwhile excitement has quieted down around *Protocol Engineering*. At the end of this book we want to discuss the reasons for this and give some prospects on future developments.

Protocol Engineering combines aspects of telecommunication, distributed systems, software engineering, and theoretical computer science. This made it attractive for many researchers and initiated a lot of research work. Communication protocols though may be, as repeatedly emphasized in the book, very complex. Already relatively simple protocols like the XDT protocol show how difficult it is to properly understand the process flow in a communication protocol. The complexity of protocol procedures, their partial concurrency, nondeterministic behavior, and various requirements regarding performance, reliability, integration into the execution environment, etc. make protocol development complicated. The proof of the correct functioning of a protocol is therefore difficult and currently feasible only for less complex protocols. Theoretical research has yielded many contributions to tackle the related problems, but it has never really succeeded in meeting the demands of practical protocol development. Many approaches use simplifying assumptions or are proved with less complex protocols. Thus, few approaches come to practical importance.

A systematic engineering design of communication protocols requires formal methods because exact design decisions, verification proofs, exact coding, and efficient tests are only possible based on precise descriptions and unambiguous interpretations. The use of formal methods forms therefore the basis of *Protocol Engineering*. Several formal description techniques and various approaches have been investigated. The usefulness of formal techniques in the protocol development process and for precise protocol specifications has been demonstrated in many ways. Despite the obvious advantages of formal description techniques and the state of development they have reached, they are only of limited use for practical protocol development. The majority of protocols are designed ad hoc and rarely described formally. If applied, formal description techniques are mainly used as a supplement to support, for instance, single stages, e.g., test case derivations. The reason for this is that some aspects relevant in practice have been underestimated in theoretical research. We comment on some of these reasons in the following:

- **User acceptance**
  The utility of formal description techniques and their applicability to real pro-tocol developments has not been demonstrated convincingly for many potential users. The arguments usually given are high learning efforts, high development costs for specifications, lack of tool support, and inadequate efficiency of de-rived implementations. We address these aspects subsequently. The significant time pressure under which developers often work causes them to shy away from the alleged overhead in the use of formal description techniques. The nu-merous success stories for the application of formal description techniques in practice cannot belie this fact. Often formal methods experts have a decisive part in such case studies.

- **Learning efforts**
  Formal description techniques require a certain effort to learn the language and associated semantic model. This effort is comparable to that of learning a pro-gramming language. It is often shied away from, especially when the benefit seems not to have been convincingly demonstrated, yet.

- **Specification development effort**
  The development of a formal description based on a given informal specifica-tion requires an effort which should not be underestimated. Since most formal description techniques represent constructive methods (cp. Section 7.3), the ef-fort can be compared with that of an implementation. It can take several weeks or months. Specifications with a size from 2000 to 10,000 lines are not un-common. The high cost stems from the complexity of the protocol procedures, the compliance with the formal semantics of the applied technique, and the time needed to validate the specification. The size of real-life formal protocol specifications also explains why more abstract description techniques, such as LOTOS, have failed to find wide practical application, while techniques with graphical support, such as SDL, MSC or increasingly UML, are more popular.

- **Tool support**
  The success and acceptance of formal description techniques depend crucially on the availability of tools that support their application. The size of formal protocol descriptions and the complexity of the different verification and vali-dation methods are not controllable without the support of tools. Only through tools is a convenient and efficient application of formal description techniques possible. They automate procedures that are difficult to perform manually and thus shorten the development time significantly. Tools at the same time also al-low users who are less familiar with the theoretical background to access for-mal description techniques. Figure 15/1 shows the possible application areas of tools in the protocol development. Tool development is not part of the stand-ardization of formal description techniques. A variety of tools have been devel-oped to support the various phases of the protocol development process. Most of them were created in universities or in the academic environment. These tools are mostly prototypes, which even though sometimes very mature seldom meet the requirements of commercial usage. Often the conditions for their

maintenance and further development are lacking. Some mature tools were mentioned in previous chapters. The most famous tools are the LOTOS/LTS toolset CADP (*Construction and Analysis of Distributed Processes*) [CADP] and the model checker SPIN [Holz 04]. Commercial tools were developed for the languages SDL, MSC, ASN.1, TTCN-2, and TTCN-3, but they are not focused only on *Protocol Engineering* applications. A general problem with many tools is that the familiarization effort may be pretty high. Another problem is the lack of continuous support for the entire protocol development process. Many tools are targeted to specific applications and development phases.

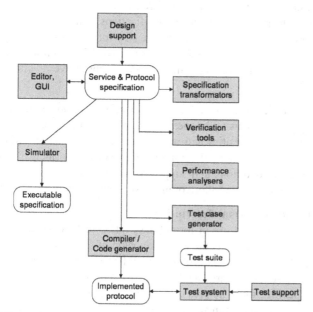

Figure 15/1: Application areas of tools in protocol development

- **Continuous technology support**
  As just mentioned for tool support, formal description techniques do not support the whole protocol development process. Many stages, especially verification and testing, often require special input notations which mean an additional expense to transform the specification. These transformations cannot always be executed automatically.
- **Insufficient implementation support**
  Automatically derived protocol implementations are primarily used for prototyping because their efficiency is not sufficient for network operation. In networks manually coded protocols are deployed. Thus, the protocol is "described" in fact twice: once in the design specification, and once in the encoding process in the given programming language. Since the costs for writ-

ing the specification, as discussed above, are as high as that of the implementation, the elaboration of the formal specification is often omitted.

- **Availability of formal descriptions**

  One of the crucial problems in the use of formal description techniques is that there are too few formal protocol descriptions available, particularly of Internet protocols. Due to the high development effort, they are, if at all, generally only available after the first implementations. This reduces their importance as reference specifications, since the benefits of formal descriptions for the protocol development process cannot be fully exploited. In addition, many specifications are elaborated at universities and research institutions and are often not complete enough to serve as reference specifications. Often formal specifications are an informative supplement. A positive step forward was made by the *European Telecommunications Standards Institute* (ETSI) which allows the use of formal techniques, in particular SDL, either as normative or informative (see [ETSI 99-2].

The successful deployment of formal description techniques implies the willingness to apply them. This willingness is given more in the vicinity of the developers, especially at universities and research institutions, than anywhere else. In order to place the development of communication software principally on a formal basis, a number of conditions and supportive measures are necessary to help to overcome the aforementioned shortcomings. We finally summarize them:

- **Early provision of formal descriptions**

  Prerequisite for a broad use of formal description techniques and the full utilization of all their benefits is the early provision of formal descriptions for newly developed communication protocols and distributed systems. Specially written formal descriptions are needed that are provided with the design as a reference specification. The provision should be made by recognized bodies so that these specifications can serve as a basis for a large number of protocol implementations. As long as this is not the case, the effect of formal description techniques in protocol development will remain limited.

- **Further development of description techniques**

  The continuous development of formal description techniques is an essential prerequisite for their widespread use in practical protocol development. Here it is especially necessary to adapt the techniques to new requirements. In research, such issues are usually quickly taken up and elaborated in extension and amendment proposals. But only a few later go into new official language extensions. Another important aspect is the development of language solutions that support the intuitive thinking of the protocol developer. Although controversially discussed in the *Protocol Engineering* area UML may play an important role in this context because it provides sufficient means to describe communication protocols and their services and attracts broad research activities.

- **Teaching formal description techniques**
  The application of formal description techniques requires the willingness on the part of the protocol developer to learn them. The teaching of formal description techniques already during education may, as experience with programming languages shows, support this readiness. This approach is, however, ultimately only successful if the benefits of its application can be demonstrated convincingly.

- **Case studies**
  Case studies will continue of one of the most important means of demonstrating the applicability of formal description techniques. Further experience reports will undoubtedly support broader usage.

- **Tool support**
  Tool development, as argued above, plays a key role in the enforcement of formal description techniques. The widespread use of formal description techniques in particular needs tools which continually evolve. This is usually the case with commercial products or tool sets developed in research institutions over a longer period of time, such as CADP or SPIN. Furthermore, these tools should be easy and intuitive to operate so that their use does not depend on the expertise of a few developers.

- **Automation of the protocol development process**
  The real breakthrough would be a largely automated protocol and system development process which consistently supports all phases as a computer-aided design process which combines various methods in a single technological process together with an automated mapping between different presentation forms. That would relieve the engineer from many troublesome transformation steps, and allow him/her largely to make design changes only in the specification. With current formal description techniques, such a full automation is difficult to realize. This requires a more general approach which in particular supports various presentations. The UML research may be helpful for this purpose.

In the development and application of formal description techniques great progress has been made over the last 15 to 20 years. Many approaches have been developed and their applicability proved. Large contributions have been made to theory. Some proposed methods are successfully applied in practice. Nevertheless, it may be asked at the end of this book, why a limited engineering problem like protocol design and development has not been solved yet. The reason is that many approaches presented in this book aim primarily at the development of the related theory rather than solving the engineering problem. So *Protocol Engineering* will continue to pose interesting questions for future research.

Glossary

ASN.1 (*Abstract Syntax Notation One*): Informal notation of ISO and ITU-T to describe abstract syntaxes. It consists of two components: the abstract syntax notation and the coding rules. The latter can be chosen freely, the most famous coding rules are the *Basic Encoding Rules* (BER). ASN.1 was originally developed for the transformation of different data representations in heterogeneous computer networks as defined in layers 6 and 7 of the OSI reference model. Later it became a popular notation for describing the data formats (PDUs, service primitives) of communication services and protocols. ASN.1 is being combined with other formal description techniques and notations, such as TTCN and SDL.

Automatic repeat request (*ARQ*): Protocol function which automatically triggers the retransmission of a lost or corrupted PDU in a stream of PDUs. The retransmission is triggered by a time-out due to a missing acknowledgement. There are two methods: *go back N* and *selective repeat*. With *go back N*, all PDUs starting from the missing N^{th} PDU are retransmitted, whereas *selective repeat* only retransmits the missing PDU.

Behavior tree: Graphical representation of behavior expressions used in process calculi. A behavior tree is a transition-oriented representation of the (in general infinite) behavior which contains the possible sequence of actions. The edges correspond to actions, the nodes to states, which, however, are not explicitly denoted. The root of the tree is the initial state. Alternative behavior is represented by different branches

Bisimulation: A binary relation between state transition systems associating systems which behave equally in the sense that one system simulates the other and vice-versa. Bisimilar systems must be able to simulate in any state the possible behavior of the other system and always return to a bisimilar state. There are two variants of bisimulation: strong and weak bisimulation. *Strong bisimulation* takes internal actions into account, while *weak bisimulation* lifts this restriction.

Certification: Administrative process for the award of a certificate that confirms the conformance of a protocol implementation with the associated protocol standard.

Communication architecture: Defined architecture of protocol layers for computer networks which determines the functionality of the layers as well as the principles of interaction between them. Communication architectures define architectural elements for describing the interaction between layers, such as service access points. The OSI reference model is an example of a communication architecture.

Communication protocol: see *Protocol*

Communication service: see *Service*

Communication software: Software that implements a protocol stack. It is embedded in the operating system.

Conformance test: Test to check whether a protocol implementation is compliant with the associated specification. With standardized protocols, compliance with the protocol standard is tested. Conformance is a necessary prerequisite for the interoperability of different protocol implementations. The conformance test is a black box test that proves whether the implementation behaves externally as specified. It forms the basis of protocol testing.

Connection: Logical relation between two service users for the duration of the communication that is established between the associated service access points. Protocols are differentiated regarding the establishment of a connection into connection-oriented and connectionless protocols. Connection-oriented protocols guarantee a reliable transmission of the data by preserving the transmission order. A connection must be explicitly set up before data transmission and released afterwards.

Constructive description methods: Specification methods for communication protocols that describe the protocol through an abstract model whose execution determines how the communicating entities behave. The description represents a quasi-implementation of the protocol on a more abstract level. Executable prototypes can be derived from the specification to validate the design. Examples of constructive description methods are finite state machines and labeled transition systems.

CTMF (*Conformance testing methodology and framework*)**:** General framework of ISO for conducting conformance tests. It defines the notion of conformance and the steps needed to assess the conformance of a protocol implementation. Further, it provides methods, procedures, and guidelines for the practical execution of conformance tests in test laboratories. The methodology is described in the ISO standard IS 9646. CTMF represents the basis of conformance testing and has sustainably influenced research on protocol testing. It was later joined by FMTC (*Formal Methods in Conformance Testing*) which describes the use of formal methods in conformance testing.

Descriptive description methods: Description methods for communication protocols that formulate properties the protocol to be designed should meet. These properties are safety and liveness properties. The properties are usually expressed in a temporal logic. The advantage of descriptive methods is the explicit specification of desired properties the design should meet and their verification for appropriateness under complete abstraction from an implementation. The derivation of implementations from a descriptive specification, however, is difficult.

E-LOTOS (*Enhanced LOTOS*): Enhancement of the FDT LOTOS. It contains among other things a number of extensions, such as predefined data types, the introduction of time, and a generalized parallelism operator. The enhancement did not find a broad application.

Estelle (*Extended State Transition Language*): One of the three standardized formal descriptions techniques developed in the 1980s. It was standardized by ISO for the description of distributed concurrent information processing systems, especially communication services and protocols. Estelle was defined as an extension of ISO-Pascal level 0 by means for the description of distributed systems using a hierarchical structure of communicating extended finite state machines. The language is not used any more.

Extended finite state machine (*EFSM*): Extension of the finite state machine by variables to store context information. A context is given by the current values of the variables. Extended finite state machines is the most popular description method for communication protocols. They form the basis for the semantic model of the FDTs Estelle and SDL. But EFSM descriptions may also become very complex.

Ferry clip method: Frequently used method for implementing the feedback between the test system and system under test (SUT) in distributed test settings. It uses an out-of-band signalization for transporting test data and test outcomes between them. In the test system an active ferry clip, which is connected with the lower and the upper tester, controls the communication. The counterpart is the passive ferry clip in the SUT which interacts with the IUT. All abstract test methods can be implemented using the ferry clip method.

Finite state machine (*FSM*): Models behavior by an automaton composed of a finite number of states, transitions between the states, and actions, e.g., inputs and outputs. Finite state machines are a popular method for describing the behavior of protocol entities. The number of states, however, may soon become very large so that they are limitations on their applicability for larger protocol and system descriptions because the representation often becomes too complex. Extended finite state machines are preferred instead. Finite state descriptions are used as a basis for test case derivations.

Flow control: Protocol function to regulate the number of PDUs exchanged between sender and receiver entity. It protects the receiver entity from being overloaded with PDUs it cannot process. There are two kinds of flow control: window-based and rate-based flow control. The former is a pure end-to-end relation which indicates the number of PDUs to be sent by a "window" of sequence numbers which smoothly moves on when the reception of a PDU is confirmed. Rate-based flow control additionally takes the network load into account by admitting only so many PDUs to the network that they can pass smoothly through it. The allowed rate cannot exceed the number of PDUs accepted by the receiver entity.

Formal description technique (*FDT*): Description technique with a formally defined syntax and semantics. The formal semantics ensures a unique interpretation of the specification and represents the basis for tool developments. Examples are the classical standardized specification languages Estelle, LOTOS, and SDL.

Fragmentation: see *Segmentation*

Go back N: see *Automatic repeat request*

Handshake: Protocol function used to synchronize communicating entities. One differentiates between 2-way and 3-way handshakes. The latter is needed for duplex communication.

Implementation specification: Documentation of the implementation design. It forms the basis for the coding of the protocol. The implementation specification is typically a refinement of the protocol specification. In contrast to the protocol specification, however, it is focused on a target execution environment.

Implementation relation: Asymmetric relation between a specification and an implementation that determines under what conditions the implementation can be considered as conformant to the specification. It defines the dynamic conformance requirements that determine the permissible observable behavior of the implementation. Implementation relations are particularly used in process calculi to describe the relationship between a specification and a refined, more deterministic presentation – the implementation.

IUT (*Implementation under test*): Reference to the (protocol) implementation to be tested.

Interleaving: Often applied semantic model in Formal Description Techniques for concurrent processes. It interprets the concurrent execution as a linear order of events in which the executed events of the processes "interleave", i.e., they appear arbitrarily ordered with respect to one another. All interleaving sequences represent possible externally observable behavior of the system. The other semantic model is true concurrency, which, however, is less applied in the FDT context.

Internal event: Means for describing events which originate nondeterministically inside the specified systems, e.g., system failures. Internal events are handled differently in different formal description techniques, e.g., through spontaneous transitions in automata representations or as an explicit internal action in algebraic descriptions.

Interoperability test: Test to examine the interaction capability of different implementations of the same protocol. The need for interoperability tests mainly results from the use of protocol options which, if selected differently, may lead to conformant but not interoperable implementations.

Layer: Important element of the hierarchical structuring of communication or protocol architectures. A layer comprises all entities of the given communication or protocol architectures that cooperate in providing a service using a communication protocol. It provides one or more services to the upper layer. A layer may contain several communication protocols which use the service(s) of the underlying layer for communication. The service(s) is usually accessible at defined access points.

Layered architecture: Defined architecture of protocol layers for computer networks. A layered architecture defines the functionality of the layers as well as the principles of interaction between them. It does not prescribe how the architecture is implemented in a computer system. There are two ways of defining layered architectures. *Communication architectures* use architectural elements for describing the basis model elements, e.g., entities, service access points, and others. *Protocol architectures* define a dedicated layering of protocols which are often used for a certain class of applications. One further distinguishes between closed and open architectures. *Closed architectures* are targeted to a specific application field. They take the specific requirements of the application area into account. A special variant of closed architectures are the *producer-related* architectures (proprietary architectures), which are aligned with the hardware and software products of a certain company. *Open architectures* define uniform principles for communication among heterogeneous computer systems. Any computer system that follows these principles can be integrated into the network. Open architectures require standardized communication protocols.

Liveness properties: Important properties in the design of communication protocols and distributed systems. Together with safety properties they are the subject of the verification process. Liveness properties state that eventually something good happens. They ensure that the specified events eventually occur and the desired states are reached. Liveness properties describe the expected (good) system properties that the system must consequently satisfy. In descriptive specification methods they are usually expressed in temporal logic formulae. Properties, such as livelock freedom, resynchronization, and termination are, for instance, liveness properties.

LOTOS (*Language of Temporal Ordering Specification*): Algebraic formal description technique for the description of distributed systems; was standardized by ISO. LOTOS is based on the process calculus CCS of Milner for the behavioral description and the algebraic data specification language ACT ONE for the data description. It distinguishes two language versions: *Basic LOTOS* for the description of the process interactions and *Full LOTOS* which additionally includes the data description.

LTS (*Labeled Transition System*): Operational semantics of *Basic LOTOS*. An LTS is defined as a quadruple of a nonempty set of states, a set of observable actions, a set of transition relations, and the initial state.

Model checking: Automated proof technique that systematically checks whether a system design satisfies claimed properties. It can be applied in connection with finite state machines, Petri nets, and labeled transition systems. The properties to be checked are formulated in a temporal logic. Model checking applies state space exploration (see *reachability analysis*) to prove the property. If the property is not fulfilled a counterexample is formulated. Model checking has become a popular and preferred method for verifying communication protocols, distributed systems, and circuit designs.

MSC (*Message Sequence Charts*): Standardized graphical description technique of the ITU-T for the representation/visualization of communication procedures. The language has two levels: Basic and High-level MSCs. *Basic MSC* allows only the presentation of selected communication procedures, while *High-level MSC* describes the composition of MSCs for complete system descriptions. MSC has mainly been used in the SDL context. It was integrated in UML 2 as sequence diagrams.

Nondeterminism: Description principle in formal descriptions which does not determine the occurrence order of events. Two kinds of nondeterminisms are applied in service and protocol specifications: simultaneous occurrence of events and different follow-up events for the same event. Nondeterminism is applied in more abstract specification levels; it is generally resolved towards the implementation.

OSI reference model (*Open Systems Interconnection Reference Model*): Reference model of the ISO for setting up open heterogeneous networks. It lost its practical importance with the breakthrough of the Internet. Its importance now lies in the theoretical contributions of its development.

Petri net: Graphical description method for modeling systems with concurrent processes by using places, transitions, and tokens that are transported by switching the transitions between the places and thus simulating the system operations. Petri nets represent a more general form of state-transition models. They combine an intuitive graphical representation with an analyzable mathematical formalism. Beside the basic form of place/transition nets other kinds of Petri nets are used, such as timed Petri nets, product nets, colored Petri nets, and others. Due to their high abstraction degree Petri nets are less applied for protocol description. They are mainly used for verification and performance analysis purposes.

PICS (*protocol implementation conformance statement*): Statement on a protocol implementation to be tested by the implementer which documents implementation decisions in a questionnaire form, such as the protocol classes and options used, the value ranges of the parameters, e.g., the PDU sizes, or the time-out values set.

PIXIT (*protocol implementation extra information for testing*): Additional information on a protocol implementation to be tested that has to be filled out along with the PICS for the conformance test. It contains information about the system under test (SAP addresses, information about the realization of the upper tester in the SUT), administrative information (IUT identification, respective PICS form), etc.

Protocol: Behavior convention for communication between hosts in a computer network that defines the temporal order of the interactions as well as the format (syntax and semantics) of the messages exchanged. A protocol provides one or more services. It can accordingly be divided into several phases. If the communication behavior of both sides is equal the protocol is called symmetric, otherwise asymmetric.

Protocol architecture: Defined layering of protocols which are often dedicated to a certain application field. Protocol architectures differ from communication architectures by the fact that the interfaces between the protocols are defined by the protocols themselves and not by some general architectural elements like service access points or a defined layer concept. In the Internet context protocol architectures are mainly used.

Protocol data unit (PDU): Data unit exchanged in a communication protocol. It consists of a header, which contains control data, and a user data part, which transports data of the service user. Sometimes, but seldom, also a trailer with further control data is added. Depending on the protocol, PDUs are named differently, e.g., packets, segments, messages, and so on. The user data part is also called the payload.

Protocol function: Basis protocol mechanism that is used in many protocols. Typical examples of protocol functions are connection management, flow control, and error control.

Protocol profile: Tailored protocol hierarchy dedicated to a certain application that specifies the protocol options and versions used in the different layers. Protocol profiles were mainly defined and used in the OSI context.

Protocol specification: Informal or formal description of the protocol procedures. It describes the temporal order of interactions between peer entities and defines the format of the messages exchanged. The protocol specification defines among other things how the entities react to service primitives, incoming PDUs, or internal events. The protocol specification is basically the "implementation" of the service specification.

Protocol stack: Colloquial term for a dedicated protocol hierarchy in a communication or a protocol architecture that refers to the protocols used.

Protocol validation: Process of evaluating the functional and nonfunctional properties of the design and the implementation of a protocol with respect to the user requirements. The protocol validation comprises all activities of the protocol development process which serve this purpose, such as prototyping, performance analysis, and the various forms of protocol testing.

Protocol verification: Evidence of the correctness of the protocol design by means of formal proof techniques. The aim of the protocol verification is to prove the correctness, completeness, and consistency of the protocol specification. It subdivides into the *verification of general properties* that must be met regardless of the specific semantics of the designed protocol, and the *verification of specific properties* that are determined by the semantics of the designed protocol.

Prototyping: Commonly used method for protocol validation through executing the protocol specifications on a computer. It is supported by most FDT compilers.

Reachability analysis: Verification method for distributed systems and protocols described by means of state-transition systems. It checks the reachability of all states by exploring the state space of the system. The analysis is based on the generation of the reachability graph. The reachability analysis allows the detection of general properties, such as deadlock freedom, livelock freedom, non-reachable actions, and others. The exhaustive exploration of the state space is limited by the state space explosion problem. Reachability analysis is one of the most commonly used verification methods for communication protocols. It is also applied in model checking.

Reachability graph: Graph generated by executing a distributed system or a protocol. It contains all reachable states as nodes and the associated state transitions as edges. The reachability graph is generated for reachability analysis, model checking, and Petri net-based verification. The generation of the reachability graph is limited by the state space explosion problem.

Reference model: As a rule an informal description of a communication architecture. A reference model describes the components of the communication architecture and the interaction principles applied. It further defines the number of layers and their functionality. The terminology applied is often different in the various models. Usually the reference model also specifies the protocols that are deployed in the different layers. The most common examples of such reference models are the ISO OSI reference model and the B-ISDN reference model.

Safety properties: Important properties in the design of communication protocols and distributed systems. Together with liveness properties they are the subject of the verification process. Safety properties state that nothing bad happens. They formulate conditions that are needed to avoid unwanted (bad) system behavior and that consequently the system may not violate. In descriptive specification methods they are usually expressed in temporal logic formulae. Properties, such as no unreachable actions and deadlock freedom are, for instance, safety properties.

SDL (*Specification and Description Language*): Standardized formal description technique of the ITU-T for telecommunications systems and communication protocols based on extended finite state machines. SDL is a graphical, object-oriented language. There are two notation forms: the graphical notation SDL/GR and the phrase notation SDL/PR, which is primarily used for tool development. The language development began in the 1970s. For a long time, SDL was updated in a cycle of four years. The currently used version is SDL 2000. A version 2010 is being approved.

Segmentation: Protocol function used to decompose an (N)-SDU or PDU into several (N-1)-PDUs which are transferred independently and then reassembled into the original data unit in the receiver entity. A special variant of segmentation is *fragmentation*, applied in the IP protocol. Here no new packet header is formed; instead an entry in the IP header is used to transport the fragment parameters. Fragmentation is needed because a *maximum transfer unit* (MTU) is used in the Internet which defines the maximum packet size that can be transmitted over a link.

Selective repeat: see *Automatic repeat request*

Sequence number: Parameter in the PDU header used to number the PDUs sent in order to re-establish their order at the receiver side. Sequence numbers are also used for acknowledgements, usually increased by one. Sequence numbers are assigned modulo if the range is exhausted. In conjunction with an abrupt connection release this may cause inconsistencies. These problems can be avoided by using timestamps and freezing connection references.

Service: Function or capability provided by a computer network or communication system. Services are subdivided in the manner of the service provision into symmetric and asymmetric services. *Symmetric services* are services that simultaneously provide the offered service at two or more service access points. *Asymmetric services* are services that follow the client/server paradigm, i.e., there is a user – the client – that issues a service request and a system in the network – the server – that provides this service. Client and server use a communication service for their interaction. Most application and network services are of an asymmetric nature. Communication services in contrast provide a symmetric service.

Service interface: Interface between the service users and the service provider, where the service is made available.

Service primitive: Abstraction for describing the interactions between the service users and the service provider at the service interface. Service primitives do not prescribe how these interactions have to be implemented.

Service specification: Description of the interactions at the service interface. It includes the description of the services provided, the respective service primitives, their parameters, and the presentation of the interactions at the service access points including causal dependencies between them. A distinction is made between local and global behavior. The *local behavior* describes the interactions at a service access point. The *global behavior* specifies the causal dependencies between the local interactions at the corresponding service access points.

Service access point (*service access point*, SAP): Point in the service interface where a service user can access the service provided.

SLTS (*Structured Labeled Transition System*): Operational semantics of *Full LOTOS*. It extends an LTS by the internal action *i* and a many-sorted algebra for data description.

State space explosion problem: Limitation of reachability graph generation due to lack of memory. When generating a reachability graph the states must be stored to avoid multiple analyses and to support backtracking. This can lead to a very high demand on memory which eventually prevents an exhaustive state exploration.

TCP/IP protocol suite: Layered architecture of the Internet. It is a protocol architecture which has been established around the core Internet protocols: the connectionless network protocol IP (*Internet Protocol*), the connection oriented transport protocol TCP (*Transmission Control Protocol*), and the connectionless transport protocol UDP (*User Datagram Protocol*).

Temporal logics: Special type of modal logics. Temporal logics represent the most important descriptive description method for communication protocols and distributed systems. They provide a formal system for describing systems with respect to time to represent desired properties as well as causal and temporal dependencies between them. Temporal logics are divided into linear-time and branching-time temporal logics. The former are preferred for use in the protocol area.

Test case: Part of a test suite which comprises all testing activities regarding a given test purpose. A test case represents an experiment that is executed on the IUT to check whether it meets a certain property defined in the specification.

Test method: Test architecture that determines how an IUT and the test system interact. The term *test method* is preferably used compared to test architecture.

Test purpose: Property defined in the protocol specification, e.g., a connection set up, which is tested by a test case.

Test suite: Set of all test cases needed for the complete test of an implementation. Test suites are differentiated with respect to their ability to recognize erroneous implementations into exhaustive, sound, and complete test suites.

Test verdict: Final expression of the test result. Mainly, three test verdicts are used: *pass* – if the test was passed successfully, *fail* – if the test was failed, and *inconclusive* – if the test outcome is not unique. A test verdict is assigned to each test case. The final test verdict of a test suite is determined by summing up the test verdicts of the test cases according to a given set of rules.

Time sequence diagram: Informal graphical representation to describe the interactions between service users and service provider at the service interface including existing dependencies. They are also used to represent interactions between several protocol layers. Time sequence diagrams only describe a selected interaction sequence. For representing dependencies between different time sequence diagrams, additional means are needed, e.g., state diagrams for each service access point.

Timer: Clock used in protocols to supervise the arrival of acknowledgements and to avoid deadlock situations. When the specified waiting time is exceeded a timeout is triggered that allows us to invoke an alternative reaction. The definition of appropriate time-out intervals may be complicated.

Transparency: Principle applied in protocol design which means that user data are not accessible to the service provider, i.e., they are not used for controlling the protocol procedures. The user data must be delivered unchanged to the receiver. To implement this principle the user data, called the *service data unit*, are supplemented by protocol control fields, which are called the *protocol control information* or the header. The protocol control information and the service data unit form a protocol data unit. The principle of transparency forms the basis for the "tunneling" concept applied in the Internet, when data are passed through a network with another protocol architecture.

TTCN-2 (*Tree and Tabular Combined Notation*)**:** Test description language developed in the context of the OSI conformance testing methodology (Part 3 of the ISO 9646 standard). The characteristic elements of TTCN-2 are behavior trees and tables. It uses a snapshot semantics to define how to interpret the test cases. Although a follow-up version has been defined TTCN-2 is still in use in practice.

TTCN-3 (*Testing and Test Control Notation*)**:** Follow-up version of TTCN-2 developed by the European Telecommunications Standards Institute (ETSI) which is no longer confined to the testing of OSI protocols. It supports a wide range of tests (network-integration tests, end-to-end tests, interoperability tests, performance tests) and various application areas (ISDN, ATM, Internet, middleware). This was achieved through a fundamental revision of the language, whereby the basic TTCN-2 concepts, behavior tree and table notation, have been largely abandoned. TTCN-3 has more the character of a modern programming language than a specification language.

XDT (*eXample Data Transfer*) **protocol**: Teaching protocol used in this book as an example protocol to demonstrate protocol principles and specification techniques. XDT is a connection-oriented data transmission protocol which transfers a large file over an insecure medium. It applies the *go back N* principle for data retransmission. XDT is more complex than other example protocols, such as the alternating bit protocol or the INRES protocol. Specifications of XDT in various formal description techniques and methods can be found under http://www.protocol-engineering.tu-cottbus.de/index_xdt.htm.

References

[Abbo 93]   Abbott, M.; Peterson, L.: Increasing Network Throughput by Integrated Protocol Layers. IEEE/ACM Transactions on Networking 1 (1993) 5.

[Ahlg 96]   Ahlgren, B.; Björkman, M; Gunningberg, P.: Integrated Layer Processing can be hazardous to your performance. In: Dabbous, W.; Diot, C. (eds.): Protocols for High-Speed Networks V. Chapman & Hall, London, pp. 127-136, 1996.

[Ande 06]   Anderson, J.A.: Automata Theory with Modern Applications. Cambridge University Press, Cambridge, 2006.

[Alon 04]   Alonso, G.; Casati, F.; Kuno, H.; Machiraju, V.: Web Services. Springer, 2004.

[Baie 08]   Baier, C.; Katoen, J.-P.; Larsen, K.G.: Principles of Model Checking. MIT Press, Cambridge, 2008.

[Baum 94]   Baumgarten, B.; Giessler, A.: OSI Conformance Testing Methodology and TTCN. Elsevier Science, Amsterdam, 1994.

[Baus 93]   Bause, F.; Buchholz, P.: Qualitative and Quantitative Analysis of Timed SDL Specifications. In: Gerner, N.; Hegering, H.G.; Swoboda, J. (eds.): Communication in Distributed Systems. Informatik Aktuell. Springer, pp. 486-500,1993.

[Baus 02]   Bause, F.; Kritzinger, P.S.: Stochastic Petri Nets - An Introduction to the Theory. Vieweg, Wiesbaden, 2002.

[Bess 02]   Besse, C.; Cavalli A.; Kim, M.; Zadi, F.: Automated Generation of Interoperability Tests. In: Schieferdecker, I.; König, H.; Wolisz, A.: Testing of Communicating Systems XIV. Kluwer Academic, Dordrecht, pp. 169 – 184, 1999.

[Bill 99]   Billington, J.; Diaz, M.; Rozenberg, G. (eds.): Application of Petri Nets to Communication Networks. LNCS 1605. Springer, 1999.

[Bill 04]   Billington, J.; Gallasch, G.E.; H. Bing: A Coloured Petri Net Approach to Protocol Verification. In: Desel, J.; Reisig, W.; Rozenberg, G.: ACPN 2003, LNCS 3098, Springer, pp. 210–290, 2004.

[Bill 08]   Billington J.; Vanit-Anunchai S.: Coloured Petri Net Modelling of an Evolving Internet Protocol Standard: The Datagram Congestion Control Protocol. Fundamenta Informaticae 88 (2008) 3: 357-385.

[Boch 87]   von Bochmann, G.; Verjus, J.-P.: Some Comments on "Transition-oriented" vs. "Structured" Specification of Distributed Algorithms and Protocols. IEEE Transactions on Software Engineering SE-13 (1987) 4: 501 - 505.

[Börg 05]   Börger, E.: The ASM method: A Tutorial Introduction. In: Gramlich, B. (ed.): Frontiers of Combining Systems, LNAI 3717, Springer, pp. 264-283, 2005.

[Bolo 87]   Bolognesi, T.; Brinksma, E.: Introduction to the ISO Specification Language LOTOS. Computer Networks and ISDN Systems 14 (1987): 25-59.

[Booc 05]   Booch, G.; Rumbaugh, J.; Jacobson, I.: The Unified Modeling Language User Guide. Addison-Wesley, Reading, 2005.

[Bowm 06]   Bowman, H.; Gomez, R.: Concurrency Theory. Springer, 2006.

[Bozg 01]   Bozga, M.; Graf, S.; Mounier L.; Ober, I. ; Roux, J.-L.; Vincent, D.: Timed Extensions for SDL. LNCS 2078, Springer, pp. 223-239, 2001.

[Brin 97]   Brinksma, E.; Heerink , L.; Tretmans, J.: Developments in Testing Transition Systems. In: [Kim 97], pp. 143-165.

[Brya 86]   Bryant, R. E.: Graph-Based Algorithms for Boolean Function Manipulation. IEEE Transactions on Computers C-35 (1986) 8: 677-691.

[Brya 92]   Bryant, R. E.: Symbolic Boolean Manipulation with Ordered Binary Decision Diagrams. ACM Computing Survey 24 (1992) 3: 293-318.

[Büto 96]   Bütow, M.; Mestern, M; Schapiro, C.; Kritzinger, P. S.: Performance Modelling with the Formal Specification Language SDL. In: [Gotz 96a], pp. 213 - 228.

[Cava 97]   Cavalli, A.; Sarma, A. (eds.): SDL'97 Time for Testing. Elsevier Science, Amsterdam, 1997.

[CADP]   CADP toolbox. http://www.inrialpes.fr/vasy/cadp/.

[Cerf 74]   Cerf, V; Kahn, R.: A Protocol for Packet Network Interconnection. IEEE Transactions on Communications COM-22 (1974): 637 - 648.

[Choi 87]   Choi, T. Y.: Sequence Method for Protocol Construction. In: von Bochmann, G.; Sarikaya, B. (eds.): Protocol Specification, Testing, and Verification VII. North-Holland, Amsterdam, pp. 307-321, 1987.

[Chow 78]   Chow, T. S.: Testing Software Design Modeled by Finite-State Machines. IEEE Transactions on Software Engineering (1978) 3: 178-187.

[Chow 85]   Chow, C.; Gouda, M.G.; Lam, S.S.: A Discipline for Constructing Multiphase Communication Protocols. ACM Transactions on Computer Systems 3 (1985) 4: 315-343.

[Cind]   Cinderella SITE. http://www.cinderella.dk/index.htm .

[Clar85]   Clark, D. D.: The Structuring of Systems Using Upcalls. In: Proceedings of the 10th ACM SIGOPS Symp. Operating System Principles, 1985.

[Clar 89]   Clark, D.; Jacobson, V.; Romkey, J.; Salwen, H.: An Analysis of TCP Processing Overhead. IEEE Communications Magazine, June 1989, 23 - 29.

[Clar 00]   Clarke, E.; Grumberg, O.; Peled, D.: Model Checking. MIT Press, Cambridge, 2000.

[DeNi 84]   De Nicola, R.; Hennessy, M.: Testing Equivalences for Processes. Theoretical Computer Science 34 (1984): 83-133.

[Dold 03]   Doldi, L.: Validation of Communications Systems with SDL: The Art of SDL Simulation and Reachability Analysis. Wiley, Chichester, 2003.

[Dors 05]   Dorsch, J.; Ek, A.; Gotzhein, R.: SPT - The SDL Pattern Tool. In: Amyot, D.; Williams, W. (eds.), System Modeling and Analysis. LNCS 3319, Springer, pp. 50-64, 2005.

[Dsso 99]   Dssouli, R.; von Bochmann,G.; Lahav,Y. (eds.): SDL'99 The Next Millennium. Elsevier Science, Amsterdam, 1999.

[Dubu 00]   Dubuisson, O.: ASN.1 - Communication Between Heterogeneous Systems. Morgan Kaufmann, San Diego, 2000. http://www.oss.com/asn1/dubuisson.html.

[Eben 05]   Ebendt, R.; Fey, G.; Drechsler, R.: Advanced BDD Optimization. Springer, 2005.

[Ehri 85]   Ehrig, H.; Mahr, B.: Fundamentals of Algebraic Specification 1. Springer, 1985.

[Emer 90]   Emerson, E.A: Temporal and Modal Logic. In: van Leeuwen, J. (ed.): Handbook of Theoretical Computer Science. Elsevier Science, Amsterdam, pp. 997-1072, 1990.

[Esch 00]   Eschbach, R., Glässer, U., Gotzhein, R., Prinz, A.: On the Formal Semantics of SDL-2000: A Compilation Approach Based on an Abstract SDL Machine. In: Y. Gurevich, Kutter, P.W.; Odersky, M; Thiele, L. (eds.): Abstract State Machines - Theory and Applications. LNCS 1912, Springer, 2000.

[ETSI 99]   Information Technology - Open Systems Interconnection Conformance Testing Methodology and Framework; The Tree and Tabular Combined Notation (TTCN) (Ed. 2++), ETSI, TR 101 666, 1999.

[ETSI 99-2]   Methods for Testing and Specification (MTS); Use of SDL in ETSI deliverables; Guidelines for facilitating validation and the development of conformance tests. EG 201 383, 1999-02, (http://www.etsi.org).

[ETSI 03]   Methods for Testing and Specification; The Tree and Tabular Combined Notation version 3 (TTCN-3); Part 1: TTCN-3 Core Language. ETSI, ES 201 873-1, V2.2.1, 2003-02, (http://www.etsi.org).

[ETSI 07a]   Methods for Testing and Specification; The Tree and Tabular Combined Notation version 3 (TTCN-3); Part 5: TTCN-3 Runtime Interface (TRI). ETSI, ES 201 873-5, V3.2.1, 2007-02, (http://www.etsi.org).

[ETSI 07b]   Methods for Testing and Specification; The Tree and Tabular Combined Notation version 3 (TTCN-3); Part 6: TTCN-3 Control Interface (TCI). ETSI, ES 201 873-6, V3.2.1, 2007-02, (http://www.etsi.org).

[Fern 91]   Fernandez, J.-C.; Mounier, L.: Verifying Bisimulations on the Fly. In: Quemada, J.; Manas, J.; Vazquez, E. (eds.): Formal Description Techniques III. North-Holland, Amsterdam, 1991.

[FORTE]   Annual IFIP Working Conference on formal description techniques. In 1996 it was combined with PSTV (*Protocol Specification, Testing and Verification*). Today it belongs to the DISCOTEC conference series. Proceedings of the FORTE conference cited here are, for instance, [Gotz 96a], [Kim 01] and [Köni 03].

[Fuji 91]   Fujiwara, S.; von Bochmann, G.; Khendek, F.; Amalou, M.; Ghedamsi, A.: Test Selection Based on Finite State Models. IEEE Transactions on Software Engineering SE-17 (1991) 6: 591-603.

[Gill 62]   Gill, A.: Introduction to the Theory of Finite State Machines. McGraw-Hill, New York, 1962.

[Gira 01]   Girault, C.; Valk, R.: Petri Nets for Systems Engineering - A Guide to Modeling, Verification, and Applications, Springer, 2001.

[Gode 96]   Godefroid, P. (ed.): Partial-Order Methods for the Verification of Concurrent Systems. LNCS 1032, Springer, 1996.

[Gone 70]   Gonenc, G.: A Method for the Design of Fault Detection Experiments. IEEE Transactions on Computers 19 (1970) 6: 551 - 558.

[Gord 00]   Gordon, S.; Billington, J.: Analysing the WAP Class 2 Wireless Transaction Protocol Using Coloured Petri Nets. In: Nielsen, M; Simpson, D. (eds.): Application and Theory of Petri Nets 2000. LNCS 1825, Springer, pp. 207-226, 2000.

[Gotz 92]   Gotzhein, R.: Temporal Logic and Applications - a Tutorial. Computer Networks and ISDN Systems, 24 (1992): 203 – 218.

[Gotz 96a]   Gotzhein, R.; Bredereke, J. (eds.): Formal Description Techniques IX. Theory, Application and Tools. Chapman & Hall, London, 1996.

[Gotz 96b]   Gotzhein, R.; Bredereke, J.; Fischer, S.; Effelsberg, W.; Koenig, H.; Held, Th.: Improving the Efficiency of Automated Protocol Implementation Using Estelle. Computer Communications 19 (1996): 1226-1235.

[Gotz 99]   Gotzhein, R.; Schaible, P.: Pattern-based Development of Communication Systems. Annales des Telecommunications 54 (1999) 11-12: 508-525.

[Gotz 03]   Gotzhein, R.: Consolidating and Applying the SDL-Pattern Approach: a Detailed Case Study. Journal on Information and Software Technology (JIST) 45 (2003) 11: 727-741.

[Grab 97]   Grabowski, J.; Scheurer, R.; Zhen R. D.; Hogrefe, D.: Applying SAMSTAG to the B-ISDN protocol SSCOP. In: [Kim 97].

[Groz 96]   Groz, R.; Charles, O.; Renevot, J.: Relating Conformance Test Coverage to Formal Specifications. In [Gotz 96a].

[Hao 04]   Hao, R..; Lee; D; Sinha, R. K.; Griffeth, N.: Integrated System Interoperability Testing with Applications to VoIP. IEEE/ACM Transactions on Networking 12 (2004) 5: 823 – 836.

[Haug 01]   Haugen, Ø.: MSC-2000 Interaction Diagrams for the New Millennium. Computer Networks 35 (2001) 6: 721-732.

[Heaf 93]   Heafner, J.; Lotridge, G.: Economic and Practical Issues of Interoperability Testing. In: Proceedings of the ISO/IEC Workshop on Worldwide Recognition of OSI Test Results. Brussels, 1993.

[Heck 91]   Heck, E.; Hogrefe, D.; Müller-Clostermann, B.: Hierarchical Performance Evaluation Based on Formally Specified Communication Protocols. IEEE Transactions on Computers 40 (1991) 4: 500 - 513.

[Hein 98]   Heiner, M.: Petri Net Based System Analysis without State Explosion. In: Proceedings of High Performance Computing'98, Boston, Massachusetts, USA, 1998.

[Hein 08]   Heiner, M.: Gilbert, D., Donaldson, R.: Petri Nets for Systems and Synthetic Biology. In: Bernardo, M.; Degano, P.; Zavattaro, G. (eds.): SFM 2008, LNCS 5016, Springer, pp. 215-264, 2008.

[Held 95]   Held, Th.; Koenig, H.: Increasing the Efficiency of Computer-Aided Protocol Implementations. In: Vuong, S.; Chanson, S. (eds.): Protocol Specification, Testing and Verification XIV. Chapman & Hall, London, 1995, pp. 387 - 394.

[Henk 97]   Henke, R.; Koenig, H.; Mitschele-Thiel, A.: Derivation of Efficient Implementations from SDL Specifications Employing Data Referencing, Integrated Packet Framing and Activity Threads. In [Cava 97], pp. 397 - 414.

[Henn 85]   Hennessy, M.; Milner, R.: Algebraic Laws for Nondeterminism and Concurrency. Journal of the ACM 32 (1985) 1: 137-161.

[Henn 02]   Henniger, O.: Test generation from Specifications in Estelle and SDL. Ph.D. thesis, Brandenburg University of Technology Cottbus, 2002 (in German).

[Herm 98]   Hermanns, H.; Herzog, U.; Mertsiotakis, V.: Stochastic Process Algebras - Between LOTOS and Markov chains. Computer Networks and ISDN Systems 30 (1998): 901-924.

[Herr 00]   Herrmann, P.; Krumm, H.: A Framework for Modeling Transfer Protocols. Computer Networks 34 (2000) 2: 317-337.

[Herr 02]   Herrmann, P.; Krumm, H.; Drögehorn, O.; Geisselhardt, W.: Framework and Tool Support for Formal Verification of High Speed Transfer Protocol Designs. Telecommunication Systems 20 (2002) 3-4: 291-310.

[Higa 93]   Higashino, T.; Okano, K; Imajo, H.; Taniguchi, K.: Deriving Protocol Specifications from Service Specifications in Extended FSM Models. In: Proc. of 13th International Conference on Distributed Computing Systems (ICDCS-13), 1993, pp. 141–148.

[Hint 01]   Hintelmann, J.; Hofmann, R.; Lemmen, F.; Mitschele-Thiel, A.; Müller-Clostermann, B.: Applying Techniques for the Performance Engineering of SDL Systems. Computer Networks 35 (2001): 647-665.

[Hoar 85]   Hoare, C.A.R.: Communicating Sequential Processes. Prentice Hall, Englewood Cliffs, New Jersey, 1985.

[Holz 91]   Holzmann, G.J.: Design and Validation of Computer Protocols. Prentice Hall, Englewood Cliffs, 1991.

[Holz 04]   Holzmann, G.J.: The SPIN Model Checker Primer and Reference Manual. Addison-Wesley, Boston, 2004.

[Hopc 07]   Hopcroft, J.E.; Motwani, R.; Ullman, J.D.: Introduction to Automata Theory, Languages and Computation. Addison-Wesley Longman, Amsterdam, 2007.

[Hutc 91]   Hutchinson, N.C.; Peterson, L.L.: The x-Kernel: An Architecture for Implementing Network Protocols. IEEE Trans. on Software Engineering 17(1991)1: 64-76.

[ISO 7498]   ISO, Information Processing Systems - Open Systems Interconnection - Basic Reference Model. ISO 7498, 1984.

[ISO 8072]   ISO, Information Processing Systems - Open Systems Interconnection - Transport Service Definition. IS 8072, 1986.

[ISO 8807]   ISO, Information Processing Systems - Open Systems Interconnection - LOTOS - A Formal Description Technique Based on the Temporal Ordering of Observational Behaviour. IS 8807, 1988.

[ISO 8824]   ISO/IEC 8824 (1998)/ITU-T Recommendation X.680-683 (1997), Information Technology - Abstract Syntax Notation One (ASN.1).

[ISO 8825]   ISO/IEC 8825 (1998)/ITU-T Recommendation X.690-691(1997), Information Technology - ASN.1 Encoding Rules.

[ISO 9646]   ISO, Information Processing Systems - OSI Conformance Testing Methodology and Framework. IS 9646, 1986.

[ISO 13245]   ISO, Information Processing Systems - Formal Methods for Conformance Testing. ISO CD 13245-1, 1997.

[ISO 15437]   ISO, Information Technology – E-LOTOS. IS 15437, 2001

[ITU-T 100]   ITU-T Recommendation Z.100: Specification and Description Language SDL. 2006.

[ITU-T 100F]   ITU-T Recommendation Z.100 Annex F: SDL Formal Definition.

[ITU-T 105]   ITU-T Recommendation Z.105: Use of SDL with ASN.1. 1999.

[ITU-T 109]   ITU-T Recommendation Z.109: SDL Combined with UML. 2006/07.

[ITU-T 120]   ITU-T Recommendation Z.120: Message Sequence Charts (MSC), 1999.

[ITU-T 161]   ITU-T Recommendation Z.161: Testing and Test Control Notation version 3: TTCN-3 Core Language, 2007.

[ITU-T 292]   ITU-T Recommendation X.292: OSI conformance testing methodology and framework for protocol Recommendations for ITU-T applications - The Tree and Tabular Combined Notation (TTCN), 2002.

[Jaco 88]   Jacobson, V.: Congestion Avoidance and Control. In: Proceedings of SIG-COMM'88 Conference, ACM, pp. 314-329, 1988.

[Kali 10]   Kaliappan, P.S., König, H., Schmerl, S.: Model-Driven Protocol Design Based on Component Oriented Modeling. In: Dong J.S.; Zhu, H.: Formal Engineering Methods and Software Engineering. LCNS 6447, Springer, pp. 613-629, 2010.

[Kant 96]   Kant, C.; Higashino, T.; von Bochmann, G.: Deriving Protocol Specifications from Service Specifications Written in LOTOS. Distributed Computing (1996) 10: 29-47.

[Kim 97]   Kim, M.; Kang, S.; Hong, K. (eds.): Testing of Communication Systems. Vol. 10. Chapman & Hall, London, 1997.

[Kim 01]   Kim, M.; Chin, B.; Kang, S.; Lee, D. et al.: Formal Techniques for Networked and Distributed Systems. Kluwer, Boston, 2001.

[Köni 97]   König, H.; Ulrich, A.; Heiner, M.: Design for Testability: A Step-wise Test Procedure. In [Kim 97], pp. 125-140

[Köni 00]   Koenig, H.; Langendoerfer, P.; Krumm, H.: Improving the Efficiency of Automated Protocol Implementations Using a Configurable FDT Compiler. Computer Communications 23 (2000) 12: 1179-1195.

[Köni 03]   König, H.; Heiner, M.; Wolisz, A. (eds.): Formal Techniques for Networked and Distributed Systems - FORTE 2003. LNCS 2767, Berlin, 2003.

[Krae 09a]   Kraemer, F. A.; Slåtten, V.; Herrmann, P.: Tool Support for the Rapid Composition, Analysis and Implementation of Reactive Services. The Journal of Systems and Software 82 (2009): 2068-2080.

[Krae 09b]   Kraemer, F.A.; Bræk, R.; Herrmann, P.: Compositional Service Engineering with Arctis. In: Teletronikk, Special Issue on Model-Driven Security - Integrating Availability in System Development, Telenor, 1 (2009): 135-151.

[Krög 07]   Kröger, F.; Merz, S.: Temporal Logic and State Systems. Springer, 2008.

[Krum 90]   Krumm, H.: Projections of the Reachability Graph and Environment Models. In: Sifakis, J. (ed.): Automatic Verification Methods for Finite State Systems. LNCS 407, Berlin, 1990.

[Kuro 08]   Kurose, J. F.; Ross, K. W.: Computer Networking. Pearson Education, 2008.

[Lai 98]   Lai, R.; Jirachiefpattana, A.: Communication Protocol Specification and Verification. Kluwer, Boston, 1998.

[Lam 84]   Lam, S. S.; Shankar, A. U.: Protocol Verification via Projections. IEEE Transactions on Software Engineering 10 (1984) 4, 325-342.

[Lamp 94]   Lamport, L.: The Temporal Logic of Actions. ACM Transactions on Programming Languages and Systems 16 (1994) 3: 872-923.

[Lang 99a]   Langendoerfer, P.; Koenig, H.: COCOS - A Configurable SDL Compiler for Generating Efficient Protocol Implementations. In [Dsso 99], pp. 259-274

[Lang 99b]   Langendoerfer, P.; Koenig, H.: Automated Protocol Implementation Based on Activity Threads. In: Proceedings of the IEEE International Conference on Network Protocols (ICNP'99), Toronto, IEEE Press, pp. 3-10, 1999.

[Lano 09]   Lano, K.: UML 2 Semantics and Applications. Wiley, New York, 2009.

[Larm 99]   Larmouth, J.: ASN.1 Complete. Morgan Kaufmann Publisher, San Diego, 1999 http: //www.oss.com/asn1/larmouth.html .

[Ledu 92]   Leduc, G.: A Framework Based on Implementation Relations for Implementing LOTOS Specifications. Computer Networks and ISDN Systems 25(1992)1: 23-41.

[Lee 97]   Lee, D.; Netravali, A. N., Sabnani, K. K., Sugla, B. B. and John, A.: Passive Testing and Applications to Network Management. In: Proceedings of IEEE International Conference on Network Protocols (ICNP'97), pp. 113–122, 1997.

[Lee 02]   Lee, D.; Chen, D.; Hao, R.; Miller, R.; Wu, J. and Yin, X.: A Formal Approach for Passive Testing of Protocol Data Portions. In: Proceeding of IEEE International Conference on Network Protocols (ICNP 2002), pp. 122–131, 2002.

[Leon 97]   Leonard, L.; Leduc, G.: An Introduction to ET-LOTOS for the Description of Time-Sensitive Systems. Computer Networks and ISDN Systems 29 (1997): 271-292.

[Mann 92]   Manna, Z.; Pnueli, A.: The Temporal Logic of Reactive and Concurrent Systems. Springer, 1992.

[Math 08]   Mathur, A. P.: Foundations of Software Testing. Pearson Education. Upper Saddle River, 2008.

[Mauw 96]   Mauw, S.: The Formalization of Message Sequence Charts. Computer Networks and ISDN Systems 28 (1996) 12: 1643 – 1657.

[Mauw 99]   Mauw, S.; M.A. Reniers: Operational Semantics for MSC'96. Computer Networks 31 (1999) 17: 1785-1799.

[McMi 93]   McMillan, K.L.: Symbolic Model Checking: An Approach to the State Explosion Problem. Kluwer Academic, Dordrecht, 1993.

[Miln 89]   Milner, R.: Communication and Concurrency. Prentice Hall. Englewood Cliffs, 1989.

[Mits 99]   Mitschele-Thiel, A.; Müller-Clostermann, B.: Performance engineering of SDL/MSC systems. Computer Networks 31 (1999): 1801-1815.

[Mits 01]   Mitschele-Thiel, A.: Systems Engineering with SDL: Developing Performance-Critical Communication Systems. Wiley, New York, 2001.

[Mura 89]   Murata, T.: Petri Nets: Properties, Analysis, and Applications. Proceedings of the IEEE 77 (1989) 4: 541-580.

[Netr 03]   Netravali, A. N.; Sabnani, K. K.; Viswanathan R.: Correct passive testing algorithms and complete fault coverage. In: [Köni 03], pp. 303-318.

[NuSMV]   NuSMV symbolic model checker. http://nusmv.fbk.eu/ .

[Pete 07]   Peterson, L.L., Davie, B. S.: Computer Networks. A Systems Approach (Morgan Kaufmann Series in Networking), Elsevier, 2007.

[Petr 94]   Petrenko, A.; von Bochmann, G.; Dssouli, R.: Conformance Relations and Test Derivation. In [Rafi 94], pp. 157 - 178.

[Petr 96]   Petrenko, A.; von Bochmann,G.; Yao, M.: On Fault Coverage of Tests for Finite State Specifications. Computer Networks and ISDN Systems 29 (1996): 81-106.

[Piat 83]   Piatkowski, T. F.: Protocol Engineering. Proc. ICC, Boston, 1983.

[Popo 06]   Popovic, M.: Communication Protocol Engineering. CRC Press, Boca Raton, 2006.

[Prob 91]   Probert, R. L.; Saleh, K.: Synthesis of Communication Protocols: Survey and Assessment. IEEE Transactions on Computers 40 (1991) 4: 468-475.

[Rafi 94]   Rafiq, O. (ed.): Protocol Test Systems VI. North-Holland, Amsterdam, 1994.

[Rama 85]   Ramamoorthy, C. V.; Dong, S. T.; Usada, Y.: An Implementation of an Automated Protocol Synthesizer (APS) and its Application to the X.21 Protocol. IEEE Transactions on Software Engineering SE-11 (1985) 9: 886 - 908.

[Reed 01]   Reed, R.: Notes on SDL-2000 for the New Millennium. Computer Networks 35 (2001) 6: 709-720.

[RFC 768]   RFC 768; User Datagram Protocol. 1980.

[RFC 793]   RFC 793; Transmission Control Protocol. 1981.

[RFC 1122]   RFC 1122: Requirements for Internet Hosts - Communication Layers. 1989.

[RFC 1323]   RFC 1323: TCP Extensions for High Performance. 1992.

[RFC 1889]   RFC 1889; RTP: A Transport Protocol for Real-Time Applications. 1996.

[RFC 2205]   RFC 2205: Resource ReSerVation Protocol (RSVP) - Version 1 Functional Specification. 1997.

[RFC 3286]   RFC 3286: An Introduction to the Stream Control Transmission Protocol (SCTP). 2002.

[Sari 87]   Sarikaya, B.; von Bochmann, G.; Cerny, E.: A Test Design Methodology for Protocol Testing. IEEE Trans. on Software Engineering SE-13 (1987) 5: 518-531.

[Sari 93]   Sarikaya, B.: Principles of Protocol Engineering and Conformance Testing. Ellis Horwood, New York, 1993.

[Schi 08]   Schieferdecker, I.; Grabowski, J.; Vassiliou-Gioles, T.; Din, G.: The Test Technology TTCN-3. Formal Methods and Testing. LNCS 4949, Springer, pp. 292-319, 2008.

[Seol 04]   Seol, S.; Kim, M.; Chanson, S.T.; Kang, S.: Interoperability Test Generation and Minimization for Communication Protocols Based on the Multiple Stimuli Principle. IEEE Journal on Selected Areas in Communications 22 (2004) 10: 2062-2074.

[Shar 08]   Sharp, R.: Principles of Protocol Design. Springer, 2008.

[SDL Forum]   Conference series of the SDL Forum Society which takes place every two years. It is dedicated to current issues concerning the application and further development of SDL and nowadays of other related language, such as UML, MSC, ASN.1, and TTCN. (see http://www.sdl-forum.org). [Cava 97] and [Dsso 99] are proceedings of this conference series.

[Somm 00]   Sommerville, I.: Software Engineering. Addison-Wesley, Reading, 2000.

[Stai 97]   Stainov, R.: IPnG - The Next Generation Internet Protocol. International Thomson, Bonn, 1997 (in German).

[Stal 08]   Stallings, W.: Data and Computer Communications (8th edition). Prentice Hall, Upper Saddle River, 2008.

[Svob 89]   Svobodova, L.: Implementing OSI Systems. IEEE Journal on Selected Areas in Communications 7 (1989) 7: 1115 - 1130.

[Tabo 99]   Tabourier, M.; Cavalli, A.: Passive Testing and Application to the GSM-MAP Protocol. Information and Software Technology 41 (1999): 813–821.

[Tane 02]   Tanenbaum, A.S.; van Steen, M.: Distributed Systems - Principles and Paradigms. Prentice Hall, Upper Saddle River, 2002.

[Tane 03]   Tanenbaum, A. S.: Computer Networks (4th ed.). Pearson Education, Upper Saddle River, 2003.

[Tane 10]   Tanenbaum, A. S.; Wetherall, D.J.: Computer Networks (5th ed.). Pearson Education, Upper Saddle River, 2010.

[TestCom]   Proceedings of the annual IFIP Conference TestCom (*International Conference on Testing Communication Systems*) (formerly IWPTS (*International Workshop on Protocol Testing Systems*) and IWTCS (*International Workshop on Testing Communication Systems*). Cited volumes of this conference series are [Rafi 94] and [Kim 97].

[Tret 96a]   Tretmans, G.J.: Conformance Testing with Labelled Transition Systems: Implementation Relations and Test Generation. Computer Networks and ISDN Systems 29 (1996) 1: 49-79.

[Tret 96b]   Tretmans, G. J.: Test Generation with Inputs, Outputs, and Repetitive Quiescence. Software – Concepts and Tools 17 (1996): 103-120.

[Tret 00]   Tretmans, J.: Specification Based Testing with Formal Methods: A Theory. In Tutorial Notes FORTE/PSTV 2000, Pisa, 2000.

[Turn 93]   Turner, K. J. (ed.): Using Formal Description Techniques. Wiley, New York, 1993.

[Ural 92]   Ural, H.: Formal Methods for Test Sequence Generation. Computer Communications 15 (1992) 5: 311 - 325.

[Valm 92]   Valmari, A.: A Stubborn Attack on State Explosion. Formal Methods in System Design 1 (1992) 4, 297-322

[Vard 94]   Vardi, M.Y.; Wolper, P.: Reasoning About Infinite Computations. Information and Computation 115 (1994): 1-37.

[Vasi 73]   Vasilevski, M. P.: Failure Diagnosis of Automata. Kibernetika, No. 4, pp. 98 - 108 (in Russian), 1973.

[Viho 01]   Viho, C.; Barbin, S.; Tanguy, L.: Towards a Formal Framework for Interoperability Testing. In: [Kim 01], pp. 53-68

[Viss 88]   Vissers, C. A.; Scollo, G.; van Sinderen, M.: Architecture and Specification Style in Formal Descriptions of Distributed Systems. In: Sabnani, K. (ed.): Protocol Specification, Testing, and Verification VIII. North-Holland, Amsterdam, 1988.

[Viss 92]   Vissers, C. A.; Pires, L. F.; van de Lagemaat, J.: Lotosphere - An Attempt Towards a Design Culture. Proceedings LOTOSPHERE Workshop, Pisa, 1992.

[Vuon 90]   Vuong, S. T.; Chan, W. W. L.; Ito, R.: The UIOv-Method for Protocol Test Sequence Generation. In: de Meer, J.; Effelsberg, W.; Mackert, L. (eds.): Protocol Test Systems. North-Holland, Amsterdam, 1990.

[Vuon 94]   Vuong, S. T.; Loureiro, A.; Chanson, S.: A Framework for the Design for Testability of Communication Protocols; In [Rafi 94], pp. 89-108.

[West 89]   West, C. H.: Protocol Validation in Complex Systems. In: Proceedings of 8th ACM Symposium on Principles of Distributed Computing, Austin, Texas, USA, 1989.

[Will 05]   Willcock, C.; Deiß, T.; Tobies, S.; Keil, S.; Engler, F.; Schulz, S.: An Introduction to TTCN-3. Wiley, New York, 2005.

[Wet 05]   de Wet, N.; Kritzinger, P.S.: Using UML Models for the Performance Analysis of Network Systems. Computer Networks 49 (2005) 5: 627-642.

[Woli 93]   Wolisz, A.: A Unified Approach to Formal Specification of Communication Protocols and Analysis of their Performance. SAMS 13 (1993): 59 - 88.

[Wu 01]   Wu, J.; Zhao, Y., Yin, X.: From Active to Passive: Progress in Testing of Internet Routing Protocols. In: [Kim 01], pp. 101–116.

[Yama 07]   Yamaguchi, H.; El-Fakih, K.; von Bochmann, G.; Higashino, T.: Deriving Protocol Specifications from Service Specifications Written as Predicate/Transition-Nets. Computer Networks 51 (2007): 258-284.

[Zafi 80]   Zafiropulo, P.; West, C.H.; Rudin, H.; Cowan, D.D.; Brand, D.: Towards Analyzing and Synthesizing Protocols. IEEE Transactions on Communications COM-28 (1980) 4: 651 - 660.

[Zeng 86]   Zeng, H. K.; Rayner, D.: The Impact of the Ferry Concept on Protocol Testing. In Diaz, M. (ed.): Protocol Specification, Testing, and Verification IV. North-Holland, Amsterdam, 1986, pp. 533 - 544.

Abbreviations

ASCII	American Standard Code for Information Interchange
ARP	Address Resolution Protocol
ARQ	Automatic Repeat Request
ASM	Abstract State Machine
ASN.1	Abstract Syntax Notation One
ASP	Abstract Service Primitive
ATM	Abstract Test Method *or* Asynchronous Transfer Mode
ATS	Abstract Test Suite
BDD	Binary Decision Diagram
BGP	Border Gateway Protocol
B-ISDN	Broadband ISDN
BER	Basic Encoding Rules
CADP	Construction and Analysis of Distributed Processes
CCS	Calculus of Communicating Systems
CEP	Connection End Point
CLS	Canonical LOTOS Specification
CRC	Cyclic Redundancy Check
CSMA/CD	Carrier Sense Multiple Access with Collision Detection
CTL	Computational Tree Logic
cTLA	compositional Temporal Logic of Actions
CTMF	Conformance Testing Methodology and Framework
CP	Coordination Point
CORBA	Common Object Request Broker Architecture
DNA	Digital Network Architecture
DS	Distinguishing Sequence
EFSM	Extended Finite State Machine
Estelle	Extended State Transition Language
ETS	Executable Test Suite
ETSI	European Telecommunications Standards Institute
FDT	Formal Description Technique
FEC	Forward Error Control
FIFO	First In First Out
FMCT	Formal Methods in Conformance Testing
FSM	Finite State Machine
FTP	File Transfer Protocol
HTTP	Hypertext Transport Protocol
IAP	Implementation Access Point
ICMP	Internet Control Message Protocol
IEEE	Institute of Electrical and Electronics Engineers

IETF	Internet Engineering Task Force
IGMP	Internet Group Management Protocol
ILP	Integrated Layer Processing
IOTS	Input/Output Transition System
IP	Internet Protocol
IPv4	IP version 4
IPv6	IP version 6
IS	International Standard
ISDN	Integrated Services Digital Network
ISO	International Organization for Standardization
ITU-T	International Telecommunication Union - Telecommunication Standardization Sector
IUT	Implementation Under Test
LAN	Local Area Network
LNCS	Lecture Notes in Computer Science (Springer)
LLC	Logical Link Control
LOTOS	Language of Temporal Ordering Specification
LT	Lower Tester
LTL	Linear Temporal Logic
LTS	Labeled Transition System
MAC	Medium Access Control
MPLS	Multi-Protocol Label Switching
MSC	Message Sequence Charts
MTC	Main Test Component
MTU	Maximum Transfer Unit
NIST	National Institute of Standards and Technology
OBDD	Ordered Binary Decision Diagram
OSI	Open Systems Interconnection
OSI/RM	Open Systems Interconnection Reference Model
OSPF	Open Shortest Path First
PCI	Protocol Control Information
PCO	Points of Control and Observation
PDU	Protocol Data Unit
PICS	Protocol Implementation Conformance Statement
PIXIT	Protocol Implementation Extra Information for Testing
POTS	Plain Old Telephone Service
PPP	Point-to-Point Protocol
PROMELA	Process Meta Language
PTC	Parallel Test Component
QoS	Quality of Service
RARP	Reverse Address Resolution Protocol
RFC	Request for Comments
RIP	Routing Information Protocol
RPC	Remote Procedure Call

RSVP	Resource Reservation Setup Protocol
RTP	Real-time Transport Protocol
SAP	Service Access Point
SC	State Cover
SDL	Specification and Description Language
SDL/GR	Specification and Description Language/ Graphical Representation
SDL/PR	Specification and Description Language/Phrase Representation
SDU	Service Data Unit
SIP	Session Initiation Protocol
SLIP	Serial Line IP
SLTS	Structured Labeled Transition System
SMTP	Simple Mail Transfer Protocol
SNA	Systems Network Architecture
SOAP	(originally) Simple Object Access Protocol
SP	Service Primitive
SPIN	Simple Promela Interpreter
SUT	System Under Test
TC	Transition Cover
TCP	Transmission Control Protocol or Test Coordination Procedure (in the context of [ISO 9646])
TLA	Temporal Logic of Actions
TTL	Time-to-Live
TMP	Test Management Protocol
TTCN	Tree and Tabular Combined Notation or Testing and Test Control Notation (since version 3)
UDP	User Datagram Protocol
UIO	Unique Input/Output (sequences)
UML	Unified Modeling Language
URI	Unique Resource Identifier
UT	Upper Tester
WAN	Wide Area Networks
WWW	World Wide Web
XDT	eXample Data Transfer (-Protocol)
XML	Extensible Markup Language
YL	Loop-back Test Method
YT	Transverse Test Method

Index

A

Separating 96
Protocol development process **283 ff**,
286 ff, 289, 291, 295, 299 ff, 341,
351, 485 ff
Protocol design 12, 146, 211, 259, 275,
285, 287, **289**, 291, 299 ff, 304,
341, 342, 351, 352, 385, 416, 489
analytical 289, 291
synthetic 289 ff
Protocol engineering 129, 148, 259,
289, 320, 342, 351, 391, 485 ff
Protocol function 32, 71, **77**, 83, 88, 93,
94, 118, 291, 377, 498
Protocol implementation 67, 94, 193,
286, 287, 298, 300, 351, **354 ff**,
359, 372, 374, 379, 386 ff, 394, 409
ff, 441 ff, 485 ff
automated 353, **378 ff**, 487 ff
parallel 377
Protocol implementation conformance
statement **409 ff**, 497
Protocol implementation extra information for testing **409 ff**, 497
Protocol number **74**, 109, 113
Protocol option 55, 66, 95, 111, 285 ff,
352 ff, 386, 387, 392, 409, 441 ff
Protocol phase **18**, 38, 216, 297
Protocol profile **66**, 442, 498
Protocol specification **33 ff**, 42, 131 ff,
140, 151, 180, 284 ff, 289 ff, 295,
297, 299 ff, 305, 319 ff, 330, 341,
351 ff, 373, 379, 385 ff, 388 ff, 394,
442, 485, 486, 498
Protocol stack **67**, 359, 443, 498
Protocol testing 286, 299, **385 ff**, 391,
492, 498
passive 448 ff
Protocol validation 299, 498
Protocol verification 285, 287, **299 ff**,
302, 310, 311, 330, 331, 385, 498
deductive 301 ff, 329 ff
general properties **300 ff**, 304, 315,
319
special properties **300 ff**, 304, 319

Prototyping 299, 315, **351**, 378 ff, 487,
498

Q

Quality of Service **11 ff**, 31, 85, 109
QUEST 348 ff

R

Reachability analysis **301 ff**, 304 ff,
320, 329, 331, 333, 499
Reachability graph **302 ff**, 309, 317 ff,
330, 446, 499
Reference model **67 ff**, 70, 72, 127, 499
OSI 3, 8, 12, 53, 66, **68 ff**, 72, 73,
76, 112, 127, 259, 497
B-ISDN 68, **75**
Refinement relation 321
Refusal semantics 327
Registration 414
Representation
behavior-oriented **133 ff**, 137, 145,
146
communication-oriented **133 ff**,
145, 146
Reset capability **416**, 418
Robustness test 286, 387

S

Safety property 136, **152 ff**, 155, 314,
499
SDU   see *Service data unit*
SDL 35, 42 ff, 68, 141, 156, 159, **160
ff**, 198 ff, 259, 274, 276, 290 ff,
296, 342, 344 ff, 382, 438, 486 ff,
499
Address information 168, 176
Agent 161, **162 ff**, 164 ff
any 170
any-type 183
Block **162 ff**, 164, 166 ff, 180
Branching 170